MARK'S JESUS

Mark's Jesus

Characterization as Narrative Christology

Elizabeth Struthers Malbon

BAYLOR UNIVERSITY PRESS

Cover Design by Cynthia Dunne, Blue Farm Graphic Design
Cover Image: Georges Rouault, French, 1871–1958, *Ecce Dolor, plate eight from the Passion*, 1936; published 1939, Color aquatint on tan laid paper, 306 × 212 mm (image); 312 × 220 mm (plate); 445 × 343 mm (sheet), Gift in memory of Kay Goodman King from the A. Peter Dewey Memorial Fund, 1946.66.8, The Art Institute of Chicago. © 2009 Artists Rights Society (ARS), New York/ADAGP, Paris. Photography © The Art Institute of Chicago.
Composition prepared by Newgen–North America.

Library of Congress Cataloging-in-Publication Data

Malbon, Elizabeth Struthers.
    Mark's Jesus : characterization as narrative christology / Elizabeth Struthers Malbon.
        p. cm.
    Includes bibliographical references and indexes.
    ISBN 978-1-60258-247-7 (hardback : alk. paper)
    1. Jesus Christ—Person and offices—Biblical teaching. 2. Bible. N.T. Mark—Criticism, Narrative. 3. Bible. N.T. Mark—Theology. 4. Narrative theology. I. Title.
    BT203.M29 2009
    226.3'066   dc22
                                                                2009022596

Printed in the United States of America on acid-free paper with a minimum of 30% pcw recycled content.

In fond memory of my parents

Roberta Diamond Struthers
1915–1997

Orville W. Struthers
1916–1995

from whom I received many blessings
and who themselves received the blessing
of not outliving their children

and in honor of and concern for
all the parents of the 33 students and faculty
who were killed on April 16, 2007
on the campus of Virginia Tech
who have not received this blessing—

may they receive other blessings.

CONTENTS

ACKNOWLEDGMENTS

The research and writing leading to this book have been spread over a decade—a decade that has included many other demands on my time and energy and thus interruptions in my work. During this time I have benefited from the support and critique of others in a variety of ways.

I have enjoyed financial support for research from Virginia Polytechnic Institute and State University in the form of a study-research leave at the beginning of the project (Spring 1998) and a research assignment near its close (Fall 2006), as well as two Humanities Summer Stipends (2001, 2005) and an international travel grant (July 2007).

As I have explored the implied audience of Mark's Gospel, I have been able to discuss my explorations with a number of real audiences. I have had the advantage of comments, questions, and critiques from audiences of papers presented to both international and regional meetings of the Society of Biblical Literature—in Knoxville, Tennessee (March 1998); Rome, Italy (July 2001); and Vienna, Austria (July 2007). I am especially grateful to my hosts on four occasions of invited lectures on ideas now further developed here: Kari Syreeni of Uppsala University, Sweden (March 1998); Troels Enberg-Pedersen of the University of Copenhagen, Denmark (April 1998); Philip Kenneson and Mark Matson of Milligan College, Tennessee (February 2003); and John Kelsay and Walter Moore of Florida State University, Tallahassee (for the John Priest Memorial Lecture, January 2006). Perhaps not all these audiences still remember their contributions to my thinking, but I remember.

I have reached additional audiences through invitations to contribute to three *Festschriften* and an anniversary volume of *Biblical Interpretation*. Grateful acknowledgment is made to the following publishers for permission to present here, substantially revised, material published in an earlier form:

Westminster John Knox Press: "The Christology of Mark's Gospel: Narrative Christology and the Markan Jesus." Pp. 33–48 in *Who Do You Say That I Am? Essays on Christology* (in honor of Jack Dean Kingsbury). Edited by Mark Allan

Powell and David R. Bauer. Louisville: Westminster John Knox, 1999. (Early sketch for the book, especially chapter 3.)

Perspectives in Religious Studies: "'Reflected Christology': An Aspect of Narrative 'Christology' in the Gospel of Mark." *Perspectives in Religious Studies* 26, in honor of Edgar V. McKnight (1999): 127–45. (Early versions of chapter 5 and a portion of chapter 1.)

Brill: "Narrative Christology and the Son of Man: What the Markan Jesus Says Instead." *Biblical Interpretation* 11 (2003): 373–85. (Early version of half of chapter 4.)

T&T Clark, an imprint of Continuum International Publishing: "Markan Narrative Christology and the Kingdom of God." Pp. 177–93 in *Literary Encounters with the Reign of God* (in honor of Robert C. Tannehill). Edited by Sharon H. Ringe and H. C. Paul Kim. New York/London: T&T Clark International, 2004. (Early version of half of chapter 4.)

Sheffield Phoenix Press: "The Jesus of Mark and the 'Son of David.'" Pp. 162–85 in *Between Author and Audience in Mark: Narration, Characterization, Interpretation.* Edited by Elizabeth Struthers Malbon. Sheffield: Sheffield Phoenix Press, 2009. (Small parts of chapters 2 and 3.)

Brill: "New Literary Criticism and Jesus Research." In *The Handbook of the Study of the Historical Jesus, Vol. 1: How to Study the Historical Jesus.* Edited by Tom Holmén and Stanley E. Porter. Leiden, The Netherlands: Brill, forthcoming. (Early version of one subsection of Implications.)

At the end of this long process I have received an enormous boost from the attention and care of a handful of readers of the penultimate draft of the book, in whole or in part. On very short notice Paul Achtemeier, Joanna Dewey, and Joel Williams read two or more chapters each and offered important suggestions for additions, deletions, and clarifications. In an equally tight time frame, both Gene Boring and David Rhoads read the entire manuscript and offered comment and critique on each chapter. Although it is I who am in a position to recognize and appreciate the contributions of these five readers, it is you, my next readers, who will be the beneficiaries of their insight and generosity.

In a category by himself is Carey Newman, whose engaging interest and energetic investment in this work—as reader and editor—has been amazing. Thanks to him, this project with many interruptions and a long development has come to a dramatic conclusion with deliberate speed. Others at Baylor University Press have made important contributions to that final process; I am pleased to thank Elisabeth Wolfe for editorial and preproduction work, Diane Smith and Jennifer Hunt for work throughout the production process, and

Cynthia (Cindy) Dunne, Blue Farm Graphic Design, for the cover design. I am happy to acknowledge the attentive and thoughtful copyediting and production work of Jay Harward of Newgen–North America and, even after all of these readers reading, the careful work of freelance proofreader Christine Gever. I have welcomed the assistance of Virginia Tech student Emi Scott in preparing the bibliography and indexes.

Thus *Mark's Jesus* reflects the long hours and years of solitary research and writing *and* the engaging conversations with other scholars, in person and electronically, that are *both* indispensable to such work. I am grateful to all who have made possible my access to both.

Abbreviations

BETL	Biblioteca ephemeridum theologicarum lovaniensium
BibInt	*Biblical Interpretation*
BNTC	Black's New Testament Commentaries
BTB	*Biblical Theology Bulletin*
BThSt	Biblische-theologische Studien
CBQ	*Catholic Biblical Quarterly*
EvT	*Evangelische Theologie*
GBS	Guides to Biblical Scholarship
Gk	Greek
HBT	*Horizons in Biblical Theology*
HCBD	*HarperCollins Bible Dictionary*
HCSB	*HarperCollins Study Bible*
HTR	*Harvard Theological Review*
Int	*Interpretation*
JAAR	*Journal of the American Academy of Religion*
JBL	*Journal of Biblical Literature*
JETS	*Journal of the Evangelical Theological Society*
JR	*Journal of Religion*
JSNT	*Journal for the Study of the New Testament*

JSNTSup	Journal for the Study of the New Testament: Supplement Series
MT	Masoretic Text
NovT	*Novum Testamentum*
NRSV	New Revised Standard Version
NS	New Series
NTS	*New Testament Studies*
SBL	Society of Biblical Literature
SBLDS	Society of Biblical Literature Dissertation Series
SBT	Studies in Biblical Theology
SNTG	Studies in New Testament Greek
SNTS	Studiorum Novi Testamenti Societas
SNTSMS	Society for New Testament Studies Monograph Series
STRev	*Sewaneee Theological Review*

CHARACTERIZATION OF JESUS AS NARRATIVE CHRISTOLOGY

To be blessedly fallible,
to have the capacity to subvert manifest senses,
is the mark of good enough readers
and good enough texts.

Frank Kermode[1]

About halfway through the Gospel of Mark the main character, Jesus, asks his disciples, "Who do people say that I am?" (8:27) and then, more pointedly, "But who do you say that I am?" (8:29).[2] These questions have continued to challenge the Markan audience of hearers and readers for nearly two thousand years. As members of that audience, we would do well to listen carefully to the whole story for cues about the appropriate *process* of responding.

Jesus' disciples report that people do not agree on who Jesus is. Some say that he is John the Baptist (raised from the dead); others, that he is (the returned) Elijah; still others, one of the prophets (8:28). None of these answers is confirmed as adequate in the Markan narrative—although "prophet" comes

---

1. Frank Kermode, *The Genesis of Secrecy: On the Interpretation of Narrative* (Cambridge, Mass.: Harvard University Press, 1979), 14.

2. Except where otherwise indicated, all biblical translations are from the New Revised Standard Version (NRSV), copyright 1989 by the Division of Christian Education of the National Council of the Churches of Christ in the United States of America.

1

closest (6:4), and the Markan Jesus does not seem satisfied with them for he asks another question: "But who do *you* say that I am?" Peter, who throughout the narrative serves as the spokesperson for the disciples, answers, "You are the Christ [NRSV Messiah]" (8:29). This answer would seem to settle the matter. The narrator had begun the story with the application of the title Christ to Jesus: "The beginning of the gospel [NRSV good news] of Jesus Christ, the Son of God" (1:1). Thus the implied audience—that is, the audience implied or suggested by the text itself, the audience necessary for the narrative to be heard or read—knows that Peter's answer conforms to an overarching point of view of Mark's Gospel. But the story does not stop there, and whatever pause a twenty-first-century audience may experience is more a product of the fragmentation of the Gospel in weekly lectionary readings and in study Bibles than part of the natural flow of the narrative.

The first surprise is that the Markan Jesus does not commend Peter for his presumably correct answer.[3] Certainly the Markan Jesus does not condemn Peter for his response; rather, Jesus commands silence from all his disciples on this issue of who he is: "And he sternly ordered them not to tell anyone about him" (8:30). If Jesus is the Christ, why is this fact not to be proclaimed by the disciples at this point? "Christ," from the Greek *Christos*, translates the Hebrew word transliterated "messiah," meaning "anointed one," that is, one called by God to a special task, such as kingship or prophecy. Halfway through the Markan narrative, how much do Peter and the disciples know and understand about Jesus' special task?

Immediately after Jesus' command not to tell, the narrator continues:

Then he [Jesus] began to teach them that the Son of Man must undergo great suffering, and be rejected by the elders, the chief priests, and the scribes, and be killed, and after three days rise again. He said this all quite openly. And Peter took him aside and began to rebuke him. But turning and looking at his disciples, he rebuked Peter and said, "Get behind me Satan! For you are setting your mind not on divine things but on human things" (8:31-33).

Thus the second surprise is that Jesus (as the Son of Man or, translated more literally, the Son of Humanity) is to suffer—not, apparently, what Peter had intended in calling Jesus the Christ. The third surprise is that Peter is rebuked by Jesus (a strong word used for Jesus' response to demons and unclean spirits) as "Satan." The Markan narrative suggests that there is more to knowing who Jesus is than coming up with a correct title. There is at least the requirement of

3. It is not fair to bring into our reading of Mark's Gospel what Jesus says to Peter in Matthew's Gospel (Matt 16:17-19). Each gospel has its own powerful and unique way of telling the story. Along with most New Testament scholars, I conclude that Mark's Gospel was written prior to Matthew—and Luke and John—and was a literary source for Matthew and Luke.

engagement with the whole story of Jesus—as it fits into the story of God and influences the stories of Jesus' followers.[4]

History, Theology, Story

Hearers and readers of Mark's Gospel throughout the centuries have not only answered the Markan Jesus' question—"Who do you say that I am?"—differently, they have also asked quite different types of questions about the Markan Gospel that recounts this story. Some scholarly readers of Mark have asked, Who is the historical figure that lies behind this conversation? In fact, this search for the historical Jesus brought the Gospel of Mark into prominence in the eighteenth century when, as a result of source criticism and the growing acceptance of Markan priority as part of the two-source hypothesis, Mark's Gospel was presumed the best historical source among the gospels simply because it appeared to be the earliest.[5] Other scholarly readers of Mark have asked instead, What is the Christology supported by this Markan text? "Christology" is a term applied to theological reflection on the ongoing responses to these two questions of the Markan Jesus: Who do people say that I am? Who do you say that I am?

However, both the historical question and the theological question are problematic when applied to Mark's Gospel. The presumed "historicity" of the Gospel of Mark did not survive as well as the theory of Markan priority; scholars learned, as early as the work of William Wrede on "the messianic secret" in Mark (1901),[6] that just being first written did not mean that Mark was written in a disinterested way or without its own theological agenda, even if different from those of Matthew and Luke. Although Mark's Gospel continues to be of great interest to scholars and others interested in the quest for the historical Jesus, nearly all interpreters recognize that material from Mark's Gospel needs to be carefully sifted and subjected to additional tests for historicity as part of this quest. (We will return to this issue briefly in the final chapter.)

Certainly, to presume uncritically that the Jesus portrayed in Mark's Gospel represents the historical Jesus is problematic. So also, applying the term "Christology" to Mark's Gospel is problematic—and in two ways. First, the term is anachronistic when applied to a first-century text; Christology as an explicit category of thought is a development of later centuries of the Christian tradition. Second,

---

4. Cf. John R. Donahue, S.J., "Jesus as the Parable of God in the Gospel of Mark," in *Interpreting the Gospels* (ed. James Luther Mays; Philadelphia: Fortress, 1981), 148–67, see 148–49; first published in *Int* 32 (1978): 369–86.

5. For a brief and lively overview, see Janice Capel Anderson and Stephen D. Moore, "Introduction: The Lives of Mark," in *Mark and Method: New Approaches in Biblical Studies* (2nd ed.; ed. Janice Capel Anderson and Stephen D. Moore; Minneapolis: Fortress, 2008), 1–27, esp. 5–6.

6. William Wrede, *The Messianic Secret* (trans. J. C. C. Grieg; Cambridge and London: James Clarke, 1971). See Anderson and Moore, "Introduction," 6–7.

Christology is usually discussed in propositional language—even when such language is paradoxical (e.g., Jesus is fully human *and* Jesus is fully divine). This is the language of the great creeds of Christendom, such as the Nicene Creed. But it is not the language of Mark's Gospel—or of the biblical tradition as a whole for that matter![7] Perhaps it is because the "titles" that are applied to the Markan Jesus (Christ, Son of God, Son of Man, et al.) *seem* somewhat like propositional language or the language of the later creeds that the "Christological titles" in Mark have been the focus of many explorations of Markan Christology.[8]

The problem shared by both the pursuit of Mark's Gospel as a source for information about the historical Jesus and its exploration as a source for Christological affirmations is that what is overlooked, if not overwhelmed, is the Gospel of Mark itself! My goal in this book is to give serious, sustained attention to the story of Jesus told in the Gospel of Mark and the way of its telling. For me the Gospel of Mark is not a resource to be mined for historical nuggets or Christological jewels; it is the ground on which we walk.

Such a study, one that attends to the literary nature of the Gospel of Mark as a narrative, is not, of course, a completely new venture. Robert Tannehill's seminal essay in *Semeia* in 1979 introduced into the discussion the term "narrative christology."[9] Tannehill's pioneering move was to focus not on titles abstracted from the narrative but on actions embedded in the plot: "We learn who Jesus is through what he says and does in the context of the action of others."[10] (As a

---

7. As Herbert N. Schneidau observes, "narrative is of the essence, if one may use the term, of the Bible, it is not merely a vehicle or adjunct or epiphe[n]omenon. This point needs emphasis because it tends to be eclipsed by the assumption that the Bible consists of a set of doctrinal propositions, with illustrative stories: of all the *idées reçues* about the Bible, this one is surely the most stultifying." From "Biblical Narrative and Modern Consciousness," in *The Bible and the Narrative Tradition* (ed. Frank McConnell; Oxford: Oxford University Press, 1986), 132–50, quotation from 132.

8. But not all, of course. Leander E. Keck, for example, has long argued against such a way of doing New Testament Christology; see "Toward the Renewal of New Testament Christology," *NTS* 32 (1986): 362–77, esp. 368–70; "Christology and History: A Review Essay," *Theology Today* 57 (2000): 232–38; "The Task of New Testament Christology," *Princeton Seminary Bulletin* 26 NS (2005): 266–76. In fact, Keck claims that "probably no other factor has contributed more to the current aridity of the discipline than this fascination with the palaeontology of christological titles" ("Toward the Renewal," 368).

9. Robert C. Tannehill, "The Gospel of Mark as Narrative Christology," *Semeia* 16 (1979): 57–95, quotation from 57. See also Robert C. Tannehill, "The Disciples in Mark: The Function of a Narrative Role," *JR* 57 (1977): 386–405. Both essays have been republished in Robert C. Tannehill, *The Shape of the Gospel: New Testament Essays* (Eugene, Ore.: Cascade Books, 2007). On this contribution of Tannehill, see Elizabeth Struthers Malbon, "Markan Narrative Christology and the Kingdom of God," in *Literary Encounters with the Reign of God* (in honor of Robert C. Tannehill; ed. Sharon H. Ringe and H. C. Paul Kim; New York/London: T&T Clark International, 2004), 177–93, esp. 177–83.

10. Tannehill, "Narrative Christology," 58.

deliberate reminder that in my book I will be discussing not Christology in its usual sense as a branch of theology that is then *applied* to the Gospel of Mark but narrative christology that moves within the Markan story, I will not capitalize christology.) In 1982, the narrative critical approach to Mark's Gospel, and to its central character Jesus, was introduced to a broader audience by the publication of *Mark as Story: An Introduction to the Narrative of a Gospel* by David Rhoads and Donald Michie.[11] In 1983, Jack Dean Kingsbury attempted "a balancing act" in *The Christology of Mark's Gospel*: "while keeping the reader in touch with the plot of Mark by tracing the development of the motif of the secret of Jesus' identity, I have also attended to what I perceive to be the more stubborn problem of ascertaining the meaning and function of the major titles of majesty."[12] This is a difficult balancing act, and, in my judgment, Kingsbury's attention to the theological issue of Christological titles outweighs his attention to the literary issue of narrative functions and roles.[13] By the year 2000, the narrative critical approach to christology is categorized as one of three main approaches by Jacob Chacko Naluparayil in a review article on "Jesus of the Gospel of Mark":

Main approaches to the christological titles can be divided into three categories: (1) seeking the meaning to the christological titles outside the text [usually a

---

11. David Rhoads and Donald Michie, *Mark as Story: An Introduction to the Narrative of a Gospel* (Philadelphia: Fortress, 1982). A second edition has now appeared: David Rhoads, Joanna Dewey, and Donald Michie, *Mark as Story: An Introduction to the Narrative of a Gospel* (2nd ed.; Minneapolis: Fortress, 1999).

12. Jack Dean Kingsbury, *The Christology of Mark's Gospel* (Philadelphia: Fortress, 1983), ix.

13. In Kingsbury's more popular treatment of Markan christology, *Conflict in Mark: Jesus, Authorities, Disciples* (Minneapolis: Fortress, 1989), we hear an echo of Tannehill's more narrative terms "commissions" and "task." With Kingsbury, compare W. R. Telford, *The Theology of the Gospel of Mark* (New Testament Theology; Cambridge: Cambridge University Press, 1999), who, in discussing "The Person of Jesus" (30–54), also focuses on Christological titles but raises questions about their literary settings in the Markan narrative; Telford operates within the framework of redaction criticism and concludes that the author of Mark presents a Pauline-influenced Gentile Christian suffering Son of God Christology over against a Jewish-Christian Son of David and apocalyptic Son of Man Christology. For an insightful critique of "The Quest for Christological Titles," see the introductory chapter of Edwin K. Broadhead's *Naming Jesus: Titular Christology in the Gospel of Mark* (JSNTSup 175; Sheffield: Sheffield Academic, 1999). See also John Donahue's overview of four "presentations" of the Jesus of Mark in his recent study: Jesus as Hellenistic Savior; Jesus as the Fulfillment of the Old Testament; Jesus, Messiah, Son of God, Son of Man (focused on "titles"); Jesus as Prophetic Teacher and Apocalyptic Seer ("Jesus as the Parable of God," 149–55). Suzanne Watts Henderson concludes her study of discipleship passages in Mark 1–6 with this statement: "faithful discipleship can best be understood not as the correct appraisal of Jesus' Christological identity, but as the disciples' collective participation in Jesus' Christological mission" (*Christology and Discipleship in the Gospel of Mark* [SNTSMS 135; Cambridge: Cambridge University Press, 2006], 241).

historical focus]; (2) finding the key in the theological interests of the author, often
in conjunction with redaction criticism [a theological focus]; and (3) in conjunction with narrative criticism, looking for the meaning of the titles within the narrative as they are defined by the act of narration [a literary focus].[14]

But the hold of Christological titles and the pull of the quest for the historical Jesus are strong, and appropriate attention has yet to be paid to how
the story of Jesus unfolds in the Gospel of Mark. Even if Mark's Gospel is to
be a resource for another type of study—whether historical or theological—it
deserves to be read literarily and carefully as the narrative document it is. And,
in fact, as narrative critics and their audiences have generally found, such careful
attention to the narrative for its own sake is repaid in greater appreciation of the
mystery of the Gospel of Mark. This is my goal.

Narrative Criticism and the Characterization of Mark's Jesus

As a narrative critic of the Gospel of Mark, I have been asking the question,
"*How* does the story mean?"[15] Although I recognize the importance of the first-
century historical context of Mark's Gospel on the one hand, and, on the other,
the religious significance of Mark's Gospel for two thousand years of Christian faith, my own research concerns the Gospel's literariness, its narrativity,
its working as a story—with settings, characters, plot, and rhetoric—all communicated from an implied author to an implied audience. Because these terms

14. Jacob Chacko Naluparayil, "Jesus of the Gospel of Mark: Present State of Research,"
Currents in Research: Biblical Studies 8 (2000): 191–226, quotation from 192 (note the focus on christological titles). Although Naluparayil discusses, under the category of narrative
critical approaches, some of the earlier work of Broadhead, he does not list Broadhead's
more recent book, *Naming Jesus: Titular Christology in the Gospel of Mark.* Although it might
appear from the subtitle—and the table of contents, seeming to list sixteen "christological
titles"—that this small and intriguing book by Broadhead focuses on "christological titles" in
isolation from their Markan narrative contexts, such an interpretation is nearly the opposite
of Broadhead's meaning: "There are no titles which are inherently and unambiguously christological; they become so only within defined social and literary contexts. Because of this
recognition, it is perhaps more accurate to speak of 'Titular Christology' rather than 'Christological Titles.' Titular Christology recognizes that the titles, along with various other materials, have been taken up as strategic elements in the characterization of Jesus" (28). "Titles
prove to be one element in complex patterns of narrative characterization" (28). Broadhead's
book is not an attempt to portray a narrative christology but "a formalist description of the
narrative titles set against a *traditionsgeschichtliche* (history of traditions) context" (30).
15. Elizabeth Struthers Malbon, "Narrative Criticism: How Does the Story Mean?" in
Mark and Method: New Approaches in Biblical Studies (2nd ed.; ed. Janice Capel Anderson
and Stephen D. Moore; Minneapolis: Fortress, 2008 [first published in 1992]), 29–57. The
1992 version is republished as the first chapter in Elizabeth Struthers Malbon, *In the Company of Jesus: Characters in Mark's Gospel* (Louisville: Westminster John Knox, 2000), 1–40.

are presupposed in the present study, a word must be said about how they are being used.

In the model of a narrative text frequently used by narrative critics, based on the model of literary critic Seymour Chatman,[16] a narrative is understood as a communication between an implied author and an implied reader or implied audience. (Although Chatman referred to the "implied reader," many narrative critics now use "implied audience" in recognition of biblical narratives' originating oral/aural contexts. The Gospel of Mark was written to be heard.) "The implied author is a theoretical construction based on the requirements of knowledge and understanding presupposed in a narrative; in other words, the implied author is the one who would be necessary for a particular narrative to be told or written. The implied audience is the one that would be necessary for a particular narrative to be heard or read."[17] Both the implied author and the implied audience are considered internal (although constructed and theoretical) aspects of the narrative. The narrator and the narrator's counterpart, the narratee, are also internal to the narrative, but the real author and the real audience are external to the narrative. "Narrative critics are wary of what is called the 'intentional fallacy' (overvaluing the presumed motivation of the 'real' author) and the 'affective fallacy' (overvaluing the response of the 'real' audience), but of course they realize that basic information about the cultural context is essential to any interpretation"[18]—and that each narrative critic is one among many members of many real audiences.

Thus there are three embedded communicating pairs, one external to the narrative (real author/real audience) and two internal to the narrative (implied author/implied audience and narrator/narratee). Although my work is not focused on the real author or the real audience, I recognize that without both of those we would not have the luxury of focusing on the textual continuum: implied author/narrator/characters/narratee/implied audience.[19] The Markan narrator depicts the action of the Markan Jesus (a character) to the narratee,

---

16. Seymour Chatman, *Story and Discourse: Narrative Structure in Fiction and Film* (Ithaca: Cornell University Press, 1978).

17. Elizabeth Struthers Malbon, "Narrative Criticism: How Did the Theory Develop and What Are Its Main Features?" in *Searching for Meaning: A Practical Guide to New Testament Interpretation* (by Paula Gooder; London: SPCK, 2008; Louisville: Westminster John Knox, 2009), 80; cf. Malbon, "Narrative Criticism," 33. A diagram of Chatman's model, as modified by narrative critics, appears at each of these points.

18. Malbon, "Narrative Criticism: How Did the Theory Develop," 80–81; cf. Malbon, "Narrative Criticism," 33.

19. Stephen H. Smith, *A Lion with Wings: A Narrative-Critical Approach to Mark's Gospel* (Sheffield: Sheffield Academic, 1996), 29, presents a modification (following Vorster and Staley) of the diagram of Chatman as an inverted pyramid, with the characters appearing "at the lowest level, for they are confined by the temporal and spatial constraints of the story-world."

but both the Markan narrator and the Markan Jesus, each of whom has his own point of view, are being used by the Markan implied author to communicate with the Markan implied audience. The relationships of these three—the implied author, the narrator, and the character Jesus—will be of special interest to me in this study. All are part of the narrative world, which is my focus here rather than the real world of the first-century Gospel of Mark. I am also particularly interested in the relationship of the story level of the narrative (where the narrator recounts the words and actions of the various characters in relation to each other) to the discourse level of the narrative (where the implied author communicates with the implied audience through the overall arrangement of the story elements).

More detailed discussions of the other terms mentioned above as elements of narrative—settings, characters, plot, rhetoric—are readily available in several introductions to narrative criticism in biblical studies generally and narrative criticism of the Gospel of Mark in particular.[20] All these elements will be relevant at some point in the present work, and their Markan significance will be exemplified as my argument unfolds. I began my scholarly work on the Gospel of Mark by investigating the significance of the spatial settings throughout which the characters move in Mark's story.[21] Since then I have made some com-

---

20. General introductions to biblical narrative criticism: David M. Gunn, "Narrative Criticism," chapter 10 (with Hebrew Bible examples) in *To Each Its Own Meaning: An Introduction to Biblical Criticisms and Their Application* (revised and expanded ed.; ed. Steven L. McKenzie and Stephen R. Haynes; Louisville: Westminster John Knox, 1999), 201–29; Daniel Marguerat and Yvan Bourquin, *How to Read Bible Stories: An Introduction to Narrative Criticism* (with the collaboration of Marcel Durrer; illus. Florence Clerc; trans. John Bowden; London: SCM, 1999); Mark Allen Powell, *What Is Narrative Criticism?* (GBS; Minneapolis: Fortress, 1990); James L. Resseguie, *Narrative Criticism of the New Testament: An Introduction* (Grand Rapids: Baker Academic, 2005). Markan introductions to narrative criticism: Paula Gooder, "Narrative Criticism," chapter 10 of *Searching for Meaning: A Practical Guide to New Testament Interpretation* (by Paula Gooder; London: SPCK, 2008; Louisville: Westminster John Knox, 2009), 80–87, 220; Daniel J. Harrington, S.J., "Literary Studies," chapter 2 of *What Are They Saying about Mark?* (2nd ed.; Mahwah, N.J.: Paulist, 2004), 10–28; Malbon, "Narrative Criticism"; Rhoads, Dewey, and Michie, *Mark as Story*; Smith, *A Lion with Wings*. For a helpful overview that provides a framework for appreciating narrative criticism among many critical approaches, see Anderson and Moore, "Introduction." For critiques of narrative criticism, see Stephen D. Moore, *Literary Criticism and the Gospels: The Theoretical Challenge* (New Haven: Yale University Press, 1989)—largely from the point of view of deconstruction, and Petri Merenlahti, *Poetics for the Gospels? Rethinking Narrative Criticism* (Edinburgh: T&T Clark, 2002)—largely from the point of view of ideological criticism, as well as the opening chapter (by Petri Merenlahti and Raimo Hakola) and closing chapter (by David Rhoads) of David Rhoads and Kari Syreeni, eds., *Characterization in the Gospels: Reconceiving Narrative Criticism* (JSNTSup 184; Sheffield: Sheffield Academic, 1999).

21. See especially Elizabeth Struthers Malbon, *Narrative Space and Mythic Meaning in*

ments on Markan plot and rhetoric,[22] but chiefly I have been observing Markan characters and have written on the disciples and the crowd,[23] the women characters and the broader category of fallible followers,[24] the Jewish leaders,[25] and the so-called minor characters[26]—nearly all the characters around Jesus.[27] It is from this perspective that I have more recently turned my attention to the Gospel's central character, Jesus.[28]

Since 1993, three substantial books on the characterization of the Markan Jesus have appeared[29] whose titles and subtitles may suggest more overlap with my current project than turns out to be the case: Ole Davidsen, *The Narrative Jesus: A Semiotic Reading of Mark's Gospel*;[30] Jacob Chacko Naluparayil, *The Identity of Jesus in Mark: An Essay on Narrative Christology*;[31] and Paul Danove, *The Rhetoric of the Characterization of God, Jesus, and Jesus' Disciples in the Gospel of Mark*.[32] A brief look at each of these three books will help set the scene for

---

Mark (San Francisco: Harper & Row, 1986; volume 13 of The Biblical Seminar; Sheffield: Sheffield Academic, 1991).

22. Elizabeth Struthers Malbon, "Echoes and Foreshadowings in Mark 4–8: Reading and Rereading," *JBL* 112 (1993): 213–32; Malbon, "Narrative Criticism."

23. Elizabeth Struthers Malbon, "Disciples/Crowds/Whoever: Markan Characters and Readers," *NovT* 28 (1986): 104–30; Malbon, "Texts and Contexts: Interpreting the Disciples in Mark," *Semeia* 62 (1993): 81–102.

24. Elizabeth Struthers Malbon, "Fallible Followers: Women and Men in the Gospel of Mark," *Semeia* 28 (1983): 29–48; Malbon, "The Poor Widow in Mark and Her Poor Rich Readers," *CBQ* 53 (1991): 589–604.

25. Elizabeth Struthers Malbon, "The Jewish Leaders in the Gospel of Mark: A Literary Study of Marcan Characterization," *JBL* 108 (1989): 259–81.

26. Elizabeth Struthers Malbon, "The Major Importance of the Minor Characters in Mark," in *The New Literary Criticism and the New Testament* (ed. Elizabeth Struthers Malbon and Edgar V. McKnight; JSNTSup 109; Sheffield: Sheffield Academic, 1994; Valley Forge, Pa.: Trinity, 1994), 58–86.

27. The six essays listed in notes 23–26, plus the 1992 version of the essay listed in note 15, are republished together as *In the Company of Jesus: Characters in Mark's Gospel* (Louisville: Westminster John Knox, 2000).

28. For a list of articles on the characterization of the Markan Jesus that began as the first draft of this book, then developed separate lives as articles or chapters—several in *Festschriften*—and have now been thoroughly reworked in this book, see the Acknowledgments.

29. Concerning a fourth book, P. Muller, *"Wer ist dieser?" Jesus in Markusevangelium* (BThSt 27; Neukirchen-Vluyn, Germany: Neukirchner Verlag, 1995), the reader is referred to the review of Naluparayil listed in note 14 above.

30. Ole Davidsen, *The Narrative Jesus: A Semiotic Reading of Mark's Gospel* (Aarhus, Denmark: Aarhus University Press, 1993).

31. Jacob Chacko Naluparayil, *The Identity of Jesus in Mark: An Essay on Narrative Christology* (Studium Biblicum Franciscanum Analecta 49; Jerusalem: Franciscan Printing Press, 2000).

32. Paul L. Danove, *The Rhetoric of the Characterization of God, Jesus, and Jesus' Disciples in the Gospel of Mark* (JSNTSup 290; New York: T&T Clark, 2005).

what I propose in my exploration of the characterization of Jesus in the Gospel of Mark.[33]

Ole Davidsen's *The Narrative Jesus: A Semiotic Reading of Mark's Gospel* presents an intricate interpretation of aspects of the Markan Jesus based on an elaboration of the theoretical work of Claude Bremond on narrative "roles" and "programs" and of A.-J. Greimas on semiotic squares (although that term is not used here). Davidsen identifies the three basic roles of the Markan Jesus as the wonder-worker, the proclaimer, and the savior. He is interested not in the movement between events of the narrative but in the deeper working out of the basic semiotic program of Jesus in the role of savior; Jesus' roles as wonder-worker and proclaimer are understood to be subsidiary to that underlying semiotic structure. "The term *narrative christology*," for Davidsen, "refers to the gospel narrative's teaching on Christ, God's anointed, his person and his acts. This teaching . . . must be reconstructed on the basis of a narrative analysis of the story's universe,"[34] which, in Davidsen's analysis, is many levels of abstraction away from the story itself.[35] Davidsen concludes that "[n]arrative exegesis

---

33. This is not the place to review broadly how narrative critics have explored characterization in biblical narratives or even the gospels. The reader who wishes a compact overview is referred to Rhoads, Dewey, and Michie, *Mark as Story*, 98–103, and the literature cited there. In the space of a few pages the major issues of characterization are raised: "showing" vs. "telling" about characters, consistency of characters, readers' inferences about characters, social locations of characters, characters as types in ancient literature, characters and the narrative's standards of judgment, comparison and contrasts among characters in a narrative, traits of characters, and audience identification with characters. A helpful chapter on characters or characterization, with references to literary critical and biblical critical studies, also appears in each of the following books: Marguerat and Bourquin, *How to Read Bible Stories*; Powell, *What Is Narrative Criticism?*; Resseguie, *Narrative Criticism of the New Testament*; Smith, *A Lion with Wings*—all cited in full in note 20 above. Two anthologies of biblical narrative critical work focused on characterization are Elizabeth Struthers Malbon and Adele Berlin, eds., *Characterization in Biblical Literature*, Semeia 63 (1993), and Rhoads and Syreeni, eds., *Characterization in the Gospels: Reconceiving Narrative Criticism*. For a reader-response approach to characterization, see John A. Darr, *On Character Building: The Reader and the Rhetoric of Characterization in Luke-Acts* (Louisville: Westminster John Knox, 1992); Darr, "Narrator as Character: Mapping a Reader-Oriented Approach to Narration in Luke-Acts," *Semeia* 63 (1993): 43–60; and Fred W. Burnett, "Characterization and Reader Construction of Characters in the Gospels," *Semeia* 63 (1993): 1–28.

34. Davidsen, *Narrative Jesus*, 333, italics original; see also his reference to "semiotic or narrative criticism, one of whose tasks is to explain in detail the extent to which the gospel of Jesus Christ symbolizes or semiotizes our historical reality" (372).

35. Like most interpreters, Davidsen makes no distinction between the Markan implied author and the narrator: "By the story-teller, or Mark, therefore is meant the narrator . . ." (*Narrative Jesus*, 28). Davidsen does refer occasionally to "the implicit reader" (e.g., 179, 184) and at least once to the narratee (333). Doing without the distinction between implied author and narrator seems to lead to blurring the distinction between the implied author

thus seems to be a particularly appropriate methodical basis for the establishment of a New Testament theology."[36] A second book on Jesus in Mark, equally extensive and equally theological, focuses less on christology as soteriology than Davidsen does[37] and more on Christology as identity.

Jacob Chacko Naluparayil's *The Identity of Jesus in Mark: An Essay on Narrative Christology* opens with a review of the problem of the identity of Jesus in Mark; however, there is then a long detour to discuss and debate issues of sources and redaction. (Like most narrative critics, I will begin with the Markan narrative in the Greek text that has come down to us and not debate redactional issues.) Naluparayil examines the points of view of what he terms five "individuals"—the narrator, God, Jesus, the disciples, and the Jewish leaders—on two "planes": the identity plane (their point of view about Jesus) and the ideological plane (their evaluative viewpoint). His conclusion that the points of view of God, Jesus, the narrator, and the implied reader converge echoes that of Norman Petersen in 1978.[38] Finally, Naluparayil investigates the character Jesus directly by identifying separately the traits of Jesus from the views of other characters and the traits of Jesus from what he does and says. Then he "brings together" these two lists of traits, along with "other evidences appearing in the narrative that would assist our comprehension of Jesus' character traits"[39]—a less-than-clear method—into a list of "prominent traits" and the "designation" that together "answer the question 'what Jesus is like.'"[40] Naluparayil's overall conclusion is that "'the Son of Man' functions in the narrative as the designation, as the locus of all the above-said divine character traits of the protagonist, as the name of the divine person."[41] In my judgment Naluparayil, like Kingsbury, allows a christological title (for him "Son of Man," a designation privileged by Jesus; for Kingsbury "Christ" and "Son of God," privileged by the narrator)

---

and the characters: "But whether or not an embedded enunciative or utterative speech is concerned it is the narrator who supplies the voice"(177); "When the narrative Jesus speaks it is Mark who speaks, hidden behind a narrated actor. When the disciples speak it is similarly Mark who speaks, hidden behind narrated actors" (362). In my work I will be making careful distinctions among these various voices.

36. Davidsen, *Narrative Jesus*, 360, n. 5. Davidsen can also express the implicit dangers: "When exegesis falls to temptation and hypostatizes, it also fails to appreciate its own task and tends to carry out a static and abstract-dogmatic discourse" (320).

37. Davidsen, *Narrative Jesus*, 339: "As already said, christology and soteriology are two aspects of the same matter."

38. Norman R. Petersen, "'Point of View' in Mark's Narrative," *Semeia* 12 (1978): 97–121. In my final chapter, I will discuss my disagreement with Petersen on the point paralleled by Naluparayil.

39. Naluparayil, *Identity of Jesus*, 540.

40. Naluparayil, *Identity of Jesus*, 540.

41. Naluparayil, *Identity of Jesus*, 547. For more details, see my review of Naluparayil, *The Identity of Jesus in Mark*, in *Biblica* 4 (2001): 569–73.

and concern for abstract (essentialist) christological categories like "identity" to outweigh narratological concerns like plot and characterization.[42]

Paul Danove's *The Rhetoric of the Characterization of God, Jesus, and Jesus' Disciples in the Gospel of Mark* is smaller in length than the works of Davidsen and Naluparayil. However, in one way it is broader in scope: it deals not only with the characterization of Jesus but also with the characterization of God and the disciples, which the other two authors also recognize as related.[43] Repetition is key to this method:[44] repetition of words and phrases because such "repetition is able to develop specialized meaning or connotations for particular words and phrases,"[45] but also "nonverbal repetition," that is, repetition of "constructs abstracted from the narration."[46] Danove notes, however, that his "proposed method ultimately grounds the contribution of both verbal and nonverbal rep-

42. In the terms of literary theorist Menakhem Perry, it would appear to me that Christologies based on titles interpret Mark's Gospel as having "'model'-oriented motivations" whereas a narrative christological interpretation such as Tannehill's assumes "[r]hetorical or reader-oriented motivations: the structure of the text-continuum here is not motivated in terms of a model which the text imitates and the reader must identify or in terms of a frame which the reader has to construct. Here the text is grasped as a message which is supposed to be experienced" ("Literary Dynamics: How the Order of a Text Creates Its Meanings [with an Analysis of Faulkner's 'A Rose for Emily']," *Poetics* 1 [1979]: 35–64 and 311–61, quotation from 40).

43. In this book Danove draws together and develops four previously published studies— on the characterization of God, Jesus, the disciples, and the women at the tomb (here treated as a "recapitulation" of the characterization of the disciples)—and frames them with a careful delineation of his method of analysis at the beginning and, at the end, a consideration of applications and implications of the four studies of characterization. See Paul Danove, "The Narrative Function of Mark's Characterization of God," *NovT* 43 (2001): 12–30; Paul Danove, "The Rhetoric of the Characterization of Jesus as the Son of Man and Christ in Mark," *Biblica* 84 (2003): 16–34; Paul Danove, "A Rhetorical Analysis of Mark's Construction of Discipleship," in *Rhetorical Criticism and the Bible: Essays from the 1998 Florence Conference* (ed. Stanley D. Porter and Dennis L. Stamps; JSNTSup 195; Sheffield: Sheffield Academic, 2002), 280–96; Paul Danove, "The Characterization and Narrative Function of the Women at the Tomb (Mark 15,40-41, 47; 16,1-8)," *Biblica* 77 (1996): 375–97. To Danove's "A Rhetorical Analysis of Mark's Construction of Discipleship," compare his "The Narrative Rhetoric of Mark's Ambiguous Characterization of the Disciples," *JSNT* 70 (1998): 21–38; in the former article Danove states that "[e]lements of the analysis receive alternative development" in the latter. Danove's method of analysis depends on his earlier work, *Linguistics and Exegesis in the Gospel of Mark: Applications of a Case Frame Analysis and Lexicon* (JSNTSup 218; SNTG 10; Sheffield: Sheffield Academic, 2001).

44. Danove, *Rhetoric of Characterization*, 12: "Of the panoply of potential manifestations of the semantic rhetoric available to the original readers and interpreters, only those discernible in the text remain; and, of these, repetition constitutes the least contentious, most pervasive, and most directly accessible."

45. Danove, *Rhetoric of Characterization*, 3.

46. Danove, *Rhetoric of Characterization*, 5–6.

etition in linguistic concepts."[47] He employs the terms "authorial audience" and "narrative audience" in the sense proposed by Peter Rabinowitz,[48] and the distinction is critical for Danove's work because he seeks to show how the "pre-interpreted" or "preexisting" beliefs of the authorial audience (which are evoked by "neutral repetition") are sometimes reinforced (by "sophisticated repetition") and sometimes challenged (by "deconstructive repetition"), thus forming the "cultivated beliefs" encouraged in the narrative audience through the narrative rhetoric. Danove's work is quite detailed and methodical; however, it offers few insights on the characterization of Jesus in Mark's Gospel that have not long been presented by both redaction critics and narrative critics, although it does confirm such insights by an alternate method, one that is linguistically based.[49] I find it problematic that Danove, like Davidsen, Naluparayil, and many other Markan commentators, makes no distinction between the levels of the reporting of the words—no distinction between the words of the narrator and the words of Jesus, and for Danove, not even a distinction between the words of Mark's Gospel telling the story of Jesus and the words of Jesus telling the parable of the wicked tenants. In my hearing of Mark's Gospel, all words are not created (or spoken) equal.

In relation to the work of Davidsen, Naluparayil, and Danove, my interest is considerably more exegetical than theoretical. My question is, How does the Gospel of Mark characterize Jesus? not, How can characterization be theorized within narrative criticism or within linguistically based rhetoric? or, How can a particular theoretical construction of characterization be applied to Mark's Gospel or Mark's Jesus? In addition, and especially in contrast to the work of Davidsen and Naluparayil, my work is more literary than theological.[50] Again, my

47. Danove, *Rhetoric of Characterization*, 6.

48. Peter J. Rabinowitz, "Truth in Fiction: A Reexamination of Audiences," *Critical Inquiry* 4 (1974): 121–41, esp. 126–33.

49. Overall, this firm linguistic base seems to me to constrain unduly Danove's work on the characterization of Jesus in Mark's Gospel. The observations and arguments are so based on statistical word studies that the resultant picture of both rhetoric and characterization is atomistic. Others studying rhetoric do look more broadly at both the text and the context—for example, Vernon K. Robbins, *Jesus the Teacher: A Socio-Rhetorical Interpretation of Mark* (Philadelphia: Fortress, 1984); Whitney Taylor Shiner, *Follow Me! Disciples in Markan Rhetoric* (SBLDS 145; Atlanta: Scholars Press, 1995); Whitney Shiner, *Proclaiming the Gospel: First-Century Performance of Mark* (Harrisburg, Pa.: Trinity, 2003). Others studying characterization do look at units larger than words, such as the speech and actions of characters within the plot.

50. Danove mentions but does not develop the theological application of his method in *The Rhetoric of Characterization*, but I am made nervous by his assertion that "[t]he development of a single, integrated, and coherent method for analyzing the semantic and narrative rhetoric of repetition and the narrative rhetoric and function of characterization has significant implications for articulating rigorous and specific statements of Mark's theology, christology, and mathetology [having to do with the disciples and discipleship]. . . . [T]he

question is, *How* does the Gospel of Mark characterize Jesus? not, *What* is the
Christology of Mark's Gospel? However, a crucial theoretical issue is raised by
my literary interest in the *how*, rather than the *what*, of Jesus' characterization.
I am seeking to understand *how* narrative christology works in Mark's narrative
and not *what* the Christology of Mark's Gospel is within a theological system.
Although interpreters interested in the *what* of Markan christology also read
the Markan narrative, their conclusions are usually distilled in discursive language in relation to theological issues raised elsewhere. Interpreters interested in
the *how* of Markan narrative christology focus on the emergence of meaning in
the experience of reading itself, guided by multiple dimensions of the narrative
and producing no concept or idea precipitated out as separate from its narrative
manifestation. In this regard, my recurrent dialogue partners throughout this
book are John Donahue, Gene Boring, and Edwin Broadhead through their
published works on Markan christology and the Markan narrative.[51]

Thus I will not be making any statements about "the roles that *constitute*
the narrative Jesus" (Davidsen[52]) or "the identity of Jesus" (Naluparayil). Although the Markan Jesus' question, "*Who* do you say that I am?" is perhaps the
key question, in different ways, for Davidsen and Naluparayil, the question that
is key for me is "*How* does the Gospel of Mark suggest who Jesus is?" To answer
this question I will, unlike Danove, not focus on the linguistic level of verbal
and nonverbal repetition but on aspects of the narrative level, making careful
observations about who says what to whom about the Markan Jesus when and
under what circumstances, as well as what the Markan Jesus says in response
and instead. Thus my investigation of the characterization of Jesus in Mark's
Gospel is based on a fairly simple observation about characters in narratives:
characters are known by what they say and by what they do and by what others
(the narrator and other characters) say and do to, about, or in relation to them.

---

method provides access to a large quantity of grammatically justified semantic data about the
characters that may be placed in the service of theological interpretation. . . . For example, . . .
[t]he capacity of the proposed method to clarify the manner in which all of the referenced beliefs are related to these thirty-five actions and attributes [of God, as presented in his chapter 2]
and the manner in which these beliefs are organized into a unified framework for interpretation establishes the possibility for developing a very detailed and nuanced statement of
Mark's theology" (*Rhetoric of Characterization*, 164).

51. John R. Donahue, S.J., "Jesus as the Parable of God"; Donahue, "A Neglected Factor in the Theology of Mark," *JBL* 101 (1982): 563–94; M. Eugene Boring, "The Christology of Mark: Hermeneutical Issues for Systematic Theology," *Semeia* 30 (1984): 125–53;
Boring, "Markan Christology: God-Language for Jesus?" *NTS* 45 (1999): 451–71; Edwin K.
Broadhead: *Teaching with Authority: Miracles and Christology in the Gospel of Mark* (JSNTSup
74; Sheffield: Sheffield Academic, 1992); Broadhead, *Prophet, Son, Messiah: Narrative Form
and Function in Mark 14–16* (JSNTSup 97; Sheffield: Sheffield Academic, 1994); Broadhead, *Naming Jesus*.

52. Davidsen, *Narrative Jesus*, 33, emphasis added.

The table below shows how these categories ("say" and "do"/"main character" and "others") are interrelated in focusing on characterization of the main character in a narrative.

Characterization of the Main Character in a Narrative

	OTHERS	MAIN CHARACTER
SAY(S)	what other characters and the narrator say to and about the main character	what the main character says
DO(ES)	what other characters and the narrator do in relation to the main character	what the main character does

This table will be adapted to the specific case of the characterization of Jesus in the Gospel of Mark.

In focusing on the particularity of who says what rather than on the generality of what is said, I will be calling attention to some applications of the theory of "point of view." Norman Petersen's 1978 article "'Point of View' in Mark's Narrative"[53] served to introduce many New Testament scholars to the theoretical work of Boris Uspensky on point of view.[54] Although Petersen was right to note that the overarching ideological (or evaluative) point of view of the narrative is, in the words of the Markan Jesus, the importance of "thinking the things of God" rather than "thinking the things of human beings," in my investigation I have come to realize that the conclusion of Petersen (and most narrative critics) that the "point of view" of the Markan narrator (and implied author) is

---

53. See note 38 above.

54. Boris Uspensky, *A Poetics of Composition: The Structure of the Artistic Text and Typology of a Compositional Form* (trans. Valentina Zavarin and Susan Wittig; Berkeley: University of California Press, 1973). In my final chapter I will deal directly with Petersen's application of Uspensky's categories to Mark's Gospel; however, it is not my intention to evoke Uspensky's specific theory when using the phrase "point of view" periodically in my work, since the phrase is also meaningful in a more general way. On the few occasions when I am using the phrase technically, I will use "point of view." A clear and vigilant presentation of Uspensky's work can be found in Gary Yamasaki, *Watching a Biblical Narrative: Point of View in Biblical Exegesis* (New York and London: T&T Clark, 2007), 30–34, but also throughout the book in pointing out how various subsequent interpreters "misunderstand" Uspensky. In Yamasaki's words, "the essence of point of view" is "the narrator leading the audience to see the events of the story line as filtered through the consciousness of one of the characters, or simply through the consciousness of the narrator" (94–95).

completely aligned with the "point of view" of the Markan Jesus misses a key element in the characterization of Jesus in Mark. Ever since Chatman's model was
introduced, narrative critics have had readily available the theoretical distinction between the implied author and the narrator; we have simply not always
taken advantage of it. My exploration of the characterization of Mark's Jesus has
renewed my appreciation for this theoretical distinction between the implied
author, who controls all the characters and all their points of view (in the usual,
not technical, sense of the phrase), and the narrator, who may be conceived as
functioning somewhat like a character and, like a character, manifests a point of
view. The importance of maintaining this theoretical distinction will come into
increasingly sharper focus as we move through the material, and I will address
the issue explicitly in the final chapter. A second theoretical issue that can only
be raised as a question at the end of this study is the complexity of categorizing
and interrelating layers or strands within a narrative—whether literary strands,
such as multiple points of view, or "historical" layers, such as "the historical
Jesus" and "the Markan redactor."

Characterization of Jesus as Narrative Christology

Characterization is a term used in narrative criticism; Christology is a term
used in theology; narrative christology is a term introduced by Robert Tannehill as a corrective for the imposition of theological categories onto the
characterization of Jesus in the narrative of Mark.[55] A narrative christology
of Mark follows the cues of the Markan narrative. Remembering the experience of the character Peter, a narrative christology of Mark looks for something more than coming up with the correct title. As Gene Boring writes in
his essay on "The Christology of Mark": "While Mark does not do christology
without considerable attention to titles, neither does he make finding the appropriate title for Jesus the primary method of christology, precisely because
pronouncing the correct title can still be a profound misunderstanding (8:27-
31)."[56] What leads to understanding is engagement with the story. As Boring
continues:

55. Reginald Fuller notes that a tension between story (narrative) and thought (theology) is manifest in the word "christology" itself: "But the very fact that christology conceals
a combination of two very different ideas, one of them Hebraic, denoting appointment for a
particular role in (salvation) history, and the other a Greek word, denoting reflection and ra-
tiocination, suggests something of a paradox. We must not exaggerate the difference between
Hebraic and Greek thought, but there is a difference, for example, between Aristotle's *Metaphys-
ics* and the book of Deuteronomy!" ("Christology: Its Nature and Methods," in Reginald H.
Fuller and Pheme Perkins, *Who Is This Christ? Gospel Christology and Contemporary Faith*
[Philadelphia: Fortress, 1983], 1–2).
56. Boring, "Christology of Mark," 133. Note that Boring also does not capitalize
christology.

> Mark is a theologian who writes a story. His christology is a narrative christology. . . .
> It is thus not the case that the sixteen chapters of Mark's narrative are only the raw
> materials for christology, awaiting some explanation in propositional language to
> explicate a "real" christology based on Mark's narrative. Mark's narrative is already
> a christology.[57]

And as Edwin Broadhead asserts, "Christology is characterization."[58] My book
is one reading of this narrative christology of Mark's Gospel understood as the
way in which the Markan Jesus is characterized—thus, my subtitle, *Characterization as Narrative Christology.*

Michael Cook argues not only that narrative is essential to Markan christology but that narrative is central to *all* christology. Cook writes of *Christology
as Narrative Quest.*[59] Such an argument is beyond the scope of the present work:
Cook's focus is Christology; mine is the Markan narrative. But both Cook and
Boring present strongly the philosophical, epistemological, and literary evidence that indicates that the only christology to be attributed fairly to Mark's
Gospel is narrative christology, in the sense expressed by Tannehill when he
introduced the term in 1979. My goal is to investigate the characterization of
Jesus in Mark's Gospel as narrative christology.

As Pheme Perkins notes in an essay on "Mark as Narrative Christology,"
"Narrative by its very nature always suggests more than it spells out explicitly.
Differences in presentation depend in part on those details to which a given
interpreter or a given method is sensitive."[60] As a narrative critic, I am interested
in all the ways the narrative employs to disclose its central character, Jesus, but
I will, of course, be sensitive only to certain details, and I will be unable here
even to comment on all of those. The centrality of Jesus in the Markan narrative makes discussion of this character more complex than discussions of the
other characters. To share my reflections more clearly, I present them in five
specifically Markan categories based on the four basic ways characters become
known to an audience explained above: characters are known by what they say
and by what they do, and by what others (the narrator and other characters)
say and do to, about, or in relation to them. The table below shows how these

57. Boring, "Christology of Mark," 136–37. See also Boring, "Markan Christology."

58. Broadhead, *Teaching with Authority*, 25. Broadhead's comment should be read in
context: "Because the content, the processes and the results of the Gospels are all literary in
nature, a crucial consequence follows: Christology is characterization." The broader context
of this sentence is Broadhead's introductory chapter, which is also relevant to mine.

59. Michael L. Cook, S.J., *Christology as Narrative Quest* (Collegeville, Minn.: Liturgical Press, 1997). See especially chapter 1, "The Centrality of Narrative in Christology," and
chapter 2, "A Biblical Image: 'The Beloved Son' in the Gospel of Mark." In chapters 3, 4,
and 5, Cook explores images of Christ in the Nicene-Constantinopolitan Creed, the *Summa
Theologiae* of Thomas Aquinas, and Mexican American experience of "the rejected prophet."

60. Pheme Perkins, "Mark as Narrative Christology," in Fuller and Perkins, *Who Is This
Christ?* 77.

categories ("say" and "do"/"Jesus" and "others") are worked out in this narrative christology of Mark's Gospel, with the numbers in parentheses representing the chapters in this book.

Characterization of Jesus in Mark's Gospel as a Multilayered Narrative Christology

	OTHERS	JESUS
SAY(S)	what other characters and the narrator say to and about Jesus: projected christology (2)	what Jesus says in response to other characters: deflected christology (3)
		what Jesus says instead of what other characters and the narrator say: refracted christology (4)
DO(ES)	what other characters do that mirrors what Jesus says and does: reflected christology (5)	what Jesus does: enacted christology (1)

The five categories—enacted, projected, deflected, refracted, reflected—are not simply formal categories like "say" and "do" but also suggest the content of what I have come to realize about Mark's Gospel and Mark's Jesus in attending to those formal categories in my reading. (If these five categories—which I have had years to think about and learn to say without tripping!—seem confusing at first, perhaps returning to this table occasionally throughout the book will be of help in relating them meaningfully.) For practical purposes that are stated in chapters 1 and 5, my investigations of the category of "doing," both what Jesus does and what other characters and the narrator do in relation to him, are more circumscribed here than my analyses of the category of "saying."

Thus my current project is to present a multilayered Markan narrative christology, focusing not only on what the narrator and other characters say about Jesus (projected christology), but also on what Jesus says in response to what these others say to and about him (deflected christology), what Jesus says instead about himself and God (refracted christology), what Jesus does (enacted christology), and *how* what other characters do is related to what Jesus says and does (reflected christology). Just as it makes a significant difference to the Markan Jesus who is doing the speaking—Who do *people* say that I am? Who do *you* say that I am?—so "who is speaking" makes a significant difference in my examination of the characterization of the Markan Jesus, and care will be taken throughout to attend to who is speaking to whom and under what narrative circumstances as crucial evidence of the implied author's communication with the implied audience. These five categories of christology are really five distinctive yet complementary aspects of a Markan narrative christology, and they form the five central chapters of this book. Because the five categories are intended as heuristic devices in the process of presenting a considerable amount of material, they should not be reified. Because the five ways of looking at Mark's Jesus interrelate and overlap, some material is explored in more than one chapter. I will use the phrase "the Markan Jesus" to refer to the character Jesus who speaks and acts in Mark and the phrase "Mark's Jesus" to refer to the fuller characterization of Jesus not only by his own words and actions but also by what the other characters and especially the narrator say and do in relation to him; thus "Mark's Jesus" is the portrait painted by the implied author.

I trust it is obvious—not only to those who are familiar with the enormous scholarly literature on Jesus in the gospels but also to those who have read or heard the enormously powerful Gospel of Mark—that I cannot discuss here everything the Markan Jesus says and does and everything the narrator and other characters say and do to, about, or in relation to him. I make no pretense to exhaust the subject matter of the characterization of the Markan Jesus as narrative christology. Rather I will try not to exhaust my audience! Here is where the epigraph to this chapter, a statement by literary critic Frank Kermode, who has sensitively and imaginatively explored the Gospel of Mark, is most appropriate: "To be blessedly fallible, to have the capacity to subvert manifest senses, is the mark of good enough readers and good enough texts." The Gospel of Mark is more than a "good enough" text and is well known both "to be blessedly fallible" and "to subvert manifest senses." I aspire to be a "blessedly fallible" but "good enough" reader. I aspire "to subvert manifest senses" in part by distinguishing some ideas and categories that have not always been clearly distinguished in the scholarly discussion of Mark (e.g., narrator and implied author) and relating some ideas and categories that have rarely been related in the scholarly discussion of Mark (e.g., "Son of Humanity" and "kingdom of God" as reflecting the unique point of view of the Markan Jesus). I come to this project not as a theologian (or "Christologian"!) and not as one trained in the quest for the historical Jesus but as a Markan narrative critic exploring the characterization of the central character, Jesus—thus my title, *Mark's Jesus.*

CHAPTER 1

ENACTED CHRISTOLOGY: WHAT JESUS DOES

Enacted christology explores the actions of the Markan Jesus as they contribute to a narrative christology. Because actions are both essential and central to narratives, enacted christology is also essential and central to narrative christology, making this a good place to begin. At the most elemental level, what the Markan Jesus does is preach and teach (about the in-breaking of God's rule), exorcise and heal (as an exemplification of the in-breaking of God's rule), and insist on and practice service to those with the least status in society and thus suffer persecution and death by the authorities of that society (as an exemplification of the implications of the in-breaking of God's rule in the present age).[1]

Much has been written about each of these activities, thus there is no need to repeat that information and commentary here. Certain questions will be ignored here in order to focus on other questions. This decision does not intend to invalidate other researchers' questions, any more than other researchers' questions invalidate my own. I will *not* be examining the historical background

---

1. See Joanna Dewey and Elizabeth Struthers Malbon, "Mark," in *Theological Bible Commentary* (ed. Gail R. O'Day and David L. Petersen; Louisville: Westminster John Knox, 2009), 311–24. For the arguments behind this reading of the meaning of Jesus' death in its Markan narrative context, see Sharyn Dowd and Elizabeth Struthers Malbon, "The Significance of Jesus' Death in Mark: Narrative Context and Authorial Audience," *JBL* 125 (2006): 271–97, republished in *The Trial and Death of Jesus: Essays on the Passion Narrative in Mark* (ed. Geert Van Oyen and Tom Shepherd; Leuven, Belgium: Peeters, 2006), 1–31.

of Jesus as teacher, preacher, exorcist, healer, or one who serves and is persecuted in first-century Jewish Hellenistic culture in Roman-ruled Palestine, or
the tradition history of these accounts as they come to be included in Mark's
Gospel—as rich as the research in these areas has been.[2] Further, although it
would be appropriate to begin by examining each action of the Markan Jesus
in its chronological or diachronic order in the narrative, it would also be a
daunting task and one that other scholars have already attempted in various
ways.[3] Thus here I am taking on the somewhat smaller task of focusing on
a more generalized view, attending not to all the details of Mark's story per
se (Jesus' individual actions) but to Mark's plot and the discourse level of the
narrative—the how and the why of the way these actions of the Markan Jesus are narrated. Even within this broad task, I will focus on one diachronic
query (what types of activities does the Markan Jesus do when) and one synchronic query (what does the Markan Jesus do in relation to whom). Both
queries are in keeping with my literary or narrative critical approach, although
they begin my discussion of what Jesus does at a higher level of abstraction
from the Markan narrative than does my analysis of what Jesus and others say.
The diachronic ("through time") query will explore how interpreters have understood the overall Markan outline as a way of commenting on the plot, that
is, the unfolding and connection of the events of the story in their narrated
order, from 1:1 through 16:8. The synchronic ("same time") query will examine how the Markan Jesus relates to the entire cast of narrative characters
considered as a set. It is from this background of enacted christology, that is,
understanding how Jesus is characterized by the way his actions are narrated
in relation to other characters, that we will move in later chapters to a more
detailed exploration of what the Markan Jesus and other characters and the
narrator say.

---

2. Adela Yarbro Collins, *Mark: A Commentary* (Hermeneia; Minneapolis: Fortress,
2007), serves as a convenient overview of and gateway to this literature. See also the recently
published collection of essays by Paul J. Achtemeier, *Jesus and the Miracle Tradition* (Eugene,
Ore.: Cascade Books, 2008).

3. For my brief critique of the analysis of the Markan Jesus' "roles" by Ole Davidsen (*The
Narrative Jesus: A Semiotic Reading of Mark's Gospel* [Aarhus, Denmark: Aarhus University
Press, 1993]) and the rhetorical analysis of repeated verbs denoting Jesus' actions by Paul L.
Danove (*The Rhetoric of the Characterization of God, Jesus, and Jesus' Disciples in the Gospel
of Mark* [JSNTSup 290; New York: T&T Clark, 2005], esp. 60–66), see the Introduction.
For a meticulous and intriguing "formalist" narrative critical analysis of the actions of the
Markan Jesus and of other characters in reference to him, see the pair of books by Edwin K.
Broadhead: *Teaching with Authority: Miracles and Christology in the Gospel of Mark* (JSNT-
Sup 74; Sheffield: Sheffield Academic, 1992); and *Prophet, Son, Messiah: Narrative Form and
Function in Mark 14–16* (JSNTSup 97; Sheffield: Sheffield Academic, 1994). Here Broad-
head combines interest in narrative, the characterization of Jesus, and christology.

What Jesus Does When

At the level of the sentence, Mark's Gospel is frequently grammatically paratactic, connecting parallel elements with a simple coordinating conjunction: this and this and this. At the level of the plot, Mark's Gospel does manifest in some ways the episodic nature of oral narrative:[4] this happens, then this happens, which might be considered analogous to grammatical parataxis. The term "episodic," however, does not quite do justice to the situation, for in the Markan narrative as a whole there are overarching themes that connect episodes and intriguing patterns of subordination by grouping, foreshadowing, echoing,[5] and otherwise interconnecting events as part of the rhetorical outreach to the implied audience at the discourse level of the narrative. Thus the Markan narrative as a whole could be considered hypotactic rather than paratactic by extending the grammatical analogy. In hypotaxis, certain elements of sentences are placed under main clauses by subordinating clauses, thus relating elements

---

4. Joanna Dewey points out, following Walter J. Ong, *Orality and Literacy: The Technologizing of the Word* (London and New York: Methuen, 1982), that "oral narrative style tends to be additive rather than subordinate, simply adding one phrase, sentence or episode to another, rather than relating them in subordinating or analytic ways" ("Mark as Aural Narrative: Structures as Clues to Understanding," *STRev* 36 [1992]: 45–56, quotation from 48). On oral compositional techniques in Mark, see further Joanna Dewey, "Oral Methods of Structuring Narrative in Mark," *Int* 53 (1989): 32–44; Dewey, "Mark as Interwoven Tapestry: Forecasts and Echoes for a Listening Audience," *CBQ* 53 (1991): 221–36, esp. 234–36; and Dewey, "The Gospel of Mark as an Oral-Aural Event: Implications for Interpretation," in *The New Literary Criticism and the New Testament* (ed. Elizabeth Struthers Malbon and Edgar V. McKnight; JSNTSup 109; Sheffield: Sheffield Academic, 1994; Valley Forge, Pa.: Trinity, 1994), 145–63, esp. 148–50. See also Dewey's more recent argument, on the basis of the work of Thorlief Boman and others, that "[s]tudies from the fields of folklore, oral tradition, and oral history all suggest that traditions are likely to coalesce into a continuous narrative or narrative framework quite quickly. . . . All agree against the form-critical assumption of transmission of disparate small episodes" (Joanna Dewey, "The Survival of Mark's Gospel: A Good Story?" *JBL* 123 [2004]: 495–507, quotation from 500, 501). Dewey concludes that "Mark could be entirely an oral composition which was at some point dictated to a scribe; however, the text of the gospel as we have it seems to indicate some use of writing to create such an elegant structure as 2:1–3:6, or to create structural and *verbal* parallels in episodes far distant. The gospel then is close to oral composition but shows some indication of writing" ("Mark as Aural Narrative," 47). For groundbreaking work on issues of orality and literacy in Markan scholarship, see Werner H. Kelber, *The Oral and the Written Gospel: The Hermeneutics of Speaking and Writing in the Synoptic Tradition, Mark, Paul, and Q* (Philadelphia: Fortress, 1983), and Kelber, "Jesus and Tradition: Words in Time, Words in Space," *Semeia* 65 (1994): 139–67.

5. The echo principle is fundamental to oral composition. See Eric Havelock, "Oral Composition in the *Oedipus Tyrannus* of Sophocles," *New Literary History* 16 (1984): 175–97, and Dewey, "Mark as Interwoven Tapestry."

in more complex ways than do coordinating conjunctions like "and." Actually I think "hypertactic," although not a recognized term, might be more descriptive of Mark's narrative than hypotactic; the Greek prefix "hypo-" means "under," but "hyper-" means "over." Even more obvious than subordination of episodes *under* a strict classification system that divides Mark's narrative are *over*arching themes and emphases that link episodes and unite the narrative.[6] There is much more to the way the story is told and the plot unfolds than a paratactic this happens, then this happens. The proliferation of Markan outlines offered by interpreters bears witness to this "hypertactic" presentation or multidimensional plotting.[7] A preliminary word about the complexities of making Markan outlines will serve as an introduction to my contribution to this task, an ongoing task not only because of the "hypertactic" Markan narrative but also because of the changing needs and desires of Markan interpreters.

ON MAKING MARKAN OUTLINES

New Testament scholar Joel Williams opens an article presenting a Markan outline of his own with some useful comments on the problems of Markan outlines. Although Williams does not presume to offer an itemized list of such problems, I have isolated the following from his essay as reminders for us all:

> "An outline cannot display all the possible relationships that exist between passages in Mark's Gospel" partly because "[o]utlines struggle to show relationships that head in opposite directions."[8]

> "[D]ivisions are more obvious in an outline than they are in the narrative itself," thus "the segmenting in an outline has the potential to conceal the connections between major units."[9]

> "[O]utlines often do not display the presence of transitional passages, episodes that draw a major section to a close at the same time that they introduce a new one."[10]

---

6. What I mean by "hypertactic" appears to be close to what Joel F. Williams refers to as "the artful arrangement of episodes" whereby "Mark arranged analogous or similar [or, I would add, contrasting] episodes into recognizable literary patterns in order to provide structure for the major units in his narrative and to identify some of the primary concerns of the story" ("Does Mark's Gospel Have an Outline?" *JETS* 49 [2006]: 505–25, quotation from 510).

7. Joanna Dewey has undertaken a survey of seventeen Markan outlines ranging from B. W. Bacon to P. J. Achtemeier, the results of which she summarizes in "Mark as Interwoven Tapestry," 221–22 n. 3. Dewey concludes from this survey that "[o]verall, the degree of consensus is not impressive" (222). Williams ("An Outline?" 506 n. 3) discusses the differences between "[t]wo of the most well known attempts to understand the outline of Mark's Gospel," the form-critical work of C. H. Dodd and the redaction-critical work of Norman Perrin.

8. Williams, "An Outline?" 507.

9. Williams, "An Outline?" 507.

10. Williams, "An Outline?" 507.

I concur wholeheartedly with each of these statements and believe that such statements should be reiterated whenever any outline of any literary work is presented. Williams offers helpful Markan examples of each of these problem areas, but he concludes that, even with these limitations, there is merit in the making of a Markan outline.

In his reflections on Markan outlines, Williams is in dialogue with Joanna Dewey's discussion of "Mark as Interwoven Tapestry." Dewey argues "that the Gospel of Mark does not have a single structure made up of discrete sequential units but rather is an interwoven tapestry or fugue made up of multiple overlapping structures and sequences, forecasts of what is to come and echoes of what has already been said."[11] In addition, she argues that the Gospel of Mark is this way because "such a nonlinear recursive compositional style is characteristic of aural narrative."[12] Although Williams seems to suggest that Dewey's assertion is that the Gospel of Mark does not have an outline, what Dewey argues is "that the Gospel does not consist of a single linear structure."[13] I suspect Williams' question—"Does Mark's Gospel *Have* an Outline?"[14]—is not the one to ask.

Both Dewey and Williams offer a visual image that enriches our reflection on this issue. Dewey's image of Mark's Gospel as an interwoven tapestry is based on her understanding of what the Gospel is trying to do:

> Mark's problem, after all, was not to divide the Gospel into separate sequential units. Rather, Mark's task was to interweave and integrate disparate and episodic material into a single narrative whole, to bridge breaks rather than to create them. Mark is telling a story for a listening audience, not presenting a logical argument. Arguments may be clouded by the lack of a clear linear outline, but stories gain depth and enrichment through repetition and recursion.[15]

---

11. Dewey, "Mark as Interwoven Tapestry," 224. Sherman E. Johnson presents the image of an oriental carpet in *A Commentary on the Gospel According to St. Mark* (London: Adam & Charles Black, 1960), 24; and Howard Clark Kee develops the image of a fugue in *Community of the New Age: Studies in Mark's Gospel* (Philadelphia: Westminster, 1977), 64, 75. Dewey's complaint of most other scholars is that they "assume that Mark must have a single linear outline or structure, whether elegantly rhetorical or rather haphazard" (224).

12. Dewey, "Mark as Interwoven Tapestry," 224. B. M. F. van Iersel, writing in "Concentric Structures in Mark 1:14–3:35 (4:1) with Some Observations on Method," trans. W. H. Bisscheroux, *BibInt* 3 (1995): 75–97, argues that concentric structures present in an ancient text without any graphic signs for guidance assisted the reciter of the text to structure it for presentation (80).

13. Dewey, "Mark as Interwoven Tapestry," 225.

14. Williams, "An Outline?" title, emphasis added.

15. Dewey, "Mark as Interwoven Tapestry," 224. Dewey develops this image of an interwoven tapestry from "Sherman Johnson's metaphor of an oriental carpet with crisscrossing patterns" (224 and n. 15).

Williams offers an image of Mark's Gospel and a related image of an outline of
Mark's Gospel:

> Mark's Gospel is like a path, a road on which readers can travel, walking with Jesus
> and experiencing his life, death, and resurrection. As with any journey, this one has
> a starting point, travel time, and a destination. . . . If Mark's Gospel is like a path,
> then an outline of the book is like a road map. It guides the traveler along the path,
> identifying important turns, intersections, and points of interest. Any map is a
> simplified representation, so that it does not replace the journey itself but helps the
> traveler to make sense of the trip. . . . A road map does not identify every possible
> back road or dirt path, nor does it point out every conceivable building or destina-
> tion. . . . An outline is not an exhaustive explanation of all possible relationships
> and transitions within Mark's Gospel. . . . Undoubtedly, a map tells us something
> about the interests and priorities of both the map-maker and those who use it, but
> that does not mean the map is unrelated to the lay of the land.[16]

Although Dewey's image of Mark as an interwoven tapestry seems too dif-
fuse for Williams, Williams' image of Mark as a road is surely too linear for
Dewey.

I find myself in the middle of this conversation. I find "interwoven tapestry" a wonderfully appropriate image for Mark's Gospel, although I would
probably develop the musical image of a fugue that Dewey also suggests, following Howard Clark Kee.[17] Nevertheless, and like Williams, I do find it useful
to present an outline of the Gospel of Mark. And, like Williams, I too have
concluded that anyone who presents such an outline has an obligation to state
what that particular outline is designed to make clear. Williams reaches this
conclusion by taking note of Dewey's argument:

> Yet Dewey's argument provides a useful caution. Mark's Gospel does contain over-
> lapping patterns, and the reality of these overlapping structures means that any
> interpreter who suggests an outline must identify the purpose for the outline.
> What features of Mark's Gospel is the outline intended to clarify? The outline can
> then be judged on the extent to which it fulfills its purpose and on the degree to
> which it sheds light on meaningful features in Mark's Gospel.[18]

---

16. Williams, "An Outline?" 505, 508.

17. Kee, *Community of the New Age*. Dewey admits that "a fugue is, perhaps, the better
metaphor, for Mark certainly contains development and dramatic climax as well" ("Mark as
Interwoven Tapestry," 234).

18. Williams, "An Outline?" 508. Dewey's countersuggestion would seem to be to focus not on the narrative's divisions but "on the interconnections, on the repetitions, and the
variations in the repetition" ("Mark as Interwoven Tapestry," 235). Perhaps some form of
outlining might help bring out just such interconnections and repetitions with variations,
especially for today's more visually oriented audience. Dewey notes that "[a] scholar's outline
of Mark tells us more about which aspect of the Gospel narrative is his or her focus than it
does about Mark's structure" ("Mark as Interwoven Tapestry," 235). Perhaps Williams and I

In my view, it is not necessarily Mark's Gospel that *has* an outline, certainly not a single, simple outline; it is Markan interpreters who *offer* multiple outlines as they pick up different threads of the interwoven tapestry or listen to different strains of the fugue that is Mark's Gospel.[19] Making an outline of a narrative is a heuristic task—first for the maker herself or himself and then for anyone else who reads it; a thoughtfully constructed outline can help interpreters appreciate various dimensions of the narrative and its interpretation. No such outline is to be taken as *the* correct one. Yet the goal of the procedure is to reveal something about the narrative even as it reveals something about the interpreter of the narrative.

A MARKAN OUTLINE FOR CONSIDERING ENACTED CHRISTOLOGY

What my Markan outline seeks to make clear is how the actions of the Markan Jesus contribute to Markan narrative christology in the form of enacted christology and to do this without requiring an analysis of each action or each episode in detail—a task that would prove impossible for my current project. I need to look at the types of actions of the Markan Jesus and their broad sweep in the narrative. I will present my Markan outline in several forms, beginning with a schematic diagram to suggest the basic structure of the entire narrative, moving to a simple and then a more detailed overall outline that focuses on interconnections of subsections, and concluding with two examples of even more detailed outlines of large sections of the Gospel.

First, my schematic diagram is to be read from left to right and from top to bottom.[20] The pattern of intercalation, the insertion of one episode into another

---

mean to turn this disadvantage to an advantage by insisting that scholars make plain which aspects of a narrative and its interpretation any particular outline is intended to bring out.

19. So also Michael L. Cook, S.J., *Christology as Narrative Quest* (Collegeville, Minn.: Liturgical Press, 1997), 73–74: "Admittedly the value of a proposed structure for the entire gospel is that it fits our hermeneutical condition as text-centered. Oriented around a print culture, it is we who need a table of contents, as it were, an outline that allows us to see how the individual parts relate to the whole. Mark certainly did not provide one, so any such proposal is a hypothetical construction from the text itself."

20. I first presented this schematic diagram in a footnote in an article examining another Markan rhetorical technique often identified in small scale (duality—with the second element representing an addition rather than a straightforward repetition) that occurs as well in large scale: Malbon, "Echoes and Foreshadowings in Mark 4–8: Reading and Rereading," *JBL* 112 (1993): 213–32; for the schematic diagram, see 214 n. 11, where it is offered as "a rough 'score' or a general 'image,'" reaching for both musical and visual analogies. The analogy of a musical score, which is read both diachronically (from start to finish) and synchronically (from top to bottom, reflecting what all the instruments play simultaneously), was applied by Claude Lévi-Strauss to myth; see Elizabeth Struthers Malbon, *Narrative Space and Mythic Meaning in Mark* (San Francisco: Harper & Row, 1986; volume 13 of The Biblical Seminar; Sheffield: Sheffield Academic, 1991).

SCHEMATIC DIAGRAM
Mark's Gospel

1–3	4:1-34	4:35–8:21
	8:22–10:52	
11–12	13	14–16

kingdom and community	authoritative teaching	restoring health/suffering persecution
(established and new)	(seedtime/on the way/harvest)	(Jews and Gentiles)

for interpretive purposes—for example, the insertion of the story of the healing of the hemorrhaging woman into the story of the healing of Jairus' daughter (5:21-24/25-34/35-43)—is often recognized as a recurrent Markan rhetorical technique.[21] My schematic diagram calls attention to the entire Markan Gospel as a series of large-scale intercalations.[22] Mark 4:1-34, the parables discourse, is intercalated between chapters 1–3 and 4:35–8:21. Likewise, Mark 13, the eschatological discourse, is intercalated between chapters 11–12 and 14–16.[23] Mark 8:22–10:52, the "way" section, in which the Markan Jesus, while on the way to Jerusalem with his disciples, teaches them and other followers repeatedly that "the son of humanity [*ho huios tou anthrōpou*] must suffer,"[24] is intercalated between these two larger and composite sections, 1:1–8:21 and 11–16.

---

21. On Markan intercalation see, e.g., James R. Edwards, "Markan Sandwiches: The Significance of Interpolations in Markan Narratives," *NovT* 31 (1989): 193–216; Geert Van Oyen, "Intercalation and Irony in the Gospel of Mark," in *The Four Gospels 1992: Festschrift Frans Neirynck* (ed. F. Van Segbroeck et al.; Leuven, Belgium: Leuven University Press, 1992), II: 949–74; and Tom Shepherd, "The Narrative Function of Markan Intercalation," *NTS* 41 (1995): 522–40, who argues that each intercalation, through "dramatized irony" (538, following D. C. Muecke, *The Compass of Irony* [London: Methuen, 1969]), links with Christology (540). For a playful and philosophical look at Markan intercalation as "an emblem of many conjunctions and oppositions, which are found at all levels of the discourse" (137), see the work of literary critic Frank Kermode, *The Genesis of Secrecy: On the Interpretation of Narrative* (Cambridge, Mass.: Harvard University Press, 1979), chapter 6, "The Unfollowable World," 125–45.

22. Bas van Iersel also notes that "the whole book is structured by means of sandwich construction" (*Reading Mark* [trans. W. H. Bisscheroux; Collegeville, Minn.: Liturgical Press, 1988], 20), although the overall pattern of the intercalation of intercalations is not so easy to see in his various outlines, which give considerable other details and organize the entire Gospel concentrically; see *Reading Mark*, 18–30, and *Mark: A Reader-Response Commentary* (trans. W. H. Bisscheroux; Sheffield: Sheffield Academic, 1998), 68–86.

23. Kermode, *Genesis of Secrecy*, views chapter 13, as a major intercalation between chapters 1–12 and 14–16, as "the largest of his intercalations, in fact, an analepsis that is certainly homodiegetic, an incursion of the future, properly terrible, properly ambiguous, into a narrative which proleptically shapes and sanctifies it" (128; see also 134).

24. Dewey notes that, of the seventeen Markan outlines she surveyed, "eighty-two per-

Listing the sections of this schema vertically (see Outline 1) masks somewhat the large-scale intercalations (although indentation and the brackets on the
left attempt to suggest that aspect), but it allows me to introduce titles for the
various sections in order to call attention to additional connections between
them based on the actions of the Markan Jesus.

The brackets on the right make obvious several connections between sections that the titles intend to suggest. Chapters 1–3, "Jesus, kingdom, and community," focus on Jesus' proclamation of the "kingdom" or rule of God, his
manifestation of the in-breaking of God's rule in powerful acts of healing and
teaching, his formation of a new community by calling disciples and other followers, and his struggles with the leaders of the established (Jewish) community, centered in Galilee.[25] On the basis of these actions of the Markan Jesus,
chapters 1–3 are related to chapters 11–12, "Jesus and the established community," in which Jesus enters Jerusalem and, after an apparent welcome, challenges the temple in symbolic ways and then is challenged by representatives of
the established (Jewish) community.[26] Thus chapters 1–3 and 11–12, the left-
hand column in the schematic diagram above, concern the Markan Jesus' actions in proclaiming the in-breaking "kingdom" (rule of God) and challenging
community—both the established community and a new community that is
coming into being around that proclamation.[27]

---

cent thought there was a distinct section in the middle of the Gospel, beginning at either
8:22 or 8:27 and ending at 10:45 or 10:52" ("Mark as Interwoven Tapestry," 221).

25. On cohesiveness and concentric structures in Mark 1–3, see van Iersel, "Concentric
Structures." Although I am not entirely convinced by the concentric structures van Iersel
designates at 1:14-45 and 3:7–4:1, there is much agreement between us on larger issues,
e.g., the importance of attending to markers at the macro-level before focusing on markers
at the micro-level, the similarities between chapters 4 and 13, the creation of two sections
(1:14–4:1 for van Iersel, 1:1–3:35 for me; 4:35–8:21) around chapter 4, and the thematic
focus of chapters 1–3 (or 1:14–4:1) on authority in relation to the old and the new.

26. On the Markan arrangement of episodes in chapters 11–12, see Stephen H. Smith,
"The Literary Structure of Mk 11:1–12:40," *NovT* 31 (1989): 104–24, who sees a three-day
temporal scheme that results, somewhat complicatedly, in an introduction (11:1-11) and
two triads (11:12–12:12), followed by two more triads (12:13-44). Smith's observations are
interesting, although perhaps not totally convincing; however, his language of "Christians"
and "Jews" and "Jewish-Christians" and "Jewish non-Christians" seems anachronistic and
problematic.

27. Through a detailed formalist analysis of the "miracle" stories of Mark's Gospel,
Broadhead also links mighty deeds, teaching, discipleship, and opposition in the characterization of Jesus by his actions. The connections are encoded in the title and subtitle of
Broadhead's book: *Teaching with Authority: Miracles and Christology in the Gospel of Mark.*
The Markan Jesus' teaching/preaching is "characterized both by its quality (authority)"—
demonstrated in "acts of power" and in discipleship demands—"and by its result (opposition)" (*Teaching with Authority,* 86; see also 216).

OUTLINE 1
Mark's Gospel

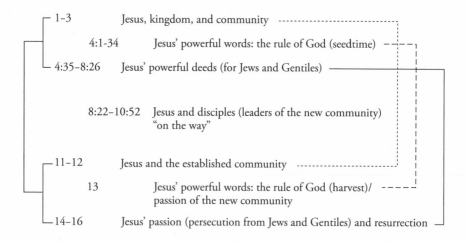

1–3   Jesus, kingdom, and community

4:1-34   Jesus' powerful words: the rule of God (seedtime)

4:35-8:26   Jesus' powerful deeds (for Jews and Gentiles)

8:22-10:52   Jesus and disciples (leaders of the new community) "on the way"

11–12   Jesus and the established community

13   Jesus' powerful words: the rule of God (harvest)/ passion of the new community

14–16   Jesus' passion (persecution from Jews and Gentiles) and resurrection

Mark 4:35–8:26, "Jesus' powerful deeds (for Jews and Gentiles)," presents the Markan Jesus in a series of mighty deeds (Gk *dynameis*) of healing and feeding that restore health to both Jews and Gentiles, centered around the Sea of Galilee, which itself is the scene of two *dynameis* and a significant conversation that draws these events together. In addition, 4:35–8:26 includes events that contribute to and/or foreshadow Jesus' growing struggle with the leaders of the established community: Jesus' rejection in his hometown, John's beheading by Herod, and Jesus' disagreements with the Pharisees.[28] The final section, chapters 14–16, "Jesus' passion (persecution from Jews and Gentiles) and resurrection," echoes the events of 4:35–8:26 and, in some ways, turns them upside down. Instead of powerfully restoring Jews and Gentiles to health, the Markan Jesus is persecuted to the death by powerful leaders of the Jewish and Gentile establishment; nevertheless, the resurrection marks a final reversal that suggests the paradox of the power of God's rule. Thus 4:35–8:21 and 14–16, the right-hand

28. It is interesting to compare the careful, detailed, composition-critical examination of Mark 4:1–8:26 by Norman R. Petersen, "The Composition of Mark 4:1–8:26," *HTR* 73 (1980): 185–217, with my own literary-critical analysis of 4:1–8:21 ("Echoes and Fore-shadowings") and Dewey's orality-critical article "Mark as Interwoven Tapestry" more than a decade later. The language shifts from "minimal composition units," "sources," and "compositional structure" to "echoes" and "forecasts"; the focus shifts from segmentation to interconnection. One comment of Petersen's, however, is especially interesting in relation to later research on oral and aural narrative: "Parallelism interrupts the merely sequential flow of content through a systematic repetition that requires readers and hearers to move forth and back through the text rather than simply straight through it" (203).

column in the schematic diagram above, concern the Markan Jesus' actions in restoring health and suffering persecution, among Jews and Gentiles. (The fact that the schematic diagram refers to 4:35–8:21 and Outline 1 refers to 4:35–8:26 is a mark of the strong connection of 8:22-26 with both what precedes it, stressed in Outline 1, and what follows it, stressed in the schematic diagram.)

In the center column of the schematic diagram are three sections that present authoritative (not to be confused with authoritarian!) teaching of the Markan Jesus: 4:1-34, the parables discourse, focused on images of seedtime; chapter 13, the eschatological (concerning "last things") discourse, focused on images of harvest;[29] and—in the middle of the middle—8:22–10:52, the "way" section, focused, literally and symbolically, on transitions. In 8:22–10:52, Jesus and his disciples are moving from Galilee, where his restoring power used for those in need had usually been accepted, to Jerusalem, where his insistence on serving those of greater need and lower status challenges the status quo and those in power, with serious implications for both Jesus and his followers. One narrative detail concerning these three teaching sections is important to highlight: in each case the Markan Jesus is said to "sit"—the authoritative position for teaching, according to the Gospel's first-century context. Jesus sits in "a boat on the sea" at 4:1 to present the parables of seeds sown in the earth; Jesus sits "on the Mount of Olives opposite the temple" at 13:3 to present images of the future of the heavens and the earth and its peoples.[30] And, although the Markan Jesus could obviously not be sitting for his whole journey to Jerusalem in the "way" section, he is said

29. Among the similarities linking the two units, van Iersel includes their composition as "spoken text," their positions in the middle of the two halves of Mark's Gospel, their "explicit signals which give the words spoken to the characters in the story a validity that extends to the readers outside it," their "signals relating to a hidden meaning, which in due time is to be brought to light by the listeners" ("Concentric Structures," 85), and their narrative frames (see 82–86). Van Iersel finds it "peculiar that in studies about the structure of Mark the effect of the presence of the two great speeches on the book's structure is seldom or never taken into account" ("Concentric Structures," 84 n. 27; van Iersel cites E. Haenchen's work as an exception). Other significant exceptions are Ched Myers, who calls chapter 4 "the first sermon on revolutionary patience" and chapter 13 "the second sermon on revolutionary patience" (*Binding the Strong Man: A Political Reading of Mark's Story of Jesus* [Maryknoll, N.Y.: Orbis, 1988]), and M. Eugene Boring, *Mark: A Commentary* (The New Testament Library; Louisville: Westminster John Knox, 2006), 4–6.

30. Mark's Gospel employs two different verbs for "to sit" or "to sit down." The verb used at 4:1 and 13:3 is the intransitive verb *kathēmai*, and these are the only two times it is applied to the Markan Jesus (also noted by van Iersel, "Concentric Structures," 86). However, the Markan Jesus does apply the verb to "the Son of Man seated at the right hand of the Power," a composite quotation of or allusion to Dan 7:13 and Ps 110:1 in Mark 14:62. The image of sitting comes from Psalm 110:1, where the Septuagint (Ps 109:1) has the imperative of *kathēmai*. Sitting is associated with authority. Interestingly enough, the longer ending of Mark's Gospel applies the other Greek verb for sitting, *kathizō* (on which, see the following note), to the risen "Lord Jesus" who "sat down at the right hand of God" (16:19).

to sit in a house in Capernaum with his disciples at 9:35 to present the image
of a child, a powerless one, one who must serve, as "the greatest."[31] These three
occasions of Jesus sitting mark three intercalated sections of authoritative—and
also always surprising—teaching concerning the in-breaking rule of God in this
age and the next. Thus 4:1-34, 8:22–10:52, and chapter 13, the center column
in the schematic diagram above, concern the Markan Jesus' actions in offering
authoritative, surprising, challenging teaching to his followers.[32]

As expected, there is much, and much of importance, about the Markan
narrative that is not revealed or suggested in this schematic diagram and brief
outline (Outline 1)—for example, no "prologue" is isolated[33] and the parallels between the baptism (1:9-11) and the transfiguration (9:2-8) are hidden;
they would be brought out when attending to what is said to the Markan Jesus
rather than what he does.[34] However, what is brought to awareness here is that

31. Here the other of the two Greek words for sitting found in Mark is used: *kathizō*.
Kathizō can be used transitively to mean "to cause to sit down," but here it is used intran-
sitively to mean simply "to sit down." This Greek verb is applied to the Markan Jesus three
times: at 9:35, in the central teaching section; at 11:7, when Jesus sits on the colt at his
entrance into Jerusalem; and at 12:41, when he sits down opposite the treasury and observes
the poor widow contributing her two coins. Mark 12:41 is a transitional scene that follows
Jesus' challenges by the leaders of the Jewish establishment while he was "walking in the
temple" (11:27) and leads directly to chapter 13, the eschatological discourse, which Jesus
delivers "sitting [from *kathēmai*] on the Mount of Olives opposite the temple" (13:3), just
after he had "sat down [from *kathizō*] opposite the treasury." In that transitional moment
in 12:41, Jesus points out to his disciples that the poor widow placing her two coins in the
treasury is giving "her whole life" (Gk *holon ton bion autēs*, 12:44). On the symbolic and
narrative effect of Mark's only three uses of the term "opposite" (*katenanti*)—11:2; 12:41;
13:3—see Stephen Smith, "Mark 11:1–12:40," 110.

32. As Cook notes, "In Mark Jesus is the only one who teaches, and it is C (8:27–10:45),
the center and key of the entire gospel, that articulates the most important and fundamental
content of that teaching. . . . Thus the image of Jesus as teacher functions as the 'hermeneutical bridge' to Mark's way of doing christology" (*Christology as Narrative Quest*, 76, citing, in
relation to the final statement, M. Eugene Boring, "The Christology of Mark: Hermeneutical
Issues for Systematic Theology," *Semeia* 30 [1984]: 125–53).

33. The Markan prologue has been of great interest in Markan scholarship. See, e.g.,
M. Eugene Boring, "Mark 1:1-15 and the Beginning of the Gospel," *Semeia* 52 (1990):
43–81, and the literature cited there, as well as note 37 below.

34. For a quite different outline, especially of the first half of Mark, see Eduard Schweizer, "The Portrayal of the Life of Faith in the Gospel of Mark," in *Interpreting the Gospels*
(ed. James Luther Mays; Philadelphia: Fortress, 1981), 168–82; first published in *Int* 32
(1978): 387–99, who stresses the human rejection of Jesus, that is, what others do in relation to Jesus rather than what Jesus does, as I am stressing here. Schweizer's outline of
Mark's entire Gospel is also available in English in "Mark's Theological Achievement" (trans.
R. Morgan), in *The Interpretation of Mark* (2nd ed.; ed. William A. Telford; Edinburgh: T&T
Clark, 1995), 63–87; first published in *EvT* (1964): 337–55. An almost identical overall
outline appears in Norman Perrin, "Towards an Interpretation of the Gospel of Mark," in

Mark's narrative of the actions of Jesus, the basis of enacted christology, is a double-sided story: (1) Jesus comes as a powerful teacher, preacher, exorcist, and healer of both Jews and Gentiles as he proclaims and enacts the in-breaking rule of God (1–3/4:1-34/4:35–8:21, the first row of the schematic diagram); (2) Jesus challenges the societal status quo and thus those established in power, both Jews and Gentiles (8:22–10:52, the center row, column, and point), and is eventually persecuted and killed by them, although that too is reversed (11–12/13/14–16, the final row of the schematic diagram). My schematic diagram seeks to illustrate the overall pattern of the intercalation of large sections and their synchronic as well as diachronic relationships. Diachronically the plot line of powerful teaching and healing (1:1–8:21) is followed by the plot line of suffering persecution at the hands of the powerful for the sake of the powerless (11–16). Within each of these plot lines, a central teaching section is intercalated, chapters 4 and 13. But *the* central teaching section (8:22–10:52), which intersperses teaching and action in itself, is intercalated between these two plot lines. The schematic diagram has the advantage of making central visually what is central to enacted christology: the two plot lines are centered on (chapters 4 and 13) and connected by (8:22–10:52) the Markan Jesus' challenging teaching.[35]

A further iteration of my Markan outline (Outline 2), with subsections and thus more detail, serves to bring attention to additional connections, but it should not change the impact of the more foundational schematic diagram.[36] As with Outline 1, the brackets on the left indicate large-scale intercalations or

Christology and a Modern Pilgrimage: A Discussion with Norman Perrin (ed. Hans Dieter Betz; rev. ed.; Missoula, Mont.: SBL and Scholars Press, 1974; first published in 1971), 1–52; see esp. 3–5. Schweizer acknowledges "a few additions [to his revised outline in 1979] due to Perrin (1971)" ("Mark's Theological Achievement," 86 n. 52).

35. Perhaps my schematic diagram can also suggest why some commentators present a basically three-part Markan outline (e.g., Robert C. Tannehill, "The Gospel of Mark as Narrative Christology," *Semeia* 16 [1979]: 57–95; Boring, *Mark*, 4–6) and others suggest a basically two-part outline (e.g., Jack Dean Kingsbury, *The Christology of Mark's Gospel* [Philadelphia: Fortress, 1983]; Williams, "An Outline?"), reading the center row with the third row, as I do in my term "double-sided story" above, to emphasize the change in focus from the Markan Jesus' power in healing and teaching to his suffering persecution.

36. To my Outline 1 and Outline 2, compare and contrast the outlines proposed by van Iersel, whose goal is to show consistent concentric structuring throughout Mark in considerable detail. Van Iersel's outlines have been published in many forms, but two of the most accessible are *Mark*, 68–86, and *Reading Mark*, 18–30; see my review of *Mark* in *Biblica* 81 (2000): 285–90. My research on Markan narrative space in the late 1970s, culminating in my dissertation in 1980 (part of which was published as *Narrative Space* in 1986), paralleled in significant ways the working out of a five-part topographic Markan framework by van Iersel; see esp. *Narrative Space*, 141–68. In fact, van Iersel cites and adapts two diagrams from my unpublished dissertation in his 1982 article "De betekenis van Marcus vanuit zijn topografische structuur," *Tidschrift voor Theologie* 22 (1982): 117–38, see 118–19.

OUTLINE 2
Mark's Gospel

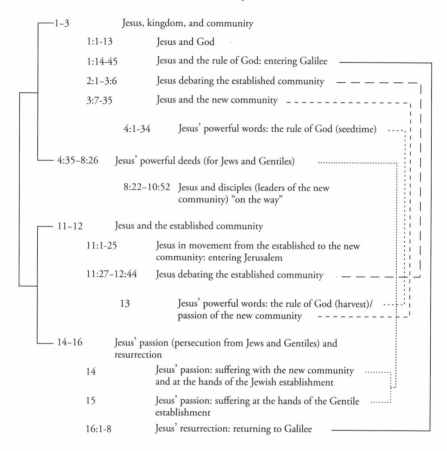

┌─1–3   Jesus, kingdom, and community

     1:1-13   Jesus and God

     1:14-45   Jesus and the rule of God: entering Galilee

     2:1–3:6   Jesus debating the established community

     3:7-35   Jesus and the new community

               4:1-34   Jesus' powerful words: the rule of God (seedtime)

└─ 4:35–8:26   Jesus' powerful deeds (for Jews and Gentiles)

               8:22–10:52 Jesus and disciples (leaders of the new
                           community) "on the way"

┌─ 11–12   Jesus and the established community

     11:1-25   Jesus in movement from the established to the new
                      community: entering Jerusalem

     11:27–12:44   Jesus debating the established community

               13   Jesus' powerful words: the rule of God (harvest)/
                           passion of the new community

└─ 14–16   Jesus' passion (persecution from Jews and Gentiles) and
                resurrection

     14   Jesus' passion: suffering with the new community
                      and at the hands of the Jewish establishment

     15   Jesus' passion: suffering at the hands of the Gentile
                      establishment

     16:1-8   Jesus' resurrection: returning to Galilee

frames, and the brackets on the right signal several connections between sections that the titles intend to suggest.

Within the overarching frame indicated by the brackets on the left of Outline 2, several sections and subsections are especially interrelated, as suggested by their titles and the brackets on the right. The ending of Mark's Gospel, as many interpreters have observed, sends the implied audience back to its beginning. At 1:14 Jesus comes into Galilee as a return, having previously gone from Nazareth to the Jordan to be baptized by John (1:9). At 16:7, the young man at the empty tomb reminds Jesus' followers that "he is going ahead of you to Galilee." Thus 1:14-45 (or 1:1-15[37]) is connected with 16:1-8. Mark

---

37. Mark 1:14-15 serves as a hinge or transition; see Augustine Stock, O.S.B., "Hinge Transitions in Mark's Gospel," *BTB* 15 (1985): 27–31, who, in turn, is following the five-

2:1–3:6, Jesus' debating with the scribes and Pharisees in Galilee,[38] is quite clearly linked with Jesus' debating with the chief priests, scribes, and elders, Pharisees and Herodians, Sadducees, and one of the scribes in the temple in Jerusalem at 11:27–12:44.[39] Perhaps less obvious, but equally significant, the subsection 3:7-35, which closes with Jesus' recognizing as family "whoever does the will of God," is joined thematically with chapter 13 in its functioning as the passion of the community (note especially 13:9-13, 14, 37).[40] Those who do the will of God, like Jesus (see 14:36, Jesus' prayer at Gethsemane), will find themselves persecuted by those who are challenged by such actions. As mentioned in relation to Outline 1 above, Jesus' parables discourse (4:1-34), focusing on the rule of God in its mysterious beginnings in this present age, is closely tied (by content and position) to Jesus' eschatological discourse (chapter 13), focusing on the rule of God in power at the end of this age. In the former case, the internal (and implied) audience is repeatedly admonished to "hear"; in the latter case, the audience is repeatedly warned to "watch," yet another way of linking and highlighting these two discourses for the understanding of the implied audience.[41] And again we may relate Jesus' powerful deeds for Jews and

---

part topographic framework (with four hinges) of Bas van Iersel, "De betekenis." Thus it is not too surprising that some outlines attach 1:14-15 to 1:1-13 and others to what follows. I have attached it to what follows because it opens the section in which the in-breaking "kingdom of God," first proclaimed at 1:15, is central, that is, 1:14-45. However, were I focusing on the framing of the entire Gospel, I would likely link 1:14-15 with 1:1-13 in order to consider 1:1-15 in relation with 16:1-8, both of which mention a return to Galilee. Dewey notes that, of the seventeen Markan outlines she surveyed, seventy percent "agreed that there was a break at 1:14 or 1:16 after the prologue in Mark 1" ("Mark as Interwoven Tapestry," 221). For Dewey's own list of the "multiple verbal and content connections, repetitions and anticipations, echoing backwards and forwards in the narrative" at 1:14-15, see "Mark as Interwoven Tapestry," 226.

38. The unusual phrase "scribes of the Pharisees" occurs at 2:16. The Pharisees are said to go out (leaving Jesus) to conspire with the Herodians at 3:6, which is echoed at 12:13.

39. Dewey considers that "11:11, the first entry into the temple, forms a narrative frame around the Jerusalem public ministry with 13:1-2, the final exit from the temple. The frame is similar to that around 2:1–3:6, in which 3:7 resumes the crowds coming to Jesus of 1:45" ("Mark as Interwoven Tapestry," 232). For Joanna Dewey's detailed analysis of 2:1–3:6, and also some analysis of 12:1-40, see *Markan Public Debate: Literary Technique, Concentric Structure, and Theology in Mark 2:1–3:6* (SBLDS 48; Chico, Calif.: Scholars Press, 1980). Stephen Smith points out that "Jesus' controversy with his adversaries in Mark 11, 12, in marked contrast to 2:1–3:6, is consistently conducted in the absence of any followers" ("Mark 11:1–12:40," 113).

40. On chapter 13 as the passion of the community and part of the "double ending" of Mark (along with chapters 14–16), see Malbon, *Narrative Space*, 151–52 and 199–200 n. 6 and the literature cited there (Perrin, Trocmé, Pesch, Kermode). See also Helen R. Graham, "A Passion Prediction for Mark's Community: Mark 13:9-13," *BTB* 16 (1986): 18–22.

41. Williams (e.g., "An Outline?" 512) also notes many of these parallels between

Gentiles (4:35–8:26) to their seeming reversal in Jesus' passion, his persecution at the hands of Jews and Gentiles, and the final reversal represented by the
resurrection (14–16).

Of course, many rhetorical and/or thematic connections in Mark's Gospel
are simply not drawn out in this (or any one) outline. Here I am concentrating on the actions of the Markan Jesus—what Jesus does, and especially what
Jesus does when—as a way of understanding how the plot (that is, the actions
in their narrated order) and the discourse level of the narrative (for example,
how actions and events are grouped, foreshadowed, and echoed for rhetorical
effect) lead the implied audience to a view of enacted christology. The dominant
impression is of the Markan Jesus' relentless proclamation of the in-breaking
rule of God, in spite of the ever clearer consequences of this proclamation in the
sphere of the rule of powerful men. Also highlighted is the difficulty of others
(both characters and the implied audience) in appreciating and appropriating
the implications of such a proclamation. Markan enacted christology is surprising and challenging in asking characters and the implied audience to hold
together these seemingly contradictory manifestations of the in-breaking rule of
God.[42] But these conclusions are hardly startling to contemporary Markan interpreters. Here my outline, focused on Jesus' actions (rather than, for example,
christological titles) confirms what other interpreters and other outlines have
also noted: the powerful one who teaches and heals with God's authority accepts
his persecution and death at the hands of men in authority as the will of God.

In moving from my brief outline to my somewhat longer Markan outline,
I subdivided only three sections: chapters 1–3, 11–12, and 14–16. While it is
probably understandable why I left undivided the parables discourse (4:1-34)
and the eschatological discourse (13) for my broad purpose here, one might
wonder why I did not further subdivide the intriguing narrative sections, 4:35–
8:26 (or 4:35–8:21 in the schematic diagram) and 8:22–10:52. I did try, but
these two sections are so complex and so often examined in detail that I was not
successful in devising simple subdivisions. Instead I will present a separate outline for each of these two significant sections as final ways of exploring Markan
enacted christology through a look at what Jesus does when. My purpose is heu-

---

chapters 4 and 13; however, I find that his designation of the two chapters as "transitions"
(the same term is also, and understandably, applied to 1:14-15; 8:22-26; and 10:46-52)
underestimates their place and weight in the Markan narrative.

42. Broadhead builds a careful and detailed argument of the way Mark's narrative
prepares its readers for this christological surprise from the very beginning, by "an extensive, reciprocal realignment" of images of Jesus as teacher, prophet, or miracle worker with
"passion Christology" (*Prophet, Son, Messiah*, 258; see also *Teaching with Authority*, 83–84).
Broadhead presents this view over against Theodore Weeden's view of Mark's "corrective"
christology—now generally rejected by Markan interpreters, that is, the notion that "Mark"
replaces a miracles-based christology with a cross-based christology; see Theodore J. Weeden,
Sr., *Mark—Traditions in Conflict* (Philadelphia: Fortress, 1971).

ristic; the exercise may help us understand and interpret the "hypertactic" plot and the discourse level of the Markan narrative. I will look at the central section, 8:22–10:52, first; it is perhaps the section of Mark first and most often pointed out by interpreters as carefully organized and not just haphazardly "collected."

As literary criticism was growing out of and away from redaction criticism, Norman Perrin showed that the whole central section of Mark's Gospel is organized around three recurrences of a passion prediction, each followed by a depiction of discipleship misunderstanding and further discipleship instruction.[43] Markan interpreters have continued to build on and refine that observation, as does my next outline (Outline 3).[44]

At this point, reading the outline should be fairly obvious. The section is organized by the three passion prediction units, each marked with an asterisk. Each passion prediction unit has its three parts: passion prediction, misunderstanding, discipleship instruction. In the second unit, the misunderstanding and instruction subsections are doubled; in the third unit, the passion prediction is elaborated. The brackets to the left indicate the framing of the entire section by the two stories of the healing of blindness, the only two stories of the healing of blindness in Mark's Gospel. The first of these paired stories is itself twofold: Jesus heals the blind man of Bethsaida in two stages, an obvious symbolic foreshadowing of the work the Markan Jesus has to do next with his disciples with regard to the necessity of the persecution and suffering of the "son of humanity." This twofold story is also a perhaps not-so-obvious echo of the work he has just done in relation to introducing them to his powerful healing and feeding of Gentiles as well as Jews.[45] Physical sight as a figure for insight is a commonplace in the ancient—and even the postmodern—world.

The first two passion prediction units are also framed within the larger frame. The first unit is framed by Peter's confession of Jesus as the "Christ" and Jesus' transfiguration with its confession of Jesus as "my Son" by the voice (of God). (In the next chapter we will discuss these two titles projected onto Jesus

43. Norman Perrin, *What Is Redaction Criticism?* (Philadelphia: Fortress, 1969), 40–56. Of course, Perrin was illustrating redaction criticism and thus focused on how Mark's editing of tradition shows his theology. Narrative criticism generally works with the received text as a whole. For Perrin's more detailed analysis of 8:22–10:52, see "Towards an Interpretation," 6–21.

44. A simplified version of this outline appears in Elizabeth Struthers Malbon, *Hearing Mark: A Listener's Guide* (Harrisburg, Pa.: Trinity, 2002), 71; for a fuller discussion of 8:22–10:52, see 55–73.

45. Dewey argues that this echo would be heard by a listening audience: "Since the hearers have recently heard two stories of the disciples afraid on the boat (4:35-41; 6:45-52), and two stories of miraculous feedings of thousands (6:30-44; 8:1-10), a second difficult healing using spittle [7:31-37; 8:22-26] would not be unexpected. The healing at Bethsaida is the third item in a sequence of doublets. . . . The healing of the blind man at Bethsaida is thoroughly intertwined with the preceding material" ("Mark as Interwoven Tapestry," 229, 230).

OUTLINE 3
Mark 8:22–10:52

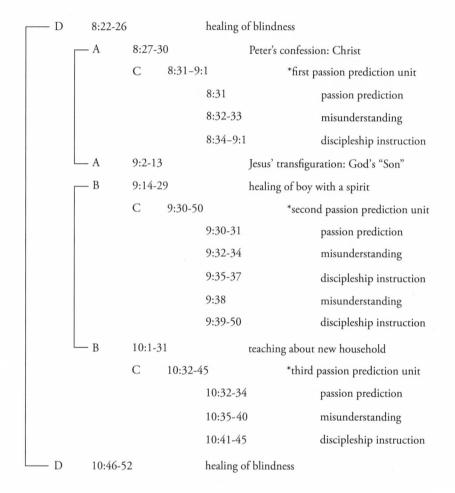

D	8:22-26	healing of blindness
A	8:27-30	Peter's confession: Christ
C	8:31–9:1	*first passion prediction unit
	8:31	passion prediction
	8:32-33	misunderstanding
	8:34–9:1	discipleship instruction
A	9:2-13	Jesus' transfiguration: God's "Son"
B	9:14-29	healing of boy with a spirit
C	9:30-50	*second passion prediction unit
	9:30-31	passion prediction
	9:32-34	misunderstanding
	9:35-37	discipleship instruction
	9:38	misunderstanding
	9:39-50	discipleship instruction
B	10:1-31	teaching about new household
C	10:32-45	*third passion prediction unit
	10:32-34	passion prediction
	10:35-40	misunderstanding
	10:41-45	discipleship instruction
D	10:46-52	healing of blindness

A = re-view of chapters 1–3 (now especially for followers)
B = re-view of chapters 4–8 (now especially for followers)
C = pre-view of chapters 11–16 (especially for followers)
D = view of proper viewing

by these two characters in confirmation of the narrator's confession of these two titles projected onto Jesus at 1:1.) I have suggested in the key at the bottom of Outline 3 that Peter's confession serves almost as a "re-view" of chapters 1–3, Jesus' powerful words and deeds; that is the part of Jesus' story that Peter understands at the time of his confession. The transfiguration and the statement of the voice (of God) may also serve as a confirmation of what the narrator, God, and the unclean spirits know in chapters 1–3, but they also suggest what the narrator, God, and the Markan Jesus know about what is hinted in chapters 1–3 and will happen in chapters 11–16. This is not something that can be understood by a human character until the crucifixion (15:39). The second passion prediction unit is framed by a healing story (9:14-29) and a teaching segment (10:1-31), although I am using "frame" here as a metaphor in the sense of "surrounding" and not as a technical literary term. Except for the framing stories of the healing of blindness, 9:14-29, the healing of the boy with a spirit is the only healing story in the entire second half of the Gospel; and this teaching segment, 10:1-31, is the only teaching segment in 8:22–10:52 not directly presented as the third part of a passion prediction unit;[46] thus both seem carefully placed. Because healing and teaching are important aspects of chapters 4–8, this frame might be said to serve as a "re-view" of those chapters, now especially for followers. (Let the reader understand: all analogies break when pushed.) The passion prediction units, especially but not solely the passion predictions themselves, then serve as a "pre-view" of chapters 11–16, especially for followers. And the two stories of the healing of blindness that frame the whole section give us a view of proper viewing: listen twice to see clearly—then follow Jesus on the way.

Mark 8:22–10:52 illustrates once again the strong interconnections of the actions of the Markan Jesus: the one who is called "Christ" and "Son of God," the one powerful in healing and teaching, is the very one who insists that he and his followers must serve those with the least power even at the risk of persecution by those with the most power. Enacted christology affirms the centrality of that paradox. Mark 8:22–10:52, especially Peter's confession and the transfiguration with its voice from heaven, also raises questions about projected christology (based on what others say to and about the Markan Jesus) that will be considered in the next chapter.

Finally we take a somewhat more detailed look at the other section of my longer Markan outline (Outline 2) that I did not find possible to subdivide easily, 4:35–8:26. As I have observed elsewhere:

> Mark 4–8 is a section in which most interpreters have heard multiple echoes. The scholarly discussion of these echoes, however, has shifted from the debate over the hypothetical sources of the real author (Achtemeier on pre-Marcan miracle catenae), to the isolation of the compositional techniques of the real or implied author (Neirynck on duality in Mark), to the consideration of the effect on the implied or real reader (Fowler on reader response criticism of Mark).[47]

---

46. Presumably one could argue that 10:1-31 is a continuation of the discipleship instruction given in 9:39-50, but both the extent of the material and the disjunctions of 10:1 (Jesus' departure from that place and arrival in "the region of Judea and beyond the Jordan" and the gathering of the crowds "again") argue against such a designation.

47. Malbon, "Echoes and Foreshadowings," 213–24, where full details of the cited authors' works are given.

My contribution to this intensive scholarship has been to observe that a smaller narrative pattern repeated at the level of the story is repeated in larger narrative scale at the level of the discourse in Mark 4–8.

> Marcan commentators have often analyzed the pattern of public pronouncement [e.g., 4:1-9] and private explanation [4:10-20] in the Gospel. What is less obvious is that 4:35–8:21 seems also to echo 4:1-34, more faintly, yet more grandly: 4:35–8:21 is a structural magnification of the twofold pattern of 4:1-34. What happens at the level of the story in 4:1-34 is echoed by what happens at the level of the discourse in 4:35–8:21. Marcan commentators have often noted that the miracles of Mark 4–8, especially the two sea miracles and the two feedings, function very much like the parables as they are presented in Mark 4. . . . What I wish to add to this widely shared perception is that the Marcan *dynameis*, taken not individually but together in their narrative arrangement in the story-as-discoursed, are also subject to the same pattern of presentation-plus-additional-explanation as the parables. The Marcan Jesus tells, then explains, a parable; the Marcan implied author tells, then explains by additional telling, a story.[48]

Outline 4 seeks to illustrate this observation based on rereadings of Mark 4–8.[49]

Outline 4 is to be read in this way: Mark 7:14-23 echoes 4:1-34 in smaller scale, and Mark 4:35–8:21 echoes 4:1-34 in larger scale; that is, initial parabolic words (4:1-9) or works (4:35–6:44) are followed by additional explanatory words (4:10-20) or works (6:45–8:12), with comments or questions about the disciples' understanding near the midpoint (4:10-13; 6:51-52).[50] Note that the additional works, 6:45–8:12 (along with the final boat scene, 8:13-21), make up the "detour"[51]—from the Markan Jesus' attempt to send his disciples "ahead to the other side, to Bethsaida" at 6:45 to their eventual arrival there with Jesus at 8:22. As the Markan Jesus provides the additional instruction his disciples need, the Markan implied author seems to do the same for the implied audience. The overall narrative impact of this arrangement is that

> [a] surrounding echo effect is produced by the final scene of Jesus in the boat on the sea, questioning the disciples, at 8:13-21, and the initial scene of Jesus in the

48. Malbon, "Echoes and Foreshadowings," 218–19.
49. Note that the subtitle of my article "Echoes and Foreshadowings in Mark 4–8" is "Reading and Rereading." Van Iersel, "Concentric Structures," 81, notes that "at a first reading such [text] signals [of structural elements] are recognized only at [the] micro-level, simply because the reader or hearer is unable to look or hear ahead, let alone have an overview of the whole text. Not until a considerable part of the text or the whole book has been read is it possible to recognize in retrospect their macro-syntactic function in major portions of the text or the whole book." Outline 4 here was originally Figure 2 in Malbon, "Echoes and Foreshadowings," 220.
50. See Malbon, "Echoes and Foreshadowings," 225.
51. See Elizabeth Struthers Malbon, "The Jesus of Mark and the Sea of Galilee," *JBL* 103 (1984): 363–77.

OUTLINE 4
Mark 4:1–8:21

4:1-9	Parable of sower *SEA SERMON
4:10-20	Explanation of parable(s)

4:21-	Additional parables and
34	Additional explanations

4:35-41	*SEA CALMING
5:1-20	Healing Gerasene demoniac
5:21-24a	Jairus' request for healing/
5:24b-34	Healing hemorrhaging woman/
5:35-43	Healing Jairus' daughter
6:1-6	(Rejection in the *patris*)
6:7-13	(Sending out of the twelve/
6:14-29	Herod and the death of John/
6:30	Return of the apostles)
6:31-44	*FEEDING THE 5000*

6:45-52	*SEA WALKING
6:53-56	Healings at Gennesaret
7:1-13	(Argument with Pharisees and scribes on the tradition of the elders/

7:14-15 (16)	Parable on defilement/
7:17-23	Explanation of parable)

7:24-30	Healing Syrophoenician woman's daughter
7:31-37	Healing deaf man in the Decapolis
8:1-9	*FEEDING THE 4000*
8:10-12	(Pharisees' request for a sign)

8:13-21	*SEA CONVERSATION

boat on the sea, teaching the crowd, at 4:1-9. The "sea conversation" echoes the "sea sermon," and together they enclose Mark 4:1–8:21. . . . Perhaps the two-stage healing of the blind man at Bethsaida, often—and convincingly—interpreted as an allusion forward to Peter's half-sight/half-blindness as expressed in 8:29 and 32, is also an allusion backward to 4:1–8:21, where Jesus repeatedly works in two stages so that the disciples may see and see clearly.[52]

Thus my previous work on "Echoes and Foreshadowings in Mark 4–8" is congruent with my present observation of the "hypertactic" aspect of the Markan plot and the discourse level of the narrative. The Markan narrative continually anticipates and recapitulates both the events of the plot and the significance of those events for the overall meaning of the story-as-discoursed. Years ago, Frans Neirynck observed "a sort of homogeneity in Mark from the wording of sentences to the composition of the gospel."[53] Neirynck examined this homogeneity in terms of the historical interests of redaction criticism, but I concur with his observation from the literary point of view of narrative criticism. In addition, Eric Havelock, a pioneer in orality criticism, has observed that oral composition operates on the echo principle:

> What is to be said and remembered later is cast in the form of an echo of something said already; the future is encoded in the present. All oral narrative is in structure continually both prophetic and retrospective. . . . Though the narrative syntax is paratactic—the basic conjunction being "and then," "and next"—the narrative is not linear but turns back on itself in order to assist the memory to reach the end by having it anticipated somehow in the beginning.[54]

This is what I am calling the "hypertactic" aspect of Mark's plot and the discourse level of the narrative: events and explanations are subordinated and coordinated in complex ways in the narrative rhetoric of Mark's Gospel.

Enacted christology depends on this "hypertactic" rhetorical effect in building its image of Jesus based on what he does. Enacted christology concerns not just the separate or collected actions of the Markan Jesus as teacher, preacher, exorcist, healer, server, and persecuted sufferer. It also—and especially—addresses the interconnections and development of these actions as they are narrated in a plot that consistently anticipates, insinuates, and recapitulates its message: the Markan Jesus who proclaims and participates in the in-breaking of the rule

52. Malbon, "Echoes and Foreshadowings," 225–26.

53. Frans Neirynck, *Duality in Mark: Contributions to the Study of the Markan Redaction* (BETL 31; Leuven, Belgium: Leuven University Press, 1972), 37.

54. Havelock, "Oral Composition," 183. I quoted this passage in "Echoes and Foreshadowings" (229), and Dewey quotes it as well in "Mark as Interwoven Tapestry"; for a comment on the echoes between our two articles, including their titles and subtitles, see Malbon, "Echoes and Foreshadowings," 212 n. 5.

of God, restoring health to the powerless ill and hungry, both within his own group and beyond it, insists on continuing to serve those with the least status in society and teach whoever wishes to do the will of God to do the same, even at the clear risk of losing his life at the hands of the established powers, and accepts that risk as the will of God. This is how the Markan Jesus is characterized by his actions; this is what the enacted christology of Mark's Gospel proclaims.

We move now from this diachronic query (what types of activities does the Markan Jesus do when) to a synchronic query (what does the Markan Jesus do in relation to whom). Both queries are intended to shed light on enacted christology, which focuses on what the Markan Jesus does. The synchronic query will explore how the Markan Jesus, in his actions, relates to the entire cast of characters in the Markan narrative considered as a set with subsets.

What Jesus Does in Relation to Whom

In their wonderfully useful introduction to Markan narrative criticism, *Mark as Story*, David Rhoads, Joanna Dewey, and Donald Michie concentrate on the analysis of conflicts in their discussion of plot.[55] Kingsbury titles a book *Conflict in Mark*.[56] Both Ched Myers and Richard Horsley focus primarily on conflict with the Roman imperial authorities as it is implicit and explicit in the Markan narrative.[57] My own observations about conflict between Jesus and the character groups of Mark parallel many of the suggestions of Rhoads, Dewey, and Michie.[58] Conflict with the other characters is basic to the action of the Markan Jesus and thus to enacted christology. To understand enacted christology, we must understand with whom the Markan Jesus comes into conflict and why.

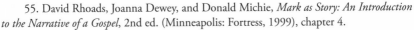

The Background Conflict with the Transcendent Characters

The background conflict underlying Mark's Gospel is that between the king- dom of God and the kingdom of Satan. The "kingdom of God has come near" (1:15), and for Satan's kingdom the "end has come" (3:26). Everything else that happens in Mark is to be understood against this transcendent background. After the superscription or title (1:1), the narrative opens with "As it is written," a formula for introducing a biblical quotation. The composite quotation

---

55. David Rhoads, Joanna Dewey, and Donald Michie, *Mark as Story: An Introduction to the Narrative of a Gospel*, 2nd ed. (Minneapolis: Fortress, 1999), chapter 4.

56. However, Kingsbury focuses each chapter on *one* character or character group, rather than on groups in conflict: the story of Jesus, the story of the authorities, the story of the disciples. The "story of Jesus" in *Conflict in Mark* is largely a version of *The Christology of Mark's Gospel* for an audience of "pastors and students."

57. Ched Myers, *Binding the Strong Man*; Richard A. Horsley, *Hearing the Whole Story: The Politics of Plot in Mark's Gospel* (Louisville: Westminster John Knox, 2001).

58. See also Dewey and Malbon, "Mark."

that follows (conflating Isaiah 40:3 with Exodus 23:20 and Malachi 3:1) points particularly to John the baptizer as the forerunner of Jesus ("As it is written . . . [so] John the baptizer appeared . . ."), but it also sets the tone for the entire narrative: what follows in this story occurs "as it is written" in the Bible, the revealing of God's will for the people of God. Thus the background conflict, the foundational conflict underlying the story, is God's: God struggles with Satan through the main character Jesus.

First, God has a scene with Jesus, the baptism (1:9-11). It is one of only two Markan scenes in which God participates as a character, or at least as a voice (the other being the transfiguration).[59] God commissions Jesus as "my Son" (1:11). Then, Satan has a scene with Jesus, testing him (1:12-13). It is extremely short and decisive from the point of view of indicating the readiness of the Markan Jesus to participate in this cosmic conflict: in the wilderness, Satan tests (Gk *peirazomenos*) Jesus for forty days, one day for each year of Israel's testing in the wilderness; Jesus passes the test; not only do "the angels" (from God's side) "minister to" or serve (Gk *diēkonoun*) Jesus, but "the wild beasts" (more representative of Satan's side) are peaceably "with" him.[60] But it is clear from

---

59. However, as Gene Boring notes, "Mark's narrative is thoroughly theocentric and permeated with God language" (M. Eugene Boring, "Markan Christology: God-Language for Jesus?" *NTS* 45 [1999]: 451–71, quotation from 451). See also Boring, "Christology of Mark," 136–45. John R. Donahue, S.J., notes that this Markan God language occurs, "[a]s one would expect," mostly "on the lips of Jesus" ("A Neglected Factor in the Theology of Mark," *JBL* 101 [1982]: 563–94, quotation from 566), thus it will be discussed when we turn, in chapters 3 and 4, to what Jesus says. Donahue also notes "the sober and reserved way Mark speaks of God" (569), avoiding anthropomorphism (567) and stressing transcendence. The fact that God is present as a character only twice in Mark, and then only to hearing not to sight, is consistent with the overall approach Donahue describes.

60. Ernest Best argues that, although Mark's Gospel does not make explicit the outcome of the temptation account within that account, the outcome is made clear elsewhere in the Gospel, especially in 3:19b-35: Jesus defeats Satan decisively in the wilderness and thus removes Satan as a powerful antagonist in the rest of Mark's Gospel (*The Temptation and the Passion: The Markan Soteriology* [SNTSMS 2; 2nd ed.; Cambridge: Cambridge University Press, 1965], esp. 3–18 for Best's position and 18–23, where Best argues against James M. Robinson, *The Problem of History in Mark* [Philadelphia: Fortress, 1982]). However, the situation is more complex than that. Elizabeth Shively cautions against reading an initial cosmic "victory" as a final victory, arguing on the basis of a careful literary analysis that the apparent contradiction between the parables of the divided house and kingdom and the parable of the strong man in Mark 3:23-27 in fact creates "a tension of power between Satan and the Spirit that is manifested in the ministry of Jesus" ("The Story Matters: Solving the Problem of the Parables in Mark 3:23-27," in *Between Author and Audience in Mark: Narration, Characterization, Interpretation* [ed. Elizabeth Struthers Malbon; New Testament Monographs 23; Sheffield: Sheffield Phoenix, 2009], 122–44, quotation from 131). Still, it is fair to say that the Markan narrative indicates a victory for Jesus in the testing; the Markan Jesus is portrayed as proven worthy of engaging in this cosmic conflict on the side of God and against Satan.

the link that connects the two scenes that the Markan Jesus was well equipped for the contest: "And the Spirit immediately [after God's words at the baptism] drove him out into the wilderness" (1:12). In the previous scene, God's scene with Jesus, "the Spirit" had descended from the split-apart heavens into Jesus (Gk *eis*). The Spirit is a manifestation of God's presence, which goes with Jesus as he is driven out (Gk *ekballei*) into the wilderness. This cosmic conflict of God and Satan is the deep background for all of Mark's Gospel and the immediate background for the opening of Jesus' ministry with his proclamation that "[t]he time is fulfilled, and the kingdom of God has come near" (1:15).

Given this beginning at the transcendent level—Jesus as the protagonist dealing directly with God and Satan—the implied audience is not too shocked to learn from the narrator that other transcendent beings, the demons and unclean spirits, know of Jesus' role in the cosmic conflict (1:24, 34; 3:11; 5:7). The Markan Jesus tries to contain their knowledge at the same time he attempts to constrict the kingdom they represent (as will be discussed later as part of deflected christology, what Jesus says in response). As even the scribes know, the demons are in league with the ruler of demons, whom the scribes call Beelzebul (3:22), a Jewish insult to a "pagan" god by applying his name to Satan. As the Holy Spirit manifests God's presence, so the unclean spirits and demons manifest the presence of Satan. The Holy Spirit drives Jesus out (1:12, *ekballei*), but Jesus drives out the unclean spirits (1:34, 39; 3:22). The Markan Jesus' "hard saying" about blasphemy against the Holy Spirit as an "eternal sin" is uttered in response to the scribes' 180-degree reversal in evaluating the work of the Holy Spirit as demonic (3:28-30). The Markan Jesus, who is depicted as living and dying as a human being, is also shown to act directly with a range of suprahuman and nonhuman, or transcendent, beings,[61] whose relations might be suggested in a simple diagram (Diagram 1).

"Jesus" appears below the line in Diagram 1 because his humanity distinguishes him from the others. "Jesus" appears at the center of the line because he interacts directly with each character or group, not because he occupies a "mediate" position between God and Satan, for there is no such position. Rather, God and Satan struggle through Jesus; with God, Jesus will win. The cosmic struggle

---

61. Workable terminology is not easy to find. John R. Donahue, S.J., notes that "Son of God" is "expressed by a voice from the heavens or by those with some kind of preternatural knowledge," and he also refers to "'otherworldly' salutations of Jesus [that] reappear throughout the narrative (1:24; 3:11; 5:7; 9:7)" ("Jesus as the Parable of God in the Gospel of Mark," in *Interpreting the Gospels* [ed. James Luther Mays; Philadelphia: Fortress, 1981], 148–67; quotations from 158, 164–65; first published in *Int* 32 [1978]: 369–86). Petersen, commenting on the knowledge of Jesus shared by God and the unclean spirits, refers to them as "transcendent beings" ("Composition of Mark 4:1–8:26," 213). I am using "transcendent" here to suggest the dramatic connection between characters whose knowledge (and very being) goes beyond, or transcends, human knowledge (and being): God, the (Holy) Spirit, angels, unclean spirits/demons, Satan.

DIAGRAM 1
The Markan Jesus and the Transcendent Characters

Satan   unclean spirits/demons   angels   Holy Spirit   God

|---|

Jesus

between God and Satan is manifest in Mark's narrative through the exceptional protagonist Jesus, who, under the power of God's (Holy) Spirit, proclaims God's kingdom and overthrows the unclean spirits, signaling that Satan's kingdom is coming to an end. The christological implications of this narrative are obvious. Jesus' conflicts on this transcendent level form the backdrop against which the other conflicts of the narrative are acted out. Theologically they are fundamental, but dramatically they are in the background.

THE MIDDLE-GROUND CONFLICT WITH THE AUTHORITIES

In the middle ground is the conflict between Jesus and the authorities—throughout the narrative, the Jewish authorities (scribes and Pharisees in the first half; chief priests, scribes, and elders in the passion narrative), and at the end of the narrative, the Roman authorities (Herod, Pilate, and his soldiers). Although this conflict is undoubtedly important within the plot of the Markan narrative, I must take issue with Kingsbury's generalization concerning it: "The major conflict is between Jesus and Israel, made up of the religious authorities and the Jewish crowd."[62] Several problematic issues are involved.

First, the application of the term "religious" to the Jewish (literally Judean) authorities is anachronistic and Westernizing in Mark's first-century context, where neither "religion" nor "politics" were distinctive or separate spheres and where Jewish/Judean personnel held positions at the pleasure of the dominating Roman Empire.[63] The second problem with Kingsbury's formulation is the linking of "the religious authorities" and "the Jewish crowd." Although it is true that chief priests, scribes, and elders are able to manipulate the crowd at the very end, earlier in the narrative the crowd responds positively to Jesus.[64]

---

62. Kingsbury, *Conflict*, 63.

63. For an impassioned critique of the application of the term "religion" to Mark's Gospel, see Horsley, *Hearing the Whole Story*, 27–51. Horsley also critiques the use, in reference to Mark's Gospel, of the terms "Christian," "Christianity," "Jew," and "Judaism," which I do avoid, as well as "Jewish," which I have found more difficult to avoid, although I never use it in a way that would include scribes and Pharisees but exclude Jesus and his disciples.

64. See Elizabeth Struthers Malbon, "Disciples/Crowds/Whoever: Markan Characters

The third problem is labeling this forced pairing (that is, "the religious authorities and the Jewish crowd") as "Israel." Although the chief priests, scribes, and elders (but not the crowd) might be said to represent "the establishment" within Israel (over against Jesus *and* the crowd!), Jesus, the crowd, and the disciples are no less a part of "Israel" in Mark's narrative than "the religious authorities." This label does a great disservice to the Gospel. In addition, labeling "the religious authorities" as "Israel" gives little or no recognition to the fact that, in the first-century world of Mark's narrative, they are political appointees of the Roman imperial system. The fourth problem is labeling the conflict with the authorities as "the major conflict." "Major" is a term difficult to apply to one aspect without undercutting another significant aspect. Kingsbury does not mind undercutting the significance of the Markan conflict between Jesus and the disciples because in his interpretation, "[e]xcept perhaps for Judas, the disciples do not materially influence the plot, or flow of events, of Mark's story."[65] A similar situation occurs with Richard Horsley, who, although extremely sensitive to the political implications of the conflict with the Judean rulers, is so focused on the conflict with the Roman Empire as the major conflict in Mark that he downplays the conflict with the disciples, stressing only their failure.[66] But the labeling of Jesus' conflict with the authorities (in their complex "religious" and political alliances) as "the major conflict" also undercuts the significance of the foundational (but background, not minor) conflict between God and Satan. Thus I find it more helpful to regard the conflict between Jesus and the authorities as the conflict of the middle ground.

Many commentators have noted that Jesus' conflict with the authorities that climaxes at Jesus' crucifixion is manifest as early as the set of five controversy stories at 2:1–3:6, with its own (and foreshadowing) climax at 3:6—"The Pharisees went out and immediately conspired with the Herodians against him, how to destroy him." The working out of their conspiracy is alluded to soon thereafter by the narrator as he recounts Jesus' calling of the twelve, including

---

and Readers," *NovT* 28 (1986): 104–30, republished in *The Composition of Mark's Gospel: Selected Studies from Novum Testamentum* (ed. David E. Orton; Leiden, The Netherlands: Brill, 1999), 144–70, and also in Malbon, *In the Company of Jesus: Characters in Mark's Gospel* (Louisville: Westminster John Knox, 2000), 70–99. See also Joel F. Williams, *Other Followers of Jesus: Minor Characters as Major Figures in Mark's Gospel* (JSNTSup 102; Sheffield: Sheffield Academic, 1994).

65. Kingsbury, *Conflict*, 89.

66. Horsley, *Hearing the Whole Story*, 79–97, on the disciples, and 99–119, on "the overall plotting of Mark's story [that] focuses on Jesus' renewal of Israel in opposition to the rulers" (119). Horsley regards "Mark's narrative [as] a highly credible account of the emergence and expansion of just such a [renewal] movement" (117) and interprets Mark's story as "calling a particular Jesus movement or set of communities back to the egalitarian ideal with which it began, over against the inner circle of the twelve who became the revered heads of the movement(s)" (96).

"Judas Iscariot, who betrayed him" (3:19). But the Markan Jesus has already alluded to his death metaphorically in the central controversy story of the set: "The wedding guests cannot fast while the bridegroom is with them, can they? As long as they have the bridegroom with them, they cannot fast. The days will come when the bridegroom is taken away from them, and then they will fast on that day" (2:19-20).[67] Or it may be that the narrator makes the first allusion to Jesus' passion, if that passion (the climax of the middle-ground conflict) is seen against the background of the conflict between God and Satan: "And the Spirit immediately drove him out into the wilderness . . . [where he was] tempted by Satan . . ." (1:12-13).[68] Jesus' conflict with the authorities, like his conflicts with the demons and unclean spirits, reflects the more fundamental conflict between God and Satan. Yet Mark's narrative does not set up an allegory; the authorities are no more Satan that the Markan Jesus *is* God.

"Middle ground" is not an unproblematic term itself, for the middle-ground conflict of Jesus and the authorities, foreshadowed from the beginning, seems to take center stage at 2:1–3:6 (the set of five controversy stories) and again at 11:15–12:44 (Jesus' action and teaching in the temple) and 14:43–15:39 (Jesus' arrest, "trials," and crucifixion). Mark's *story* is a given: Jesus dies at the hands of Jewish/Judean and Roman authorities. Thus the conflict between Jesus and the authorities comes into its own in the passion narrative. But Mark's *plot* first introduces this conflict against the background conflict of God and Satan (1:9-13 or 1:9-15 or 1:1-15) and then frames it by introducing the story of Jesus and the disciples (1:16-20, Jesus calling his disciples, including Peter) before the conflict with the authorities and, following the conclusion of the conflict with the authorities, closing the narrative with a final reference to the disciples (16:7, the young man's echo of Jesus' words, 14:28, to the disciples, especially Peter;[69] see also 15:40–16:8, stories of followers' responses). Thus the conflict of Jesus and the authorities is the middle-ground conflict, with the cosmic conflict of God and Satan in the background and, in the foreground, the conflict between Jesus and the disciples. The Markan narrative presents, develops, and intertwines all three levels of conflict, so interpreters who isolate one level as the major conflict and ignore the other two do the narrative an injustice.

67. For a discussion of this allusive bridegroom imagery in Mark and John, see Annalisa Guida, "From *Parabolē* to *Sēmeion*: The Nuptial Imagery in Mark and John," in *Between Author and Audience*, 103–20.

68. One might even argue that the first allusion to Jesus' passion is given by the character God, in the words of the voice from heaven, "You are my Son, the Beloved" (1:11), which echo the words of God to Abraham in Gen 22:2: "Take your son, your only son Isaac, whom you love. . . ." See Dowd and Malbon, "The Significance of Jesus' Death in Mark," 273–74.

69. Boring also calls attention to 1:16-20 and 16:1-8 in noting that Mark "is a narrative about Jesus-in-relationship-to-the-disciples" ("Christology of Mark," 143).

The Foreground Conflict with the Disciples

The conflict between God and Satan is clearly a mismatch in God's favor in Mark's Gospel, and the conflict with the authorities, although not without its intrigue, leads to a known outcome: the seeming victory of the authorities, Jesus' crucifixion, is overturned by the victory of God, Jesus' resurrection. Thus the conflict between the Markan Jesus and the disciples is of greatest dramatic interest for the implied author and the implied audience. Jesus and the disciples are the only "round" characters in the Markan narrative.[70] The other characters are "flat": the unclean spirits are always evil; the Pharisees are always conspiring. The disciples change. They respond to Jesus' call; they follow and listen to him; they teach and cast out demons on his authority; they question him; they misunderstand him; they question themselves; they still follow him. Jesus suggests that they will be scattered like sheep whose shepherd is struck down (14:27) but that, later, they will be "gathered" from the ends of the earth and heaven (13:27). They do scatter. One betrays him; one denies him; all abandon him—but he does not abandon them; he is going before them to Galilee, as he told them (14:28; 16:7). The dynamic portrayal of the disciples in their relation to Jesus is one of the reasons the implied audience is most drawn into their conflict.

The disciples in Mark have been much commented on in recent years. But even more recently, Markan scholars have commented on the connections between the Markan understanding of discipleship and Markan christology—especially narrative christology.[71] The disciples are only disciples in relation to Jesus. A disciple is to be a reflection of his or her teacher. Thus Jesus' discipleship instruction also implies a christology, one that can be reflected in the actions of his followers—the disciples, other followers, and even the implied audience.

It is Jesus' developing relationship with the disciples that is plotted *over* the story of Jesus' ministry and passion. Once Jesus' proclamation that "the kingdom of God has come near" (1:15) signals the decisive beginning of the victory of God over Satan, Jesus calls his first disciples (1:16-20). The Markan Jesus does not set out on a solo mission and only at some later point involve others.

---

70. Elizabeth Struthers Malbon, "The Jewish Leaders in the Gospel of Mark: A Literary Study of Marcan Characterization," *JBL* 108 (1989): 259–81, esp. 277–81, republished in Malbon, *In the Company of Jesus*, 131–65.

71. See, e.g., Paul L. Danove, *The Rhetoric of the Characterization of God, Jesus, and Jesus' Disciples in the Gospel of Mark* (JSNTSup 290; New York: T&T Clark, 2005); Suzanne Watts Henderson, *Christology and Discipleship in the Gospel of Mark* (SNTSMS 135; Cambridge: Cambridge University Press, 2006), esp. 245–500; and Ira Brent Driggers, *Following God through Mark: Theological Tension in the Second Gospel* (Louisville: Westminster John Knox, 2007). Precursors were Tannehill, "Narrative Christology"; Tannehill, "The Disciples in Mark: The Function of a Narrative Role," *JR* 57 (1977): 386–405; and Donahue, "Neglected Factor," esp. 581–92.

The proclamation of God's in-breaking kingdom demands and creates community immediately. The disciples are with Jesus through the whirlwind of activities of chapter 1 (*kai euthus, kai euthus*; and immediately, and immediately) and are intertwined in the controversy stories of 2:1–3:6. Mark 3:7-35 focuses on the disciples and broadens the category of followers to "[w]hoever does the will of God" (3:35). The disciples are Jesus' continual partners for chapters 4–8, where his struggle to teach them, through some impressive rhetoric of the Markan implied author, that there is enough bread and teaching for Gentiles as well as for Jews comes to a climax in the third boat scene (8:14-21) and Jesus' unanswered question: "Do you not yet understand?" (8:21).

Then begins the special section for Jesus and his disciples, 8:22–10:52. As noted above, this "way" section is framed by the only two Markan stories of the healing of blindness and punctuated by the three passion prediction units. From the two-stage healing of the blind man of Bethsaida, the implied audience learns that sight, like insight, may take a second effort. With the disciples, who are given discipleship instruction three times, the implied audience learns that followers of one willing even to suffer persecution in order to serve must be ready to serve and possibly suffer persecution themselves. Peter's initial struggle with this teaching of Jesus leads to mutual rebuking and Peter being called "Satan" by Jesus (8:33), bringing the background conflict of God and Satan to the foreground in a brief but powerful scene.[72] When Bartimaeus receives his sight and follows Jesus "on the way," he presents not only a contrast with the disciples that shows them in a negative light but a positive symbolic model of the possibility of discipleship. The disciples, too, enter Jerusalem with Jesus at chapter 11, making way in the temple for the authorities to share the spotlight with Jesus. But chapter 13, the eschatological discourse, belongs to the disciples again, as does the future that it sets forth. Scenes with the anointing woman, the final Passover meal, and Jesus' prayer in Gethsemane give center stage to Jesus and the disciples again, before the authorities seem to be in charge in the arrest, trials, and crucifixion scenes.

But in the end is the beginning: the women at the cross and tomb, followers from the beginning, and Joseph of Arimathea, here at the end "waiting expectantly for the kingdom of God" (15:43), remind the implied audience of Jesus' initial proclamation of the "kingdom of God" (1:15) and his concomitant calling of disciples (1:16-20). The Markan Jesus, true to his word, does not abandon those who have abandoned him. That Jesus is still going before his disciples, his fallible followers, to Galilee (16:7; cf. 14:28) is a narrative christological confession of some import. "Who can forgive sins but God alone?" (2:7). "[T]he Son of Man has authority on earth to forgive sins." (2:10). "The

---

72. Williams comments, "Satan's role is played out by a human being who foolishly speaks from a human perspective. In the introduction, Mark places the story of Jesus within the context of the conflict between God and Satan but then shows how this story is played out in the lives of ordinary people who come into contact with Jesus" ("An Outline?" 514).

time is fulfilled, and the kingdom of God has come near; *repent*, and believe in the *good news*" (1:15). The disciples—women and men—have a renewed opportunity to repent and trust in the good news of the in-breaking rule of God that the Markan Jesus proclaims.

As is probably clear from what I have sketched here, I find an expansive movement in Mark's narrative from the twelve disciples, to the women disciples, to the followers, to certain "minor" characters, to the crowd, to the implied audience.[73] It is this expanded and expansive group to which I have given the name "fallible followers."[74] At any moment in their relationship with Jesus, fallible followers might range from disciples betraying or denying Jesus, to disciples healing in Jesus' name, to suppliants trusting in Jesus' power, to exemplars modeling Jesus' self-giving service. Diagram 2 suggests the range of the human characters' responses to the Markan Jesus.

"Jesus" appears above the line in Diagram 2 because he is the defining character, the human character over against whom all other human characters are defined. It is not possible to place on this line "the authorities" because the individuals in this somewhat variegated group of Markan characters do not all play the same role in relation to Jesus. Most of them, most of the time, are indeed opponents; but Mark's narrative presents three significant exceptions: the synagogue leader Jairus; the scribe "not far from the kingdom of God"; and Joseph of Arimathea, "a respected member of the council." When Kingsbury, among others, dismisses these characters from the category of "the authorities" that does include the chief priests, scribes, and elders, he fills in a significant fissure in Mark's largely stereotypical portrayal of the Jewish authorities and thus makes the stereotype monolithic to be sure.[75] But in Mark's narrative, Jairus is a suppliant, asking for healing and life for his daughter, with exemplary faith. The scribe in dialogue with Jesus may be a suppliant asking for teaching, but he is clearly exemplary in not being far from the kingdom of God. Joseph of

73. Dewey notes: "Ancient aural narrative permits different perspectives even with an omniscient narrator because of the listeners' sequential identification with the different characters as they are portrayed in performance. Identification occurs successively—that is, the performer and the audience identify in turn with each character." ("Mark as Aural Narrative," 55).

74. Malbon, "Fallible Followers"; "Disciples, Crowds, Whoever"; and "The Major Importance of the Minor Characters in Mark," in *The New Literary Criticism and the New Testament*, 58–86, republished in Malbon, *In the Company of Jesus*, 189–225.

75. Certainly, Markan characterization relies on "types," as did ancient literature in general; however, Mark's Gospel does seem to go out of its way to present a few "atypical" Jewish authorities that interfere with the implied audience's tendency to stereotype; see Malbon, "Jewish Leaders," 275–81, or Malbon, *In the Company of Jesus*, 157–65. For a compact but excellent review of ancient typological characterization, see Abraham Smith, "Tyranny Exposed: Mark's Typological Characterization of Herod Antipas (Mark 6:14-29)," *BibInt* 14 (2006): 263–66.

DIAGRAM 2
The Markan Jesus and the Human Characters

Jesus

|--|

opponents   disciples   suppliants   exemplars

                           ⟨------------ fallible followers ------------⟩

Arimathea asks for nothing but Jesus' body, which he lays in a tomb, while wait-ing expectantly as an exemplar for all (see 13:37) for the kingdom of God. All three *reflect* the christology by which the Markan narrative characterizes Jesus, a topic to be pursued in a later chapter.

We can overlay the two lines of Markan characters, transcendent and hu-man, to achieve Diagram 3. The placement of "Jesus" in the center of the dia-gram indicates that he is the central character, the one character who has direct interaction with all the others. The placement of "Jesus" in the center of the diagram should not be read as a suggestion of two natures, divine and hu-man, in the creedal sense developed in Christian councils centuries after Mark's narrative![76] "Transcendent" here is not equivalent to "divine"; in fact, "divine" seems not to be a functional category for Mark's Gospel.[77] "Transcendent" re-fers to the suprahuman characters, whether good (God, Holy Spirit, angels) or evil (unclean spirits/demons, Satan), because they share knowledge beyond (or "transcendent" to) the human characters other than Jesus. Despite Jesus' own knowledge, however, in Mark's Gospel "Jesus" is a human character, although an extraordinary human character who is in communication with suprahuman characters in a way no other human characters in this narrative are.

The length of the two lines is meant to suggest that the range of the tran-scendent characters is broader than that of the human characters. In the larger scheme of things (the Markan narrator's background), the high priest (an oppo-nent) is closer to the anointing woman (an exemplar) than Satan is to God—or than the high priest is to Satan. Because both the high priest and the anointing

76. Cf. Boring, "Christology of Mark," 136. Contra M. Philip Scott, O.C.S.O., "Chi-astic Structure: A Key to the Interpretation of Mark's Gospel," *BTB* 15 (1985): 17–26, who has no problem interpreting the Markan Jesus in terms of Johannine preexistence, Chalcedo-nian theology of the two natures, and the terms of the Nicene Creed (see 20, 23, 24).

77. As Boring notes, "Mark emphasizes the absoluteness of the one God (2.7; 10.18), is the only NT author to quote the Shema directly (12.29-32), and thus does not and cannot have a general category 'divine' into which God and other divine beings (Christ, angels) can be placed" ("Markan Christology," 456–57).

DIAGRAM 3
Markan Characters

Satan	unclean spirits/demons		angels	Holy Spirit	God

├ --- |

Jesus

├ --- ┤

	opponents		disciples	suppliants	exemplars	

〈 -------- fallible followers -------- 〉

woman have their "place" in relation to Jesus, this observation is not without
narrative christological import. The characters at the center, Jesus and the disciples, are the rounded ones, the ones who can change, who can falter, who can
grow in understanding. Peter's denial can be seen in relation to Jesus' initial
prayer in Gethsemane; Peter's abandonment can be heard in relation to Jesus'
cry of despair from the cross. Jesus is unique in Mark's narrative; there is no
mistaking that. But in showing that even Jesus had to struggle to follow God's
will, the implied author shows understanding of human misunderstanding and
weakness and offers hope of reconciliation not only to the disciples, and Peter,
but also to the implied audience.[78]

One additional overlay on the diagram will put the three dramatic conflicts
in relationship with each other (Diagram 4). This diagram does *not* present
an ontological schema.[79] Mark's narrative is obviously the story of Jesus. Everything revolves around him. All the human characters find their places in
relation to him. But the Markan Jesus finds his place in relation to God—and
the struggle between Satan and God that occurs when God's kingdom comes
near.[80] As I will discuss later in relation to deflected and refracted christology,

---

78. Cf. Petr Pokorny: "On the literary level this kenotic christology of Jesus' solidarity
with sinful humans left its traces in Mark's representation of other human characters. . . .
[T]he role of Peter, . . . the role of the other poor or socially insignificant people, women or the
sick ones—[these] all are features untypical for literature dealing with heroic figures. The ordinary, sinful people, who in the aretalogies belonged to the hero's scenery, move in the centre
stream of the narrative and into the centre of the divine movement" ("Markan Christology,"
unpublished paper distributed to members of the Mark Seminar of the SNTS, 1998, 6).

79. Boring demonstrates that "[i]t is possible to construct from Markan data an ontological scale that represents Mark's presumed understanding of deity and humanity, and
then to fit Mark's Christology into this 'great chain of being,'" but also that this would be "to
impose an alien schema on Markan thought" ("Markan Christology," 451, 456).

80. Cf. Cook (*Christology as Narrative Quest*, 78): "The most fundamental question is
not about Jesus' own sense of personal identity but about his relationship to God."

DIAGRAM 4
Markan Characters and Conflicts

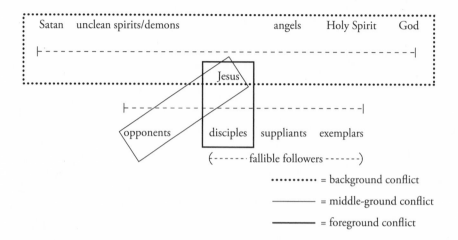

although the Markan narrator is eager to proclaim Jesus as "Christ, the Son of God," the Markan Jesus is reticent to accept such titles, preferring to deflect attention from them, and ready and willing to challenge and refract their meanings. In examining enacted christology, we see that the Markan narrator is very much aware of the background against which the Markan Jesus attempts to deflect attention and honor from himself to God: the cosmic conflict of God with Satan. From his position as the character in the center of the Markan narrative, Jesus wants to talk about God's kingdom; such talk has different consequences for each character and character group, including Jesus! From his position at the edge of the narrative, the narrator wants to talk about Jesus—Jesus talking about God's kingdom, to be sure, but also Jesus as responded to by opponents and followers and Jesus as talked about by other characters as well as by the narrator.

It is thus for the narrator (and the narratee, as well as the implied author and the implied audience) that the terms *background, middle ground*, and *foreground* apply as discussed here. For the Markan Jesus, the conflict between God and Satan is not quite so far back! The Markan Jesus takes a broader view than the opponents, who see him as opposing God, and a broader view than the disciples, who do "not yet understand" (8:21) that Jesus asks the impossible only because "for God all things are possible" (10:27). The Markan Jesus even takes a broader view than the Markan narrator, who paints the cosmic story of God as the background and clears the stage in order to narrow the spotlight's focus on the central character, Jesus. But that central character, Jesus, continually draws the disciples, the fallible followers, and the implied audience into the broader story of God.

Conclusion

In our quest to explore a Markan narrative christology, it is appropriate to have begun with the aspect of narrative christology I have termed enacted christology—a christology based on what the Markan Jesus does. Because of the impossibility of dealing in detail with all the individual actions of Jesus in Mark's story, I have focused here on Mark's plot and the discourse level of the narrative, that is, on the actions as arranged by the implied author in communication with the implied audience. Specifically I made two queries of the Gospel narrative—one diachronic ("through time") and one synchronic ("same time"). Asking first the diachronic question, "What types of activities does the Markan Jesus do when?" and recognizing that various Markan outlines serve as heuristic devices, I presented several outlines to highlight the "hypertactic" plot of Mark's Gospel, a plot in which actions and events are interconnected in complex ways that influence the discourse level of the narrative—the implied author's conversation with the implied audience. Asking then the synchronic question, "What does the Markan Jesus do in relation to whom?" I examined how the Markan Jesus relates to the entire cast of characters in the Markan narrative by considering three levels of conflict in which Jesus is engaged—the background (but foundational) conflict among the transcendent characters, the middle-ground conflict with the authorities, and the foreground conflict with the disciples. The actions of the Markan Jesus—whether investigated synchronically by abstracting a system of transcendent and human characters or diachronically by focusing on the unfolding plot with its echoes and foreshadowings—are the data of enacted christology. One important way of characterizing Jesus is by what he does; this aspect of characterization of the Markan Jesus is what I mean by enacted christology.

We began our look at enacted christology with this observation: at the most elemental level, what the Markan Jesus does is preach and teach (about the in-breaking of God's rule), exorcise and heal (as an exemplification of the in-breaking of God's rule), and insist on and practice service to those with the least status in society and thus suffer persecution and death by the authorities of that society (as an exemplification of the implications of the in-breaking of God's rule in the present age). We conclude with a reiteration of a more complex observation. Enacted christology concerns not just the separate or collected actions of the Markan Jesus as teacher, preacher, exorcist, healer, server, and persecuted sufferer, but also the interconnections and development of these actions as they are narrated in a plot that consistently anticipates, insinuates, and recapitulates its message: the Markan Jesus who proclaims and participates in the in-breaking of the rule of God, restoring health to the powerless ill and hungry, both within his own group and beyond it, insists on continuing to serve those with the least status in society and teach whoever wishes to do the will of God to do the same, even at the clear risk of losing his life at the hands of the established powers, and accepts that risk as the will of God.

CHAPTER 2

PROJECTED CHRISTOLOGY: WHAT OTHERS SAY

Traditionally, examinations of Markan Christology have focused on the "titles" applied to Jesus by others in the narrative, especially "Christ" and "Son of God," although "Son of Man" (or, more literally translated, "Son of Humanity"), used only by Jesus in Mark, and Jesus' actions have not been ignored. My work on narrative christology decenters this way of abstracting "titles" from the narrative and discussing their meaning outside of their narrative contexts, whether in a history of religions context or in a theological-philosophical context. It would be impossible, of course, to ignore the "titles" altogether because they are an integral part of the narrative, or to ignore their potential meanings in their broader cultural contexts for the Markan implied audience.[1] What others in the narrative say to and about Jesus is naturally of great importance to a Markan narrative christology, but it is not to be given priority or dominance. Projected christology, that is, the view of Jesus that is projected onto him by the narrator and the characters internal to the story, is one of several aspects of narrative christology. Care is taken to note who says what to or about Jesus and under what circumstances in the narrative. An important distinction is

---

1. Narrative critic David Rhoads speaks not of "titles" but of "epithets," referring to the way in which they depict traits or relationships or functions rather than focusing on status and identity; see David Rhoads, Joanna Dewey, and Donald Michie, *Mark as Story: An Introduction to the Narrative of a Gospel* (2nd ed.; Minneapolis: Fortress, 1999), 98–115, on the character Jesus.

between what the narrator says and what the characters say, because the implied
author of Mark does give the narrator a privileged position. Do the comments
of characters presented in direct discourse fit with or exist in tension with the
narrator's generalizations? Do different categories of characters make similar or
differing comments to or about Jesus? How is the implied audience encouraged
to relate to the different character groups and their comments? These are the
questions under investigation here. We begin with a look at what the narrator
says about Jesus, followed by examinations of what various character groups
say to or about Jesus—to the extent possible, in their chronological order of
introduction into the story.

What the Narrator Says about Jesus

Because there is much to say—and much that has been said—about what the
narrator says about Jesus in Mark 1:1, we will focus on this allusive and elusive
opening line in one subsection and explore what the narrator says in his more
usual way in the rest of Mark's Gospel in a second subsection.

WHAT THE NARRATOR SAYS ABOUT JESUS IN MARK 1:1

The tremendous amount of attention given to Mark 1:1, not only in investigations of Markan christology but in Markan commentary in general, is not misplaced; the opening verse is both complicated and crucial in a number of ways:
"The beginning of the good news [Gk *euangelion*, gospel] of Jesus Christ, the
Son of God." First, there is a textual problem: the phrase "Son of God" is lacking in some ancient manuscripts. As a literary critic of the New Testament and
not a textual scholar, I defer to the comments of Bruce Metzger on this issue:

> The absence of *huiou theou* [Son of God] in . . . [Codex Sinaiticus, Codex Koride-
> thianus, 28ᶜ, and other ancient manuscripts] may be due to an oversight in copy-
> ing, occasioned by the similarity of the endings of the *nomina sacra* [sacred name;
> that is, the ending of *Christou*, Christ, resembles the ending of *huiou theou*, Son of
> God, and may have led a copyist to think he had finished with *theou* when he had
> only copied *Christou*]. On the other hand, however, there was always a temptation
> (to which copyists often succumbed) to expand titles and quasi-titles of books.
> Since the combination of B D W *al* [Codex Vaticanus, Codex Bezae Cantabrigien-
> sis, Codex Freerianus, and other ancient manuscripts] in support of *huiou theou* is
> strong, it was not thought advisable to omit the words altogether, yet because of
> the antiquity of the shorter reading and the possibility of scribal expansion, it was
> decided to enclose the words within square brackets.[2]

2. Bruce M. Metzger, *A Textual Commentary on the Greek New Testament* (United Bible
Societies, 1971), 73. As Henry Barclay Swete put it years ago: "The evidence for the omission
of these words is weighty but meagre" (*The Gospel According to Mark* [London: Macmillan,
1913]; repr., *Commentary on Mark* [Grand Rapids: Kregel Publications, 1977], 2). For a

The New Revised Standard Version does not use square brackets for 1:1, as it does for the shorter and longer additions to the ending of Mark, but it does note that "other ancient authorities lack *the Son of God.*" The phrase "Son of God" at 1:1 makes excellent sense in terms of Markan christology,[3] which could be used to argue either for its original inclusion or for its later addition! Thus, knowing that the textual evidence is inconclusive, I am following the NRSV's pattern of raising the question but including "Son of God" in my literary analysis of 1:1.

Second, there is a grammatical problem with verse 1 in relation to verses 2-3 and 4: scholars debate just how these verses are to be divided into sentences and connected to each other. Because ancient Greek manuscripts lacked punctuation and spacing that we depend on for clarity, modern editions of Greek texts, as well as contemporary English translations, have inserted such features. Mark 1:1 is distinctive in the narrative for its lack of a verb; for this reason, I follow a standard scholarly edition of the Greek text[4] and the NRSV in reading 1:1 by itself. I consider this opening phrase a proclamation that serves as a title for the work.[5] (The current title, "The Gospel According to Mark," is not as old as the text of the Gospel.) Some commentators and readers supply a "This is" before 1:1, which weakens the proclamation/title to a simple declarative sentence. Other commentators connect 1:1 to the biblical quotation that follows it, rather than connecting that quotation to verse 4, reading, "The beginning of the good news about Jesus the anointed one, the son of God, was just as it is written in Isaiah the prophet: . . . . It was John baptizing in the desert and

decision not to consider "Son of God" part of Mark 1:1 in a commentary, see Adela Yarbro Collins, *Mark: A Commentary* (Hermeneia; Minneapolis: Fortress, 2007), 130; for her more detailed evaluation of the textual evidence on Mark 1:1, see Adela Yarbro Collins, "Establishing the Text: Mark 1:1," in *Texts and Contexts: Biblical Texts in Their Textual and Situational Contexts: Essays in Honor of Lars Hartman* (ed. Tord Fomberg and David Hellholm; Oslo: Scandinavian University Press, 1995), 111–27.

3. Vincent Taylor, *The Gospel According to St. Mark* (2nd ed.; New York: St. Martins, 1966; repr., Grand Rapids: Baker Book House, 1981), 152, after noting the absence of "the Son of God" in certain ancient manuscripts, concludes that "[t]here are strong reasons, however, for accepting the phrase as original, in view of its attestation [in other ancient manuscripts], its possible omission by homoioteleuton [error due to similar word endings], and the use of the title in Mark's Christology."

4. Kurt Aland et al., ed., *The Greek New Testament* (3rd ed.; New York: United Bible Societies, 1975).

5. Cf. Taylor, *St. Mark*, 152: "The verse is probably intended by Mark as a title, as the absence of the article before *archē* [beginning] may indicate." M. Eugene Boring, "Mark 1:1-15 and the Beginning of the Gospel," *Semeia* 52 (1990): 43–81, presents a detailed argument that 1:1 is Mark's title to the whole narrative, based on the options among the textual variants, the possible syntactical construals of 1:1-4, and the meaning of 1:1 as a title to the whole narrative (47–53).

proclaiming a baptism of turning around for pardon of sins."[6] As can be seen
in this translation by David Rhoads, attaching the quotation to 1:1 entails, in
addition to adding a verb between verses 1 and 2, making some change in 1:4.
With the Greek text and the NRSV, I connect the quotation (about which more
will be said below) grammatically to the statement about John: "As is it written
in the prophet Isaiah, . . . [so] John the baptized appeared in the wilderness. . . ."
For our purpose in exploring the aspect of Markan narrative christology that
I am calling projected christology, what is important is understanding 1:1 as
the narrator's opening line—the narrator's way of arresting the attention of the
narratee.

In comparison with what the narrator says in the rest of Mark's Gospel, 1:1
is unique. All other words voiced by the narrator are straightforward narration
of Jesus' actions (including speaking), or the actions of others in relation to
Jesus, or the actions of John the baptizer and others in relation to John as parallel to Jesus. Except for 1:1, all the statements of the narrator about Jesus relate
what Jesus did, where he went, what he said and to whom, etc.[7] In performance,
Mark 1:1 was no doubt voiced in such a way as to gather attention for the listening experience. As Philip Ruge-Jones observes,

> This verse is dramatically set off from the text that follows it by its sound qual-
> ity. After the opening word in Greek, the next six consecutive words all end with

---

6. Rhoads, Dewey, and Michie, *Mark as Story*, 10.

7. The parenthetical phrase embedded in Jesus' eschatological discourse at 13:14 is exceptional in another way, being addressed directly to the "reader": "(let the reader understand)." The Markan narrator provides explanations to his audience in a number of places
(see below for examples); however, as Whitney Shiner notes, "Mark breaks more completely
out of his narrative in the apocalyptic discourse" at 13:14 (*Proclaiming the Gospel: First-
Century Performance of Mark* [Harrisburg, Pa.: Trinity, 2003], 176). Shiner explains that
"'reader' in the ancient world often meant those listening to someone else performing a
work of literature. . . . The phrase would be more accurately translated, 'Let the one whom I
am addressing understand.' . . . More idiomatically, it could be translated, 'Understand this
carefully'" (177). "Mark uses the singular 'addressee' in order to include each reader or listener individually. As we learned from [Longinus'] *On the Sublime* [26.3], the singular form
of address involves the audience more fully than does the plural. . . . The closest analogy to
the 'understand carefully' passage is the stereotyped phrase with which many of the parables
end, 'Let one with ears to hear, hear!' (4:9, 23; 7:16)" (177). Among other Markan explanations to the listeners, Shiner lists translations of foreign words (5:41; 7:34; 14:36; 15:22;
15:34), "explanations" (hardly neutral) of Pharisaic/Jewish practices (7:3-4), and comments
on the cause of actions, whether emotional (9:6; 16:8), natural (11:13), or occupational
(1:16) (176). Also comparable to 13:14 as the narrator's commentary, but without the direct
reference to the reader, is 7:19: "(Thus he declared all foods clean.)" Within this entire range
of direct addresses to the audience, 1:1 is unique in being presented at the head of the work,
being presented alone as an incomplete sentence, and being focused on the categories in
which Jesus is to be understood.

an "ou" sound: Ἀρχὴ τοῦ εὐαγελίου Ἰησοῦ Χριστοῦ υἱοῦ Θεοῦ, helping the phrase stand out dramatically from both normal speech and the next part of the story, but also wooing the audience into a moment unto itself that marks the transition into a storied reality.[8]

Although, for the most part, the Markan narrator tells the story in the chronological order of its occurrence, 1:1 is not offered as a statement of chronology but as a generalization about Jesus by the narrator that the unfolding story will support and fill out. Never again does the narrator attribute these or any other "titles" to Jesus, that is, as narrator, rather than in the reported speech of other characters. It is no wonder scholars of Markan christology have been impressed by this powerfully effective opening.

Each word of this opening proclamation—"The beginning of the gospel of Jesus Christ, the Son of God"—is worthy of further reflection;[9] however, here we can only comment briefly on Jesus, Christ, and Son of God. The Greek text of the Gospel of Mark has eighty occurrences of the name Jesus, seventy-five of which are the narrator's, and none of which are the disciples', the crowds', the Jewish authorities', or the Roman authorities'.[10] Unlike Matthew's Gospel,[11] Mark's Gospel does not offer any explanation of the name Jesus. Frequently the narrator simply uses "he" for Jesus—and others as well, a confusing situation that is sometimes amended by translators for clarity.[12] At Jesus' first appearance on the scene, the narrator does explain that "Jesus came from Nazareth [Gk *apo Nazaret*] of Galilee" (1:9), and the narrator employs the designation "Jesus the Nazarene" (Gk *ho Nazarēnos*) at 10:47 in reference to what the blind man of Jericho heard.

8. Philip Ruge-Jones, "Omnipresent, not Omniscient: How Literary Interpretation Confuses the Storyteller's Narrating," in *Between Author and Audience in Mark: Narration, Characterization, Interpretation* (ed. Elizabeth Struthers Malbon; New Testament Monographs 23; Sheffield: Sheffield Phoenix, 2009), 29–43, quotation from 33.

9. See Elizabeth Struthers Malbon, *Hearing Mark: A Listener's Guide* (Harrisburg, Pa.: Trinity, 2002), 11–14.

10. The 75 uses of "Jesus" by the Markan narrator are found in 1:1, 9, 14, 17, 25; 2:5, 8, 15, 17, 19; 3:7; 5:6, 15, 20, 21, 27, 30, 36; 6:4, 30; 8:27; 9:2, 4, 5, 8, 23, 25, 27, 39; 10:5, 14, 18, 21, 23, 24, 27, 29, 32, 38, 39, 42, 47a, 49, 50, 51, 52; 11:6, 7, 22, 29, 33a, 33b; 12:17, 24, 29, 34, 35; 13:2, 5; 14:6, 18, 27, 30, 48, 53, 55, 60, 62, 72; 15:1, 5, 15, 34, 37, 43. There is also one use of "Jesus" by the narrator of the longer ending of Mark: 16:19. The five uses of "Jesus" in Mark in direct discourse by characters are at 1:24 (unclean spirit in the Capernaum synagogue), 5:7 (Gerasene demoniac), 10:47b (Bartimaeus)—three suppliants, 14:67 (servant-girl of the high priest), and 16:6 (young man at the empty tomb).

11. See Matt 1:21, presented as the words of the angel of the Lord to Joseph in a dream: "She will bear a son, and you are to name him Jesus, for he will save his people from their sins." *Jesus*, the Greek form of the Hebrew name *Joshua*, is derived from the Hebrew for "he saves."

12. The NRSV adds "Jesus" in fifteen places in Mark, each marked with a translator's footnote, except at 1:16; 2:4; and 8:17.

The term "Nazarene" is also linked with the name Jesus in the direct discourse of an unclean spirit in Capernaum (1:24, *Nazarēne*), a servant-girl of the high priest in Jerusalem (14:67, *tou Nazarēnou*), and the young man at the empty tomb (16:6, *ton Nazarēnon*).[13] The narrator's use of the designator "Nazareth" at 1:9 serves to situate Jesus more fully as a character whose first reported action is to come from Galilee to the Jordan, from which he soon returns to Galilee (1:14) for largely the first half of the Gospel, before journeying to Jerusalem at the end—until the final reported return to Galilee (16:6-7; cf. 14:28). This return to Galilee is reported by the young man at the tomb, also combining "Jesus" with "Nazarene" (16:6). At 14:67 (cf. 14:70) the linking of Jesus with Nazareth serves, in the speech of the high priest's servant, to link Peter with Jesus—to Peter's dismay. The narrator's use of "Jesus the Nazarene" at 10:47a provides an interesting contrast with Bartimaeus' shouting out to "Son of David, Jesus" (10:47b, following the Gk order, against the NRSV), which we will discuss below. The contrast at 1:24 is internal to the unclean spirit in the synagogue in Capernaum: "Jesus Nazarene" and "the Holy One of God," but this juxtaposition is no more startling than the initial one of the narrator: "Jesus" and "Christ, the Son of God" (1:1); in each case a name, Jesus, is linked with a role, Christ, Son of God, or Holy One of God.

It is essential for twenty-first-century readers to avoid the anachronism of assuming the distinction Jesus/Christ or Jesus/Son of God (or, as will become obvious later, Son of Humanity/Son of God) signifies the distinction between "Jesus' humanity" and "Jesus' divinity" as developed in Christian creeds in the fourth century and beyond. This distinction is simply not yet an issue in Mark's first-century Gospel, and the terms "Christ," "Son of God," and "Son of Humanity" simply do not have Markan meanings that fit those categories.[14] The scholarly literature on the range of first-century meanings of these terms is vast and can only be alluded to here. Only a brief suggestion of the possible backgrounds of the terms "Christ" and "Son of God" for Mark's implied audience will be attempted.[15] Because the terms were fluid, it is really the Markan narrative itself that must provide the clues for what the narrator means by the

13. Thus three of the five uses of "Jesus" in Mark not attributed to the narrator are linked with "Nazarene." The non-linked uses are 5:7, the Gerasene demoniac, and 10:47b, Bartimaeus, which follows immediately the narrator's use of "Nazarene" at 10:47a.

14. As Reginald H. Fuller points out, "The traditional dogmatic Christology of Nicea (A.D. 325) and Chalcedon (A.D. 451) and of subsequent orthodoxy rests upon the Johannine development from a functional to a metaphysical Christology" ("son of God," in *The HarperCollins Bible Dictionary* [ed. Paul J. Achtemeier; San Francisco: HarperSanFrancisco for the SBL, 1996], 1053).

15. Thus my interest is more in line with Dieter Zeller's investigation of the reception history and the presuppositions of the implied audience than with Ferdinand Hahn's investigation of the history of the tradition (see below) in terms of the origin of ideas and their influence on authors (Zeller, "New Testament Christology in Its Hellenistic Reception," *NTS*

opening statement. Clearly the title (1:1), like the entire Gospel, has its deepest meaning when reheard or reread.[16]

Because, as Joseph Fitzmyer points out, "the Greek *christos* was used in the Septuagint (LXX) to translate Heb[rew] *mashiah*,"[17] it is the use of the term *mashiah* in the Hebrew Scripture that must serve as the background for the use of the term "Christ" in Mark's Gospel. Fitzmyer offers this summary definition: "an anointed agent of God appointed to a task affecting the lot of the chosen people."[18] The term's early usage in the Hebrew Bible is somewhat various:

> Though the Hebrew verb *mashiah* was often used of the anointing of men as kings over Israel (e.g., Saul, 1 Sam. 9:16; David, 2 Sam. 2:4, 7; Ps. 89:20; Solomon, 1 Kings 1:39, 45; Jehu, 1 Kings 19:16) or as priests (Aaron and his sons, Exod. 40:15; 28:41), the title *mashiah* occurs less often. At first, it was employed for unnamed historic kings of Israel (1 Sam 2:10; Pss. 2:2; 20:6; 28:8; 84:9) or for named kings, Saul (1 Sam. 12:3, 5; 24:7 [MT; 24:6 NRSV]), David (2 Sam. 19:22 [MT; 19:21 NRSV]; 22:51; 23:1; Pss. 18:50; 89:38, 51; 132:10, 17), Solomon (2 Chron. 6:42), Zedekiah (Lam. 4:20), and even the pagan king Cyrus (Isa. 45:1). In the postexilic period, when the monarchy was no more, it was used of the high priest (Lev. 4:3, 5, 16; 6:22). Rarely it was applied to patriarchs or prophets (Ps. 105:15; 1 Chron. 16:22); once it may refer to Israel itself (Hab. 3:13).[19]

In the postexilic period, prophets did give voice to the promise of a future "David," "but, significantly, the title *mashiah* was not associated with his coming, even if he was called 'a righteous shoot' of David (Jer. 33:15). . . . [See also Ezek 37:24.] None of the prophetic books of the OT [Old Testament] uses *mashiah* as a title for such a coming king."[20]

A change comes about with the apocalyptic book of Daniel. "In the second century B.C., the future 'David' becomes an 'anointed one.' . . . [In Dan 9:25] For the first time in the OT the title appears, now in the sense of a future, expected anointed leader."[21] Fitzmyer continues,

> If there had been no clear teaching about the coming of a Messiah in OT writings prior to the book of Daniel, the promise of a future "David" and the Danielic promise of a coming "anointed one, a prince" clearly fed into that Palestinian

---

47 [2001]: 312–33), although I do even less justice to the Hellenistic reception than to the Jewish roots of Mark's Gospel here.

16. On reading and rereading in Mark's Gospel, see Elizabeth Struthers Malbon, "Echoes and Foreshadowings in Mark 4–8: Reading and Rereading," *JBL* 112 (1993): 213–32, esp. 212 and 228–30.

17. Joseph A. Fitzmyer, S.J., "messiah," *HCBD*, 678.

18. Fitzmyer, "messiah," *HCBD*, 677.

19. Fitzmyer, "messiah," *HCBD*, 677.

20. Fitzmyer, "messiah," *HCBD*, 677–78.

21. Fitzmyer, "messiah," *HCBD*, 678.

Jewish belief current at Qumran in the first century B.C. about the coming of (an) individual(s) called "Messiah" (with a capital M).[22]

Further development of the term "anointed one" ("messiah" or "*christos*") may be seen in the first-century BCE *Psalms of Solomon* (17:32; 18:5) and in the *Similitudes of Enoch* (*1 Enoch* 37–71; see *1 Enoch* 48:10 and 52:4; not attested in the Qumran Aramaic form of the book). According to Fitzmyer, "the real focus of attention" in *1 Enoch* is the "exploration of the Danielic image, 'Son of Man,' . . . yet it provides a transitional usage between the corporate sense of 'Son of Man' (Dan. 7:13) and the use of this phrase for an individual in the NT (for Jesus), who is also called Messiah."[23] At the close of his survey of the early usage of "messiah," Fitzmyer posts this warning: "'Messianic' has become a rubber-band adjective, often applied to expected figures who were not really 'messiahs' in pre-Christian Jewish tradition." For example, "the figure to whom the titles 'Son of God' and 'Son of the Most High' are given in 4Q246 [*Apocryphon of Daniel*] should not be referred to as a Messiah; they are not 'messianic' titles in the Jewish tradition."[24]

In the New Testament, the term "*christos*" continues to be linked with additional terms. In fact, Fitzmyer argues that the term "King of the Jews" first brought the term "messiah" (*christos*) into association with Jesus:

> Although "Messiah" did not unambiguously denote a person who would claim the political position of "king of Israel," Jesus' execution as "the King of the Jews" (Mark 15:2, 26) makes that association with the title likely (recall the mockery scene, Mark 15:32). In fact, it was probably the title on the cross that became the catalyst for the use of "Messiah" as a title for Jesus crucified and raised from the dead.[25]

Such a historical reconstruction or history of the tradition conclusion is beyond the scope of the present work. Because Mark's Gospel was written and first heard in this broad period when the meaning and function of "messiah" (*christos*) was undergoing development, we will regard the term's use in the Hebrew Scripture, including its Danielic development, as the basic background for understanding its use in Mark's Gospel and attend to how it is used in Mark's narrative as the guide for any further meaning.[26] The situation with the term "Son of God" is similar.

22. Fitzmyer, "messiah," *HCBD*, 678.
23. Fitzmyer, "messiah," *HCBD*, 678.
24. Fitzmyer, "messiah," *HCBD*, 678.
25. Fitzmyer, "messiah," *HCBD*, 678.
26. For an overview of the development of the term "messiah" in the New Testament, see Fitzmyer, "messiah," *HCBD*, 678–79, and the literature cited there. For a tradition-historical examination of the term "Christos" in the New Testament, see Ferdinand Hahn, *The Titles of Jesus in Christology: Their History in Early Christianity* (New York: World Publishing, 1969; first published in German in 1963), chapter 3, "Christos," 136–239.

For a one-sentence commentary on the narrator's use of "Son of God" in Mark 1:1, one could hardly do better than Clifton Black: "*Son of God*, a significant title for Jesus in Mark (1.11; 3.11; 5.7; 9.7; 12:6; 14.61; 15:39), apparently connotes an obedient servant within God's salvation history (see also 2 Sam 7.13-14; Ps 2.7; Hos 11.1; Wis 2.18)."[27] A relationship of obedience is also central for Reginald Fuller's summary definition of "son of God" in the Bible: "a person or a people with a special relationship to God, often with a special role in salvation history."[28] The use of the term in Hebrew Scripture, which was, of course, the only Scripture for the early Christian community, including Mark's author and first audience, provides the crucial background for the use of the term in Mark's Gospel. In the Hebrew Scripture "and pre-Christian Judaism," Fuller points out,

> there are four notable uses of the term "son of God." First, it is predicated of Israel constituted as a nation through the Exodus (e.g., Exod. 4:22; Hos. 11:1). Second, it is a title given to the monarch at the time of enthronement (e.g., Ps. 2:7, a coronation psalm). Third, angels are called "sons of God" (e.g., Job 38:7, NRSV note). Fourth, in the apocryphal/deutero-canonical Wisdom of Solomon it is applied to the righteous individual (Wisd. of Sol. 2:18, RSV; NRSV: "child"). Primarily it denotes not physical filiation but a divine call to obedience in a predestined role in salvation history.[29]

The use of the term after the Hebrew Bible is somewhat less clear. Fuller notes that it is "a matter of dispute whether the term 'son of God' was already current in pre-Christian Judaism as a messianic title as Mark 14:16 [surely an error for Mark 14:61] would seem to suggest."[30] I would not regard the words of the high priest as a character in Mark's Gospel—"Are you the Christ [NRSV Messiah], the Son of the Blessed One?" (Mark 14:61)—as evidence of a pre-Christian use of "son of God" as a messianic title. However, other evidence cited by Fuller does seem to support a more circumscribed conclusion: "Yet in view of the discovery of Ps. 2:7 with a messianic interpretation in the Dead Sea Scrolls (4QFlor [*Florilegium* or *Midrash on Eschatology*] 10–14) it is probably safe to conclude that it was just coming into use with this meaning during the period

---

27. C. Clifton Black, "Notes on the Gospel According to Mark," *The HarperCollins Study Bible: NRSV* (New York: HarperCollins, 1993), on 1:1.

28. Fuller, "son of God," *HCBD*, 1051.

29. Fuller, "son of God," *HCBD*, 1051. A similar stress on obedience results from looking at the "son of God" relationship from the other side, from the significance of the term "father" applied to God, as Joachim Jeremias notes: "No one who is familiar with Judaism at this period will be astonished to find that the obligation to obey the heavenly father is vigorously stressed" as one of "two characteristics" of "what Jesus' Jewish contemporaries meant to express by giving God the name of father" (*The Central Message of the New Testament* [New York: Charles Scribner's Sons, 1965], 15).

30. Fuller, "son of God," *HCBD*, 1051.

of Christian origins."[31] Because Mark's Gospel was written and first heard in this period when the meaning and function of "son of God" was undergoing development, we will regard the term's use in the Hebrew Scripture as the more settled background for understanding its use in Mark's Gospel and attend to how it is used in Mark's narrative as the guide for any further meaning.[32]

What is obvious is that the narrator's opening line, the title of the narrative (1:1), is both allusive and elusive: it alludes to previous uses of "Christ" and "Son of God" in Jewish Scripture (for Mark's author and audience, in the form of the Septuagint) and tradition, and it resists easy comprehension and full definition at this beginning point. Thus the implied audience, and commentators as well, must attend to the further uses of "Christ" and "Son of God," as well as to the entire unfolding of the Markan narrative with its competing voices of other characters, in order to come closer to understanding the import of the narrator's first words about Jesus. As we have noted, the narrator's first words (1:1) are exceptional; we turn now to the narrator's more usual way of speaking about Jesus.

WHAT THE NARRATOR SAYS ABOUT JESUS IN THE REST OF THE GOSPEL

Because most of Mark's Gospel is in the voice of the narrator, and the story the narrator is telling is the story of Jesus, most of what the narrator says is about what Jesus does. However, because we have already surveyed "what Jesus does" in the previous chapter on enacted christology, we need not summarize that material here. Much of what Jesus does is speak, and in the two following chapters we will consider "what Jesus says" (deflected christology and refracted christology); the words of the Markan Jesus provide some interesting contrasts with the words of the Markan narrator. Nevertheless, we owe most of what we know about Jesus to the narrator. For the most part, this narrator prefers to show rather than to tell the implied audience about Jesus. Jesus is shown through his actions, his speech, and the reactions in word and speech that he elicits from other characters. The narrator does not apply many evaluative words and phrases directly to Jesus but usually attributes such evaluation to those who respond to Jesus. For example, the narrator does not assert that "Jesus taught them brilliantly"; rather, he notes that "they were astounded at his teaching" (1:22). Yet the narrator does offer some "inside views" of Jesus—brief descrip-

---

31. Fuller, "son of God," *HCBD*, 1051–52, although see Fitzmyer's warning about the interpretation of 4Q246, *Apocryphon of Daniel*, quoted above.

32. For an overview of the development of the term "Son of God" in the New Testament, see Fuller, "son of God," *HCBD*, 1052–53, and the literature cited there. For a tradition-historical examination of the term "Son of God" in the New Testament, see Hahn, *Titles of Jesus*, chapter 5, "Son of God," 279–346. For a brief reception history of "Son of God" in Mark for a Hellenistic audience, see Zeller, "Hellenistic Reception," 325–29, and the literature cited there.

tions of Jesus' emotions or perception and knowledge.[33] In fact, the ability to present inside views is one that is shared by the narrator and Jesus.[34]

On several occasions, the narrator names explicitly the emotion Jesus is experiencing. At 1:41, the narrator names the emotion that accompanies Jesus' healing touch: "Moved with pity, Jesus stretched out his hand and touched" the leper.[35] At 6:34, the narrator names the emotion that accompanies Jesus' teaching—and then his miraculous feeding—of a crowd of five thousand: "and he had compassion for them, because they were like sheep without a shepherd; and he began to teach them many things."[36] At 3:2, the narrator sets the scene in the Capernaum synagogue by presenting an inside view of those who "watched him to see whether he would cure him on the sabbath, so that they might accuse him"; then the narrator reports that Jesus "looked around at them with anger; he was grieved [Gk *sullupoumenos*] at their hardness of heart" (3:5). Much later, in the Gethsemane scene, the Markan Jesus expresses grief in his own words: "I

33. Robert M. Fowler, *Let the Reader Understand: Reader-Response Criticism and the Gospel of Mark* (Minneapolis: Fortress, 1991), discusses Mark's "inside views" in four categories: perceptions, emotions, knowledge and motivation, and interior or private speech (120–26), following the fourfold categorization of Thomas E. Boomershine: perceptions, emotions, inner knowledge/motivation, and inner statements ("Mark, the Storyteller: A Rhetorical-Critical Investigation of Mark's Passion and Resurrection Narrative" [Ph.D. dissertation, Union Theological Seminary, New York, 1974], 273–75). Joel F. Williams, "Jesus' Love for the Rich Man (Mark 10:21): A Disputed Response toward a Disputed Character," in Malbon, ed., *Between Author and Audience*, 145–61, provides, in the appendix to his article (160–61), a detailed chart of the Markan references to inside views of all the characters, utilizing three categories: perception, cognition, and emotion/reaction.

34. Pilate also seems to share this ability: "For he realized that it was out of jealousy that the chief priests had handed him over" (15:10; see also 12:12, "When they [chief priests, scribes, and elders] realized that he had told this parable against them, they wanted to arrest him, but they feared the crowd. So they left him and went away"). One might counter that Pilate shows no great ability in noticing signs of jealousy in the Jewish leaders, but the same could be said of some of the Markan Jesus' inside views, such as seeing the faith of those who dig through the roof for the sake of the paralyzed man (2:5) or knowing the hypocrisy of the flattering Pharisees and Herodians (12:15). Fowler, *Let the Reader Understand*, 123, considers the shared "mind-reading powers" of the narrator and Jesus a mark of "the ideological alignment of the narrator with his protagonist Jesus." As will become clear, one of the most significant conclusions I have come to in my research on Markan narrative christology is that the narrator and the character Jesus are not so completely aligned but present a certain tension in their views. The transcendent knowledge of the unclean spirits and demons, to be discussed below, is not the same as an "inside view"; they see not what Jesus is thinking but who Jesus is in relation to God.

35. As the NRSV translators note, other ancient authorities read "anger" rather than "pity," a rather different emotion.

36. For an intriguing analysis of Jesus' emotional response of "love" toward the rich man, see Williams, "Jesus' Love for the Rich Man."

am deeply grieved [Gk *perilupos*]" (14:34), echoing the psalmist's prayer.[37] The emotion of amazement is attributed to Jesus by the narrator at the conclusion of the scene of Jesus' rejection in his hometown: "And he was amazed at their unbelief" and was limited in doing deeds of power there (6:6)—an ironic contrast to the narrator's frequent inside views of the amazement of the crowds at Jesus' deeds of power and teaching (see 1:22, 27; 2:12; 5:20, 42; 6:2; 7:37; 11:18; 12:17).[38] Jesus' emotion is not so explicitly named at 8:12, "he sighed deeply in his spirit," but the context of argument with the Pharisees and Jesus' concluding words—"no sign will be given to this generation"—suggest discouragement, perhaps indignation. Indignation is named by the narrator at 10:14, here aimed at the disciples who are trying to prevent people from bringing children to Jesus: "But when Jesus saw this, he was indignant." Pity, compassion, anger, grief, amazement, discouragement, indignation—these are powerful human emotions, and the Markan narrator, who is certainly not effusive, makes a point to attribute them to the Markan Jesus directly and explicitly with inside views.

When the narrator tells what Jesus perceives or knows, the narrator is giving the narratee an inside view of Jesus' inside view of other characters.[39] At 2:5, the narrator reports that "Jesus saw their faith"; naturally it is assumed that Jesus saw the action of the friends of the paralyzed man in digging through the roof, but seeing often signifies a more significant perception as well. A similar case occurs at 12:34, "[w]hen Jesus saw that he [the exceptional scribe] answered wisely," echoing the scribe's similar perception of Jesus at 12:28. Jesus' "knowing their hypocrisy," narrated at 12:15, also combines external observation—their overblown attempt at flattery (12:14) gives away the questioning Pharisees and Herodians—and internal realization. At 2:8 the narrator presents a more obvious inside view, claiming Jesus' perception is not based on public action: "At once Jesus perceived in his spirit that they were discussing these questions among themselves." At 5:30, it is inner awareness of an inner event that the narrator reports of Jesus: "Immediately aware that power had gone forth from him" in response to the touch of the hemorrhaging woman, Jesus said, "Who touched my clothes?" Interestingly enough, who touched his clothes is not reported as something Jesus knows internally.

One of the narrator's most impressive inside views of Jesus is an extremely early one. After the first mention of Jesus' action in the narrative—"In those days Jesus came from Nazareth of Galilee and was baptized by John in the

---

37. Ps 42:5, 11 and 43:5, NRSV "cast down." LXX Ps 41:6, 12 and 42:5, *perilupos*.

38. Also noted by Edwin K. Broadhead, *Teaching with Authority: Miracles and Christology in the Gospel of Mark* (JSNTSup 74; Sheffield: Sheffield Academic, 1992), 115.

39. Janice Capel Anderson calls these "complex inside views": "cases where the narrator implies or tells the implied reader that Jesus has an inside view of a third party. The narrator knows that Jesus knows" (*Matthew's Narrative Web: Over, and Over, and Over Again* [JSNTSup 91; Sheffield: Sheffield Academic, 1994], 70, see 69–74).

Jordan" (1:9)—a public action, the narrator goes on to say, "And just as he was coming up out of the water, he saw the heavens torn apart and the Spirit descending like a dove on him" (1:10). No reference to others seeing this sight is made; no responses of others to this drama are narrated. The narrator then adds, "a voice came from heaven" (1:11). For a clearer inside view the narrator could have said, "Jesus heard a voice from heaven." However, the voice—to be discussed below in terms of what (God) says to and about Jesus—does speak in the second person singular, that is, to Jesus, and no response to the voice is reported by the narrator. This situation of the baptism underscores the situation with all the narrator's inside views of Jesus: not only the narrator but, through the narrator, the narratee is privileged to see these inside views.[40]

By these inside views of Jesus, the Markan narrator tells the narratee that Jesus is aware of the varying responses to his words and actions, from the responses of eager suppliants to those of agitated opponents. Nevertheless, the narrator relies more on showing than telling to communicate his story about Jesus, giving more inside views of characters other than Jesus—suppliants, disciples, and opponents—than of Jesus himself.[41] The narrated portions of Mark comprise three broad categories: (1) what the narrator says about Jesus, at which we have been looking; (2) what the narrator says about others' reactions to

40. As Fowler notes, "No one in the story, except Jesus, witnesses the descent of the spirit in 1:10. . . . Uptake occurs only at the level of discourse, and none, except possibly for Jesus, occurs at the level of story" (*Let the Reader Understand*, 18). Fowler is employing "uptake" in the sense given to it by J. L. Austin, *How to Do Things with Words* (Cambridge, Mass.: Harvard University Press, 1975), 117–18. Perhaps because of "the introspective conscience of the West," to use the powerful phrase of Krister Stehdahl, modern Western readers attribute a certain profundity to inside views—or even to the narrator's views in general. My daughter illustrated this point to me with a conversation in the car when she was sixteen. "Wouldn't it be nice to have your own narrator?" she said to me. When I asked just what she meant she supplied an example: "As she drove past the apartments, her mind wandered to thoughts of creation and existence." I must have replied, "That's profound," because she responded, "It's a narrator; of course it's profound!" (recorded in writing, at my request, on a Lowe's receipt for spring bedding plants, June 1, 2005—and now I have become my daughter's hoped-for narrator!).

41. For commentary on these inside views, see Fowler, *Let the Reader Understand*, 120–26. Because "inside views" are important to Fowler's overall reader-response critical argument, it may be that he applies the criteria for determining an "inside view" more liberally than others. One of the narrator's inside views of the disciples is especially interesting since it anticipates by a couple of chapters a direct question of Jesus to the disciples—narrator at 6:52: "for they did not understand about the loaves, but their hearts were hardened"; Jesus at 8:17: "Why are you talking about having no bread? Do you still not perceive or understand? Are your hearts hardened?" As Norman R. Petersen has noted, "Thus the reader here learns from the narrator what the character Jesus only verbalizes six episodes later" ("The Composition of Mark 4:1–8:26," *HTR* 73 [1980]: 185–217, quotation from 209).

Jesus, to which we have alluded; and (3) what the narrator says about John the baptizer and reactions to him, to which we now turn.

What the Narrator Says about John the Baptizer and Implies about Jesus

After the narrator's dramatic announcement of 1:1, "The beginning of the good news of Jesus Christ, the Son of God," one might expect the narrator to bring his main character onto the stage. Instead, the narrator presents the prophet "Isaiah," who points first of all to John the baptizer. The rhetoric of Mark is one of juxtaposition. Two statements or two events or two characters are juxtaposed in a way that entices the audience to puzzle out their connection. The title of the narrative is juxtaposed with a biblical quotation, suggesting to the audience that the story of Jesus as the Christ, the Son of God, is to be understood against the background of the continuing action of God with the people of God (Israel), as proclaimed by the prophets.[42] Jesus the Christ (Messiah) is juxtaposed with John the baptizer, to whom the biblical quotation points and who, in turn, points to Jesus. There is even a juxtaposition internal to the biblical quotation in 1:2-3 because, while the narrator's text refers directly to the prophet Isaiah, the quotation as given conflates material from Isaiah 40:3 with material from Exodus 23:20 and Malachi 3:1, all in their forms in the Septuagint, the Greek translation of the Hebrew Bible. This textual juxtaposition may be in part a reflection of the way the Bible was known to and used by the author and his audience in the oral tradition, as well as differing assumptions about "accuracy" in "quoting" sources.[43] But the juxtaposition of the composite biblical quotation and the title of the work, and the juxtaposition of Jesus the Christ and John the baptizer, engage the implied audience in active listening.

Even more interesting than the composite nature of the biblical quotation is its divergence from two of its Septuagintal sources in significant ways. The first

42. See Joel Marcus, *The Way of the Lord: Christological Exegesis of the Old Testament in the Gospel of Mark* (Louisville: Westminster John Knox, 1992), for a detailed and thorough—although perhaps too rigid—reading of Mark's Gospel as biblical exegesis, that is, as his subtitle states: "Christological Exegesis of the Old Testament." Marcus interprets Mark 1:2-3 as "The Gospel According to Isaiah" (12–47).

43. Howard Clark Kee argues that the synthetic quotation in 1:2-3 illustrates the Markan process of "interpretation of scripture by scripture" also known from the Qumran community ("The Function of Scriptural Quotations and Allusions in Mark 11–16," in *Jesus und Paulus: Festschrift für Werner Georg Kümmel zum 70. Geburtstag* [ed. E. Earle Elllis and Erich Grässer; Göttingen, Germany: Vandenhoeck & Ruprecht, 1975], 165–88, 177 for 1:2-3). However, the Gospels of Matthew and Luke do "correct" the quotation by dropping the portions from Malachi and Exodus; cf. Matt 3:3 and Luke 3:4-6, where the Isaiah quotation is extended.

part of the composite quotation follows the Septuagint (LXX) of Exodus 23:20 quite closely; "sending my messenger" is also a part of LXX Malachi 3:1. However, the Markan composite quotation changes the Septuagint's designation of whose way is to be prepared: not "the way before me" (that is, God, who is the speaker; so Mal 3:1 LXX and also the Hebrew) but "your way." And who is this "you"? Whose way is being prepared? The quotation has been opened up to a referent other than God.[44] Concerning the Isaiah 40:3 portion of the composite quotation, we note first that the Septuagint differs from the Hebrew in connecting "in the wilderness" to the location of the voice rather than to the message of the voice. The Hebrew is represented in the NRSV: "A voice cries out: 'In the wilderness prepare the way of the Lord . . . ,'" whereas Mark 1:3 reads, "the voice of one crying out in the wilderness: 'Prepare the way of the Lord . . . ,'" following the Septuagint exactly. In Mark's narrative, this reading underscores the connection of John the baptizer, who "appeared in the wilderness, proclaiming" (1:4), with "the voice of one crying out in the wilderness" (1:3), a link the narratee completes. However, in the second line of Isaiah 40:3, Mark diverges from the Septuagint where it follows the Hebrew, represented by the NRSV: "make straight . . . a highway for our God." Rather than "of our God" (*tou theou hēmōn*), Mark reads "of him," that is, "his." This small change has a potentially enormous significance because grammatically the substantive referent of "his" is "the Lord" in the preceding line: "Prepare the way of the Lord, make his paths straight." Because John the baptizer seems to be the one who is, in the wilderness, preparing the way for someone (not "me," God, as in Mal 3:1 in the LXX, but "you"), and Jesus is the one who comes (1:9), the narrator seems to have opened the possibility for the narratee to think of Jesus as "the Lord."[45] In addition, "the way" (a part of both the Mal 3:1 and the Isa 40:3 references) turns out to be a theologically charged location for the Markan Jesus, as repeatedly reported by the narrator in 8:22–10:52. The suggestion that Jesus is Lord is not explicit, but it fits with the Markan rhetoric of juxtaposition.

Except for this both composite and complex quotation of Isaiah, the Markan narrator never voices the term "Lord." However, on several additional occasions the narrator seems to invite the narratee to link the term with Jesus, while leaving ambiguous what the character involved may think about it. In the first-century world, *kyrios* (lord) could mean sir, master (as it does for the Markan Jesus at 2:28; 11:3; 12:9; and 13:35; cf. the single Markan use of a related verb at 10:42; and as it does for the Syrophoenician woman at 7:28), or God, using an honorific title instead of the personal name (as it does when Jesus quotes

---

44. Taylor, *St. Mark*, 153: "Mark's version is manifestly a re-interpretation of the prophecy in a Messianic sense."

45. Hahn asserts that 1:3 is a "characteristic instance of this sort of application to Jesus of Septuagint statements with *kyrios*" (*Titles of Jesus*, 108).

Scripture at 12:11, 29-30, and 36-37, or refers to God at 5:19 and 13:20; and when the crowd in Jerusalem quotes Scripture at 11:9).[46] At 5:19, the Markan Jesus refuses the request of the healed Gerasene demoniac to "be with him" (1:18) and says to him instead, "Go home to your friends, and tell them how much the Lord has done for you, and what mercy he has shown you"—with "Lord" clearly meaning God. However, the Markan narrator adds, "And he went away and began to proclaim in the Decapolis how much Jesus [Gk *ho Iēsous*, "the Jesus," in parallel with *ho kyrios*, "the Lord"] had done for him . . ." (5:20)—with the "Ten Cities" being considerably more that the man's "home" and "friends" and with "Jesus" taking the place of "the Lord."[47] At 13:35, near the close of the eschatological discourse, the Markan Jesus tells a parable about a householder who goes on a journey, with clear allusions to the passion narrative in the times when "the lord [NRSV master] of the house" might return. It would not take much for the Markan narratee to see (i.e., perceive, link, complete the allusion explicitly) Jesus as the coming "lord [Lord?] of the house."[48]

At 7:28, in the Syrophoenician woman's response to Jesus, "Sir" (*kyrie*, the vocative of *kyrios*), and in Jesus' self-reference at 11:3, "The master [NRSV Lord] needs" the colt, some narratees might also make a connection between Jesus and Lord, but the cases are different from those just discussed and from each other.[49] Although the narrator gives no definite signal to interpret *kyrios* as

---

46. On the philological background and history of the tradition of the use of "Lord" in the New Testament, see Hahn, *Titles of Jesus*, chapter 2, "Kyrios [Lord]," 68–135. According to Hahn, "In the sphere of the Diaspora the Septuagint *kyrios* took the place of the name Jahwe, with the result that eventually it became the standard Biblical name for God" (73). With Hahn's tradition-historical approach, searching for the origins of ideas and their influence on authors, one may contrast the reception history approach of Zeller, looking more "for the presuppositions of the implied reader and moreover for any potential contemporary reader" ("Hellenistic Reception," 314; see 315–21 on Jesus as *kyrios*).

47. Petersen, "Composition of Mark 4:1–8:26," 213, argues that the healed demoniac misunderstands and thus demonstrates the incomprehension of the people, paralleling the incomprehension of the disciples. I think it more likely that the narrator's move serves to open up for the implied audience the applicability of the term "Lord" to Jesus. Of course, the Markan Jesus and the narrator are in tension on this point.

48. Hahn does not hesitate: "That in Mk. 13:35 the householder is Jesus is obvious" (*Titles of Jesus*, 101). Hahn points out that "[u]nlike the concept of the Son of man (and however independently the church proceeded there also) the address of Jesus as Lord has its life-situation less in doctrinal elucidation, than in the cult, where it develops further into acclamation and confession" (101–2). It is worth noting that the phrase "Lord of the house" might, thus, reverberate doubly with worship, because early congregations usually met in houses and "the house" (as opposed to the synagogue or temple) is especially associated with the Markan Jesus; on this latter point see Elizabeth Struthers Malbon, *Narrative Space and Mythic Meaning in Mark* (San Francisco: Harper & Row, 1986; volume 13 of The Biblical Seminar; Sheffield: Sheffield Academic, 1991), esp. 106–40; see also note 107 below.

49. Hahn, working as a critic of the history of traditions rather than as a narrative critic,

"Lord" rather than "Sir" at 7:28, such a reading would not be inconsistent with the narrator's suggestions—and delight in ambiguity—elsewhere. However, the only time the Markan Jesus uses *kyrios* (11:3)—or "teacher" (14:14)—as a self-reference, and both with the definite article, he is giving the disciples exact words to use in making arrangements for their stay with him in Jerusalem. So when the Markan Jesus says to the disciples: say to someone that "the lord (or master)" (11:3) or "the teacher" (14:14) needs this, he is speaking the disciples' words in advance. To be sure, members of the implied audience may choose to take up these words later, but it is important to note first their specific location among the narrative voices. The narrator never applies the term "Lord" explicitly to Jesus,[50] as he does the terms "Christ" and "Son of God" at 1:1.

The narrator does link Jesus the Christ to John the baptizer by making parallel statements about them. John is reported "proclaiming a baptism of repentance for the forgiveness of sins" (1:4); Jesus is reported "proclaiming the good news of God, and saying, 'The time is fulfilled, and the kingdom of God has come near; repent, and believe in the good news'" (1:14-15). John is "handed over" (1:14, NRSV arrested); Jesus is handed over or arrested. John is killed (6:14-29); Jesus is killed. There are, of course, both significant differences—John baptizes and prepares the way; Jesus, in his preaching and healing, manifests the in-breaking rule of God—and smaller, but not insignificant, differences—John is laid in a tomb by his disciples (6:29); Jesus is laid in a tomb by Joseph of Arimathea (15:46). The implied author's way of juxtaposing the story of John and the story of Jesus is impressive. As John's appearance in the wilderness, baptizing (1:4) sets the scene for Jesus' appearance in the narrative (1:9), John's arrest sets the scene for Jesus' ministry in Galilee (1:14, "Now after John was arrested, Jesus came to Galilee, proclaiming . . ."). The details of John's arrest and beheading by Herod are not revealed until the flashback of

finds *kyrie* at 7:28 "general" and "emphatically profane" (*Titles of Jesus*, 80, 79), that is, without any suggestion of reference to Jesus as "Lord," but *ho kyrios* at 11:3 "a title of dignity in which the authority of Jesus is expressed" (83). Hahn's reasoning is based on what he sees as a historical development from its general use as an address to its absolute use (with "the"), with consequent christological import (73–89). In narrative critical terms, Hahn is reading 7:28 at the level of the story and 11:3 at the level of the discourse. Hahn sees a parallel historical development with *didaskale/ho didaskalos* (teacher/the teacher), and, accordingly, interprets Mark 14:14 (Jesus' words to his disciples concerning arrangements for a room for the Passover: "say to the owner of the house, 'The Teacher [the NRSV capitalization exaggerates] asks, Where is my guest room where I may eat the Passover with my disciples?'") as "a markedly Christological use of the title *ho didaskalos*" (77). Again, from a narrative critical point of view, this is a reading at the discourse level.

50. The fact that the narrator of the longer ending of Mark (16:9-20) has no problem applying this term to Jesus as a title ("the Lord," 16:20) or even almost as a name ("the Lord Jesus," 16:19) is one among many indications that these verses are from a different and later hand.

6:14-29, which is intercalated into the story of Jesus' sending out of the twelve (6:7-13) and their return (6:30), which follows the story of Jesus' rejection in his hometown (6:1-6). Being sent out leads to rejection, which leads to being handed over, which leads to death—for John, for Jesus, and for Jesus' disciples.[51] Thus what the narrator says about John, he implies about Jesus. Such implications apply not only to the eventual deaths of John and Jesus at the hands of easily swayed Roman officials (Herod swayed by Herodias and her dancing daughter, Pilate swayed by the Jewish authorities and the changeable crowd)[52] but to their initial success with large crowds as well: "And people from the whole Judean countryside and all the people of Jerusalem were going out to him [John], and were baptized by him in the river Jordan, confessing their sins" (1:5); "At once his [Jesus'] fame began to spread throughout the surrounding region of Galilee" (1:28).

In the quite spare presentation of the story of John, the narrator's full verse about his clothing and diet is striking. It seems obvious that the narrator as-sumes the narratee is capable of making the connection between John's food and the wilderness and John's clothes and the prophets (Zech 13:4), but es-pecially Elijah (2 Kgs 1:8). Elijah is not mentioned explicitly at this point in Mark's narrative, but the name and fame of Elijah do come up three times later in close connection with John. At 6:15-16, some people think Jesus is Elijah re-turned, but Herod thinks Jesus is John, whom he beheaded, returned. At 8:28, the disciples report that some people think Jesus is John the baptizer and others think he is Elijah. In chapter 9, after Jesus is transfigured before three of the disciples and there appear with him "Elijah with Moses" (9:4), the disciples ask Jesus, "Why do the scribes say that Elijah must come first?" (9:11). The Markan Jesus answers, "Elijah is indeed coming first to restore all things. . . . But I tell you that Elijah has come, and they did to him whatever they pleased, as it is written about him" (9:12-13). Again John, Elijah, and Scripture ("it is writ-ten") are linked, here by the Markan Jesus rather than by the Markan narrator as in 1:2-8. Although there are, as we shall see, some significant differences be-tween what the narrator says about Jesus and what the Markan Jesus says about himself, it would appear that the Markan narrator is not at odds with Jesus in thinking that John is (somehow) Elijah returned. Such a view is sympathetic with the incorporation into the "Isaiah" quotation at Mark 1:2-3 of Malachi 3:1: "See, I am sending my messenger to prepare the way before me. . . ."

---

51. For further development, see Malbon, "Echoes and Foreshadowings," 222–23, and Malbon, *Hearing Mark*, 40–43. Cf. Frank Kermode, *The Genesis of Secrecy: On the Interpreta-tion of Narrative* (Cambridge, Mass.: Harvard University Press, 1979), 129–31.

52. Abraham Smith, "Tyranny Exposed: Mark's Typological Characterization of Herod Antipas (Mark 6:14-29)," *BibInt* 14 (2006): 259–93, demonstrates persuasively "the *textured* or multi-faceted manner in which Mark constructed and exposed Herod Antipas as a tyrant" (277) and "the 'sustained verbal echoes' [that] make the authorial audience's actualization of Pilate as a tyrant figure irresistible" (283).

Malachi 4:5 also seems implied behind the Markan narrative: "Lo, I will send you the prophet Elijah before the great and terrible day of the Lord comes. . . ." But before too much attention is given to this renewed Elijah, John the baptizer, by the Markan narrator, the narrative gives John a chance to speak on his own.

What John the Baptizer Says about Jesus

Almost the only words given to John in direct speech in Mark's Gospel are the words he says about Jesus,[53] and these words emphasize John's status as forerunner and Jesus' status as the more powerful one: "The one who is more powerful than I is coming after me; I am not worthy to stoop down and untie the thong of his sandals. I have baptized you with water; but he will baptize you with the Holy Spirit" (1:7-8). In Matthew (3:7-12) and Luke (3:7-14), the audience learns something about John's preaching of repentance—not in Mark. In Luke (1:5-25, 39-80), the audience even learns something about John's prophesied and celebrated birth—not in Mark. In Mark, John appears in the wilderness as a brief visual and auditory link between what "is written" in the prophets about God's continuing activity with the people of God and Jesus as the one in whom that activity is renewed. This anticipated renewal is suggested by John's reference to Jesus baptizing with the Holy Spirit, since "Israel's re-infusion with God's Spirit was expected in the last days" on the basis of Isaiah 11:1-2 and Joel 2:28-29.[54] Thus what John the baptizer says about Jesus points to what the Spirit does and what God says.

What the Voice (of God) Says to and about Jesus

Although the Greek word for God, *theos*, appears forty-eight times in Mark's Gospel, it does not appear in the two scenes in which a voice from heaven, presumably God's, speaks. God clearly does not step onto the stage of Mark's narrative as other characters do. God is not seen, only heard—and then not by everyone.[55] To signal this important decision of the implied author in introducing

53. In the flashback to John's death at the hands of Herod in chapter 6, one line is given to John in direct speech to Herod: "It is not lawful for you to have your brother's wife" (6:18b), and this is reported as a flashback within the flashback, "For John had been telling Herod . . ." (6:18a).

54. Black, "Mark," *HCSB*, on 1:8.

55. Although God does not appear as an actor but is only heard as a voice, the (Holy) Spirit is reported to act (1:10, 12) but not to speak. As the Markan Jesus (along with the narrator and the implied audience) is apparently the only one to hear the voice (of God) at 1:11, so he is also apparently the only character to perceive the actions of the Spirit: its descent at 1:10 and its expulsion of Jesus into the wilderness at 1:12. The Spirit descends *into* Jesus (1:10, Gk *eis*) and throws him *out* into the wilderness (1:12, *ekballei*). John the baptizer points to another action of the Holy Spirit, claiming that the one coming after him

God as a character, I will enclose the term "God" in parentheses when referring to what (God) says to and about Jesus. Such reserve in speaking of God is the major observation of John Donahue's important study of God as "A Neglected Factor in the Theology of Mark": "Such reserved speech about God is strong especially in contrast to the anthropomorphism of Matthew and the interventionist or salvation history perspective of Luke."[56] Most of the references to God occur in the direct speech of the Markan Jesus and will be examined in the following chapter. Only twice does the narrator mention God directly, once in describing Jesus' message—"Now after John was arrested, Jesus came to Galilee, proclaiming the good news of God . . ." (1:14)—and once in describing the response of the people to Jesus' healing of the paralytic—"And he stood up, and immediately took the mat and went out before all of them; so that they were all amazed and glorified God . . ." (2:12). Thus the power of Jesus' teaching and his healing are attributed by the narrator to God; on this attribution the Markan Jesus would agree.

The voice that comes from heaven at 1:11 is framed by two actions of "the Spirit" in 1:10 and 1:12. "And just as he [Jesus] was coming up out of the water [of the Jordan], he saw the heavens torn apart and the Spirit descending like a dove on him" (1:10). From this report of the narrator—with no responses of others in reaction—the event is presented as an inside view of Jesus' experience, as we noted above. Indeed, the voice that comes from this split-open heaven speaks in the second person singular, that is, to Jesus: "You are my Son, the Beloved; with you I am well pleased" (1:11). Not too surprisingly, (God) seems to be quite familiar with Scripture but not constrained to quote it exactly! The first words of the voice, "You are my Son (Gk *Su ei ho huios mou*)," derive from Ps 2:7. In Psalm 2, God is described as sitting in the heavens laughing (v. 4) at the nations conspiring in vain (v. 1) and taking "counsel together, against the Lord and his anointed" (v. 2). God responds to the nations by setting his "king on Zion" (v. 6), to whom God speaks: "You are my son (LXX *Huios mou ei su*); today I have begotten you" (v. 7).[57] In recognizing Jesus as "my Son," (God) is

will baptize with the Holy Spirit (1:8). Three times the Markan Jesus comments on speech in relation to the Holy Spirit, proclaiming that, in the present, whoever speaks blasphemy against the Holy Spirit will never have forgiveness (3:29); that, in the past, David spoke by the Holy Spirit (12:36); and that, in the future, the Holy Spirit will give his disciples the words to speak in their times of trials (13:11).

56. John R. Donahue, S.J., "A Neglected Factor in the Theology of Mark," *JBL* 101 (1982): 563–94, quotation from 567.

57. Eduard Schweizer comments, "Whether the position of *huios mou* ('my son') at 1.11, which is different from the Septuagint, was first rearranged and given its present reference by Mark, or whether it already existed in this form in the tradition, we do not know. At any rate it is strongly emphasized by the change" ("Mark's Theological Achievement" [trans. R. Morgan], in *The Interpretation of Mark* [2nd ed.; ed. William A. Telford; Edinburgh: T&T Clark, 1995], 63–87, quotation from 83 n. 21; first published in *EvT* [1964]: 337–55).

continuing God's action in human history for the people of God and designating Jesus for a role in that activity.

As we noted above, the term "son of God" in Jewish Scripture is a relational term; the one who is a son to God—whether all Israel, or the king, or angels, or the righteous person—is obedient to God as God acts in history for the people of God. Michael Cook comments that "the voice from heaven is recognizing Jesus' full immersion into the baptism of John as freely given obedience."[58] The first phrase of the voice from the heaven, "You are my Son," suggests that Jesus' activity will need to be understood in relation to God's activity. The application by (God) of the term "my son" to the Markan Jesus also serves to confirm the narrator's application of the term "Son of God" to Jesus in the title of the work (1:1). Because God is the highest authority in Mark's narrative world, the voice from heaven (God) gives the narrator's assertion a high measure of authority. The Markan Jesus is the next most highly valued authority in this narrative world, but, as we will see later in exploring what the Markan Jesus says, he does not confirm the narrator's opening assertion about Jesus as the "Son of God." Thus without the confirmation of the Markan Jesus, this confirmation from (God) is crucial to the narrator's credibility. (The implied audience may wonder whether the other term linked to Jesus in the narrator's title, "Christ," will receive confirmation by another.)

The second phrase of the voice from heaven, "the Beloved (Gk *ho agapētos*)" echoes ominously Genesis 22:2 (cf. 22:12, 16), spoken by God to Abraham about Isaac: "Take your son, your only son (LXX *ton agapēton*) Isaac, whom you love (LXX *hon ēgapēsas*), . . . and offer him . . . as a burnt offering." Is (God) then the first one in Mark's narrative to allude to Jesus' death?[59] The final phrase of the voice, "with you I am well pleased (Gk *eudokēsa*)," is often compared to Isaiah 42:1, "in whom my soul delights (LXX *prosedexato*)," although it is the general idea rather than specific vocabulary that overlaps in this case (see also Isa 62:4).[60] Isaiah 42:1 is spoken by God of "my servant, whom I uphold, my

58. Michael L. Cook, S.J., *Christology as Narrative Quest* (Collegeville, Minn.: Liturgical Press, 1997), 104 n. 54.

59. Cook has no doubt: "The key image of Jesus that integrates all the factors in Mark's narrative quest is God's view of him as the 'beloved Son' who must die on the cross in order to give life to others" (*Christology as Narrative Quest*, 95). See also Sharyn Dowd and Elizabeth Struthers Malbon, "The Significance of the Death of Jesus in Mark: Narrative Context and Authorial Audience," *JBL* 125 (2006): 271–97, see 273–74, republished in *The Trial and Death of Jesus* (ed. Geert Van Oyen and Tom Shepherd; Leuven, Belgium: Peeters, 2006), 1–31, see 3–4.

60. I thank my Virginia Tech classics colleague Andrew Becker for pointing out to me that *dok-* and *dek-(s)* are etymologically related, with *dek-* coming to mean "receive" or "take" while *dok-* comes to mean "expect," then "seem" or "think." See Pierre Chantraine, *Dictionnaire étymologique de la langue grecque: Histoire des mots* (supplement under the direction of A. Blanc, C. de Lamberterie, J.-L. Perpillou; Paris: Klincksieck, 1999), 267–69 (esp. 268, column 2), 290–91.

chosen," that is, the focus is on a relationship of responsibility and obedience to God. These biblical allusions, and especially the narrative fact that it is the voice from heaven (God) that applies them to the Markan Jesus, clearly designate Jesus as having a role in the activity of God for the people of God based on a relationship of responsibility and obedience, in the pattern of Israel's relationship with God in the past.[61] Obedience to the death may be hinted, but the details of that role are not clear from the words of this voice. The action of the Spirit closes the frame (1:10, Spirit/1:11, voice/1:12, Spirit) with the clear assertion (echoing the voice's hint?) that Jesus' commission will not be an easy one: "And the Spirit immediately drove him out [Gk *ekballei*] into the wilderness."

The second Markan scene in which a voice, this time coming "from the cloud" (9:7), speaks is Jesus' transfiguration. This time the voice speaks not to Jesus but about Jesus to Peter, James, and John, whom Jesus had taken with him up the "high mountain" (9:2) where he appears transfigured and with Elijah and Moses, a cloud overshadowing them all. The voice comes from the cloud, saying, "This is my Son, the Beloved; listen to him!" (9:7), with a clear intratextual echo of the voice at Jesus' baptism. The intertextual echoes of "Son" and "the Beloved" with Psalm 2 and Genesis 22 are heard again. What is new is the intended hearers of the voice within the narrative—three of Jesus' disciples—and what they are told to do—"listen to him," that is, to Jesus. The words "my son" coming from (God) lend authority to the narrator's initial assertion of Jesus as "Son of God" (1:1), about which the Markan Jesus says nothing. But the words "listen to him" give (God's) authority to what the Markan Jesus does say. What Jesus says next is reported by the narrator as indirect speech: "As they were coming down the mountain, he ordered them to tell no one about what they had seen"—no big surprise there since the Markan Jesus has given such warnings with regularity, although usually to those whom he heals—"until after the Son of Man had risen from the dead" (9:9)—a new twist. The first surprise is that the narrator here comes close to using the Markan Jesus' unique term, "Son of Man"; however, it remains clear that the narrator intends these words as a report of Jesus' words.[62] The second surprise is that the "don't tell" warning (often discussed in terms of the "messianic secret") now has a limit—until after the resurrection. One must beware of telling the half-truth for fear of having hold of the wrong half, but after the crucifixion and the resurrection the story will be whole and may be, even must be, told. Thus the words of the voice (of God) to three of Jesus' disciples, "Listen to him," that is, to the Markan Jesus,

---

61. Rhoads, Dewey, and Michie use the terms "agent" and "ambassador" to suggest this relationship: "Jesus is the commissioned agent of God, sent as an ambassador to inaugurate God's rule" (*Mark as Story*, 104).

62. Cf. the Markan Jesus' words giving the disciples' words at 11:3 and 14:14, as discussed above.

at this point in the narrative (the "way" section) highlight the crucifixion and resurrection as the standpoint from which all of Jesus' words and actions are to be interpreted by the implied audience.

Indeed what (God) says to and about Jesus is quite limited in terms of quantity:[63] "You are my Son, the Beloved; with you I am pleased" (1:11). "This is my Son, the Beloved; listen to him!" (9:7). Even these two short statements are repetitious, further limiting the new content expressed. But their reverberations with each other, with Scripture, and with the narrator's opening line are deeply resonant. (God) confirms the narrator's application of "Son of God" to the Markan Jesus and also confirms that what the Markan Jesus does and says is pleasing to (God). Because, as we have mentioned and will discuss further in the next two chapters, the Markan Jesus and the narrator are not always in agreement, (God) serves as a mediating character between them, confirming them both in different ways. We will see in exploring what Jesus says (chapters 3 and 4) that Jesus speaks of and deflects attention to God, but here at 9:7 (God) calls attention to what Jesus says: "Listen to him!"

If the Markan implied author is reticent about introducing God into the action as a character (with only two references to the "voice"), and the Markan narrator is reticent about commenting on God in his narration (with only two references), both are even more reticent concerning God's opponent in the cosmic struggle underlying Mark's Gospel—Satan.[64] Satan never appears as a character, not even as a voice, but only through the speech of his representatives, the unclean spirits and demons, who are confronted directly by God's representative, Jesus—like obedient kings, righteous persons, angels, and all Israel before him—designated "son of God."

63. I am following the verbal cues of Mark's narrative strictly here. One could presumably argue, for example, that the voice of God is heard whenever Scripture is recited, but that would take us too far afield from this more circumscribed look at what others say to or about the Markan Jesus. Cook, with broader purposes in mind, does interpret the voice of God more metaphorically when he applies it to the beginning and ending of Mark's Gospel: Mark 1:2-13 and 15:42–16:8, "which function as prologue and epilogue respectively, show a concern to begin and end with God's voice proclaiming the good news through a messenger or herald (John the Baptist dressed in camel's hair as the voice in the desert and the young man dressed in a white robe as the voice in the tomb). In each case there is a 'going before' (1:2; 16:7) that echoes the importance of the 'way,' but whereas John's voice is superseded by God's voice (1:11) Jesus' 'going before' at 16:7 calls attention to all that has preceded in the story world and evokes the expectation of a response that now only the listener/reader can give" (*Christology as Narrative Quest*, 74).

64. As Joel Williams observes: "Mark offers inside views of Jesus and all the major character groups that interact with Jesus. . . . Yet he always presents God and Satan from the outside, without reference to their thoughts and feelings" ("Jesus' Love for the Rich Man," 151).

What the Unclean Spirits and Demons Say to and about Jesus

The unclean spirits and demons have an odd connection with God as transcendent characters, characters whose knowledge and very existence is beyond human limitations. (There does not appear to be a significant difference between the terms "unclean spirits" and "demons" in Markan usage; the terms are used interchangeably in the story of the Syrophoenician woman: 7:25, unclean spirit; 7:26, demon; 7:30, demon—all in the voice of the narrator.) In terms of the cosmic struggle that is foundational for Mark's Gospel, unclean spirits and demons are aligned with Satan over against God. But in terms of their knowledge of Jesus' role in that cosmic struggle, they share knowledge with God—knowledge learned, in their case, firsthand as combatants on the run.[65] Their position is made known early in the narrative, in the Markan Jesus' initial exorcism in the synagogue in Capernaum (1:21-28).

Even before Jesus speaks to the possessed man, the unclean spirit possessing him cries out, "What have you to do with us, Jesus of Nazareth? Have you come to destroy us? I know who you are, the Holy One of God" (1:24).[66] The unclean spirit, speaking first in the plural ("us"), seems to speak for the host of unclean spirits now engaged in the cosmic struggle renewed by God through the ministry of Jesus; he knows the answer to his own question: Yes, Jesus has come in the name and power of God to destroy all such unclean spirits and demons. Like the narrator (1:9) and a few others in the text (discussed above), the unclean spirit identifies Jesus as "Jesus the Nazarene," that is, Jesus from Nazareth, a not particularly illustrious town in the history of Israel. But, speaking in the singular, the unclean spirit also asserts his knowledge of Jesus as "the Holy One of God." Jesus' only response to the unclean spirit is to continue the struggle: "Be silent, and come out of him!" (1:25). (The Markan Jesus' re-

---

65. I suspect the *Testament of Levi* 18:12 and the *Testament of Dan* 5:10 illustrate the same cosmic background of casting out demons as the Gospel of Mark, against Hahn: "So far as the destruction of the demons is concerned, the instances adduced from the *Test. of Levi* 18, 12 and the *Test. of Dan* 5, 10f, are not convincing and do not represent actual parallels. For there quite a different understanding of the evil spirits presents itself: in the stories of exorcisms in the Gospels the *ponēra pneumata* [unclean spirits] are the authors of sickness (possession), but in the *Testaments* they are the followers of Beliar who must be vanquished by the messianic high priest in a holy war (*Test. of Dan* 5, 10); consequently the special dualistic conception of the Qumran texts is behind these statements, whilst in the exorcism narratives we are concerned with the general belief in demons of late Judaism. Accordingly these connections drop out" (*Titles of Jesus*, 232–33). I see a stronger connection between sickness, evil, and Satan as opposed to health, good, and God in Mark's Gospel—and in the first-century Mediterranean world as a whole.

66. Interestingly enough, in the portion of John's Gospel that is most parallel to Peter's confession in Mark (8:27-30), Simon Peter replies to Jesus, "We have come to believe and know that you are the Holy One of God" (John 6:69).

sponses to what the unclean spirits and demons say is examined in the following chapter.) This encounter shows the depth and scope of the struggle to anyone who witnesses it. It is not clear that anyone within the story world other than Jesus hears the speech of the unclean spirit; however, the narrator reports the amazement of the people in the synagogue at the obvious and dramatic result of the encounter: "He commands even the unclean spirits, and they obey him" (1:27).

At 1:34 the Markan narrator summarizes the apparently repeated encounters between Jesus and demons: "And he cured many who were sick with various diseases, and cast out many demons; and he would not permit the demons to speak, because they knew him." Presumably demons generally know what the unclean spirit in Capernaum knows: that Jesus is engaged with God in the cosmic struggle against Satan and his forces of evil, sickness, suffering, and death. In another summary statement, 3:7-12, the narrator allows the unclean spirits to speak in their own voice: "Whenever the unclean spirits saw him, they fell down before him and shouted, 'You are the Son of God!'" (3:11). Again, the unclean spirits manifest their transcendent knowledge of who Jesus is in relation to God; the Son fights alongside and for the Father—and they are winning. Not all the demons and unclean spirits that Jesus casts out speak in Mark's Gospel, but by means of these summary statements, all are given some voice.

A final unclean spirit who does speak out—loudly and clearly—is the one who possesses the man in the country of the Gerasenes. This time the Markan Jesus apparently speaks first, although the narrator reports Jesus' speech as an added explanation (5:8) after reporting that of the unclean spirit (5:7). This unclean spirit, perhaps knowing how things have been going for unclean spirits and demons lately, acts through the man to make a truce or a deal with Jesus: "When he saw Jesus from a distance, he ran and bowed down before him; and he shouted at the top of his voice, 'What have you to do with me, Jesus, Son of the Most High God? I adjure you by God, do not torment me'" (5:6-7). Perhaps the unclean spirit thinks that showing honor (running to meet Jesus, bowing down before him) and trying to speak in God's name will assist his plea for mercy. This unclean spirit does manage more of a conversation with Jesus than any other demon or unclean spirit, speaking in direct discourse three times. Although the unclean spirit knows Jesus' name already, Jesus asks for his,[67] and he obediently responds, "My name is Legion; for we are many" (5:9), combining singular and plural forms as did the unclean spirit in the synagogue in Capernaum. Realizing he cannot entirely win this struggle, Legion hopes at least to cut his losses by arranging to stay in his current neighborhood—"among

---

67. As Broadhead notes, "Jesus asks the name of the victim/opponent. While implying a note of mercy, the naming of an opponent also brings power over that opponent in ancient thought" (*Teaching with Authority*, 99). Of course, the demon had first "named" Jesus as part of the ongoing cosmic power struggle.

the tombs and on the mountains" (5:5), so his final plea to Jesus is, "Send us into the swine; let us enter them" (5:12). Jesus agrees to do so, but the possessed swine then rush down the steep bank and drown in the sea. The joke is on Legion, whose very name is probably an anti-Roman joke and whose final fate (shared with pigs) is probably a Jewish joke.

Jesus' silencing of the demons and unclean spirits first represents the in-breaking rule (kingdom) of God, as discussed in the preceding chapter; this is a responsibility shared with his disciples (3:15; 6:7, 13; cf. 9:38-39). But when the Markan Jesus silences the demons and unclean spirits who have expressed their knowledge of him in relation to God, another dynamic is at work (to be explored in the following chapter), a dynamic that recognizes at least two ways to misunderstand such exorcisms: the way the scribes who come down from Jerusalem misunderstand Jesus' relationship to God's adversary and thus to God (3:22-30) and the way Peter misunderstands Jesus' role in living out that relationship (8:31-33). Both misunderstandings elicit a reference to Satan, the adversary of God and thus of Jesus, by the Markan Jesus (3:23, 26; 8:33).

Unclean spirits and demons are on the side of Satan in the cosmic struggle between God and Satan, but, oddly enough, what the unclean spirits and demons say to and about Jesus is most like what (God) says in 1:11 and 9:7 and what the narrator says in 1:1.

1:1	narrator: Son of God
1:11	(God): my Son
1:24	unclean spirit: the Holy One of God
3:11	unclean spirits: the Son of God
5:7	Legion: Son of the Most High God
9:7	(God): my Son

The closest match in vocabulary, and this is not so odd, is between the narrator's title and the speech of the unclean spirits reported in a summary by the narrator: (the) Son of God (1:1 and 3:11). By means of the voice from heaven or the cloud at 1:11 and 9:7, (God) confirms this use of "Son" by both the narrator and the unclean spirits, including Legion (5:7). Only the unclean spirit in the synagogue in Capernaum does not use the term "Son," substituting the term "the Holy One." The title "the Holy One of God" is not inappropriate in a synagogue because it recalls the term "the Holy One of Israel" (sometimes shortened to "the Holy One"), a phrase "used frequently by the Hebrew prophets, especially Isaiah, as a title for Yahweh, Israel's God (Isa. 1:4; 5:19, 24; 10:17, 20; 40:25; 41:14, 16, 20; 43:3, 14-15). The phrase also appears in the Psalms (71:22; 78:41; 89:18)."[68] Legion's term, "Son of the Most High God," would make good sense in a Gentile environment with a hierarchical pantheon of

68. Paul J. Achtemeier, gen. ed., "Holy One of Israel, the," *HCBD*, 432.

gods, but it also has reverberations with Jewish Scripture (Pss 7:17; 21:7; 91:1), which it seems to have entered with the story of the Canaanite priest-king of Salem, Melchizedek (Gen 14:19-20).

To repeat, the knowledge of Jesus' role in relation to God is transcendent knowledge; thus it is shared by the transcendent characters of the Markan narrative, (God) and unclean spirits and demons, who are opposed to each other at the most basic level of the narrative. On the basis of this shared knowledge, (God) recognizes the Markan Jesus as "my Son," my deputy, and the unclean spirits and demons recognize Jesus as the Son of God, our enemy. The narrator shares this knowledge with them by virtue of his superior knowledge[69] in relation to the story, and immediately he shares it with the narratee (1:1).

What Suppliants Say to or about Jesus

Just as the unclean spirits and demons suffer a disadvantage due to the Markan Jesus' role in the cosmic struggle between God and Satan, so the suppliants, those who ask Jesus for healing or exorcism, enjoy an advantage. Suppliants are beneficiaries of Jesus' proclamation and manifestation of the in-breaking rule (kingdom) of God. Seven suppliants in Mark's narrative are provided with direct speech; six speak to Jesus, two of these in several verbal exchanges; one speaks to herself about Jesus. First a leper shows his faith in Jesus' healing power by his actions (begging and kneeling[70]) and his words: "If you choose, you can make me clean" (1:40). From the leper's point of view, Jesus' power and ability to heal are unquestioned; what is at stake is Jesus' will in this case. However, the narrator has already cued the narratee concerning Jesus' will—"Moved with pity, Jesus stretched out his hand and touched him" (1:41a)—prior to its confirmation in Jesus' words: "I do choose. Be made clean!" (1:41b). A considerably higher-status suppliant, "one of the leaders of the synagogue named Jairus" (5:22), shows the same actions of deference as the leper (falling at Jesus' feet and begging him repeatedly, 5:22-23) and similar words of faith: "My little daughter is at the point of death. Come and lay your hands on her, so that she may be made well, and live" (5:23). As it happens in the narrative, Jairus' story is delayed by the story of the faith and healing of the hemorrhaging woman, whose exemplary faith serves as a model for the further faith Jairus will need; however, he does not speak again in the narrative. In addition to being a suppliant, Jairus is also a Jewish leader; his direct speech will be reconsidered below along with other, more powerful members of the "Jewish authorities."

---

69. I avoid the problematic term "omniscience" because clearly the narrator does not know everything. See Ruge-Jones, "Omnipresent, not Omniscient." The use of the masculine pronoun for the narrator of Mark is not out of line for its first-century context.

70. "Kneeling" is lacking at 1:40 in some ancient authorities.

The hemorrhaging woman, whose story is intercalated into Jairus' story, is one of two women suppliants in Mark,[71] both of whom are given direct speech. The hemorrhaging woman's narrated speech is apparently internal, representing one of the narrator's inside views, and is presented in an explanatory "for" (Gk *gar*) phrase following her action: "She had heard about Jesus, and came up behind him in the crowd and touched his cloak, for she said, 'If I but touch his clothes, I will be made well'" (5:27-28). Hers is a bold move of gaining access to the power of the in-breaking rule of God that is available through Jesus, and it is successful. The other woman suppliant, the Syrophoenician woman, is equally bold, on behalf of her daughter. Because the Markan Jesus has already healed/raised Jairus' *daughter* (5:22-24, 35-43) and exorcised a demoniac in *Gentile* territory (5:1-20), the implied audience is perhaps taken aback by Jesus' initial rebuttal of her request to heal her Gentile daughter (7:27). But she takes the insult in stride and quickly develops the metaphor in focused pursuit of her goal for her daughter: "Sir, even the dogs under the table eat the children's crumbs" (7:28). The Markan Jesus is impressed, as we will consider further in the following chapter, saying (literally), "On account of this word, you may go; the demon has gone out of your daughter" (7:29). While the leper and Jairus demonstrate deference to Jesus and express faith in his healing power, these two women suppliants show a bolder approach and assume a knowledge of the availability of God's power that surprises even the Markan Jesus.[72]

The Syrophoenician woman opens her comeback to Jesus' not-so-polite metaphorical reference to her as a dog with the polite form of address "Sir" or "Master" (7:28). The Greek work is *kyrie* (the vocative of *kyrios*, used only here in Mark), literally "lord," and applied both to human masters (e.g., "the lord of the vineyard" [12:9] and "the lord of the house" [13:35] in Jesus' parables) and to God (e.g., in the Scriptures quoted by Jesus at 12:11, 29-30, 36-37). The NRSV is right to translate the Syrophoenician woman's use of *kyrie* as "Sir";[73]

71. Simon's mother-in-law is healed of a fever by Jesus, but others ask on her behalf (1:29-31). Jairus is a suppliant on behalf of his daughter, and the Syrophoenician woman is a suppliant on behalf of her daughter. Thus only the hemorrhaging woman is a woman suppliant who seeks healing for herself—and she does so without speaking out loud to Jesus!

72. For my slightly fuller analysis of these two women suppliants, see Elizabeth Struthers Malbon, "Fallible Followers: Women and Men in the Gospel of Mark," *Semeia* 28 (1983): 29–48, esp. 36–37, republished in Malbon, *In the Company of Jesus: Characters in Mark's Gospel* (Louisville: Westminster John Knox, 2000), 41–69, esp. 50–53.

73. Hahn argues that the "term of address is used in the most general sense, although it expresses real subordination and not only courtesy" (*Titles of Jesus*, 80). Hahn's research is from a history of traditions point of view; however, an additional comment of his on the address of the Syrophoenician woman to Jesus is interesting from a narrative critical point of view: "*rabbi/didaskale* [rabbi/teacher] has perhaps been intentionally avoided, for it is here a question of a heathen woman on whose lips the word 'Rabbi,' emphasizing as it does the special position of a Jewish teacher of the Torah, might have seemed inappropriate to the

however, the translators are also right to note that "Lord" is an alternative translation. The implied audience, understanding Greek, would be able to hear both possible meanings reverberating. "Sir" makes sense at the level of the story, but "Lord" may be suggested at the level of the discourse, with the same significant ambiguity suggested by the narrator as at 1:3 and 5:19-20, discussed above in relation to what the narrator says about John the baptizer and implies about Jesus.

The direct speech of the blind man of Bethsaida underscores the dramatic twofold nature of his healing. This healing story, unique to Mark's Gospel, focuses not on Jesus' healing power and the suppliant's faith (although these are assumed) but on the two stages of the healing process as a metaphor for two stages in the process of understanding Jesus' role and his relationship to God and God's kingdom, as discussed in the previous chapter. After Jesus' first laying of his hands on the man's eyes, he asks him, "Can you see anything?" (8:23). The man replies, "I can see people, but they look like trees, walking" (8:24). At this stage the man is a figure for all those with half-understanding, whether the disciples who do not understand that there is bread enough for both Jews and Gentiles (8:14-21) in the immediately preceding story, or Peter, who does not understand that Jesus' way of being "Christ" will involve not only power but persecution (8:27-33) in the immediately following story. After the second stage of the healing, the man sees "everything clearly" (8:25). The question for the implied audience is then, for whom is this a figure?

The remaining two suppliants with direct speech each have several exchanges with Jesus, and each also fits into more than one category of characters. The father of the boy with a spirit is presented first as "someone from the crowd" (9:17); then it is revealed that he was an unsuccessful suppliant of the nine disciples prior to becoming a suppliant of Jesus. Bartimaeus, initially a suppliant, acts like a follower at the end of his story. Both the father and Bartimaeus also address Jesus with a distinctive phrase, "Teacher" or "Son of David" and "my rabbi." With the story of the healing of the blind man of Bethsaida, the stories of the father and his possessed son and of Bartimaeus comprise the only three healing stories in the second half of Mark's Gospel, and each story contributes a significant aspect to Mark's narrative above and beyond the manifestation of the in-breaking of God's rule in the healing power of Jesus. Thus these suppliants have a bit more to say to and about Jesus.

The father of the possessed boy, like several suppliants before him, needs and shows persistence. While Jesus was away (on the mount of transfiguration) with Peter, James, and John, the father had sought healing for his son from the remaining nine disciples, as he reports to Jesus upon his return: "Teacher, I brought you my son; he has a spirit that makes him unable to speak; and

---

community which handed on this tradition" (80). In terms of the narrative, the Syrophoenician woman speaks "in character."

whenever it seizes him, it dashes him down; and he foams and grinds his teeth
and becomes rigid; and I asked your disciples to cast it out, but they could not
do so" (9:17-18). The father's use of the term "Teacher" (Gk *didaskale*) reminds
the implied audience of Jesus' first exorcism, intercalated with his teaching
with authority in the synagogue in Capernaum (1:21-29). Both teaching and
exorcising/healing are presented as manifestations of the in-breaking rule of
God. Of the twelve occurrences of the term "teacher" in Mark's narrative, the
first four occur in settings of *dynameis*, "mighty deeds" (4:38; 5:35; 9:17, 38),
and the next seven occur in settings of teaching (10:17, 20, 35; 12:14, 19, 32;
13:1; cf. the final occurrence in 14:14). "Teacher" is not an exclusive term of
any one group of characters in Mark's narrative. It is applied only to Jesus, but
the Markan Jesus is called "Teacher" by his disciples (4:38; 9:38; 10:35; 13:1;
cf. 14:14, where the Markan Jesus presents it to his disciples as what they will
say to someone), by suppliants and those associated with them (5:35; 9:17), by
the rich man (10:17, 20), and by Jewish authorities (12:14, 19, 32). The irony
in the father's calling Jesus "Teacher" while simultaneously reporting the failure
of the disciples Jesus has been trying to teach seems to be picked up by the
Markan Jesus in his generalized response to the father: "You faithless generation, how much longer must I be among you? How much longer must I put up
with you?" (9:19).[74]

But Jesus then focuses on the father and his son, following up the question
coming from his own frustration ("How much longer must I put up with you?"
9:19) with one coming from his concern for them ("How long has this been
happening to him?" 9:21a). The father answers Jesus' question, then, hesitantly,
becomes a suppliant of the teacher as he had earlier been of the students: "From
childhood. It has often cast him into the fire and into the water, to destroy him;
but if you are able to do anything, have pity on us and help us" (9:21b-22).
Jesus' response seems to be as much to his students, the disciples, as to the father: "If you are able!—All things can be done for the one who believes" (9:23).
And, in turn, the father's response serves well not just for himself but for all
followers: "I believe; help my unbelief!" (9:24). As the healing of the blind man
of Bethsaida functions as an image of second-stage insight for those who would
follow Jesus, so this father's statement serves as an emblem of the dynamic process of faith.

The response of Bartimaeus, in the second giving-of-sight story in Mark,
presents a final image for those who would see and follow Jesus: "Immediately
he regained his sight and followed him on the way" (10:52)—into Jerusalem.

---

74. Broadhead notes: "In the face of the physical crisis and the impotence of the disciples Jesus is addressed as teacher (9.17). In the aftermath of the disciples' failure, Jesus
embodies the model of teacher when he instructs his followers in the privacy of the house
(9.28-29)" (*Teaching with Authority*, 156–57).

But because Bartimaeus' initial direct speech to Jesus is considerably more problematic, a separate subsection will be devoted to this discussion.

WHAT BARTIMAEUS SAYS TO JESUS

Bartimaeus' story is the narrator's last before Jesus' final approach to Jerusalem, and, as the narrator explained that Jesus was "from Nazareth" at his entrance onto the narrative scene (1:9), so here the narrator reminds the narratee of that connection: "When he [Bartimaeus] heard that it was Jesus of Nazareth [literally "Jesus the Nazarene"], he began to shout out . . ." (10:47a). Bartimaeus' first shout is, "Son of David, Jesus [following the order of the appellations in Greek against the NRSV[75]], have mercy on me!" (10:47b), and it is unheeded by the Markan Jesus—and probably unheard because "many sternly ordered him to be quiet" (10:48a). But, as suppliants before him, Bartimaeus is persistent, crying out "even more loudly, 'Son of David, have mercy on me!'" (10:48b). This time the Markan Jesus does hear and heed the cry and asks the crowd to call Bartimaeus forward, which they do. Bartimaeus, who was sitting by the side of the road (10:46), now springs into action: "throwing off his cloak, he sprang up and came to Jesus" (10:50). Alan Culpepper has argued that the left-behind cloak "reiterates on another level Bartimaeus's radical break with his past."[76] In response to Jesus' only question to him, "What do you want me to do for you?" (10:51a),[77] Bartimaeus speaks his third and final time: "My teacher [Aramaic *Rabbouni*, literally "my rabbi"], let me see again" (10:51b). The healing is apparently instantaneous—no need for stages here.[78] The story concludes with words

75. In reversing the order of "Son of David" and "Jesus," the NRSV seems to be operating from the point of view that "Jesus" is the more familiar address; however, the Greek text of Mark may suggest that, from the point of view of the character Bartimaeus, "Son of David" (uttered first) is more familiar than "Jesus." Perhaps this is the implied audience's first clue that Bartimaeus may be making a blind guess in applying "Son of David," an honorific term he knows, to "Jesus," of whom he has heard and whom he hopes to meet.

76. R. Alan Culpepper, "Mark 10:50: Why Mention the Garment?" *JBL* 101 (1982): 131–32, quotation from 132. Culpepper continues, "The garment, therefore, represents that which the disciple leaves behind to follow Jesus. . . . [Cf. 1:18, 20; 10:28-30; 12:44; contra 10:21-22] . . . Discipleship mandates that one's former way of life can neither be patched up nor retrieved at will" (132).

77. As Adela Yarbro Collins notes, this is the same question that the Markan Jesus asks of James and John at 10:36, not long before in the story, and the two answers could hardly be more different: "Again, James and John are cast as negative models and the blind man as a positive model" (*Mark*, 511). I might add that, although Bartimaeus is certainly a positive model of persistence in reaching Jesus, it is primarily after being addressed by Jesus that Bartimaeus serves as a positive model, that is, after he drops "Son of David" and addresses Jesus as "*Rabbouni*."

78. In contrast to the two-stage healing of blindness at Bethsaida (8:22-26), although

of Jesus that remind the implied audience of earlier words to the hemorrhaging woman, "Go; your faith has made you well" (10:52a; cf. 5:34), and with Bartimaeus' action that reminds the implied audience of what is required of all followers: "Immediately he regained his sight and followed him on the way" (10:52b).

It is in his following Jesus on the way that Bartimaeus is exemplary, not in his initial—and ignored and abandoned—address of Jesus as "Son of David." Although I agree with Ian Henderson that "the single-episode, sub-apostolic characters in Mark, such as BarTimaeus, are privileged examples of valid faith affirmation,"[79] I argue that it is the action of Bartimaeus and not his initial words that are affirmed. A similar tendency of overgeneralization is seen in Stephen Ahearne-Kroll's analysis: because Bartimaeus follows Jesus on the way "this makes him a character whose opinion the reader can trust, encouraging him or her to assent to the declaration that Jesus is 'Son of David.'"[80] Perhaps we interpreters are more prone to stereotyping Mark's characters as "all right" or "all wrong" than the implied author is! Adela Yarbro Collins even suggests that "it may be . . . that the address of Jesus as son of David . . . manifests Bartimaeus's prophetic gift. In Greek myths the association of blindness with compensatory supernatural gifts was common."[81] Certainly Mark's Gospel does assume metaphorical dimensions to references to blindness and sight; however, in the only two stories of the healing of blindness in Mark it is the *healing* of blindness, the *restoration of sight*, that is the positive image. The partial sight of the man from Bethsaida is problematic, just as the half-sight of Peter's view of Jesus as Christ is, and the phrase "Son of David" appears on the lips of Bartimaeus when he is still blind, not after he is healed of his blindness by Jesus.[82]

---

there are two stages in Bartimaeus' address to Jesus: "Son of David" before encountering Jesus, "*Rabbouni*" afterward.

79. Ian Henderson, "Reconstructing Mark's Double Audience," in Malbon, ed., *Between Author and Audience*, 6–28, quotation from 24.

80. Stephen Ahearne-Kroll, *The Psalms of Lament in Mark's Passion: Jesus' Davidic Suffering* (SNTSMS 142; Cambridge: Cambridge University Press, 2007), 138–39.

81. Adela Yarbro Collins, *Mark*, 510.

82. Cf. Paul J. Achtemeier, "'And He Followed Him': Miracles and Discipleship in Mark 10:46-52," *Semeia* 11 (1978): 115–45, quotation from 131, who worries that it might be "over-subtle to point out that Bartimaeus was still blind when he called Jesus 'son of David.'" See also W. R. Telford, *The Theology of the Gospel of Mark* (New Testament Theology; Cambridge: Cambridge University Press, 1999), 36, who sees in the healing of the blindness of Bartimaeus, who calls Jesus "Son of David," "a move away from a 'Son of David' Christology, one embodied, I suspect, in the characters of the Markan text (Peter, the disciples, blind Bartimaeus and the Jewish crowd who are later to crucify him)" (37). David Rhoads has suggested to me that Bartimaeus may be interpreted as referring to Jesus as "Son of David" in the sense of simply identifying Jesus as a fellow Israelite who may help him but that the identification also seems to be a misunderstanding in line with the failure of other

Unlike the Markan Jesus and the Markan narrator, some Markan scholars have not set aside Bartimaeus' two shouts to Jesus as "Son of David." In fact, scholars often interpret this passage as if the phrase "Son of David" were accepted and supported by both the narrator and Jesus. For example, Ferdinand Hahn writes, "[I]n the gospel of Mark and also in Matthew and Luke, in connection with the son of David question, affirmations of Jesus' being Son of David are calmly and unhesitatingly accepted, and this fact cannot be argued away by simply referring to the very varied origins of the traditional material."[83] The commentary of Gene Boring, however, confirms my reading, arguing that "it is more likely that for Mark, 'Son of David' is a misunderstanding of Jesus' true identity" and adding two additional justifications for this reading: (1) "The 'Son of David' was expected to come from Bethlehem, the city of David. Yet Bethlehem is never mentioned in Mark, and Jesus is here named 'of Nazareth'" and (2) Bartimaeus "makes this acclamation while seated *beside* the way, a phrase found elsewhere in Mark only in 4:4, 15 . . . [the seeds fallen beside the way and thus unfruitful]. After his blindness is removed, he follows Jesus *on* the way as a true disciple."[84]

Here I am focusing, like Boring, on the internal, narrative evidence of how the phrase "Son of David" is functioning both at the story level and at the discourse level and not, like Hahn, on external evidence or speculation concerning what the phrase once meant or came to mean in its multiple Jewish and early

---

minor characters to understand who Jesus is (e.g., identifying him as John the baptizer, Elijah, or a prophet).

83. Hahn, *Titles of Jesus*, 252. For the details of the interpretation of Bartimaeus' cry by Hahn and others with similar views—and my critique—see the excursus at the end of my essay, "The Jesus of Mark and the 'Son of David,'" in Malbon, ed., *Between Author and Audience*, 162–85, 180–84 for the excursus, 180–83 for Bartimaeus' cry. Vernon K. Robbins, "The Healing of Blind Bartimaeus (10:46-52) in the Marcan Theology," *JBL* 92 (1973): 224–43, correctly assesses the importance of the placement of the Bartimaeus story in Mark's narrative: "The story of the healing of blind Bartimaeus stands in between and forms the transition from the discipleship teaching to the Jerusalem entry" (237). However, Robbins' treatment of "Son of David" as a positive Markan title in parallel with "Son of Man" and "Son of God" is not a convincing interpretation of the Markan narrative: "The story of blind Bartimaeus introduces a transition in christological nomenclature concerning Jesus' activity. A transition is made from the disciples' following 'in the way of the Son of Man' (8:27–10:45) toward Jerusalem to following 'in the way of the Son of David' (10:46–12:44) into Jerusalem" (241); and "Marcan redaction in the Bartimaeus story to achieve this explicit characterization [as Son of David] is analogous to Marcan redaction in 3:7-12 to bring all healing activity of Jesus into an explicit relationship with the title 'the Son of God'" (240). See also Broadhead: "The reference to Jesus as son of David [at 10:47-48] carries kingly and christological overtones and focuses the unique identity of Jesus" (*Teaching with Authority*, 165).

84. M. Eugene Boring, *Mark: A Commentary* (The New Testament Library; Louisville: Westminster John Knox, 2006), 305.

Christian contexts.[85] In Mark's Gospel, only Bartimaeus and Jesus use the term "Son of David." Although the narrative does not make clear at the story level just what Bartimaeus means by the term, when Bartimaeus uses it (10:47, 48), Jesus seems to ignore it; when Jesus uses it later he seems to do so to dispute the idea that the Messiah could be the son of David (12:35-37). What Jesus says about David (2:25) and the Son of David (12:35-37) will be discussed in the following chapter on what Jesus says in response. Given that neither the narrator nor any other character picks up the designation "Son of David" and that the Markan Jesus argues against its application to the Christ (Messiah), it would seem that the implied audience is also expected to set it aside, following the lead of the Markan Jesus and Bartimaeus—at least until a fuller discussion of it in the Markan Jesus' extremely relevant comments at 12:35-37.[86] In addition, neither the Markan Jesus nor the narrator respond to the crowd's shouting, "Blessed is the coming kingdom of our ancestor [Gk father] David!" (11:10) at Jesus' entry into Jerusalem (to be discussed below). Clearly something about "Son of David" is in the air, but, like Bartimaeus' cries, it appears to be drowned out or drift away at this point in Mark's narrative. When the phrase "Son of David" appears again (12:35-37) it is no longer a questionable acclamation offered to Jesus but an accusatory question asserted by Jesus.

When Bartimaeus is addressed directly by Jesus and replies to him, his earlier designation "Son of David" is replaced by "*Rabbouni.*"[87] The NRSV translation as "teacher" is understandable, but it fails to make connections with other references in the narrative. The word *rabbouni* occurs only here (10:51) in Mark, although "*rabbi*" does appear in the direct speech of Peter (9:5; 11:21) and Judas (14:45), both fairly late in the narrative. Rabbi (transliterated from

---

85. Such a history of the tradition is the explicit goal of Hahn, *Titles of Jesus*, chapter 4, "Son of David," 240–78.

86. David Rhoads has suggested to me that the implied audience is led to reject this title for Jesus when it first appears here because Jesus has just said that the disciples are not to be like Gentile nations (10:42-44), a clear rejection of political domination of the sort that might be encouraged by the "Son of David" image.

87. The rich man also changes his address to Jesus within his story—from "Good Teacher" to "Teacher"—but in response to the direct correction of the Markan Jesus (10:17-22). However, in each story the action of the one who encounters Jesus speaks louder to the implied audience than his words: Bartimaeus follows Jesus on the way, the rich man goes away grieving. For an intriguing analysis of Jesus' response to the rich man, see Williams, "Jesus' Love for the Rich Man." Hans Dieter Betz, "The Early Christian Miracle Story: Some Observations on the Form Critical Problem," *Semeia* 11 (1978): 69–81, see esp. 74–75, argues that the change in Bartimaeus' address of Jesus from "Son of David" to "*Rabbouni*" ("master") accompanies a genre shift in the narrative, from miracle story to call story at vv. 49–50; thus it is as a disciple that Bartimaeus addresses Jesus as "master." Achtemeier notes that the change in titles occurs at the "crucial moment": "At the crucial moment Bartimaeus calls Jesus *rabbouni* (10:51) and his faith is confirmed. These terms belong to the language of discipleship" ("'And He Followed Him,'" 115).

the Hebrew) is "properly a form of address" and "then an honorary title for out-standing teachers of the law."[88] *Rabbouni* is "a heightened form" of *rabbi*.[89] In the New Testament, "*Rabbi* is used mostly in direct address of Jesus as a person of respect or teacher."[90] As Gene Boring notes, in its Markan context *rabbouni* is "double-edged": it is "an exalted expression" but it is also related to "rabbi," which is "always used by Mark to express inadequate or failed discipleship."[91] Of course, fallible followership is the norm in Mark's narrative.[92] In addition, Bartimaeus' Aramaic name, which the narrator explains (10:46), and his Aramaic form of address for Jesus ("*Rabbouni*," 10:51) prepare the narratee for the story's movement into the Jewish capital, Jerusalem.[93] Bartimaeus' final address of Jesus as "my rabbi"/"my teacher" and his final action of following him on the way bring to a close the central teaching section of Mark's Gospel, 8:22–10:52.

Of course there are other suppliants in Mark's Gospel in addition to these seven who are given direct speech to or about Jesus. Their stories confirm the faith and persistence of all those who come to Jesus seeking healing of disease or relief from possession by unclean spirits or demons. At times the narrator also offers summary statements concerning suppliants, especially in the first six chapters of the narrative (1:34, 39; 3:7-12; 6:53-56; contrast 6:5-6). The first such summary statement sets the pattern: "And he cured many who were sick with various diseases, and cast out many demons; and he would not permit the demons to speak, because they knew him" (1:34). Direct speech in healing stories and exorcisms heightens the drama of these accounts and leads to answers to what would otherwise be hypothetical questions: Is Jesus willing to heal? (1:40). Is Jesus able to heal someone at the point of, or even after, death? (5:23). Is Jesus' healing power available without his knowledge? (5:28). Is Jesus willing to heal Gentiles? (7:28). Direct speech of suppliants also provides a symbolic dimension to certain healing stories, a dimension that points to incomplete understanding

88. William F. Arndt and F. Wilbur Gingrich, *A Greek-English Lexicon of the New Testament and Other Early Christian Literature* (2nd ed.; Chicago: University of Chicago Press, 1979), 733. Hahn notes, "The fact that *rabbi* in Greek has in part been left untranslated is an indication of the ancient character and currency of this mode of address" (*Titles of Jesus*, 74).

89. Arndt and Gingrich, *Lexicon*, 733.

90. Anthony J. Saldarini, "Rabbi, Rabbouni," *HCBD*, 909. Saldarini explains, "The NT has two forms of the title, *rabbi* and *rabbouni* (in the best manuscripts), which probably reflect first-century Hebrew and Aramaic pronunciations" (909).

91. Boring, *Mark*, 306.

92. Elizabeth Struthers Malbon, "Fallible Followers: Women and Men in the Gospel of Mark," *Semeia* 28 (1983): 23–49, republished in Malbon, *In the Company of Jesus* (Louisville: Westminster John Knox, 2000), 41–69.

93. So also Broadhead: "the use of the Hebrew form of 'teacher' [i.e., rabbi or *rabbouni*] is most appropriate in the approach to Jerusalem" (*Teaching with Authority*, 160).

or misunderstanding as something that Jesus can also heal (8:24; 9:24; 10:51). What the suppliants say to or about Jesus is that they trust him as a source of willing power for health and wholeness. Suppliants believe they can experience the in-breaking of the rule of God in the healing power of the Markan Jesus.

What the Crowds/People/Some Say to or about Jesus

This grouping of characters is the least well defined of all those we will be considering. The designation "crowd" (Gk *ochlos*) occurs 38 times in Mark's Gospel, of which only one is linked with direct discourse (3:32).[94] Occasionally speakers in this group are signified as "some" (plural; Gk *tines*, 14:4, 57, 65) or "someone" (singular; Gk *tis*, 15:36) or "others" (Gk *alloi*, 6:15; 8:28). But most frequently the English translation must simply employ "they" (or substitute "people"), reflecting the third-person plural ending of the Greek verb. Sometimes there is a significant scholarly debate over the referent of the "they." By examining these anonymous instances of direct speech together, I am not suggesting that they reflect one composite "character." Rather, they reflect the range of responses to the Markan Jesus. For ease of discussion I will examine what crowds/people/some say to or about Jesus in three sets: (1) what is said in stories of *dynameis* ("mighty deeds"), either in questioning or in acclamation; (2) what is said, as a question or remark, that shows noncomprehension; and (3) what is said in the passion narrative—much of which could also be discussed with set 2, thus illustrating that the sets are simply heuristic.

WHAT IS SAID IN STORIES OF DYNAMEIS

The responses of those who witness and acclaim the Markan Jesus' healing power remind the implied audience of the responses of the chorus in Greek drama; groups speak in one voice to show the effect and emotional impact of the actions of the main character. The first instance is an especially rich example. The Markan narrator frames Jesus' initial encounter in the synagogue in Capernaum, which includes both teaching and an exorcism, with references to the response of those present. At the beginning, straightforward narration is used in a way that suggests later conflicts: "They were astounded at his teaching, for he taught them as one having authority, and not as the scribes" (1:22). At the end, narration is combined with direct discourse: "They were all amazed, and they

94. There is direct discourse between "someone from the crowd" (a suppliant) and Jesus at 9:17 and indirect discourse between the crowd and Pilate at 15:8. For an analysis of Markan statements about the crowd, in relation to both the disciples and the implied audience, see Elizabeth Struthers Malbon, "Disciples/Crowds/Whoever: Markan Characters and Readers," *NovT* 28 (1986): 104–30, republished in *The Composition of Mark's Gospel: Selected Studies from Novum Testamentum* (ed. David E. Orton; Leiden, The Netherlands: Brill, 1999), 144–70, and also in Malbon, *In the Company of Jesus*, 70–99.

kept on asking one another, 'What is this? A new teaching—with authority! He commands even the unclean spirits, and they obey him.' At once his fame began to spread throughout the surrounding region of Galilee" (1:27-28).

This combination of narration and direct discourse is found again, expressed more compactly, at the close of the healing of the paralytic: "[T]hey were all amazed and glorified God, saying, 'We have never seen anything like this!'" (2:12). (As noted above, here the narrator makes it clear that Jesus' power in healing is recognized as coming from God, a significant comment given the immediately preceding debate about the source of the forgiveness of sins.) The third and final instance of anonymous acclamation, by those who witness the healing of the deaf man with a speech impediment in the Decapolis, also combines narration and direct speech: "They were astounded beyond measure, saying, 'He has done everything well; he even makes the deaf to hear and the mute to speak'" (7:37). Although the area of the Decapolis, "Ten (Greek) Cities," is signaled in Mark's Gospel as a Gentile area, the response of these presumably Gentile onlookers echoes (for the implied audience) Jewish Scripture, Isaiah 35:5-6a: "Then the eyes of the blind shall be opened, and the ears of the deaf unstopped; then the lame shall leap like a deer, and the tongue of the speechless sing for joy." The Markan chorus reminds the implied audience of the foundational level of the plot: Jesus' healing power is a manifestation of the in-breaking of the rule (kingdom) of God and the defeat of the Satanic forces of evil, sickness, suffering, and death.

In addition to these three instances of anonymous acclamation of the *dynameis* ("mighty deeds") of the Markan Jesus, there are three instances of anonymous direct discourse that question this power in the course of a healing story. These bits of reported speech seem to function to enliven the narrator's story, especially when we consider that the first-century performer was expected to personify the characters' direct speech.[95] At 5:35, some people come from the house of Jairus to report, "Your daughter is dead. Why trouble the teacher any further?" These words increase the drama of the event and thus the power of the eventual healing/resuscitation.[96] The other two examples are part of the story of the healing of the boy with a spirit in chapter 9. When the Markan Jesus comes down from the mount of transfiguration with Peter, James, and John, they come upon an argument and a failed exorcism by the nine remaining disciples. Because the father of the boy, who becomes a suppliant to Jesus (and as such was considered above), is first identified in the text as "one from the crowd" (Gk *eis ek tou ochlou*, 9:17), his initial words are considered again

---

95. Shiner, *Proclaiming the Gospel*, 92–93.

96. Broadhead notes: "Significantly Jesus is addressed in the face of death as *didaskalos*, 'teacher' (5.35). This renews and reinforces the presentation of Jesus as teacher with authority, especially from 4.1-34 and 4.38, and this portrait impacts the presentation of Jesus as miracle worker in 5.21–6.1a" (*Teaching with Authority*, 105–6).

here: "Teacher, I brought you my son; he has a spirit that makes him unable to speak; and whenever it seizes him, it dashes him down; and he foams and grinds his teeth and becomes rigid; and I asked your disciples to cast it out, but they could not do so" (9:17-18). These words serve to increase not only the drama of Jesus' healing but also the drama of Jesus' struggling attempts to prepare his disciples to work in his absence, which is also reflected in the father's further speech as a suppliant (discussed above). The anonymous observers of the healing, unlike the father, continue in skepticism: "[M]ost of them said, 'He is dead'" (9:26). This was also the message of those from the house of Jairus: "Your daughter is dead. Why trouble the teacher any further?" (5:35). But like Jairus, the father of the boy also troubles Jesus further, and like those from the house of Jairus, the father refers to Jesus as Teacher.[97]

What Is Said That Shows Noncomprehension

The second set of discourses crowds/people/some say to or about Jesus to be examined here is what is said, as a question or remark, that shows noncomprehension and occurs prior to the passion narrative. In the middle story of the five controversy stories chiastically presented at 2:1–3:6, "they" come to Jesus and ask, "Why do John's disciples and the disciples of the Pharisees fast, but your disciples do not fast?" (2:18). Although the focus of these five stories is the growing level of controversy between the Markan Jesus and the Jewish authorities, the authorities are designated as the subject of this question and not as those who raise it.[98] What is not comprehended by the questioners is explained by the Markan Jesus in the metaphor of the bridegroom who will be taken away, a metaphor that reveals just how serious the conflict will become and is most clear to the implied audience.

The attribution of the second instance of anonymous direct speech that manifests noncomprehension has been much argued. The translation in the

97. The father of the possessed boy and those from Jairus' house are the only suppliants (9:17) or persons associated with suppliants (5:35) who refer to the Markan Jesus as teacher. Jesus is also called "Teacher" by his disciples (4:38; 9:38; 10:35; 13:1), by the rich man (10:17, 20), and by Jewish authorities (12:14, 19, 32); the final use of the term appears in the words of the Markan Jesus (14:14), but they are words he presents to the disciples to say to someone else. As we noted above, the first four occurrences of the term "teacher" in Mark are situated in settings of *dynameis*, "mighty deeds" (4:38; 5:35; 9:17, 38) and the next seven occur in settings of teaching (10:17, 20, 35; 12:14, 19, 32; 13:1).

98. Or at least the Jewish authorities are not *clearly* designated as the questioners. It would be possible to read the Greek "they" as referring to the Pharisees, the last mentioned noun: "Now John's disciples and the Pharisees were fasting; and they [the Pharisees] came and said to him, 'Why do John's disciples and the disciples of the Pharisees fast, but your disciples do not fast?'" (2:18). However, if this were the intended meaning, the question would more appropriately be worded, "Why do John's disciples and our disciples fast, but your disciples do not fast?" Presumably the Pharisees already know why their own disciples fast!

NRSV masks two complicated issues: "When his family heard it, they went out to restrain him, for people were saying, 'He has gone out of his mind'" (3:21). As Clifton Black gently notes, "The people mentioned in 3.31 [Jesus' mother and brothers] prompt the translation of an ambiguous phrase here as *his family*."[99] The ambiguous Greek phrase, *hoi par'autou*, means literally "those around him," and it is generally taken to mean family or extended family. However, it is worth noting that in the story just prior, Jesus had called his twelve disciples "to be with him" (3:14; see also 4:10, "those who were around him [Gk *hoi peri auton*] along with the twelve"). Certainly there is in 3:20-35 an intercalation, with encounters of persons close to Jesus framing an encounter with "the scribes who came down from Jerusalem" (3:22), so that a significant contrast in response to the Markan Jesus is highlighted. The ambiguous "they" follows the ambiguous "those around him": literally, "And hearing, those around him went out to restrain him, for they were saying, 'He is beside himself'" (3:21). Because "those around him" is the substantive immediately preceding the "they," presumably the "they" could refer to "those around him."[100] However, I think it equally likely that the "for" (Gk *gar*) clause, "for they were saying 'He has gone out of his mind,'" is explaining why "those around him" came to restrain him, because what they heard was that people were saying their Jesus was crazy. Whether they believed what they heard or not, Jesus would appear to be in danger and in need of support. A certain amount of ambiguity at the story level seems to be residual in this passage.[101] What is clear for the Markan narrative at the discourse level is that anyone who thinks Jesus is crazy does not comprehend what is going on. What is also clear (as we will discuss in the following chapter on what Jesus says) is that the Markan Jesus, "looking at those who sat around him (Gk *periblepsamenos tous peri auton kuklō kathēmenous*),"[102] says, "[W]hoever does the will of

99. Black, "Mark," *HCSB*, on 3:21.

100. This is probably not the case in the similar example above: "they" are probably not "the Pharisees" at 2:18; see note 98 above.

101. The taking of this episode as reflecting a historical antagonism with Jesus' biological family is over-reading the evidence. See John Dominic Crossan, "Mark and the Relatives of Jesus," *NovT* 15 (1973): 81–113, quotation from 113: "Mark has redacted the tradition in iii 21–35 and vi 1–6 and possibly in xiii [xv] 40, 47; xvi 1 as well so that there is severe opposition between Jesus and his relatives. . . . This Markan condemnation reflects the polemic of the Markan community against the Jerusalem mother-church not only as a doctrinal debate (against the disciples) but also as a jurisdictional debate (against the relatives) as well."

102. Those sitting around him are the crowd: "A crowd was sitting around him (Gk *peri auton*, 3:32)." In addition, verse 34 has three lexical references to "around": the prefix *peri* in the verb *periblepsamenos*, "looking around"; the preposition *peri* in the phrase *tous peri auton*, "those around him"; and the adverb *kuklō*, "around," modifying the verb sitting: *periblepsamenos tous peri auton kuklō kathēmenous*. The ambiguous phrase *hoi par'autou*, "those around him," in the opening frame works extremely well with these intensified references to "around" in the closing frame to emphasize the Markan Jesus' new way of understanding

God" is family (3:34-35), making less relevant for the implied audience the absolute determination of "those around him" in 3:21.

The third instance of anonymous direct speech that manifests noncomprehension also has to do with those close to Jesus, those in his hometown synagogue: "They said, 'Where did this man get all this? What is this wisdom that has been given to him? What deeds of power are being done by his hands! Is not this the carpenter, the son of Mary and brother of James and Joses and Judas and Simon, and are not his sisters here with us?'" (6:2b-3a). These words could be interpreted as an acclamation; in fact, the narrator's statement just before them seems to suggest that interpretation: "On the sabbath he began to teach in the synagogue, and many who heard him were astounded" (6:2a). The implied audience recalls that the people in the synagogue in Capernaum were similarly astounded (1:22). However, the "who does he think he is" interpretation is given weight by the narrator's comment immediately following "their" statement: "And they took offense at him" (6:3b). The final signal that this anonymous direct speech manifests noncomprehension is given in the Markan Jesus' concluding saying: "Prophets are not without honor, except in their hometown . . ." (6:4). The unclean spirit in the synagogue in Capernaum was able to hold together "Jesus of Nazareth" and "the Holy One of God" (1:24); the members of the synagogue in Jesus' hometown (Nazareth?) are not.

In fact, just after this scene in Jesus' hometown synagogue, three groups of "others" in succession say things about Jesus that illustrate their noncomprehension. All three instances involve what "others" say about who Jesus is, as a prelude to Herod's answer to this question (to be discussed below in relation to what Roman authorities say to or about Jesus) and the flashback narration of Herod's beheading of John the baptizer in 6:14-29. "They"[103] say that in Jesus, "John the baptizer has been raised from the dead; and for this reason these powers are at work in him" (6:14). "Others" say, "It is Elijah," and still others, "It is a prophet, like one of the prophets of old" (6:15). These three answers of "others," presented here in their own voices, are reported in the direct discourse of the disciples at 8:28. Because the narrator has already associated John the baptizer with Elijah in 1:2-8, the implied audience is able to recognize the error of the first two statements. Jesus is neither John the baptizer returned from the dead nor Elijah returned from heaven, although John has come in the role of Elijah as the herald of Jesus. However, the designation of Jesus as "a prophet" by these

---

family. In fact, "those around him" at 3:21 works better to prepare for the Markan Jesus' concluding saying to and about those "around him" than would a less ambiguous phrase, such as "his mother and his brothers" (cf. 3:31). In the same way, as is generally recognized, at 6:1 the phrase he "came to his hometown [Gk *patris*]" serves to prepare for the Markan Jesus' concluding saying about "prophets [who] are not without honor, except in their hometown [Gk *patris*] . . ." (6:4).

103. Instead of "They were" at 6:14b, some ancient authorities read "He was," presumably referring to Herod in 6:14a (NRSV translator's notes).

anonymous "others," although inadequate from the overall point of view of Mark's narrative, shows some comprehension.[104] In the immediately preceding episode of rejection in his hometown synagogue, the Markan Jesus has implicitly applied this designation to himself: "Prophets are not without honor, except in their hometown . . ." (6:4; cf. 11:32, where the narrator reports "all regarded John as truly a prophet"—as a worry of the chief priests, scribes, and elders; and 13:22, where Jesus warns about "false prophets" yet to come).

A final situation (outside the passion narrative) of anonymous direct speech that shows noncomprehension is that of the rich man who asks Jesus, "Good Teacher, what must I do to inherit eternal life?" (10:17). The question is not a bad one, although, as we will consider in the following chapter, the Markan Jesus corrects the address: "Why do you call me good? No one is good but God alone" (10:18). Jesus does not object to being addressed as "Teacher," and the rich man uses "Teacher" rather than "Good Teacher" in his second address to Jesus,[105] showing at least courtesy and perhaps some learning. However, when Jesus answers by listing the commandments and the rich man replies by defending himself—"Teacher, I have kept all these since my youth" (10:20)—the implied audience is beginning to wonder about his comprehension. In the end, it is not in the rich man's speech but in his silence in response to Jesus' final comment—"You lack one thing; go, sell what you own, and give the money to the poor . . ." (10:21)—that the rich man's noncomprehension is made loud and clear by the narrator: "When he heard this, he was shocked and went away grieving, for he had many possessions" (10:22).

What Is Said in the Passion Narrative

The above type of material, anonymous direct speech that shows noncomprehension, recurs in the passion narrative as well; I am simply discussing all anonymous direct speech in the passion narrative together for ease of explanation. (The first type, what is said in stories of *dynameis*, "mighty deeds," does not, of course, recur in the passion narrative.) Two noncomprehending statements about Jesus are connected again with "Elijah." From the cross, the Markan Jesus cries out in Aramaic: "'*Eloi, Eloi, lema sabachthani?*' which means, 'My God, my God, why have you forsaken me?'" (15:34). However, "some (Gk *tines*, plural) of the bystanders" seem to hear "Eloi" as "Elijah," saying, "Listen, he is calling for Elijah" (15:35), and "someone (Gk *tis*, singular)" says, "Wait, let us

---

104. Richard A. Horsley, *Hearing the Whole Story: The Politics of Plot in Mark's Gospel* (Louisville: Westminster John Knox, 2001), argues that "Mark's story is full of, indeed permeated with, images, references, actions, and teachings that suggest that it is fully informed by the prophetic script that was so prominent among the people in first-century Palestine" (247; see esp. 231–53).

105. For a listing of other references to the Markan Jesus as "teacher," see note 97 above.

see whether Elijah will come to take him down" (15:36). The implied audience knows these hearers to be wrong linguistically and theologically. Jesus is not calling Elijah because "Elijah has [already] come, and they did to him whatever they pleased" (9:13, Jesus' speech to Peter, James, and John), and Jesus is taking up his cross as he has asked others to be prepared to do (8:34). The misguided speech of these anonymous characters serves to confirm the implied audience in its correct convictions.

Even more misguided from the overall point of view of the narrative is the statement of "some" (Gk *tines*) who, as the narrator asserts, "gave false testimony against him, saying, 'We heard him say, "I will destroy this temple that is made with hands, and in three days I will build another, not made with hands"'" (14:57b-58). Although some scholars have argued that this statement, while clearly not true of what the Markan Jesus is reported to say in Mark's Gospel, is nevertheless, and ironically, true at the level of the implied author (or, as is more likely for those scholars, "the Markan redactor"). Such scholars argue, largely on the basis of non-Markan texts, that the community of Jesus' followers constitutes the new temple "not made with hands."[106] On the other hand, I have argued elsewhere that both the immediate Markan context (both "false testimony" and "did not agree" are stated twice in 14:56-57, 59, framing the statement) and the overall Markan antitemple theme work against such an interpretation.[107] In Mark, these false witnesses are simply wrong, as are the passers-by who echo them when Jesus is on the cross: "Aha! You who would destroy the temple and build it in three days, save yourself, and come down from the cross!" (15:29b-30). The narrator comments that the passers-by "derided [or blasphemed] him, shaking their heads" (15:29a), steering the narratee to a realization that their direct speech is incorrect from the overall point of view of Mark's Gospel.

Several other instances of anonymous direct speech in the passion narrative are not so entirely "wrong" about Jesus but manifest noncomprehension because their narrative contexts seem more open to ironic interpretation of something about them that is "right." As "some" (Gk *tines*) say to the bound and blind-

106. See, e.g., John R. Donahue, S.J., *Are You the Christ? The Trial Narrative in the Gospel of Mark* (SBLDS 10; Missoula, Mont.: Scholars Press for SBL, 1973), esp. 108–9; Donahue, "Temple, Trial, and Royal Christology (Mark 14:53-65)," in *The Passion in Mark: Studies on Mark 14–16* (ed. Werner H. Kelber; Philadelphia: Fortress, 1976), 61–79, see esp. 69–71; Donald Juel, *Messiah and Temple: The Trial of Jesus in the Gospel of Mark* (SBLDS 31; Missoula, Mont.: Scholars Press for SBL, 1977).

107. See Malbon, *Narrative Space*, esp. 112, 124–25, 134–36, 194 n. 61. "The Markan Jesus rejects the institution of the temple, and it may be that the Markan narrator rejects the metaphor of the temple as well. . . . The surpassing of the temple 'made with hands,' a phrase employed with reference to idols in the Septuagint, is mandated by the logic of Mark's narrative, but the new reality is suggested by new images" (*Narrative Space*, 112), including "the house."

folded Jesus, "Prophesy!" (14:65), Peter comes onto the scene and denies Jesus (14:66-72), just as Jesus had prophesied he would (14:30). The narrator has given the narratee specific reason to hear their cry as ironically true, as a manifestation of noncomprehension at the story level and different comprehension at the discourse level. As Pilate tries to convince the crowd to call for the release of Jesus, "they" shout back, "Crucify him!" (15:13). And when Pilate questions the crowd again, "they" shout "all the more, 'Crucify him!'" (15:14). Although clearly the crowd has, at this point, come under the influence of and become one with the authorities who are Jesus' opponents, their cry manifests—again for the implied audience—the all-too-common noncomprehension of the inevitability of persecution and even death for one who lives the life the Markan Jesus chose.

"Some" (Gk *tines*) at the final meal of Jesus and his disciples in the house of Simon the leper in Bethany show noncomprehension in questioning the actions of the woman who anoints Jesus' head: "Why was the ointment wasted in this way? For this ointment could have been sold for more than three hundred denarii and the money given to the poor" (14:4b-5). Again the narrator has set the narratee up to hear their question negatively by the way of introducing it: "But some were there who said to one another in anger . . ." (14:4a). This statement of "some" apparently in the company of the disciples is comparable to statements the disciples make elsewhere, as we will see below.

The final instance of anonymous direct speech in the passion narrative to be discussed is more difficult to interpret, partly because the narrator's clues are complex. As Jesus approaches Jerusalem, he is greeted by a crowd.[108] The narrator says, "Then those who went ahead and those who followed were shouting, 'Hosanna! Blessed is he who comes in the name of the Lord! Blessed is the coming kingdom of our ancestor David! Hosanna in the highest heaven!'" (11:9-10). Is this an acclamation?[109] The narrator's word "follow" is a discipleship word in Mark's Gospel; it has positive connotations and is used of disciples and other followers—although even followers who make acclamations (e.g., Peter), especially in the second half of Mark's Gospel, do often misunderstand. Since the opening biblical quotation ("Prepare the way of the Lord," 1:3), the words

---

108. The term "crowd" (Gk *ochlos*) does not appear in this pericope; however, the terms "many" (Gk *polloi*) and "others" (Gk *alloi*) do occur in 11:8, presumably describing the same characters as those who speak in 11:9-10. However, as they speak, the characters are also labeled "those who went ahead and those who followed," which also links them with other "followers" of the Markan Jesus in some way.

109. As Robbins admits, "This is not an explicitly clear and forcefully presented acclamation of Jesus as Son of David." However, Robbins moves away from this point in his further assertion: "It is rather a declaration of the Davidic character of this action in the context of Christian expectation of the coming kingdom of God. For this reason the expression is noticeably un-Jewish and lacks in this context specific political overtones" ("Healing of Blind Bartimaeus," 240).

of the voice from heaven to Jesus ("my Son," 1:11), and Jesus' opening words ("The time is fulfilled, and the kingdom of God has come near," 1:15), Jesus has been portrayed as the one most often to speak of "the Lord" (usually quoting Scripture); thus "one who comes in the name of the Lord" (11:9) seems an apt description of Jesus. However, the crowd's call for a blessing on "the coming kingdom of our ancestor [Gk father] David" (11:10) is problematic since the Markan Jesus continually speaks of the coming and arrival of the kingdom not of David but of God and, although regarding David as a positive model (2:25), refers to and calls God, not David, "father" (13:32; 14:36). (What Jesus says is discussed in the following two chapters.) Is the crowd depicted as not hearing (literally) or not comprehending what the Markan Jesus has said about God and the kingdom of God?[110]

As we noted above, the ambiguity of the crowd's cry of blessing on "the coming kingdom of our ancestor [father] David" at Jesus' entry into Jerusalem— often noted, but not by Mark, as the city of David[111]—is anticipated by the ambiguity of the cry of Bartimaeus to Jesus as "Son of David" (10:47-48) in the immediately preceding scene outside Jericho.[112] As Boring notes, the crowd's acclamation "is in continuity with Bartimaeus's repeated identification of Jesus as 'Son of David.' . . . Though the kingdom of God proclaimed and lived out by Jesus is not the Davidic kingdom of popular expectation, Jesus does not cor-

---

110. For details of the interpretation of "our father David" at 11:10 by Hahn and others with similar views—and my critique—see the excursus at the end of my essay, "'Son of David,'" 183–84. Ahearne-Kroll senses a tension in Mark's Gospel at the point of the story of the entry into Jerusalem (*Psalms of Lament*, 144–55): a tension between "the eschatological coming of a Davidic messiah to restore Jewish independence [that] was part of the cultural landscape at the time of Mark" (147) and the narrative fact that "the evangelist also strongly conditions [this expectation] by evoking the image of the king as gentle and making Jesus' procession end in an anticlimactic way" (154). Ahearne-Kroll does not delve deeply into the crowd's phrase, "the coming kingdom of our father David," in its overall Markan context, but he does carry on an engaging dialogue with the extensive scholarly commentary on the royal imagery in the entry story in its cultural background. In fact, this background may overwhelm the Markan narrative foreground, where it may be that the Markan tension with the "Davidic" tradition is even stronger than Ahearne-Kroll suggests.

111. For example, Broadhead: "The use of son of David [by Bartimaeus] is especially proper in view of Jesus' approach to Jerusalem, the city of David" (*Teaching with Authority*, 160).

112. So also Achtemeier, "'And He Followed Him,'" 130: "Whatever the origin of these verses [11:9-10], they are notable not for the clarity with which they affirm Jesus' Davidic sonship, but rather for the unusual ambiguity with which they refer to any such relationship between Jesus and David." Yet Yarbro Collins' comment is more typical and illustrates how the usual reading of Bartimaeus' cry and "the context" (including royal imagery) is read into the crowd's cry at 11:9-10: "Although here Jesus is not hailed explicitly as king or as son of David, the context suggests that he is both. Such an inference is supported by the address of Jesus by Bartimaeus as son of David" (*Mark*, 520, cf. 581).

rect the crowd, just as he had not corrected Bartimaeus."[113] In fact, neither the Markan Jesus nor the narrator responds to Bartimaeus' application of "Son of David" to Jesus or to the crowd's acclamation. The Markan Jesus uses the term "son of David" once in an accusatory question, "How can the scribes say that the Christ [NRSV Messiah] is the son of David?" (12:35); his argument against their declaration will be considered in the following chapter on what Jesus says in response. Here we must conclude that the crowds' words about Jesus at his entry into Jerusalem are, within Mark's narrative, ambiguous at best.[114] Perhaps the implied audience is not to be so surprised when, before long, the crowd says quite different words about Jesus.

What can we conclude about what these diverse and anonymous speakers say to and about Jesus? Some acclaim his mighty deeds of healing, although some also question them. Others show their noncomprehension of Jesus' words and actions because those words and actions challenge their own expectations. Still others go further and wrongly represent him as being someone other than he is or as saying something other than he said. All add to the complex layering that is Markan projected christology, that is, narrative christology based on what others say to and about Jesus. The portrait the anonymous crowds or unnamed persons paint of the Markan Jesus in their direct speech to and about him is of one who is powerful in word and deed, always challenging, often questioned, and often misunderstood. It is a portrait not unlike that painted by the smaller group of named characters who follow the Markan Jesus.

What the Disciples Say to and about Jesus

The disciples as a group, including individuals and subgroupings, are given more occasions of direct speech than any other character group; among all the characters, only the Markan Jesus speaks more frequently.[115] Although Mark's

113. Boring, *Mark*, 316.

114. Although most scholars do not concur with this reading of "Son of David" and "the coming kingdom of our father David" as ambiguous, Yarbro Collins is representative of (and clearly reviews the arguments of) many who recognize that the Markan Jesus' entry into Jerusalem is *not* triumphal but (to use my words) ambiguous at best: "The lack of a welcome of Jesus by the leaders of the people and the anticlimactic ending of the account of his entry into Jerusalem are hints that the role Jesus will play in the rest of the narrative is not the one most often associated with the messianic son of David among Jews of the time" (*Mark*, 581–82). It appears to me that the nonresponse of the Markan Jesus and the Markan narrator to "Son of David" and "the coming kingdom of our father David" are earlier hints.

115. In counting incidences of direct speech to or about Jesus, I have, for convenience, followed the NRSV's translation and punctuation, counting as a separate incidence any direct speech that is separated by other text. Although the numbers resulting from such a procedure with a contemporary translation provide some sense of proportion, they must not

Gospel is Jesus' story, Jesus' story is thoroughly intertwined with the story of
the disciples. They accompany him throughout most of the narrative, and the
women followers are there at the cross and the tomb even after the twelve men
have fled. We will examine the direct speech of these disciples/followers in three
categories: (1) the disciples ask Jesus a question, (2) the disciples answer a question Jesus asks them, (3) the disciples make a statement to or about Jesus. Often
it is "the disciples" as a group character who are asking, answering, or stating.
Sometimes an individual disciple or a small group of them gives voice to the
question, answer, or statement. What characterizes the entire group also characterizes individuals within it to a greater or lesser extent: Peter is a frequent
spokesman, but he is fairly typical; Judas' betrayal is different in degree but not
in kind. The frequency and wide distribution of the disciples' direct speech is a
sign of the importance of discipleship to Mark's story of Jesus' proclamation of
the in-breaking rule of God.[116]

The Disciples Ask Jesus a Question

Near the beginning of the narrative, the narrator reports four events in rapid
succession: Jesus' baptism, his temptation, his initial proclamation of the good
news of the kingdom (1:14-15), and his calling of his first disciples (1:16-20).

---

be taken too seriously; lacking quotation marks, direct speech in the Greek text can be less
distinct from indirect speech. The results, in descending order of frequency, are as follows:

> 32 occurrences of direct speech by disciples (including the women at 16:3) to or about
>   Jesus
> 23 by crowds/people/some
> 20 by Jewish authorities
> 11 by suppliants
> 9 by Roman authorities
> 5 by unclean spirits/demons
> 2 by (God)
> 1 by John the baptizer

The occurrences of direct speech by the disciples are also the most widely distributed
throughout the narrative. The direct speech of John the baptizer and the unclean spirits/
demons occurs early; much of the direct speech of the Jewish authorities and almost all of
that of the Roman authorities occurs late. The suppliants speak in the first ten chapters only,
but the anonymous speakers of the crowds and the people are, like the disciples, given voice
throughout the narrative.

116. The published dissertation of Suzanne Watts Henderson is "organized around a set
of passages that feature the disciples as prominent players in the gospel drama" and based on
the observation that "the overarching claim of God's coming kingdom lends striking unity
to the gospel's relationship between Christology and discipleship from beginning to end"
(*Christology and Discipleship in the Gospel of Mark* [SNTSMS 135; Cambridge: Cambridge
University Press, 2006], quotations from 20 and 23).

Because the disciples are accompanying Jesus from the beginning and assisting him in various ways, they have numerous occasions to ask him questions. Some of these questions are quite practical, involving the details of carrying out Jesus' ministry; others are paradigmatic, suggesting deeper questions that potential followers in the implied audience must also confront. The first questions are asked by the disciples as a group, speaking as one, and occur in situations of Jesus' *dynameis*, "mighty deeds." In a boat on the Sea of Galilee during a "great windstorm," the disciples wake the calmly sleeping Jesus to ask, "Teacher, do you not care that we are perishing?" (4:38).[117] "Teacher" is the expected form of address for disciples to use, but the form of the question is unexpectedly desperate, even harsh (compare the more respectful version in Matt 8:25). Clearly the disciples do not share Jesus' calm trust in God's providence, but they do assume Jesus can do something practical about their plight. Indeed the disciples' question instigates Jesus' action in calming the sea. At the end of this story, the disciples ask another question, this time of themselves but about Jesus: "Who then is this, that even the wind and the sea obey him?" (4:41). No one within the narrative answers this rhetorical question; it seems addressed outward to the implied audience as a paradigmatic question of faith.

At 5:30-31 the disciples answer Jesus' question, "Who touched my clothes?" by asking their own practical question: "You see the crowd pressing in on you; how can you say, 'Who touched me?'" The exchange draws attention to something new in the story: Jesus' healing power is available to others even without his prior knowledge! Only the hemorrhaging woman was daring enough to assume that. At 6:37 the disciples seem to think that Jesus is too daring in his assumptions about their access to such power. When told by Jesus to give the crowd of five thousand something to eat, the disciples ask, "Are we to go and buy two hundred denarii worth of bread, and give it to them to eat?" (6:37). Again, the disciples are concerned with pragmatic, logistical matters, and this concern persists in the face of the hungry four thousand: "How can one feed these people with bread here in the desert?" (8:4). But the Markan Jesus' persistence matches that of the disciples; twice he feeds the crowds, and both times he relies on the disciples to distribute the bread and fish to all.

In chapter 9 the disciples are divided into two groups: the three, Peter, James, and John, who go up the mountain with Jesus and experience Jesus' transfiguration and the appearance of Elijah and Moses, and the nine, who

---

117. As Broadhead observes, "Significantly, the term by which the disciples address Jesus in their fear is 'teacher' (*didaskale* in 4.38). This direct address (vocative) recalls the extensive portrait of Jesus in Mk 1.1–3.7a as one who teaches with authority. At the same time the title evokes the teaching activity of 4.1-34. Thus, the miracle activity is preceded by the naming of Jesus as teacher, and it is as teacher that the disciples ask Jesus to save them. . . . Thus, the story infuses the character portrait of Jesus the teacher with a new level of authority: Jesus is the one in whom the creative power of Yahweh is now at work. Through this power Jesus will call forth the new community of faith" (*Teaching with Authority*, 95–96).

remain and are confronted with an exorcism they cannot perform. Each group
asks Jesus a question. After Moses and Elijah disappear the three want to know,
"Why do the scribes say that Elijah must come first?" (9:11). Jesus' answer suggests, at least to the implied audience if not to the three disciples, that Elijah has
come in the person of John the baptizer and has suffered "as it is written about
him" (9:13). After Jesus successfully exorcises the unclean spirit from the boy
the nine want to know, "Why could we not cast it out?" (9:28). Jesus' answer to
the nine—and more—is direct: "This kind can come out only through prayer"
(9:29). Both prayer and readiness to suffer on behalf of others are part of the
training of disciples—and all followers.

Further instruction is offered in chapter 10. At 10:26 the disciples ask
themselves a question about what Jesus has just said concerning "[h]ow hard
it will be for those who have wealth to enter the kingdom of God!" (10:23):
"Then who can be saved?" (10:26). The question might well be one shared with
the implied audience in a paradigmatic sense. The Markan Jesus answers it for
followers both inside and outside the narrative: "For mortals it is impossible,
but not for God; for God all things are possible" (10:27). At 13:4, four of the
disciples (Peter, James, John, and Andrew) request instruction about the events
of the close of the age: "Tell us, when will this be, and what will be the sign that
all these things are about to be accomplished?" Jesus' answer, his eschatological
discourse, closes by addressing not just these four but all: "And what I say to
you I say to all: Keep awake" (13:37)—a paradigmatic reminder for the Markan
implied audience.

At 14:12 the disciples speak as a group once again and return to a pragmatic,
logistical question: "Where do you want us to go and make the preparations
for you to eat the Passover?" Jesus' reply, and its immediate fulfillment in the
narrative, confirms the Markan Jesus' knowledge of what the near future holds.
While eating that meal, the Markan Jesus makes a statement about that future
so serious that it leads the twelve to ask him the same question individually:
"Jesus said, 'Truly I tell you, one of you will betray me, one who is eating with
me.' They began to be distressed and to say to him one after another, 'Surely, not
I?'" (14:18b-19). This is the last question given in the direct speech of the twelve
male disciples; the Markan Jesus has knowledge of what their near future holds
too: desertion, denial, betrayal. Only at the cross does the narrator report retro-
spectively that there had been women followers of Jesus all along (15:41) and
that some of them, including Mary Magdalene, and Mary the mother of James
the younger and of Joses, and Salome, are still there, though "looking on from a
distance" (15:40). The next day on their way to the tomb, these women followers
ask themselves a question that is essentially about Jesus: "Who will roll away the
stone for us from the entrance to the tomb?" (16:3). Their question seems to be
a practical, logistical one at the level of the story, but, at the level of the discourse,
it is difficult to imagine a member of the implied audience who does not already
know that the story is about to move way beyond such logistics. Rather, their
question serves to underlie the drama of the empty tomb, of the resurrection.

What these questions in the direct speech of the disciples suggest about them is that they are Jesus' nearly constant assistants and apprentices—frequently helpful, but far from perfect. More to the current point—projected christology—what these questions in the direct speech of the disciples suggest about the Markan Jesus is that Jesus desires, chooses, and trains assistants and apprentices—coworkers—in the work of proclaiming the in-breaking rule of God, experiences their misunderstandings and even failures in the task, and perseveres.

THE DISCIPLES ANSWER A QUESTION JESUS ASKS THEM

In addition to asking Jesus questions, the disciples, as a group and as individuals, are also asked questions by Jesus. Some of their questions are seemingly quite practical; some of Jesus' questions are seemingly just informational. For example, Jesus asks the disciples a number of questions having to do with counting. As he prepares to feed the five thousand, the Markan Jesus asks the disciples, "How many loaves have you? Go and see" (6:38). They count and answer, "Five, and two fish" (6:38). In preparation for the feeding of the four thousand, Jesus asks, "How many loaves do you have?" and they answer, "Seven" (8:5). Apparently the disciples count the baskets of leftovers in both feedings as well (the numbers are reported by the narrator) because when Jesus asks them about this later in the boat they answer, for the five thousand, "Twelve," and, for the four thousand, "Seven" (8:19, 20). The disciples are good at simple numbers. However, Jesus' final question in the boat remains unanswered in the story: "Do you not yet understand?" (8:21). The implied audience has been given enough clues to understand that the numbers of leftover baskets full of food suggest that Jesus' good news of the in-breaking of the rule of God is sufficient for sharing not only with Jews (12) but also with Gentiles (7).[118] Counting has its deeper significance.

Other answers the disciples give to Jesus' questions have to do with his role in relation to the in-breaking rule of God, and their deeper significance is immediately obvious. First, Jesus asks his disciples, "Who do people say that I am?" (8:27). To this, the disciples answer with one voice, although reflecting the multiple voices of the people, "John and Baptist; and others, Elijah; and still others, one of the prophets" (8:28). The implied audience knows the disciples to be faithful reporters of these views because the views were voiced by the people earlier in the narrative (6:14-15). And, by this point in the narrative, the implied audience is also quite clear about the inadequacy of these responses. Then Jesus asks the disciples, "But who do you say that I am?" (8:29). Peter serves as spokesperson in answering, "You are the Christ [NRSV Messiah]" (8:29). This is equally clearly a significant answer. The narrator uses the "title" Christ in the title to the work: "The beginning of the gospel [NRSV good news] of Jesus

___

118. The feeding stories and their number symbolism were discussed in relation to enacted christology in chapter 1 above.

Christ [NRSV Messiah], the Son of God" (1:1). Neither the narrator nor any character has used it since that time, until Peter's answer. It will be voiced again by the high priest at Jesus' hearing.

What Peter means by naming Jesus as the Christ is not so clear. Perhaps the implied audience is to think back over what Jesus has done in the first half of Mark's narrative—primarily teach and heal. Is the Christ, the longed-for Messiah, primarily a powerful teacher and healer? Is this what Peter confesses? But the implied audience might also remember that, even in the first half of Mark's narrative, Jesus has been involved in controversy with the Jewish establishment. How will that impact Jesus as the Christ? Because Peter's confession of Jesus as "Christ" agrees with that of the narrator (in 1:1), the implied audience accepts it as fitting, unlike the people's designations of Jesus as "John the Baptist" or "Elijah" or "one of the prophets" (although see 6:4 and the discussion above concerning Jesus' implied self-identification as a prophet). Nevertheless, the implied audience cannot help noticing Jesus' immediate response to Peter's confession as reported by the narrator: "And he sternly ordered them not to tell anyone about him" (8:30). Similar orders were given earlier to unclean spirits and demons who knew that Jesus was "of God." There is something important to understand here, but it must not be understood too quickly.

This narrative scene is followed immediately by the Markan Jesus' first passion prediction. And, as the narrator points out, Jesus says "all this quite openly" (8:32). Peter's response, taking Jesus aside and rebuking him for talking about such suffering, reveals to the implied audience the limits of Peter's view of the role of the Christ. The seriousness of this misunderstanding is reinforced by Jesus' response; in the clear presence of all his disciples, Jesus rebukes Peter with strong words: "Get behind me, Satan! For you are setting your mind not on divine things but on human things" (8:33). It is no wonder that many Markan scholars make this short series of scenes (including the symbolically rich two-stage healing of blindness just before Peter's confession) the center of their discussion of Markan christology. It seems natural to focus christology on the designation "Christ." Although "Christ" is only applied to Jesus four times in Mark's Gospel,[119] each placement is a critical point: 1:1, the title; 8:29, Peter's confession; 14:61, Jesus' "trial" before the high priest; and 15:32, the mocking of Jesus by the chief priests and scribes at his crucifixion. Without denying the importance of this crucial element of Markan christology, I wish to point out that it is still one layer of a multilayered narrative christology, and what the narrator and Peter say about Jesus must be heard in relation to what Jesus says in response and instead, as well as in relation to what Jesus does and what others say and do in relation to him.

119. The two times the Markan Jesus speaks the term "Christ," 9:41 and 13:21-22, neither in direct reference to himself, are discussed later as part of deflected christology in chapter 3.

Following the aftermath of Peter's answer, "You are the Christ," the Markan Jesus dares not give the disciples any more questions to answer. What these answers to Jesus' questions in the direct speech of the disciples suggest about them is that they can understand on a first level (how many loaves? how many baskets full? who is Jesus said to be? who is Jesus?), but they are still missing something Jesus is trying to teach them. In terms of projected christology, what these answers to Jesus' questions in the direct speech of the disciples suggest about the Markan Jesus is that Jesus is trying to communicate on a deeper level, to push cultural expectations (Jewish "boundaries"; messianic expectations).

THE DISCIPLES MAKE A STATEMENT TO OR ABOUT JESUS

When the disciples answer Jesus' questions, they always get the first level right, although the deeper level seems up to the implied audience. When the disciples ask Jesus questions, they are usually being helpful, but they sometimes betray their inability to share Jesus' confidence in God's power and providence and Jesus' goals in proclaiming God's rule. When the disciples make statements to or about Jesus, their fallibility shows up the most clearly.

The first direct speech of a disciple is a statement of Simon, the first disciple called by the Markan Jesus. The morning after the narrative's first eventful day in Capernaum, while Jesus is in a deserted place praying, "Simon and his companions" hunt for him; the literal sense of the Greek verb is "track him down" (1:36). Simon says to Jesus, "Everyone is searching for you" (1:37). The words are practical in that Simon is concerned with the logistics of the already gathering crowds eager for Jesus' healing and teaching. Yet a sensitive audience—or a repeating audience—can already detect the beginnings of misunderstanding on the part of the disciples. Although Jesus returns from the deserted place after Simon's arrival, Jesus does not return to Capernaum but goes "on to the neighboring towns . . . throughout Galilee" (1:38-39).

The next statement made by the disciples to Jesus is made by all of them, also in a deserted place: "This is a deserted place, and the hour is now very late; send them [the five thousand] away so that they may go into the surrounding country and villages and buy something for themselves to eat" (6:35b-36). The disciples are unprepared for Jesus' response, based on his confidence in the power and providence of God's in-breaking rule: "You give them something to eat" (6:37). Bread, the frequent subject of Jesus' questions and the disciples' answers, is also the theme of the next statement the disciples make—to themselves but about Jesus' warning about "the yeast of the Pharisees and the yeast of Herod" (8:15): "It is because we have no bread" (8:16). However, the narrator presents an inside view of Jesus "becoming aware" of what they were talking about (8:17), which leads to the review of the numbers of baskets full of leftovers ("Twelve," "Seven"), concluding with Jesus' question, "Do you not yet understand?" (8:21). Not only do the disciples not answer that question, but as a group they do not speak in direct discourse again.

Peter, however, does continue as their spokesperson. When Peter, James, and John witness Jesus' transfiguration with Elijah and Moses, Peter says, "Rabbi, it is good for us to be here; let us make three dwellings, one for you, one for Moses, and one for Elijah" (9:5). In case the narratee might think Peter's response somehow appropriate, the narrator adds, "[for (Gk *gar*)] he did not know what to say, for they were terrified" (9:6). What the voice from the cloud then tells Peter and the other two disciples to do is not to build a dwelling for Jesus but to "listen to him!" (9:7). Later it would seem that the disciple John does not know what to say or to do either, for he says, "Teacher, we saw someone casting out demons in your name, and we tried to stop him, because he was not following us" (9:38). Jesus corrects John's action, saying, rather, "Whoever is not against us is for us" (9:40). Later still Peter's eagerness continues. After Jesus points out to the disciples "[h]ow hard it will be for those who have wealth to enter the kingdom of God!" (10:23), Peter points out to Jesus, "Look, we have left everything and followed you" (10:28). And Jesus' patience continues, assuring Peter and the disciples (and the implied audience) that all who have left family and property will receive family and property "a hundredfold now in this age . . . — with persecutions—and in the age to come eternal life. But many who are first will be last, and the last will be first" (10:30-31).

But are all the disciples listening? Not much later in the narrative, and just after the second passion prediction, James and John have an encounter with the Markan Jesus that involves three incidences of their direct speech—two statements to Jesus and one answer to his question. "Teacher, we want you to do for us whatever we ask of you" (10:35). "Grant us to sit, one at your right hand and one at your left, in your glory" (10:37). They are not asking for positions of power and prestige in this age—perhaps they have learned that much—but in the age to come. Jesus does not immediately upbraid them, although asserting that "[y]ou do not know what you are asking"; Jesus asks them, "Are you able to drink the cup that I drink, or be baptized with the baptism that I am baptized with?" (10:38). James and John answer confidently, "We are able" (10:39), although some members of the implied audience may be less confident about them. But the Markan Jesus does insist that assigning positions of power in the age to come is "not mine to grant, but it is for those for whom it has been prepared" (10:40)—prepared, that is, by God. Of course, "drinking the cup" and "baptism" are figures for suffering and death, and those who end up, not so many scenes later, at Jesus' right hand and at his left are the two insurrectionists who are crucified with him.

Next Peter takes another turn at speaking, with a statement showing surprise at a mighty deed of Jesus: "Rabbi, look! The fig tree that you cursed has withered" (11:21). This is, of course, one of many mighty deeds of Jesus witnessed by Peter. Jesus answers not just Peter but "them," the disciples: "Have faith in God" (11:22), a recurrent refrain. Later "one of his disciples" also expresses wonder to Jesus—not for one of his mighty deeds but for the grandeur of the temple: "Look, Teacher, what large stones and what large buildings!"

(13:1). Both of these disciples employ "Look" and a respectful address, "Rabbi" or "Teacher," but both miss the point. The Markan Jesus is not so surprised at the withering of the fig tree he cursed (a figure of the temple), and he is not so impressed with the temple itself, knowing that "[n]ot one stone will be left here upon another; all will be thrown down" (13:2).

Finally Peter, the first disciple chosen and the only one to confess Jesus as the Christ, becomes the first to deny Jesus, despite his two direct statements that he will never do so: "Even though all become deserters, I will not" (14:29). "Even though I must die with you, I will not deny you" (14:31). And Judas, in the passion narrative always labeled "one of the twelve" (14:10, 20, 43), betrays Jesus not with a sword but with a sign of friendship, speaking about Jesus to the chief priest, scribes, and elders: "The one I will kiss is the man; arrest him and lead him away under guard" (14:44). The last word of any disciple to Jesus is the form of address for Jesus used only by Peter and Judas in Mark's Gospel, Judas' one word of betrayal: "Rabbi!" (14:45).[120] Situational irony hangs heavy over the passion narrative. The disciples, who rightfully call Jesus "Rabbi" (9:5; 11:21; 14:45) and "Teacher" (4:38; 9:38; 10:35; 13:1; cf. 14:14), do not follow their master's teaching to the end. The one disciple who identifies Jesus as "Christ" (8:29) is unable to follow his way of life to the death.

What these statements to or about Jesus in the direct speech of the disciples suggest about them is that they are fallible in the face of the challenges of discipleship, especially the challenges involving serving those with less power and enduring persecution from those with more power. The implied audience, of course, hears not just what the disciples say to or about Jesus but what the narrator says about the disciples. The narrator reports that the disciples leave their occupations and their families to follow Jesus; they are with him extensively; they hear his teaching—sometimes addressed especially to them (parables, the way section, the eschatological discourse); they are sent out by Jesus to cast out demons, which they do successfully; they help distribute bread; they go with Jesus to Jerusalem. But they have their limits; they misunderstand Jesus' convictions and demands and, in the end, abandon, deny, and betray him. The Markan portrait of the disciples is complex, but our focus here is not the disciples and how they are portrayed but how Jesus is portrayed in the disciples' direct speech to or about him. How does what the disciples say contribute to a narrative christology? In terms of projected christology, the direct speech of the disciples to or about Jesus illustrates that the Markan Jesus realizes that what he is asking is extremely demanding and that followers are fallible. In what the Markan Jesus says to or about the disciples, it is clear that he does not give up on them (13:9-13; 14:28; cf. 16:7).

120. As was discussed above, Bartimaeus, after being healed of his blindness, uses a related form of the address rabbi: *"Rabbouni"* ("my rabbi," 10:51).

What the Jewish Authorities Say to and about Jesus

Although the Markan Jesus' disciples are indeed fallible followers, they are followers nevertheless; the Jewish authorities, on the other hand, are generally portrayed as opponents. It is worth reminding ourselves that the Jewish authorities
whom we are considering are fictive characters in Mark's narrative, not "real"
Jewish leaders in the first or any subsequent century. The relationship between
first-century history and Mark's narrative with regard to the portrayal of the
Jewish authorities is complicated and beyond the scope of the present work. As
part of a literary study, I am concentrating on the portrayal of characters, and, at
present, I am concerned with how what the Jewish authorities say to and about
Jesus adds to the characterization of the Markan Jesus. For purposes of analysis I am grouping together all the direct speech assigned in Mark's Gospel to
scribes (2:7; 3:22, 30); scribes of the Pharisees (2:16); Pharisees (2:24; 10:2, 4);
Jairus—a leader of the synagogue (5:23); Pharisees and scribes (7:5); chief
priests, scribes, and elders (11:28, 31-33); Pharisees and Herodians (12:14-
15); Sadducees (12:19-23); one of the scribes (12:28, 32-33); chief priests and
scribes (14:2; 15:32); and the high priest (14:60, 61, 63-64). In general, the
Pharisees are most active in the first half of the Gospel, and the chief priests,
scribes, and elders are most active in the passion narrative, with the scribes serving as a linking group active periodically but throughout the narrative.[121]

It is this linking group, the scribes, that first represents the Jewish authorities in direct speech to the Markan Jesus. However, even before the first appearance of scribes as characters, the narrator has set up a contrast: The people
in the synagogue in Capernaum were "astounded at [Jesus'] teaching, for he
taught them as one having authority, and not as the scribes" (1:22). The issue is
clearly authority, and Jesus and the scribes are going to be opposed. The narrator takes care to credit only "some of the scribes" (2:6) with the first opposing
comment, which is reported by the narrator as an inside (and, again, negative)
view of what the scribes are "questioning in their hearts" (2:6): "Why does this
fellow speak in this way? It is blasphemy! Who can forgive sins but God alone?"
(2:7).[122] (What the Markan Jesus, who has his own inside view of the scribes,
says is examined in the following chapter.)

Of the five stories of controversy between the Markan Jesus and the Jewish
authorities presented chiastically in 2:1–3:6, the first (just mentioned), second,

---

121. For a literary analysis of the Markan characterization of the Jewish leaders, see
Elizabeth Struthers Malbon, "The Jewish Leaders in the Gospel of Mark: A Literary Study of
Marcan Characterization," *JBL* 108 (1989): 259–81, republished in Malbon, *In the Company
of Jesus*, 131–65.

122. As Broadhead notes, "This conflict initiates the charge of blasphemy which will
eventually lead to Jesus' death (14.64). In this manner the miracle story of 2.1-13 provides a
proleptic view of the ultimate destiny of Jesus" (*Teaching with Authority*, 78).

and fourth include direct speech from the Jewish authorities. The second Jewish authorities designated as speakers are "the scribes of the Pharisees" (2:16), a unique phrase, with some ancient manuscripts reporting the more usual "the scribes and the Pharisees." Here the speech of the Jewish authorities is directed not to Jesus but to his disciples about him: "Why does he eat with tax collectors and sinners?" (2:16). Those who question Jesus in the third controversy story are an ambiguous "they" (NRSV "people"; 2:18), but the questioners of the fourth one are the Pharisees, with words about the disciples directed to Jesus: "Look, why are they doing what is not lawful on the sabbath?" (2:24). In the fifth and final controversy story of this set, no direct speech is presented for the Jewish authorities, but the narrator reports even more aggressive behavior, opening with an inside view ("They watched him to see whether he would cure him on the sabbath, so that they might accuse him"; 3:2) and closing with a statement of a plot-turning conspiracy ("The Pharisees went out and immediately conspired with the Herodians against him, how to destroy him"; 3:6). The subjects of controversy—healing and proclamation of forgiveness, eating with sinners, not fasting, plucking grain on the Sabbath, and healing on the Sabbath—are issues internal to Judaism. The Markan Jesus and the Markan Jewish authorities, in good rabbinical fashion, are arguing about how the tradition should be lived out. Neither the narrator nor the implied author attempts neutrality in the debate.

As the five controversy stories manifest not only a synchronic chiastic structure but also increasing dramatic conflict diachronically,[123] so the next two incidences of direct speech by Jewish authorities continue to heighten the conflict between them and the Markan Jesus. The speakers are no longer just the presumably local, Galilean scribes of chapter 2 but "the scribes who came down from Jerusalem," who say about Jesus (to his family?), "He has Beelzebul, and by the ruler of the demons he casts out demons" (3:22). The narrator encircles Jesus' response to their charge with their initial Beelzebul comment and this final one, narrated slightly retroactively: "for they had said, 'He has an unclean spirit'" (3:30). The unforgivable sin involves confusing the two powers opposed in a cosmic struggle—God and Satan—by linking the Markan Jesus with the wrong one.

The next Jewish authority figure given the opportunity to speak is exceptional in at least two ways: he is named—"one of the leaders of the synagogue named Jairus" (5:22)—and he is a suppliant who shows faith in Jesus' healing power. His story is intercalated with the story of another faithful suppliant, the hemorrhaging woman, as was discussed earlier in relation to what suppliants say to or about Jesus. Jairus begs Jesus "repeatedly," "My little daughter is at the point of death. Come and lay your hands on her, so that she may be made well,

---

123. Joanna Dewey, *Markan Public Debate: Literary Technique, Concentric Structure, and Theology in Mark 2:1–3:6* (SBLDS 48; Chico, Calif.: Scholars Press for SBL, 1980).

and live" (5:23). To discuss Jairus only as a suppliant and not as a Jewish leader, as some commentators do, is to reinforce a stereotype Mark's narrative seems to challenge. If any positive response toward the Markan Jesus removes a Jewish leader from the category of "the Jewish leaders," it is no wonder that the resulting portrayal of "the Jewish leaders" is entirely negative! However, in Mark's narrative, Jairus is presented as the first of three Jewish leaders who challenge the stereotypical conception of the Jewish authorities as opponents.

After the exceptional story of Jairus, the narrator returns to the theme of opposition by the Jewish authorities, linking "some of the scribes who had come from Jerusalem" (7:1; cf. 3:22) with the Pharisees, whose traditions of washing hands and foods and implements are explained parenthetically to the narratees, either on the assumption that these traditions are unfamiliar or in order to make them and their practitioners appear strange. The Pharisees and the scribes ask the Markan Jesus directly about the behavior of his disciples, "Why do your disciples not live according to the tradition of the elders, but eat with defiled hands?" (7:5). Somewhat later in the narrative, it is the Pharisees alone who question Jesus directly about his interpretation of tradition: "Is it lawful for a man to divorce his wife?" (10:2). The Markan narrator makes it known that their intention is "to test" Jesus (10:2; cf. 8:11, with no direct speech); the Markan Jesus asks the Pharisees to make known their interpretation first, and they respond, "Moses allowed a man to write a certificate of dismissal and to divorce her" (10:4). As will be discussed in the following chapter, Jesus argues against their traditional interpretation by returning to an even earlier tradition. Again, Mark's Gospel presents an intra-Jewish conflict between Jesus and the Jewish authorities on issues of the interpretation of Scripture and tradition for determining practice.

With Jesus' entry into Jerusalem, the conflict with the Jewish authorities deepens and comes to focus more on the chief priests, scribes, and elders whose power is centered in the Jerusalem temple. Here another collection of controversy stories is presented, comparable to the collection at 2:1–3:6. As Jesus is "walking in the temple" (11:27), various groups of Jewish authorities come to him asking questions, and, even though they are trying to trick him, Jesus inevitably tricks them instead in this contest of wit as well as interpretation (11:27–12:44). Just as authority was clearly manifest as the issue at the first mention of any Jewish leaders (1:22), so authority is underlined as the key issue as the narrative moves toward its climax in Jerusalem. The chief priests, scribes, and elders ask the Markan Jesus directly, "By what authority are you doing these things? Who gave you this authority to do them?" (11:28). When Jesus insists that they answer a question about the source of the authority of John the baptizer first, they are trapped into pragmatic silence, as the narrator illustrates by reporting their argument among themselves: "'If we say, "From heaven," he will say, "Why then did you not believe him?" But shall we say, "Of human origin"?'—they were afraid of the crowd, for all regarded John as truly a prophet" (11:31-32). Caught between two unthinkable options, the chief priests, scribes,

and elders avoid answering, saying to Jesus, "We do not know" (11:33), allow-
ing Jesus thereby to avoid answering their original question about the source of
his authority.

After the Markan Jesus tells the parable of the wicked tenants, which the
narrator notes "they realized that he had told . . . against them" (12:12), a second
group of Jewish authorities approaches Jesus, perhaps "sent" by the chief priests,
scribes, and elders: "Then they sent to him some Pharisees and some Herodians
to trap him in what he said" (12:13). The narrator's note about entrapment
may remind the narratee that this paired group was linked once before—in
a conspiracy to bring about Jesus' death (3:6). Certainly the narrator's comment
here makes it unlikely that the narratees will consider the flattery of the Pharisees and Herodians sincere: "Teacher, we know that you are sincere, and show
deference to no one; for you do not regard people with partiality, but teach the
way of God in accordance with truth. Is it lawful to pay taxes to the emperor, or
not? Should we pay them, or should we not?" (12:14-15). The implied audience
has been given plenty of clues to realize that, although the Jewish authorities
speak sarcastically in this case, the content of their speech is in fact true of the
Markan Jesus. Jesus preaches to, heals, and feeds both men and women, both
Jews and Gentiles, both rich and poor, always teaching the way of God as God's
rule breaks into history. The Markan Jesus springs the trap the Pharisees and
Herodians have set to get him into trouble with either the Roman authorities
or the people, and, as we will consider in the following chapter, refocuses attention on God.

The Sadducees are the next group of Jewish authorities on the scene, introduced by the narrator with reference not to their motives but to their beliefs:
"[s]ome Sadducees, who say there is no resurrection" (12:18). Of course, because the Markan Jesus has been teaching the disciples about his resurrection,
this belief puts them in opposition to Jesus. The Sadducees ask Jesus a long and
complicated hypothetical question:

> Teacher, Moses wrote for us that if a man's brother dies, leaving a wife but no
> child, the man shall marry the widow and raise up children for his brother. There
> were seven brothers; the first married and, when he died, left no children; and the
> second married the widow and died, leaving no children; and the third likewise;
> none of the seven left children. Last of all the woman herself died. In the resurrec-
> tion whose wife will she be? For the seven had married her (12:19-23).

Not surprisingly, the Markan Jesus' response refocuses attention on God as God
of the living.

The Pharisees and the Herodians call Jesus "Teacher" (12:14), as do the
Sadducees (12:19), and, as the series of conflict stories between Jesus and the
Jewish authorities in the Jerusalem temple comes to a close, so does "one of
the scribes" (12:28, 32). "Teacher" is a form address also used by the disciples
(4:38; 9:38; 10:35; 13:1; cf. 14:14), suppliants (5:35; 9:17), and the rich man
(10:17, 20), as well as by representatives of the Jewish authorities (12:14,

19, 32), so its use by a character in itself does not make clear the relationship to the Markan Jesus. It is by his additional direct speech and what the narrator and Jesus say about him that "one of the scribes" comes to be seen, like Jairus before him and Joseph of Arimathea after him, as an exceptional Jewish leader. The question this scribe poses to Jesus is one "extensively debated among the rabbis," the question about "first principles":[124] "Which commandment is the first of all?" (12:28). When Jesus responds by citing the *Shema* ("Hear, O Israel"; Deut 6:4-5), the scribe replies, "You are right, Teacher; you have truly said that 'he is one, and besides him there is no other'; and 'to love him with all the heart, and with all the understanding, and with all the strength,' and 'to love one's neighbor as oneself,'—this is much more important than all whole burnt-offerings and sacrifices" (12:32-33). The mutual commendation that concludes this encounter with one of the scribes and the Teacher ("You are right"; 12:32/"You are not far from the kingdom of God"; 12:34b) appears as a reversal of the earlier mutual rebuking of one of the disciples and his Teacher (Peter rebukes Jesus/Jesus rebukes Peter at 8:32-33). Not only the Markan Jesus but also the Markan narrator designates this scribe as exceptional: "Jesus saw that he answered wisely" (12:34a; cf. 12:28). (The third exceptional Jewish leader, Joseph of Arimathea, is marked only by the narrator [15:43] because he appears after Jesus has died, but Joseph has no direct speech.) After this encounter with the exceptional scribe, the narrator notes, "no one dared to ask him any question" (12:34c).

The next Jewish authority figures to speak are the chief priests and scribes, whose motives and words (apparently among themselves) are reported by the narrator: "The chief priests and the scribes were looking for a way to arrest Jesus by stealth and kill him; for they said, 'Not during the festival, or there may be a riot among the people'" (14:1b-2). The Jewish authorities are portrayed as relentless in their pursuit of Jesus but also as having to hesitate at times due to logistical arrangements. The plot moves forward bit by bit but not always smoothly as one character group has to deal with another. Fear of the crowds slows down the Jewish authorities' death plot against the Markan Jesus (11:18; 14:1-2); Judas' betrayal speeds it up (14:10-11, 43).

Finally it is the turn of the leading Jewish authority to speak, the high priest. Here the conflict between Jesus and the Jewish authorities reaches its climax in the questions of the high priest and the Markan Jesus' response. Jesus' silence at the hearing is depicted as frustrating for the high priest: "Have you no answer? What is it that they testify against you?" (14:60). "Are you the Christ [NRSV Messiah], the Son of the Blessed One?" (14:61). The use of the term "the Blessed One" as a circumlocution for God seems appropriate in the high priest's mouth. What seems surprising is words in the mouth of the Markan Jesus in place of the silence he has maintained up until this point. The

124. Black, "Mark," *HCSB*, on 12:28.

Markan Jesus' reply both affirms ("I am") and decenters ("You will see the Son of Man seated at the right hand of the Power"; 14:62) the high priest's question. The implications of what Jesus says in response and instead will be considered in the following two chapters.

The high priest's reference to "Christ" is only the third application of the term to the Markan Jesus, the first being the narrator's title (1:1) and the second being Peter's confession (8:29). At 1:1 the narratee cannot be sure of the narrator's meaning of "Christ" when applied to Jesus; at 8:29 and following, the narratee learns that Peter does not understand fully what the narrator and the Markan Jesus mean by the term "Christ."[125] At 14:61, the narratee realizes that the conflict of authority turns on the meaning of "Christ" when applied to Jesus. Although there was no unified Jewish expectation of a messiah (Christ) in first-century Judaism, suffering and death were not part of any of the various expectations. Mark's Gospel is dealing with this conflict of expectation and interpretation in a most dramatic way in the direct speech of the high priest and the Markan Jesus. The high priest's final words are about Jesus and to his fellow Jewish authorities: "Why do we still need witnesses: You have heard his blasphemy! What is your decision?" (14:63).

But the final direct speech of the Jewish authorities, and the final use of the term "Christ" in Mark's Gospel, is not in the question of the high priest at Jesus' hearing but in the jeering of the chief priests and scribes at Jesus' crucifixion: "In the same way the chief priests, along with the scribes, were also mocking him among themselves and saying, 'He saved others; he cannot save himself. Let the Christ [NRSV Messiah], the King of Israel, come down from the cross now, so that we may see and believe'" (15:32). The Jewish authorities here appropriately use the term "King of Israel" rather than the Roman authorities' term "King of the Jews," just as the high priest appropriately uses the Jewish circumlocution for God in the phrase "Son of the Blessed One." But it is the term "Christ," shared by the high priest and the chief priests and scribes (as well as by the narrator and Peter) that arrests the attention of the implied audience—as well as Markan scholars exploring christology.

As many readers and most commentators have noted, the passion narrative of Mark's Gospel is rich with irony. If Jesus were to save himself from the cross as the Jewish authorities taunt, he would not be the Christ that Mark's Gospel proclaims him to be and would not be following the teaching he has given his followers ("If any want to become my followers, let them . . . take up their cross"; 8:34). If Jesus were to remain silent in response to the high priest's question, "Are you the Christ?," he might not take up his cross at all. Irony involves two levels of presentation or interpretation in conflict in some way. Irony

---

125. The two times the Markan Jesus speaks the term "Christ," 9:41 and 13:21-22, neither in direct reference to himself, are discussed later as part of deflected christology in chapter 3.

is *confirmed* when the text reveals that the implied audience is in a position to perceive both levels. Irony *may be present* in places where the text makes no such revelation, but, in that case, the burden of proof is on the interpreter to provide appropriate extratextual evidence from the first-century world suggesting the implied audience's external knowledge, evidence that is also not incompatible with the intratextual evidence.[126] Mark's narrative certainly gives its implied audience enough information to know that, whatever the term "Christ" means when applied to Jesus, it is in conflict with any view that involves only power as it is known among traditional authorities, those who dominate others on the basis of their authority.

What the Jewish authorities say to or about Jesus in direct speech illustrates the conflict of interpretation and practice between them and the Markan Jesus. Various Jewish authorities confront Jesus, voicing disagreements with his interpretations of Law and his departures from some traditional practices. The controversies between Jesus and the Jewish authorities in the temple (11:27–12:44) "show Jesus' agreement with dominant Jewish views on taxes, resurrection, and the basic demand of God, unlike Mark 2:1–3:6, which shows Jesus' difference from dominant Jewish perspectives in regard to Sabbath and sin, healing and eating."[127] From both what the Jewish authorities say and what the Markan Jesus says, it is clear that the debates are within Jewish tradition, not between "Christianity" and "Judaism," both anachronistic categories for Mark's Gospel. The Markan narrator encourages an overall negative attitude toward the Jewish authorities from the beginning, especially by pointing out their less than honorable motives in their dealings with Jesus.[128] However, the Markan narrator and

126. Irony has been much discussed in literary theory and criticism, typically by way of examples from eighteenth- and nineteenth-century British and American novels with little resemblance to Mark's Gospel. Although consideration of these competing conceptualizations and categorizations of irony are far beyond the scope of my work, the first two elements of D. C. Muecke's list of three essential formal requirements of irony suggest what I am assuming about irony here. Irony must have (1) two levels, a lower and an upper level, (2) which are opposed in some way (contradiction, incongruity, or incompatibility). See *The Compass of Irony* (London: Methuen, 1969, 1980), 19–20. Concerning the two levels, Muecke notes that "[t]he upper level need not be *presented* by the ironist; it need only be evoked by him or be present in the mind of the observer" (19). It is this elusive "evocation" and "mind of the observer" that interpreters of Markan irony nearly two thousand years after the fact debate. Muecke's third essential element is "innocence," which will be discussed below in reference to the statements of the centurion and Pilate. On irony in Mark as founded on the reader knowing more than the characters, see Jerry Camery-Hoggatt, *Irony in Mark's Gospel: Text and Subtext* (SNTSMS 72: Cambridge: Cambridge University Press, 1992).

127. Joanna Dewey and Elizabeth Struthers Malbon, "Mark," in *Theological Bible Commentary* (ed. Gail R. O'Day and David L. Petersen; Louisville: Westminster John Knox, 2009), 311–24, quotation from 321.

128. The Markan narrator comments on some element of the Jewish authorities at these points, many of which have been commented on briefly above: negatively—1:22; 2:6; 3:6;

the Markan Jesus concur that there are significant exceptions to the general rule that the Jewish authorities take on the role of the Markan Jesus' opponents. But our focus here is not the Jewish authorities and how they are portrayed but how Jesus is portrayed in the Jewish authorities' direct speech to or about him. In terms of projected christology, the direct speech of the Jewish authorities to or about Jesus illustrates that the Markan Jesus challenges the status quo of his Jewish tradition from within that tradition and that the resulting conflict with the traditional authorities escalates to a life-threatening confrontation—only to become death-dealing when expanded to include the Roman authorities.

What the Roman Authorities Say to or about Jesus

The final direct speech we will examine is from the Roman authorities, the final group to take an active role in Mark's narrative, primarily in the passion story. Prior to the passion narrative, the only Roman authority figure to appear or to speak is Herod. Although at least partly "Jewish," Herod is referred to in Mark's Gospel as "King" (6:14; cf. 6:22, 25, 26, 27), an appointed position in the Roman imperium, and thus Herod serves as a representative of the Roman authorities. Herod is the Roman official whose action, not carefully planned but under the influence of others—his wife Herodias and her daughter—brings about the death of John the baptizer. In a parallel way, Pilate is the Roman official whose action, not carefully planned but under the influence of others—the Jewish authorities and the crowd—brings about the death of Jesus.[129] John's story is consistently proleptic of Jesus' story in Mark's Gospel. Herod's one line of direct speech, made in response to his hearing about the activity of Jesus, connects the two stories: "John, whom I beheaded, has been raised" (6:16). Herod is ironically wrong in his assumption that Jesus is John resurrected; it is Jesus who will be resurrected, not John. Herod's statement leads into the flashback of John's beheading, which the narrator tells in between the sending out and the return of Jesus' disciples to preach and cast out demons. Jesus' disciples go out proclaiming, as Jesus did before them, as John did before him. John was handed over and killed, as Jesus will be after him, as the disciples will be in their turn. Herod is indeed right about the close connection between John and Jesus, although wrong about the resurrection.

7:3-4; 8:11, 31; 9:14; 10:2; 11:18; 12:12, 13; 14:1-2, 10, 43, 55; 15:10, 31; positively—12:28, 34; 15:43.

129. Paul L. Danove, *The Rhetoric of the Characterization of God, Jesus, and Jesus' Disciples in the Gospel of Mark* (JSNTSup 290; New York: T&T Clark, 2005), 66 n. 20, sees a link, based on shared vocabulary, between Herod and the crowd listening to the Markan Jesus in the temple: "Repetition of listen with delight . . . directly aligns Herod and the crowd; for, just as Herod listens to John the Baptist with delight (6:20) before ordering his execution (6:27), the crowd listens to Jesus with delight (12:37) before calling for his crucifixion (15:13; cf. 15:11)."

Pilate is the dominant representative of the Roman authorities in Mark's Gospel, with five incidences of direct speech, all questions. Pilate's first two questions are addressed to Jesus: "Are you the King of the Jews?" (15:2). "Have you no answer? See how many charges they [the Jewish authorities] bring against you" (15:4). To the first question, the Markan Jesus gives a begrudging answer: "You say so" (15:2). In response to the second question, Jesus returns to silence, "so that Pilate was amazed" (15:5). Pilate's second question echoes the high priest's first question to Jesus: "Have you no answer? What is it that they testify against you?" (14:60), to which Jesus had maintained silence. Pilate's three other questions are about Jesus, addressed to the crowd, but the crowd that, as the narrator notes, was "stirred up" by the chief priests (15:11). "Do you want me to release for you the King of the Jews?" (15:9). "Then what do you wish me to do with the man you call the King of the Jews?" (15:12). "Why, what evil has he done?" (15:14). At the story level of Mark's narrative, Pilate is wrong to refer to Jesus as "the man you call the King of the Jews" (15:12) because no one in the narrative uses that term until he applies it himself. Herod is called King by the narrator at 6:14 (cf. 6:22, 25, 26, 27); followers are warned of a future time when they will stand before kings (13:9); and the chief priests and scribes later mock the crucified Jesus as "the King of Israel" (15:32), but only Pilate and the soldiers under his command call Jesus "King of the Jews" in Mark's Gospel. Perhaps the clause "the man you call" was added later; it is lacking in some ancient manuscripts.[130]

Many Markan commentators remark that this "title" applies to Jesus ironically; Jesus really is "King of the Jews," although Pilate is speaking sarcastically, not confessionally. It is not clear to me that Mark's narrative actually supports the thesis that Jesus is portrayed ironically as "King of the Jews." Despite the movement toward lessening the "blame" of the Roman authorities in order to increase the "blame" of the Jewish authorities (a movement that gains speed in the Gospels of Matthew, Luke, and John), Pilate, who introduces and influences others to apply the phrase "King of the Jews," is not a reliable character in Mark's narrative but clearly and negatively portrayed as an opponent of Jesus.

130. Metzger comments: "Although there is strong external attestation for the omission of *hon legete* [the one you call], Matthew's reading *ton legomenon Christon* [the one who is called Christ] (Mt 27.22) seems to presuppose the originality of *hon legete* in Mark. On the other hand, however, the insertion of the clause may be regarded as a scribal amelioration, introduced in order to throw the onus for the use of the title 'The King of the Jews' upon the high priests. . . . On balance the Committee judged that the least unsatisfactory solution was to include the words in the text, but to enclose them within square brackets to indicate doubt that they have a right to stand there" (*Textual Commentary*, 118). The NRSV does not use square brackets in this instance, but notes that "other ancient authorities lack *the man you call*" (on 15:12). If the clause "the man you call" were original to Mark's narrative, it is odd that it is applied by Pilate only after he has already called Jesus "King of the Jews" twice, and in the presence of the chief priests, without any such qualification (15:2, 9).

Of course, a nonreliable character could still speak words that, ironically, turn out to be true in the hearing of the implied audience. This is certainly the case with the words of some of the Pharisees and some of the Herodians to Jesus: "[Y]ou do not regard people with partiality, but teach the way of God in accordance with truth" (12:14), as discussed above. But the impartiality of the Markan Jesus, especially toward those generally marginalized—the poor, the sick, Gentiles—has been demonstrated by the actions of Jesus within the narrative.

The same is not the case with "King of the Jews." It is noteworthy, for example, that the narrator does not pick up this term as he does Christ and Son of God (1:1). Pilate's use is echoed only by the soldiers ("Hail, King of the Jews," 15:18) under his command and the inscription ("The King of the Jews," 15:26) placed on the cross on his orders. The Markan Jesus speaks consistently and insistently about the kingdom of God, that is, the ruling activity of God as king (to be examined in chapter 4 below in relation to refracted christology), leaving no room for considering himself as king. Thus if "King of the Jews" is to be applied in a positive way to Jesus, it must be seen as in tension with what the Markan Jesus says (as are "Christ" and "Son of God" to some extent, on which see the following chapter, on deflected christology) as well as not confirmed by the narrator (as "Christ" and "Son of God" are) or by (God)—as "Son" is. That would be ironic, but it is also unlikely in the Markan narrative.

I make this argument against the majority of scholars, many following such fine interpreters as Donald Juel, Frank Matera, and John Donahue, from whom I also have learned a great deal.[131] Through their careful exegesis of scriptural references and allusions in Mark, they have made plain a pattern of "royal imagery" in the passion story of Mark—from the entry on a colt to the purple robe and the crown (of thorns). Certainly such imagery is present in the narrative. However, this imagery is then interpreted, to use narrative critical terms—even though some of the scholars named here were employing redaction critical terms in their foundational studies—as evidence of the implied author's affirmation of the Markan Jesus as, ironically, "king." But this is not the only possible interpretation of "royal imagery" in the passion narrative, and there is other, contrary "evidence" in the Markan narrative as well.

Certainly the characters who call Jesus "king" (Pilate, 15:2, 9, 12, cf. 26, the inscription; Roman soldiers, 15:18; chief priests and scribes, 15:32) do so in derision.[132] In addition, trouble with kings links John the Baptist, who was handed over to King Herod and beheaded (6:14-29), Jesus, who is handed over

---

131. Donald Juel, *Messiah and Temple: The Trial of Jesus in the Gospel of Mark*; Frank J. Matera, *The Kingship of Jesus: Composition and Theology in Mark 15* (SBLDS 66; Chico, Calif.: Scholars Press for SBL, 1982); Donahue, *Are You the Christ? The Trial Narrative in the Gospel of Mark*; Donahue, "Temple, Trial, and Royal Christology (Mark 14:53-65)."

132. See also Horsley, *Hearing the Whole Story*, 250–53, who understands their "sarcastic mockery" against the background of the Markan story's "extremely unclear" relation to the messianic-kingly "script" in contrast to the "prominence" of the prophetic "script" (151).

to Pilate and crucified as "The King of the Jews" (15:26), and the followers of Jesus, who are told to expect to be hauled up before kings (13:9). "King" does not have positive connotations in Mark's Gospel. Abraham Smith notes that "[i]n a Gospel otherwise saturated with irony, it is not difficult to see Mark mocking Herod Antipas as a pretentious king" and argues persuasively that Herod is portrayed as a type of "the tyrant" and that verbal echoes between Herod and Pilate would lead the audience to apply this type to Pilate as well.[133] Smith also concludes, with special reference to 10:42-44, that "the *exposure* of tyranny in Herod was not solely a critique of a brutal 'king' but a didactic challenge to Jesus' disciples within and beyond the narrative to avoid becoming tyrants among themselves."[134] I concur completely. However, Smith still accepts the usual "royal messianism" argument: "Given the Gospel's previous and eventual portrayal of Jesus as a king (e.g., in allusions to Ps. 2 in Mark 1:11 and in the passion account), it seems clear that this Gospel, like some of the other literature of the period, envisioned two types of kingship: one, false and tyrannical; another, true and beneficial toward others. For Mark, the two types were vividly dramatized in Herod Antipas and Jesus, respectively."[135] I am arguing that in Mark's Gospel, other terms—not "king"—are found to characterize this leadership that is beneficial toward others. In addition, Smith himself notes that there are strong parallels between John the baptizer (the prophet or philosopher) in relation to Herod (the king or tyrant) and Jesus in relation to Pilate. I would argue that Smith's own evidence suggests that Jesus is presented as the type of the prophet/philosopher in relation to Pilate, the type of the king/tyrant, rather than Jesus being presented as the "good king" over against the "bad king" Herod. The leadership the Markan Jesus teaches and manifests does not fit into the type of the "king," and the metaphor is not redeemed.

Equally certainly, neither the narrator nor the Markan Jesus nor any other character ever applies the term "king" to Jesus in a positive way. All interpreters of "royal messianism" agree that the Markan Jesus challenges the conventional view of kingship.[136] But could it be that the term "king" is not simply revised and applied to the Markan Jesus but rather rejected as an appropriate designation at all? Perhaps there is a deeper irony to this imagery, not that the Markan

133. Abraham Smith, "Tyranny Exposed," 266.

134. Smith, "Tyranny Exposed," 287.

135. Smith, "Tyranny Exposed," 268 n. 35.

136. For example, Joel Marcus, *The Way of the Lord*, understands the revised "kingship" of Mark's Gospel, in the wake of the Jewish war, to be apocalyptic and heavenly rather than political and earthly. I am not so comfortable with these categories as oppositional. Stephen Ahearne-Kroll, *Psalms of Lament*, argues, on the basis of the evocation of four Psalms of Lament (LXX 21, 40, 41–42, 68) in the Markan passion narrative, that Jesus is depicted as Davidic in his suffering, rather than Davidic in the culturally presupposed sense of a strong, militaristic king; I will discuss Ahearne-Kroll's work briefly in the following chapter, in reference to the Markan Jesus' argument concerning the "Christ" and the "Son of David."

Jesus is a "king" of a different sort but that the concept of human "kingship" has, in Mark's good news of Jesus Christ, Son of God, and in Jesus' good news of the in-breaking *king*dom of God, been subverted entirely. Perhaps the Markan Gospel is as antikingship in its orientation as the antimonarchical strand of tradition in the David stories in the Hebrew Bible![137] As we will see in the following chapter, a similar argument can be made about "Son of David" on the basis of what the Markan Jesus says in response to what others say. Thus the sarcasm of the use of the term "King of the Jews" by Pilate and his soldiers is obvious within the Markan narrative, but not so its ironic, but somehow "true," application to Jesus.

Muecke asserts that "there is in irony an element of 'innocence'; either a victim is confidently unaware of the very possibility of there being an upper level or point of view that invalidates his own, or an ironist pretends not to be aware of it. There is one exception to this; in sarcasm or in very overt irony the ironist does not pretend to be unaware of his real meaning and his victim is immediately aware of it."[138] That description fits the Markan narrative at the level of the story: Pilate is not pretending to be ironic about "King of the Jews," and the Markan Jesus is quite aware of that fact; thus sarcasm is the appropriate label for Pilate's speech. At the discourse level of the narrative, some interpreters regard Pilate as the innocent victim of irony who does not understand the "true" meaning of his words, unlike the implied audience who knows Jesus is the "true" king. I am not convinced that this presumed "upper level" meaning (Jesus really is king) is actually implied. Rather, I think an even more radical meaning (the kingship model is rejected in Jesus' story) is implied in the overall Markan narrative.

The irony of the statement of the centurion is a different—and quite complex—matter: "Truly this man was Son of God [NRSV God's Son]" (15:39). Whitney Shiner presents an impressive argument, based on careful research of Hellenistic literature and a sensitive narrative critical reading of Mark's Gospel, that the centurion's "pronouncement is intentionally ambiguous and is used by Mark to allow his audience to hear a deeper meaning while leaving the veil of secrecy, an essential part of Mark's religious world view, intact."[139]

---

137. In an analogous way I noted years ago that, although some interpreters comment on the believing community as the "new temple" in Mark, they rely on extra-Markan sources to help establish their claim because the Markan Gospel actually suggests no such positive imagery for "temple" but only for "house" (Malbon, *Narrative Space*, 112, 124–25, 194 n. 61). I suspect this is because, historically, Mark's Gospel is reacting to the recent destruction of the temple by the Romans. Such an event might have an equally devastating effect on hopes for and positive imagery of "king" and "Son of David." In Mark's Gospel, all hopes focus on the "kingdom of God" and the "Son of God"/"Son of Humanity."

138. Muecke, *Compass of Irony*, 20.

139. Whitney T. Shiner, "The Ambiguous Pronouncement of the Centurion and the Shrouding of Meaning in Mark," *JSNT* 78 (2000): 3–22, quotation from 22. Shiner draws

Within the Markan narrative, the centurion, exceptional among all the other Roman authorities portrayed, uses language overlapping with the narrator as well as with transcendent characters—the voice from heaven (God) and unclean spirits/demons: Son of God. The centurion's use of the phrase "Son of God" without the definite article ("the") echoes the phrase that serves in the narrator's title (1:1), and the splitting of the heavens (1:10) at the baptism just before the voice (of God) first speaks is echoed in the splitting of the curtain of the temple (15:38) just before the centurion speaks. However, Shiner argues that "[t]hose listening to the Gospel [the real audience?] would assume that the centurion identifies Jesus as a son of god, on a Hellenistic model, rather than the Son of God, the proper Markan confession."[140]

In addition, as is often commented upon, the centurion is the first—indeed the only—human being to apply the phrase "Son of God" to Jesus in Mark's narrative, and he does so only as Jesus dies, confirming for the implied audience the hard teachings of Jesus on the inevitability of his persecution and death. Thus for the implied audience, the situation in which such a comment comes from a Roman soldier rather than from a disciple is clearly ironic, whether the centurion is understood to make it sincerely or sarcastically, because such an identification, with positive value, has already become a part of the vocabulary of the implied audience. Shiner seems to strike a balance between the alternatives of interpreting the centurion as sarcastic or sincere: the centurion is mistaken; yet "the comment is positive . . . but continues the irony through the gap between the Christian understanding of the comment and that of the centurion in the narrative world."[141] The buildup to the crucifixion begins early in Mark's

---

evidence from the syntax of the centurion's pronouncement, the presumed motivation listeners would imagine for the centurion's statement—basically the miraculous signs surrounding Jesus' death, the common figure of the reluctant executioner in martyrological literature, and the relationship of the pronouncement to the understanding of miracles and parabolic reality throughout Mark's Gospel. At some points Shiner seems to me to imagine an audience trying to round out this quite flat character in a way that I cannot so easily imagine—even coming close to committing the intentional fallacy with regard to the centurion! I am assuming that by this point in the narrative the implied audience has come to realize that its own perception is the point of the narrative. I do agree with Shiner's overall conclusion that "Mark fills the death scene with puns and irony to remind the listeners of the parabolic nature of reality" (21).

140. Shiner, "Ambiguous Pronouncement," 4.

141. Shiner, "Ambiguous Pronouncement," 4, 15. Perhaps this irony is analogous to the situation Geert Van Oyen ("Intercalation and Irony in the Gospel of Mark," in *The Four Gospels 1992: Festschrift Frans Neirynck* [ed. F. Van Segbroeck et al.; Leuven, Belgium: Leuven University Press, 1992], vol. 2, 949–74, see 972–74) persuasively describes at Mark 14:53-72, with some scholars interpreting the denial of Peter with a negative or polemic view on the disciples (the "Weeden-Kelber axis") and other scholars interpreting the scene with a more moderate view of the disciples (the "Tannehill-Malbon axis"). For a reader in the first group, not identifying with the disciples, the irony of Peter's denial is clear, but the

Gospel; the crucifixion scene is the climax. As the turning point was marked by the disciple Peter's confession of Jesus as the "Christ" (seriously incomplete prior to Jesus' passion, as Jesus' acceptance of the term only when in the custody of the high priest indicates), so the climax is marked by the Gentile centurion's recognition of Jesus as "Son of God." Both phrases of the narrative's title (1:1) are echoed for the implied audience—that is, those with ears to hear.

However, it seems to me that the implied audience is cued to interpret the centurion's statement as sincere rather than sarcastic by its fit into a pattern of words and actions by exceptional authority figures in Mark's narrative. Exceptional Jewish leaders include Jairus, a synagogue leader (5:21-24, 35-43), the scribe who asks about the "first" commandment (12:28-34), and Joseph of Arimathea (15:42-47), each of whom has been discussed above. The centurion is the sole exceptional character among the Roman authorities, but he too serves to make a noticeable crack in what would otherwise be a monolithic stereotype. Like Joseph of Arimathea, "a respected member of the [Jewish] council" (15:43), the centurion, a responsible, if low-ranking, member of the Roman imperium, endangers his station by his statement: if the dying Jesus is "Son of God," the Roman emperor is not.[142]

According to Muecke, irony contains an element of "innocence."[143] Either the mistaken centurion of Shiner's interpretation or the sarcastic centurion of some others' interpretation[144] would be "innocent" (unaware) of the upper level of meaning of "Son of God" in Mark's Gospel. If, however, the centurion is

---

reader himself or herself is not implicated; for a reader in the second group, identifying with the disciples, the irony is clear, and the reader is implicated or warned about his or her own potential discipleship failure. "But," as Van Oyen notes, "the irony about irony is that in both cases one arrives as the same conclusion" (973). Whether the disciples or the centurion are negative, positive, or mixed models themselves within the narrative, ironically the implied audience knows what to do.

142. Mary Rose D'Angelo points out an intriguing parallel with 3 Maccabees: "As Ptolemy acknowledges God's fathering of the Jews (3 Macc 6:28; 7:6), the gentile centurion acclaims Jesus as the Son of God (Mark 15:39). . . . Reading the centurion's acknowledgment in the light of the submission of gentile tyrants like Ptolemy suggests that his confession may indicate not a baptism of Roman claims by Mark but an abrogation of them. The apocalyptic vision of the 'Son of man in the glory of the father' presents an alternative to the emperor's claims to be the father and guardian of the whole world. For Mark the reign of God is opposed to the reign of Satan, . . . [and] Satan's reign is also incarnate in the things that belong to Caesar (Mark 12:13-17)" ("Theology in Mark and Q: *Abba* and 'Father' in Context," *HTR* 85 [1992]: 149-74, quotation from 159-60). However, because the Jewish authorities are portrayed more negatively in Mark's passion story than the Roman authorities, especially Pilate, the contrast between the centurion and the Romans may be less than that between Joseph of Arimathea and the other Jewish authorities.

143. Muecke, *Compass of Irony*, 20.

144. See Stephen D. Moore, "The SS Officer at the Foot of the Cross: A Tragedy in Three Acts," in Malbon, ed., *Between Author and Audience*, 44-61.

interpreted as sincere, he is not "innocent," that is, he is not unknowing about what he says. In this case the irony is not verbal irony but situational irony; the conflict or gap is not between what the centurion says and what others take him to mean but between the truth of what he says and the shock of who he is as the one who says it.

Of course the implied audience always understands the words of the characters around Jesus more fully than they do themselves. Thus for the implied audience, in the words of the centurion at Jesus' death, the two major surprises about the Markan Jesus' ministry come together: Jesus' proclamation of the good news includes Gentiles as well as Jews, and Jesus' death at the hands of the Roman authorities confirms his obedience to God as son rather than disconfirming it as might conventionally be thought. Yet only those with ears to hear and eyes to see perceive this ironic, paradoxical, parabolic sense.

What the Roman authorities say to or about Jesus in direct speech illustrates that conflict with the Jewish authorities in Roman-occupied Palestine can easily result in conflict with the political authorities. Religion and politics are not separate spheres in the ancient world (or in many areas of the contemporary world). Because the status quo is supported by intertwined arrangements by Jewish and Roman authorities, Jesus' challenge to the status quo is understood as a challenge to both. The Roman authorities, however, are portrayed as being willing (although not eager) and able to meet the Markan Jesus' challenge and its resulting disruption with crucifixion. At his death, a Roman centurion speaks in a way that connects—at least for the implied audience—Jesus' death by the Roman authorities to his obedience to the highest Jewish authority, God. But our focus here is not the Roman authorities and how they are portrayed but how Jesus is portrayed in the Roman authorities' direct speech to or about him. In terms of projected christology, the direct speech of the Roman authorities to or about Jesus illustrates that the Markan Jesus challenges the status quo of his Jewish tradition and his political situation and that the resulting conflict with the Roman authorities escalates to a confrontation that leads to his death, a death that can be understood by some as reflecting obedience to God.

Summary and Conclusion

Examining what others say to or about Jesus shows the views projected onto Jesus by the narrator and the characters of Mark's narrative. Together, these views, gathered primarily from the comments of the narrator and the direct speech of all the characters except Jesus, comprise Markan projected christology, which is one aspect of a Markan narrative christology. This consideration of projected christology as one part of narrative christology decenters a more traditional way of studying Markan christology by abstracting "titles," or even just certain titles, from the narrative and discussing their meaning outside their narrative contexts, whether in a history of religions context or in a theological-philosophical context. Projected christology also goes beyond the work of Jack Dean Kingsbury, who does attend to narrative context but who gives priority to the "christological titles" introduced by the Markan narrator in the title of the narrative (1:1). Because of its position and content, 1:1 certainly contributes substantially to a Markan narrative christology, but it does not drown out what others in the narrative say to or about Jesus or dominate the attention of the implied audience. Because of the diversity and scope of what all these others say to or about the Markan Jesus, a concluding summary is in order.

After the distinctive first line (1:1; 13:14 also being unique), the narrator's work falls into three broad categories: (1) what the narrator says about Jesus, (2) what the narrator says about others' reactions to Jesus, and (3) what the narrator says about John the baptizer and reactions to him, which sets up parallels to Jesus and reactions to him. What the narrator says about what Jesus does was considered under the heading enacted christology in the preceding chapter; what Jesus says in response and instead is considered in the following two chapters. By occasional inside views of Jesus, the Markan narrator tells the narratee that Jesus is aware of the varying responses to his words and actions—from the responses of eager suppliants to those of agitated opponents. But generally the narrator relies on showing more than telling to communicate his story about Jesus. The narrator does not say on his own, "Jesus was an amazing teacher," but rather, "They were all amazed" (1:27) at this teaching.

What the narrator says about John the baptizer, he implies about Jesus, drawing attention to the parallels between their going out to proclaim (and the overlapping content of their proclamation: repentance), their being handed over, and their deaths. What John the baptizer says about Jesus, on the other hand, draws attention to their difference: John is the forerunner, Jesus is the more powerful one coming after.

God does not appear as a character in Mark's Gospel, but a voice from heaven or from the cloud is twice heard by some of the characters, and, of course, by the implied audience. The two short statements of (God), at Jesus' baptism and transfiguration, reverberate deeply with each other, with Scripture, and with the narrator's opening line. (God) confirms the narrator's application of "Son of God" to the Markan Jesus and also confirms that what the Markan Jesus does and says is pleasing to (God) and to be listened to by others. This is a significant observation because, since, as we have mentioned and will discuss further in the next two chapters, the Markan Jesus and the narrator do not always say the same thing, (God) serves as a mediating character between them, confirming them both in different ways.

What the unclean spirits and demons say to and about Jesus is most like what (God) says in 1:11 and 9:7 and what the narrator says in 1:1. Their knowledge of Jesus' role in relation to God is transcendent knowledge, reflecting not only their transcendent nature but also their personal experience of participation in the cosmic struggle between God and Satan. On the basis of this shared transcendent knowledge, (God) recognizes the Markan Jesus as "my Son," my deputy, while the unclean spirits and demons recognize Jesus as the Son of God, our enemy.

As the unclean spirits and demons suffer a disadvantage due to the Markan Jesus' role in the cosmic struggle between God and Satan, so the suppliants, those who ask Jesus for healing or exorcism, enjoy an advantage. What the suppliants say to or about Jesus is that they trust him as a source of willing power for health and wholeness. Suppliants give voice to the belief that one can experience the in-breaking of the rule of God in the healing power of the Markan Jesus.

The speakers from the crowds, the people, or "some" are diverse and anonymous. Some acclaim his mighty deeds of healing, although some also question them. Others show their noncomprehension of Jesus' words and actions because those words and actions challenge their own expectations. Still others go further and represent him as being someone other than he is or as saying something other than he said. The portrait the anonymous crowds or unnamed persons paint of the Markan Jesus in their direct speech to and about him is of one who is powerful in word and deed, always challenging, often questioned, and often misunderstood. It is a portrait not unlike that painted by the smaller group of named characters who follow the Markan Jesus.

The disciples speak more than any other character group in Mark's narrative. This is not surprising because, although Mark's Gospel is Jesus' story, Jesus' story is thoroughly intertwined with the story of the disciples. Often it is "the disciples," as a group character, who are asking, answering, or stating. Sometimes an individual disciple or a small group of them gives voice to the question, answer, or statement. What their direct speech to or about Jesus suggests about them is that they are fallible in the face of the challenges of discipleship, especially the challenges involving serving those with less power and enduring persecution from those with more power. In terms of projected christology, their direct speech illustrates that the Markan Jesus realizes that what he is asking is extremely demanding and that followers are fallible.

Although the Markan Jesus' disciples are indeed fallible, they are still followers; the Jewish authorities, on the other hand, are generally portrayed as opponents. Their direct speech illustrates the conflict between them and the Markan Jesus on issues of interpretation of the Law and tradition in relation to practice within Jewish tradition. Even though the Markan narrator encourages an overall negative attitude toward the Jewish authorities from the beginning, the Markan narrator and the Markan Jesus concur that there are significant exceptions to the general rule that the Jewish authorities take on the role of Jesus' opponents. In terms of projected christology, the direct speech of the Jewish authorities to or about Jesus illustrates that the Markan Jesus challenges the status quo of his Jewish tradition from within that tradition and that the resulting conflict with the traditional authorities escalates to a life-threatening confrontation—only to become death-dealing when expanded to include the Roman authorities.

Prior to the passion narrative the only Roman authority figure to appear or to speak is Herod, who becomes involved in the John/Jesus parallelism by having John killed as Pilate will have Jesus killed. The direct speech of the Roman authorities illustrates that conflict with the Jewish authorities in Roman-occupied Palestine can easily result in conflict with the dominant political authorities, the occupiers. Because the status quo is supported by intertwined arrangements of Jewish and Roman authorities, Jesus' challenge to the status quo is understood as a challenge to both. The Roman authorities, however, are portrayed as being willing (although not eager) and able to meet the Markan Jesus' challenge and its resulting disruption with crucifixion. What the Roman authorities say to or about Jesus illustrates that the Markan Jesus challenges the status quo of his Jewish tradition and his political situation and that the resulting conflict with the Roman authorities escalates to a confrontation that leads to his death, a death that can be understood by some (prompted by the centurion's words) as reflecting obedience to God.

In many ways, projected christology confirms enacted christology. In introducing enacted christology, we noted that, at the most elemental level, what the Markan Jesus does is preach and teach (about the in-breaking of God's rule), exorcise and heal (as an exemplification of the in-breaking of God's rule), and insist on and practice service to those with the least status in society and suffer persecution and death by the authorities of that society (as an exemplification of the implications of the in-breaking of God's rule in the present age). In terms of projected christology, the narrator, (God), and the unclean spirits and demons give witness to Jesus' role in the cosmic struggle between God and Satan that is revealed in his proclamation and enactment of the in-breaking rule (kingdom) of God, and the suppliants experience and praise his success. The diverse and anonymous crowds/people/some and the complex disciples give voice to both the success of Jesus as bringer of God's rule and the difficulty of following his teaching and example, especially concerning service to the powerless even at the risk of persecution at the hands of the powerful. The Jewish and Roman authorities portray the difficulty of dealing with Jesus' challenges on a societal level; challengers of the status quo must not expect to be heralded by those with the most to gain by protecting the status quo. In this too, John the baptizer serves as Jesus' forerunner. What others say to or about Jesus adds both depths and highlights to the portrait painted by what Jesus does.

As should be expected, separation of the various layers of narrative christology is not easy because of their integration within Mark's narrative. However, the heuristic separation of enacted and projected christology, for example, does bring to light details about characters and relationships among characters, and between the narrator and characters, that are otherwise subdued. It has been even more difficult to separate what others say to and about Jesus and what Jesus says in response, as the many references in this chapter to material to be discussed later have made obvious. While focusing on what others say to or about the Markan Jesus, we have already had to note in advance that the Markan Jesus does not always say the same thing as other Markan characters or the Markan narrator. We now turn to an examination of what Jesus says in response to those others.

CHAPTER 3

DEFLECTED CHRISTOLOGY:
WHAT JESUS SAYS IN RESPONSE

In this chapter we will explore what the Markan Jesus says in response to those whose words to and about Jesus we examined in the previous chapter—except for his responses that include "Son of Humanity" or "kingdom of God." I will deal with the Markan Jesus' words about the "Son of Humanity" and the "kingdom of God" in the following chapter, on what Jesus says instead, because these phrases are unique to the Markan Jesus, not used by any other characters or the narrator (except for the narrator's one mention of "kingdom of God" at 15:43, just after Jesus' death). It is even less possible to be complete in examining what the Markan Jesus says in response than it was in examining what others say to or about Jesus for the simple reason that, as the main character, Jesus has more lines! Here we will focus on the responses of the Markan Jesus that consistently deflect the honor or attention offered him toward God.[1] The Markan Jesus is, of course, also the most complex character, and we will find that his responses to other characters make the entire narrative more complex and more engaging for the implied audience.

---

1. Cf. Suzanne Watts Henderson, *Christology and Discipleship in the Gospel of Mark* (SNTSMS 135; Cambridge: Cambridge University Press, 2006), 39: "Mark's large-scale narrative about Jesus . . . can be called 'Christocentric' only insofar as we recognize the story's poignant paradox: if Mark's story is about Jesus, it is about a Jesus who consistently points away from himself and toward 'what the Lord has done' (Mk. 5:19)." See also Henderson, 246–47, on "Jesus' reticence about his own identity."

At least since William Wrede's challenging work on the "messianic secret" (first published in 1901), commentators have been unable to overlook one aspect of the Markan Jesus' response to others: the puzzling commands to secrecy.[2] Scholars have not agreed on exactly which data are to be included as part of the messianic secret in Mark, nor on how these data are to be interpreted, but Kingsbury judged the issue of such importance to Markan christology that he made discussion of it primary (chapter 1) and foundational for his study of *The Christology of Mark's Gospel*.[3] Kingsbury sees the secret of Jesus' "identity" in Mark as linked more with the title "Son of God" than with the title "Messiah" (Christ); and, although he recognizes that the secret is not really a secret to the readers because the narrator makes it plain in 1:1, he takes care to show how various statements in the narrative that might seem to "break" the secret (e.g., Jesus' "Son of man" statements and Bartimaeus' cry of "Son of David") in fact do not. Kingsbury discusses the secrecy motif in terms of Jesus' "identity," and he admits, although it is not of central importance to his argument, that "it is more accurate to say that it is from the standpoint of the reader that Mark depicts the progressive disclosure of Jesus' identity."[4] In his presentation of the Christology of Mark, William Telford identifies the secrecy motif as "the literary means by which his [Mark's] 'Son of God' Christology is brought home to his readers."[5] A thoroughgoing narrative analysis suggests another way to look at the evidence of the messianic secret in Mark but confirms the importance of this material for a Markan narrative christology. We will reflect on this alternative view of the tension of the so-called "messianic secret" texts at the conclusion of this chapter.

Characters are revealed to their audience by what they say and do and by what others say and do—to and about them and in relation to them. In exploring Mark's characterization of Jesus, it is important to consider the points of view of all the characters, and in this chapter and the next we will focus on the point of view of the protagonist of the Gospel, the Markan Jesus. Mark's narrative manifests a significant gap between what the character Jesus says about himself and what other characters and the narrator say about him (projected christology). Here we will consider Jesus' responses that *deflect* away from himself the recognition, honor (sincere or sarcastic), or attention a character, group of characters, or the narrator intends to give. The words of the Markan Jesus

2. William Wrede, *The Messianic Secret* (trans. J. C. C. Grieg; Cambridge and London: James Clarke, 1971). For examples of the secondary literature, see the essays collected in *The Messianic Secret* (ed. Christopher Tuckett; Philadelphia: Fortress and London: SPCK, 1983).

3. Jack Dean Kingsbury, *The Christology of Mark's Gospel* (Philadelphia: Fortress, 1983).

4. Kingsbury, *Christology*, 90, commenting on Mark 8:27–16:8.

5. W. R. Telford, *The Theology of the Gospel of Mark* (New Testament Theology; Cambridge: Cambridge University Press, 1999), 41.

do not echo the words (titles, descriptions, assertions, questions) of the Markan unclean spirits and demons, crowds, and suppliants; John the baptizer; the disciples and other followers; the Jewish authorities; Pilate; or the centurion. We will look at the Markan Jesus' responses to each of these characters or groups in turn. Then we will explore how the relationship between the Markan Jesus and God is portrayed in the Markan narrative by the Markan Jesus' response to the voice (of God) at the baptism and transfiguration, his use of the expression *dei* (must), his reference to God as father, his use of "as it is written" in evoking Scripture, his use of theological passives, and his cry to God from the cross. We will conclude with reflection on the creative tension between the Markan Jesus and the Markan narrator concerning narrative christology.

The Markan Jesus' Responses to What Others Say

It was impossible to avoid mention of Jesus' responses to what other characters say to and about him in discussing those characters' words in the previous chapter on projected christology. Likewise, it was impossible to avoid mention of Jesus' words in discussing his actions in the chapter on enacted christology. Now, however, we are free to focus on Jesus' responses to what other characters and the narrator say to and about him and do in relation to him. We begin our look at Jesus' responses to various characters with the unclean spirits and demons, along with the crowds and suppliants. Jesus' responses to these character groups are most involved with the so-called "messianic secret."

Jesus' Responses to the Unclean Spirits and Demons, the Crowds, and the Suppliants

What the unclean spirits and demons, the crowds, and the suppliants have in common is their encounter with the Markan Jesus' healing power as a manifestation of the in-breaking rule of God. What the Markan Jesus' responses to these diverse groups of characters have in common is their insistence that God is the source of that healing power.

From the beginning, the unclean spirits (and demons) "know who" "Jesus of Nazareth" is—"the Holy One of God" who has "come to destroy" them (1:24). How they come into this knowledge is not stated explicitly, but it is implicitly connected to the coming near of the kingdom (rule) of God that Jesus proclaims (1:15) and the breaking up of the kingdom of Satan to which Jesus alludes (3:23-27).[6] In discussing enacted christology, we identified this

---

6. See Elizabeth Shively, "The Story Matters: Solving the Problem of the Parables in Mark 3:23-27," in *Between Author and Audience in Mark: Narration, Characterization, Interpretation* (ed. Elizabeth Struthers Malbon; New Testament Monographs 23; Sheffield: Sheffield Phoenix, 2009), 122–44, for an interpretation of the apparent contradiction, in Mark 3:23-27, between the parables of the divided kingdom and house and the parable of the

knowledge as transcendent because it transcends human knowledge; unclean spirits and demons share with God transcendent knowledge of Jesus' relationship to God but from their position in opposition to God in the foundational conflict of God against Satan. Three times this knowledge is narrated in direct speech: the unclean spirit possessing the man in the synagogue in Capernaum (1:24b, "I know who you are, the Holy One of God"), the unclean spirits described in a summary passage (3:11, "You are the Son of God!"), and the legion of unclean spirits inhabiting the Gerasene (5:7, "What have you to do with me, Jesus, Son of the Most High God?"). Once, the narrator simply states that "the demons . . . knew him [Jesus]" (1:34). In each of the four cases, the response of the Markan Jesus is to silence them. "But Jesus rebuked him, saying, 'Be silent, and come out of him!'" (1:25). ". . . [A]nd he would not permit the demons to speak, because they knew him" (1:34b). "But he sternly ordered them not to make him known" (3:12). And in the case of the Gerasene demoniac, after Jesus' commands ("Come out of the man, you unclean spirit!" and "What is your name?"; 5:8-9), the noisy silencing comes by their negotiated sending into the swine,[7] who rush down the steep bank and are drowned in the sea. Only one of these commands to silence is given in the direct speech of the Markan Jesus (1:25); three of the four responses of Jesus to the demons or unclean spirits are reported by the narrator, who seems thereby well aware of Jesus' reticence in being made known (at the very least by *these* characters and perhaps more broadly) as the Son or Holy One of God.

Throughout at least the first half of Mark's narrative, people in general or the crowds respond to Jesus in amazement, awe, or wonder—especially in response to his healings. Over and over again the narrator reports Jesus' commands to the healed (and their families), either in direct speech or in indirect narration or in both. "After sternly warning him [the leper] he sent him away at once, saying to him, 'See that you say nothing to anyone . . .'" (1:43-44a). "He strictly ordered them that no one should know this, and told them to give her [Jairus' daughter] something to eat" (5:43). "Then Jesus ordered them [those who witnessed the healing of the deaf man in the Decapolis] to tell no one . . ." (7:36a). "Then he sent him [the man from Bethsaida] to his home, saying, 'Do not even go into the village'" (8:26). Twice Jesus even isolates the person before the healing (7:33; 8:23), apparently to deflect attention. However, no one seems surprised when these impossible commands are not obeyed; it would be quite difficult, for example, for Jairus and his wife not to tell the mourners

---

strong man through a study of Mark's characterization of Jesus, the scribes, Satan, and the Holy Spirit throughout the narrative, arguing that it is the interrelations of these characters that clarify the narrative's comment on the tension of power.

7. Edwin K. Broadhead notes: "The absence of a healing action places the words of Jesus at the center of the healing story. This series of dialogues confirms the authority of Jesus' proclamation" (*Teaching with Authority: Miracles and Christology in the Gospel of Mark* [JSNTSup 74; Sheffield: Sheffield Academic, 1992], 101).

(5:38) that their daughter's funeral is off! But the point here is that the Markan narrator repeatedly gives evidence of Jesus' reticence to be known as a healer and his desire to deflect such attention.

Repeatedly the narrator notes that Jesus tried to escape the attentions of the crowds. Alone he "went out to a deserted place" to pray (1:35); or he invited his disciples to "[c]ome away to a deserted place all by yourselves and rest a while" (6:31). He even requested the disciples "to have a boat ready for him because of the crowd, so that they would not crush him" (3:9; cf. 4:35 and 8:13). Later "he made his disciples get into the boat and go on ahead to the other side" of the Sea of Galilee "while he dismissed the crowd" and "went up on the mountain to pray" (6:45-46). To state the obvious: the Markan Jesus' prayer was to God; his retreats from the crowd, and sometimes even from the disciples, were made to attend to God.[8] Still, the pressure of the crowd is relentless. In the "region of Tyre," Jesus "entered a house and did not want anyone to know he was there." "Yet," the narrator admits, "he could not escape notice" (7:24).

In many cases the Markan Jesus makes simple and direct statements to the suppliants who come to him for healing, or to the crowd surrounding them; the power of the in-breaking rule of God is shown in the act of healing itself. Some statements mark the beginning of the healing encounter: "Come forward"; "Stretch out your [withered] hand" (3:3, 5); "Who touched my clothes?" (5:30); "What are you arguing about with them?"; "Bring him to me"; "How long has this been happening to him?" (9:16, 19, 21); "Call him [Bartimaeus] here"; "What do you want me to do for you?" (10:49, 51). Other statements mark the successful conclusion of the healing encounter and the renewal of health and life it brings: "I say to you [the healed paralytic], take your mat and go to your home" (2:11); "Daughter, your faith has made you well; go in peace, and be healed of your disease" (5:34); "'Talitha cum,' which means, 'Little girl, get up!'" (5:41); "For saying that [literally, 'through this word'], you may go— the demon has left your daughter" (7:29); "'Ephphatha,' that is, 'Be opened'" (7:34); "You spirit that keeps this boy from speaking and hearing, I command you, come out of him, and never enter him again!" (9:25); "Go [Bartimaeus]; your faith has made you well" (10:52).

Some statements of the Markan Jesus to suppliants function to highlight the drama and difficulty of the healing process: "Why do you make a commotion and weep? The child is not dead but sleeping" (5:39); "Can you see anything?" (8:23); "You faithless generation, how much longer must I be among you? How much longer must I put up with you?" (9:19). The Markan Jesus' initial statement to the paralytic transforms the healing story into a story of

---

8. As Broadhead notes of 6:45, "The departure of the miracle worker provides more than a functional conclusion, however: Jesus goes to the mountain to pray. Thus, the story ends with Jesus in the presence of God in the place of calling and revelation" (*Teaching with Authority*, 120–21).

controversy with some of the scribes: "Son, your sins are forgiven" (2:5; the
impact of the theological passive here—forgiven *by God*—will be discussed at
the close of this chapter). Jesus' initial statement to the Syrophoenician woman
complicates the healing story into a controversy with the Gentile woman suppliant herself: "Let the children be fed first, for it is not fair to take the children's
food and throw it to the dogs" (7:27). With the Jewish man, the Markan Jesus
begins by proclaiming the word that the forgiveness of sins *by God* is available;
with the Gentile woman, having heard her "word" (Gk *logos*; 7:29), Jesus ends
by manifesting that the healing power of the rule *of God* is available not only
among Jews but also among Gentiles. Once, a statement of the Markan Jesus, addressed to a nonspecific "them" after people in his hometown synagogue
have been scandalized by him, illustrates, according to the Markan narrator, the
practical limits of God's healing power through Jesus:

> Then Jesus said to them, "Prophets are not without honor, except in their home-
> town, and among their own kin, and in their own house." And he could do no
> deed of power there, except that he laid his hands on a few sick people and cured
> them. And he was amazed at their unbelief (6:4-6).

Although Jesus proclaims the in-breaking rule of God, he does not control the
manifestation of its power. The Markan Jesus does not compel suppliants—
or God!

Occasionally the Markan Jesus' statements to those who ask for healing—
or for teaching—have a more obvious ideological weight for the implied audience. When Jesus says to Jairus, the leader of the synagogue, "Do not fear, only
believe" (5:36), Jairus is provided the opportunity to be a model of faith for
the implied audience as the woman who touched Jesus' garment was for Jairus.
Jesus' words to the man whose son had a spirit, the spirit whom the disciples
could not cast out, also function to address the implied audience on the topic of
faith: "If you are able!—All things can be done for the one who believes" (9:23).
In both cases the faith encouraged is faith in God, who is the only one by whom
"all things can be done." When a man who comes as a suppliant for teaching
("what must I do to inherit eternal life?") addresses Jesus as "Good Teacher"
(10:17), the Markan Jesus deflects the attribution of goodness from himself
to God before answering the question: "Why do you call me good? No one is
good but God alone" (10:18).[9] However, the rich man learns only not to call

9. The Gospel of Matthew presents this story differently ("Why do you ask me about
what is good?"; Matt 19:17), presumably in order to avoid having Jesus deny that he is
"good." M. Philip Scott, O.C.S.O., "Chiastic Structure: A Key to the Interpretation of
Mark's Gospel," *BTB* 15 (1985): 17–26, argues for an interpretation exactly opposite the
usual view of the Markan Jesus' theological humility and my view of deflected christology
with reference to Jesus' response to "Good Teacher." Seeing Jesus' question, "Why do you call
me good?" at 10:18 as the center of a chiasm of questions, Scott insists that Jesus' reply is not

Jesus "good"; he does not learn how to follow him. Thus the story of the rich man provides both an example of how the Markan Jesus deflects honor to God and an example of how hard it is to follow Jesus in doing that, to move beyond keeping "the commandments" (10:18-19) of God and to "sell what you own, and give the money to the poor, and . . . [thus] have treasure in heaven [that is, with God]" (10:21). For the Markan Jesus, keeping "the commandments" is a necessary but insufficient response to the in-breaking rule of God.

Sometimes the Markan Jesus offers to the crowd, unasked, teaching that serves as a transition from his controversy with the Jewish authorities to his teaching of the disciples,[10] for example, in the parables chapter (scribes: 3:19b-30/crowd: 3:31–4:9/disciples: 4:10-12) and concerning the parable (see 7:17) of what defiles a person (scribes and Pharisees: 7:1-13/crowd: 7:14-15/disciples: 7:17-23). The latter example realigns the boundaries of clean and unclean and thus, for the Markan implied author and audience, the boundaries of the community called by Jesus: "Listen to me, all of you, and understand: there is nothing outside a person that by going in can defile, but the things that come out are what defile" (7:14-15). The former example realigns the value of relationships in the rule of God: "Who are my mother and my brother? . . . Here are my mother and my brothers! [those sitting around Jesus] Whoever does the will of God is my brother and sister and mother" (3:33-35). Family relationships were primary in the first-century Mediterranean world of Mark's Gospel, but for the Markan Jesus, doing the will *of God* is now more important.

Thus the Markan Jesus explicitly and consistently deflects honor from himself as both teacher and healer to God, who alone is good and who alone can do all things. The implied audience can perceive in Jesus' apparent "shyness" not so much a "messianic secret" but a theological motive: the Markan Jesus wishes to *deflect* the attention given to him, especially as healer, to the true source of the healing, God.[11] Two occasions illustrate this point. The narration of an early

---

"self-abasement" (22) or "demurring" (23) at all because "Jesus' acts were divine—like raising the dead (5:41)—and he tells the youth that none but God does such deeds—as none but God forgives sins: 'Why do you call me good?' Work out fully the answer to that, and you will have reason to wonder if calling me 'good' is good enough" (23). Scott understands such a reading to fit with "Mark's compulsion to present Jesus as God" (23); I find the compulsion to be Scott's. See note 76 in chapter 1 for more information about Scott's presuppositions.

10. See Elizabeth Struthers Malbon, "Disciples/Crowds/Whoever: Markan Characters and Readers," *NovT* 28 (1986): 104–30, republished in *The Composition of Mark's Gospel: Selected Studies from Novum Testamentum* (ed. David E. Orton; Leiden, The Netherlands: Brill, 1999), 144–70, and also in Malbon, *In the Company of Jesus: Characters in Mark's Gospel* (Louisville: Westminster John Knox, 2000), 70–99; and Elizabeth Struthers Malbon, "Echoes and Foreshadowings in Mark 4–8: Reading and Rereading," *JBL* 112 (1993): 213–32.

11. Commenting on *theos* (God) as "A Neglected Factor in the Theology of Mark" (*JBL* 101 [1982]: 563–94), John R. Donahue, S.J., notes: "Though Jesus empowered the disciples to exorcise, he is not the distributor of this power; only contact with God in prayer evokes it.

healing of a (Jewish) leper concludes with Jesus' command for secrecy *and* his command that thanksgiving be offered to God, following Jewish sacrificial tradition: "See that you say nothing to anyone; but go, show yourself to the priest, and offer for your cleansing what Moses commanded, as a testimony to them" (1:44;[12] cf. the response of the people in the synagogue in Capernaum to Jesus' healing of the paralytic, as reported by the narrator: they "glorified God," 2:12). The narration of a later healing of a (Gentile) demoniac concludes with Jesus' command for containing the news of the exorcism (you may not go with me; "Go home to your friends") but attributing it to the Lord God: "tell them how much the Lord has done for you, and what mercy he [God] has shown you" (5:19).[13] Although reporting Jesus' attempts to direct attention to God, the narrator seems more aligned with the point of view of the Gerasene demoniac who

---

One can be empowered to exorcise without being an explicit disciple of Jesus. The important thing is contact with 'the one who sent me' [9:37]. Such a christology maintains the Markan emphasis on the transcendence of God, while not minimizing the role of Jesus as the one who uniquely speaks for God and points through himself to God" (589). The title of Donahue's essay is a reference to an earlier essay by Nils A. Dahl, "The Neglected Factor in New Testament Theology," *Reflection* (Yale Divinity School) 73 (1975): 5–8, which gives several reasons for the neglect of "God" in New Testament theology, including a "pronounced christocentricity" with roots in the nineteenth century and a "common assumption that the most important elements in the New Testament are those which are specifically Christian" (6). Donahue provides challenges to both these assumptions in his article on "God" in Mark's Gospel.

12. Some interpreters, among them Broadhead, argue that "the witness is not to the authorities, but against them" because "[t]he leper's healing provides a condemnation of the religious institutions which had declared the leper unclean" (*Teaching with Authority*, 73). According to Broadhead, "By declaring the leper clean (1.41), Jesus fulfills the duty of the priest" (*Teaching with Authority*, 74). This interpretation may be an over-reading of the narrative evidence, but in any case, the Markan Jesus' directions suggest that God is to be acknowledged as the source of the cleansing; the command to "offer," that is, sacrifice to God, makes this clear. Morna D. Hooker acknowledges that the referent of "them" in the phrase "as a testimony to them" is ambiguous: the RSV interprets "them" as "the people"; some interpreters take "them" to be the Markan Jesus' opponents, but "this group has not yet appeared in the gospel"; "The one person who has been mentioned in the story so far is the priest to whom the leper is sent, and the most natural interpretation in the context is that showing himself to him will be evidence of his cure; if Mark writes 'them' rather than 'him,' that is perhaps because the one priest is representative of them all" (*The Gospel According to Saint Mark* [BNTC; Peabody, Mass.: Hendrickson, 1991], 82). My own interpretation is matched by Hooker's: "Mark has perhaps deliberately placed this indication of Jesus' adherence to the Torah immediately before the account in 2.1–3.6 of the opposition which he encountered from those who claimed to uphold the Torah: his words show that he is in fact no transgressor of the Torah" (82).

13. Broadhead notes specifically of the healing of the Gerasene demoniac, but also more generally of the miracle stories, that "the christological consequence of the miracle stories is subverted by the narrative. Fear and faith, not acclamation, become the proper response to the power of Jesus" (*Teaching with Authority*, 114).

the narrator reports "went away and began to proclaim in the Decapolis [the "Ten Cities" were hardly his "home"] how much Jesus [the Lord?] had done for him" (5:20).[14]

JESUS' NONRESPONSE AND RESPONSE TO JOHN THE BAPTIZER

More than silencing John the baptizer as he silenced the unclean spirits and demons and tried to silence the crowds and suppliants, the Markan Jesus is silent to John's acclamation of him. John the baptizer says, "The one who is more powerful than I is coming after me" and "he will baptize you with the Holy Spirit" (1:7-8). In this way, John the baptizer takes care to distinguish himself from Jesus, thus honoring Jesus. However, the Markan Jesus is not yet on the scene when John's words are reported, thus Jesus makes no response to John's acclamation. Neither does the narrator comment on John's words ranking Jesus higher than himself, it being already clear to the implied audience that this view is supported by the implied author. The Markan Jesus' nonverbal response to John the baptizer's activity is reported by the Markan narrator to be like that of "people from the whole Judean countryside and all the people of Jerusalem [who] were going out to him, and were baptized by him in the river Jordan, confessing their sins" (1:5): "In those days Jesus came from Nazareth of Galilee and was baptized by John in the Jordan" (1:9). In the Gospel of Matthew, both John the baptizer and the narrator take steps to distinguish Jesus from the others coming to John for baptism: "John would have prevented him, saying, 'I need to be baptized by you, and do you come to me?' But Jesus answered him, 'Let it be so now; for it is proper for us in this way to fulfill all righteousness.' Then he consented" (Matt 3:14-15). Thus in relation to the scene of Jesus' baptism in the Gospel of Matthew, the Markan baptism scene itself might be understood as deflecting honor from Jesus to God. People come to John and are baptized, "confessing their sins" (Mark 1:5); Jesus comes to John and is baptized (Mark 1:9); is confessing his sins implied? This possibility worries the Matthean John the baptizer but not the Markan John the baptizer; confession of sins to God (and thus deferring to God) is clearly not a part of the baptismal experience of the Matthean Jesus, as it would seem to be of the Markan Jesus. Matthew's story of Jesus' baptism thereby stretches the distance between Jesus and other human beings and closes the distance between Jesus and God that Mark's baptismal story assumes. More than the implied author of Matthew, the implied author of Mark takes care to show God's unique transcendence; as we will see, the Markan Jesus goes even further.

Although the Markan narrator never directly reports Jesus' baptizing others by the Holy Spirit as John the baptizer projects, Jesus himself seems

---

14. See the discussion of the narrator's allusive use of "Lord" in reference to Jesus at 1:3 and 5:19-20 in the previous chapter on projected christology, in the section on what the narrator says about John the baptizer and implies about Jesus.

almost baptized with the (Holy) Spirit, which is reported as descending "into" (Gk *eis*, 1:10) him and soon thereafter directing his movement: "the Spirit immediately drove him out into the wilderness" (1:12).[15] However, the Markan Jesus later assures his followers that when they experience the future wilderness of being brought "before governors and kings" (13:9) because of their faith, they will not need to be concerned about what to say because the Holy Spirit will speak through them (13:11),[16] providing for them as the angels, that is, messengers of God, provide for Jesus in the wilderness, according to the Markan narrator (1:13). Assurance of the presence of the Holy Spirit is assurance of the presence and activity of God.

Jesus' Responses to the Disciples and Other Followers

Jesus' reticence and commands to silence—and Markan deflected christology—are not restricted to his healing ministry or to his response to the unclean sprits and demons, crowds, and suppliants. As Joel Williams notes,

> Jesus charges others to remain silent in both halves of Mark's Gospel, but the recipients of these commands change. In the first half, Jesus directs his commands to silence to the demons (1:23-25, 34; 3:11-12) and to those who have benefited from his healing ministry (1:43-44; 5:43; 7:36; 8:26). In the second half, he tells his disciples to remain silent (8:30; 9:9).[17]

Greater understanding is demanded of the disciples, and that which they are to understand grows increasingly paradoxical. With both disciples and the broader group of followers, the Markan Jesus speaks in ways that deflect attention and honor away from himself and to God.

The disciples enter Mark's story very near its beginning. The Markan Jesus' first direct speech is introduced by the narrator as "proclaiming the gospel [NRSV good news] of God" (1:14): "The time is fulfilled, and the kingdom of God has come near; repent, and believe in the gospel [NRSV good news]" (1:15). Although the internal audience of this speech is not specified, and the implied audience is certainly implicated, what follows is the first calling of disciples, who are thus immediately linked with Jesus' proclamation of the in-breaking rule of

---

15. David Rhoads wonders if John's proclamation of Jesus' baptizing with the Holy Spirit refers to the exorcisms and healings and forgiveness that Jesus offers people as expressions of the Holy Spirit that came upon him at his baptism (personal communication). If so, I would add, then the actions of the Holy Spirit through Jesus manifest the in-breaking of the rule *of God*.

16. Shively, "The Story Matters," 138, argues that when the Markan Jesus is brought before Pilate in an analogous situation "the reader imagines that it is not Jesus who speaks but the Holy Spirit" (14:62).

17. Joel F. Williams, "Does Mark's Gospel Have an Outline?" *JETS* 49 (2006): 505–25, quotation from 512.

God. This announcement of the rule of God serves as a warning to the unclean spirits and demons and an invitation to the disciples, but the focus is clearly on God. Jesus' first words to Simon and Andrew make this plain: "Follow me and I will make you fish for people" (1:17), that is, drop what you are doing now, fishing for fish as part of the economic system, and take up a new task, fishing for people as part of the eschatological judgment of God. (At 2:14, Levi, who is not listed among the "twelve," is also called by Jesus to "Follow me"; in calling a tax-collector, the Markan Jesus reveals what kind of fishing for people, what kind of end-time judgment, he understands God to demand and offer.) But just as the difficulty of Jesus' role as "Son of God" is implicated immediately after the role is introduced (with the spirit "throwing him out" into the wilderness after his baptism), so the difficulty of the disciples' understanding of Jesus' role and thus their own is implicated immediately: Jesus withdrew to a wilderness place to pray *to God*, but "Simon and his companions hunted for him [literally, tracked him down]" because everyone in Capernaum was looking for him (1:36). Jesus explains that his commission from God is broader than what the disciples realize: "Let us go on to the neighboring towns, so that I may proclaim the message there also; for that is what I came out to do" (1:38).

Interestingly enough, no direct speech of Jesus is narrated in the pericope of the appointing of the twelve; the narrator takes over the telling of this story completely, explaining that the twelve are appointed "to be with him, and to be sent out to proclaim the message, and to have authority to cast out demons" (3:14-15). That is, the disciples are to be with Jesus so that they can learn to do what the narrator has been reporting Jesus does. The narrator's stress is on Jesus; there is no mention of "God" in this pericope.

Because the parables of chapter 4 are centered on proclaiming the rule (kingdom) of God, they will be discussed in my following chapter, on refracted christology. But in noting the responses of the Markan Jesus to his disciples and followers, we must consider this challenging passage in chapter 4:

> When he was alone, those who were around him along with the twelve asked him about the parables. And he said to them, "To you has been given the mystery [NRSV secret] of the kingdom of God, but for those outside, everything comes in parables; in order that
> 'they may indeed look, but not perceive,
> and may indeed listen, but not understand;
> so that they may not turn again and be forgiven.'"
> 4:10-12

The scholarly commentary on this complicated passage is extensive;[18] here we may only note the obvious paradoxes: Jesus was alone but with others. The

18. See, e.g., the commentary of Adela Yarbro Collins, *Mark: A Commentary* (Hermeneia; Minneapolis: Fortress, 2007), 247–50, focusing on cultural contexts and traditional

twelve are presumably important, but they are mentioned after "those who were around him." The "mystery" the followers are given is in many ways not unlike the "parables" "those outside" are given—both require active interpretation and participation. Is the evocation of Isaiah 6:9-10 claiming that Jesus *intended* by telling parables to prevent understanding and thus forgiveness (which seems counter to much of the narrative) or suggesting that the inevitable *result* (known to God) of Jesus' telling the parables would be such failure to understand? The disciples are also given an additional explanation of the parable of the sower (4:13-20) and apparently hear other parables as well (4:21-32, along with the crowd? the internal audience is not made clear; see 4:33-34). In relation to deflected christology as manifested in the Markan Jesus, what is clear is the centrality of God: the parables both reveal and conceal the in-breaking rule of God for "those outside," and being "given [by God] the mystery of the rule [NRSV kingdom] of God" is, for those presumed to be insiders, less like receiving the right answer and more like perceiving good questions.[19]

The Markan Jesus' response to the disciples' struggling to understand is, as it were, "move on": "Let us go across to the other side" (4:35). Jesus calms the disturbed sea with a word, "Peace! Be still!" (4:39), but he seems to disturb the disciples, "Why are you afraid? Have you still no faith?" (4:40). As Edwin Broadhead notes, "Previously Jesus' questions within miracle stories were addressed to his opponents (2.8b-9; 3.4a); here a similar tension is narrated between Jesus and his disciples."[20] The narrator's comment and the disciples' following question first draw attention to Jesus: "And they were filled with great awe and said to one another, 'Who then is this, that even the wind and the sea obey him?'" (4:41). But they may also open to the implied audience the realization that Jesus' power over the sea can only be received from God, who has power over the sea in Scripture.[21]

Although the internal audience at 6:4 is the ambiguous "they" who have taken offense at Jesus in his hometown synagogue, because his disciples are reported to have "followed him" there (6:1) the implied audience may assume that the disciples also heard that "[p]rophets are not without honor, except in their hometown" (6:4). Within the Markan narrative, this statement seems to

---

sources, and Joel Marcus, *The Mystery of the Kingdom of God* (SBLDS 90; Atlanta: Scholars Press, 1986), 73–123, who offers a translation, literary analysis (including structure and composition history), and exegesis. See also the literature cited by Yarbro Collins and Marcus.

19. Cf. Yarbro Collins, *Mark*, 249: The Isaiah passage that is quoted in Mark "is also a way of affirming the sovereignty of God: whatever happens is God's will and human beings must accept it as such."

20. Broadhead, *Teaching with Authority*, 94.

21. For a brief discussion of Pss 107:23-32; 104:7; and 106:9 in this context, see Elizabeth Struthers Malbon, *Narrative Space and Mythic Meaning in Mark* (New Voices in Biblical Studies; New York and San Francisco: Harper & Row, 1986; volume 13 of The Biblical Seminar; Sheffield: Sheffield Academic, 1991), 77.

set the disciples up for Jesus' immediately following instructions as he sends them out; you too will be rejected, he warns: "Wherever you enter a house, stay there until you leave the place. If any place will not welcome you and they refuse to hear you, as you leave, shake off the dust that is on your feet as a testimony against them" (6:10-11). When the beheading of John the baptizer is narrated next, the implied audience realizes that the Markan implied author has connected the long experience of the prophets, that is, those who speak for God: the experience of being misunderstood and rejected—from Isaiah (Isa 6 in Mark 4:12) to John the baptizer to Jesus to the disciples.

When the Markan Jesus encourages the disciples, returned from their own successful mission of preaching and exorcizing (6:30), to "[c]ome away to a deserted place all by yourselves and rest a while" (6:31), is he encouraging them to pray to God as he did when he withdrew to a "deserted place" earlier in the narrative (1:35)? The implied audience is not told, but the withdrawal is no more successful than Jesus' earlier attempt at seclusion had been. Nor is Jesus successful when he instructs the disciples to deal with the hungry crowd directly: "You give them something to eat" (6:37). As we noted earlier in the chapter on projected christology, the disciples are able to respond appropriately only to Jesus' simplest questions: "How many loaves have you? Go and see" (6:38). (They do somewhat better when commanded, such as being sent out and distributing the loaves.) After the multiplication of the loaves for the five thousand, Jesus again seeks the company of God, the only one through whom such events can occur (see 6:41, "he looked up to heaven"): "he went up on the mountain to pray" (6:46). But first Jesus had, as the narrator comments, sent the disciples "on ahead to the other side, to Bethsaida" (6:45). At this too, the disciples do not succeed on their own. When Jesus comes to them walking on the sea, they are "terrified"; Jesus responds, "Take heart, it is I [literally "I am"]; do not be afraid" (6:50). The Markan Jesus' allusion to the voice of God from the burning bush (Exod 3:14), presenting both assurance and a commission to Moses, signals to the implied audience at least the scriptural background for understanding through whose power the sea is mastered and people are fed in the desert. The disciples, however, as the narrator admits, "were utterly astounded, for they did not understand about the loaves, but their hearts were hardened" (6:51b-52).

The failure to understand is a constant undercurrent in the Markan narrative. The next reference is in Jesus' question to the disciples after his parable of what defiles a person: "Then do you also fail to understand? Do you not see that whatever goes into a person from outside cannot defile, since it enters, not the heart but the stomach, and goes out into the sewer?" (7:18-19a). With a focus on deflected christology, we must remember that the Markan Jesus told the parable as part of his attempt to deflect attention from "human tradition" to "the commandment of God" (7:8).

In chapter 8 the implied audience is returned to the topic of misunderstanding about the loaves. In direct speech to the disciples, Jesus elaborates on his "compassion for the crowd" (8:2) and asks them simply, "How many loaves do you have?" (8:5). The disciples are equally amazed at the feeding of the four thousand (8:4), but again they assist with the distribution (8:6). On the sea again, Jesus cautions the disciples, "Watch out—beware of the yeast of the Pharisees and the yeast of Herod" (8:15). The narrator lets the narratee know that Jesus has become "aware" that the disciples are taking the saying about "yeast" literally (8:16-17), and the Markan Jesus responds to them in a passionate speech that echoes the Isaiah 6 passage he quoted in Mark 4:12, as well as echoing the narrator's earlier comment in 6:52:

> Why are you talking about having no bread? Do you still not perceive or under-stand? Are your hearts hardened? Do you have eyes, and fail to see? Do you have ears, and fail to hear? And do you not remember? When I broke the five loaves for the five thousand, how many baskets full of broken pieces did you collect? . . . And the seven for the four thousand, how many baskets full of broken pieces did you collect? . . . Do you not yet understand? (8:17-21).

What the Markan Jesus wants the disciples to understand, and what the Mar-kan implied author wants the implied audience to understand, is that God is acting here—in the feeding of both Jews and Gentiles, in Jesus' mastery over the sea to calm and protect his disciples. The rule of God that Jesus proclaims is breaking into existence in his actions for others.

Everyone who has investigated the christology of Mark's Gospel, whether narrative christology or more traditional Christology, has recognized the im-portance of 8:27-30, Peter's "confession." As we discussed earlier in relation to projected christology, the disciples answer Jesus' first question easily: "Who do people say that I am?" (8:27). Then Jesus responds with another question: "But who do you say that I am?" (8:29). Peter's answer, "You are the Christ [NRSV Messiah]" (8:29), is one the implied reader knows to be in agreement with the first appellation of the narrator's opening line (Jesus Christ, 1:1). Yet the Markan narrator comments that "he sternly ordered them not to tell anyone about him" (8:30), a passage that has long served interpreters as a linchpin of "the messianic secret." The immediately succeeding pericope contains Jesus' first passion prediction and Peter's rebuking Jesus at the thought of his suffering. Only then is the application to Peter of the immediately preceding pericope of the two-stage healing of blindness made clear to the implied audience: Peter is half-sighted, half-blind; he can see a Christ powerful in healing and teaching; he cannot see a serving and suffering Christ.

The "way" section of Mark's Gospel, 8:22–10:52, serves as the Markan Jesus' second attempt to heal that half-blindness—of Peter, of all the disciples and followers, of the implied audience. Jesus' immediate response to Peter's confusion sets the theme for this instruction: the centrality of God and the will of God. "Get behind me, Satan!" Jesus rebukes Peter, "For you are setting your mind not on divine things but on human things" (8:33). Peter's problem is that he does not understand deflected christology! The discipleship instruc-

tion section of this first passion prediction unit[22] presents the implications of
the Markan Jesus' understanding of his role and destiny for his disciples: "If
any want to become my followers, let them deny themselves and take up their
cross and follow me . . ." (8:34, see 8:34–9:1; the "Son of Humanity" reference
in 8:38—and in the other two passion predictions, 9:31 and 10:33—and the
"kingdom of God" reference in 9:1 will be discussed in the following chapter).

The next scene has also long been of interest to those exploring Markan
christology, narrative or otherwise. In the transfiguration scene a voice from
the cloud (God, 9:7) calls the Markan Jesus "my Son," echoing the voice from
heaven at the baptism scene (God, 1:11) and confirming the second appellation of the narrator's opening line (Son of God, 1:1). After the transfiguration
in the presence of Peter, James, and John, the Markan Jesus "ordered them to
tell no one about what they had seen, until after the Son of Man had risen
from the dead" (9:9). Jesus' negative commands for christological secrecy (don't
tell about me) are balanced by his positive statements of theology (tell about
God).[23] Although the disciples seem not to understand "what this rising from
the dead could mean" (9:10), the implied reader is in a position to understand
at least that it is to happen by the power of God. Jesus suggests also that both
what has already happened to Elijah/John the baptizer and what is to happen to
the Son of Humanity happen by the power of God "as it is written" (9:12 and
13), that is, written in Scripture.

Jesus comes down from the mount of transfiguration with the three to the
argument about the failed exorcism among the nine. Presumably the disciples
also are part of the internal audience of Jesus' statement to the crowd on that
occasion: "You faithless generation, how much longer must I be among you?

22. On the three parts of each of the three passion prediction units (passion prediction,
misunderstanding, discipleship instruction), see chapter 1, on enacted christology.

23. Cf. Donahue: "Both the general picture of the way Jesus speaks of God in the gospel
of Mark and the short theological treatise which Mark offers in 12:13-34 indicate that Jesus
speaks authoritatively for God and summons his hearers to a right understanding of God's
revelation in scripture" ("Neglected Factor," 581–82). Donahue also notes that the Markan
Jesus speaks both *for* God and *of* God: "There emerges therefore in Mark a dual emphasis,
the kerygmatic, the following of the crucified one, and the apologetic, following Jesus is
belief in the one God. Mark explicitly allows Jesus to be the foundation of this emphasis by
having Jesus speak *of God* throughout the gospel in the language of reverential transcendence,
while at the same time speaking *for God* with a unique authority which is the teaching of the
way of God in truth (12:14)" (581, italics original). In contrast to Donahue's interpretation
is the linguistically based (and to me unconvincing) interpretation of Paul L. Danove: "the
narrative rhetoric encourages a profound identification of Jesus with God. . . . This identification invites a response to and relationship with the character Jesus that parallels and even
coincides with the narrative audience's response to and relationship with the character God"
(*The Rhetoric of the Characterization of God, Jesus, and Jesus' Disciples in the Gospel of Mark*
[JSNTSup 290; New York: T&T Clark, 2005], 52).

How much longer must I put up with you?" (9:19). In fact, when Jesus and the disciples enter "the house" they ask him "privately" why they failed at the exorcism (9:28). Jesus' response to the disciples is one that clearly calls out to the implied audience as well: "This kind can come out only through prayer" (9:29). To state the obvious, prayer is to God; God is the continuing source of healing power to which the Markan Jesus continually directs attention.

After his second passion prediction (9:31), Jesus brings out the disciples' misunderstanding by asking them, "What were you arguing about on the way?" (9:33). They do not answer, but the narrator tells the narratee why: "But they were silent, for on the way they had argued with one another about who was the greatest" (9:34). Although no inside view of Jesus' perception of their argument is explicit, his response is clearly to their thinking. Jesus deflects attention from the disciples to himself as one who deflects attention to God: "Whoever wants to be first must be last of all and servant of all. . . . [taking a child in his arms] Whoever welcomes one such child in my name welcomes me, and whoever welcomes me welcomes not me but the one who sent me" (9:35, 37). The "one who sent" Jesus, that is, God, who alone has the power of life and renewal, calls for people to serve those who have the least power in society, with a powerless child as an example of those who are to be served.[24] This realization is not easy for anyone to see.

Discipleship instruction continues because the disciple John manifests misunderstanding in his report of stopping others who are not in their group from casting out demons in Jesus' name. Jesus' response to John is in keeping with his previous discipleship instruction, yet there is a surprising use of a significant term up to this point used only by the narrator (1:1) and Peter (8:29):

> Do not stop him; for no one who does a deed of power in my name will be able soon afterwards to speak evil of me. Whoever is not against us is for us. For truly I tell you, whoever gives you a cup of water to drink because you bear the name of Christ [literally "because you are of Christ"] will by no means lose the reward (9:39-41; see also 9:42-50).

The Markan Jesus is not at this point explicitly identifying himself as "the Christ," but he is associating the Christ with lowly service. In this instance, Jesus' followers are not exhorted to give a cup of water to others but to receive it from others who give it to those who "are of Christ." Those who are asked to

---

24. For a careful and insightful analysis of 9:37 in its Markan context see Donahue, "Neglected Factor," 587–89. As Donahue notes: "On the one hand the authority of Jesus as mediator and faithful representative is enhanced. He re-presents the sender perfectly. On the other, the rejection or acceptance of the messenger himself is lessened since the addition of 'does not receive [welcome] me' moves the attention from the fate of the messenger to the authority of the sender. In effect the role or function of Jesus as faithful messenger is heightened, while his personal fate seems somewhat less important" (589).

serve the powerless are also asked to be gracious in receiving such service from others—whoever they are. It is odd that this use of "Christ" by the Markan Jesus has received so little attention among those interested in Markan christology; it certainly illustrates the deflected christology portrayed in the Markan Jesus. For the Markan Jesus, not just our group, not just my family, but "[w]hoever does the will of God is my brother and sister and mother" (3:35).

Mark 10 deals with three important issues for the household: marriage and divorce, children, and wealth. The Markan Jesus deflects the Pharisees' interpretations of divorce (based on Deuteronomy) back to the statement about God's intention in creation in Genesis: "God made them male and female" (Mark 10:6). On this basis, Jesus responds to his disciples who ask him "again about this matter": "Whoever divorces his wife and marries another commits adultery against her; and if she divorces her husband and marries another, she commits adultery" (10:10-12). "[F]rom the beginning of creation" (10:6), husbands were not to be valued over wives. Then Jesus indignantly stops the disciples who are stopping those who are bringing little children to him, and he directs the disciples: "Let the little children come to me; do not stop them; for it is to such as these that the kingdom of God belongs. Truly I tell you, whoever does not receive the kingdom of God as a little child will never enter it" (10:14-15). Adults are not to be valued over children. Finally, after the man with "many possessions" goes "away grieving" (10:22) in response to Jesus, Jesus instructs the disciples, "How hard it will be for those who have wealth to enter the kingdom of God!" (10:23), adding in response to their own perplexity, "Children, how hard it is to enter the kingdom of God! It is easier for a camel to go through the eye of a needle than for someone who is rich to enter the kingdom of God" (10:24b-25). The rich are not to be valued above the poor. When, in their response to such a teaching, the disciples ask Jesus, "Then who can be saved?" (10:26), the Markan Jesus deflects attention from human effort to God: "For mortals it is impossible, but not for God; for God all things are possible" (10:27).

But the conversation does not stop there. Peter points out that "we have left everything and followed you" (10:28), which Jesus does not deny but reframes:

> Truly I tell you, there is no one who has left house or brothers or sisters or mother or father or children or fields, for my sake and for the sake of the gospel [NRSV good news], who will not receive a hundredfold now in this age—houses, brothers and sisters, mothers and children, and fields, with persecutions—and in the age to come eternal life. But many who are first will be last, and the last will be first (10:29-31).

Yes, whoever does the will of God will have an extended family now—and also persecutions! But doing the will of God involves reversing power expectations; whoever would be first must be first to serve those who are last.

A third time Jesus predicts his passion (10:33-34), and a third time the disciples display their misunderstanding, this time in the request of James and

John. Jesus asks them, "What is it you want me to do for you?" (10:36), a question he will repeat to Bartimaeus in the next story (10:51), receiving a significantly different answer. In response to the request of James and John for positions of honor in his "glory," Jesus comments and asks a second question: "You do not know what you are asking. Are you able to drink the cup that I drink, or be baptized with the baptism that I am baptized with?" (10:38). Jesus does not dispute their straightforward and confident answer ("We are able"; 10:39a); however, he does set it in a broader context: "The cup that I drink you will drink; and with the baptism with which I am baptized, you will be baptized; but to sit at my right hand or at my left is not mine to grant, but it is for those for whom it has been prepared" (10:39b-40)—prepared, that is, by God. The Markan Jesus deflects his disciples' concern for their own future positions of honor—and their assumption that he would have interest in and power over such future positions—to God, the only one who does have such power and the one who wills that those who would be first must be servants of all (9:35). A third and final time the Markan Jesus offers discipleship instruction, trying to clarify his challenging teaching by a contrast with the usual way of thinking about power and service:

> You know that among the Gentiles those whom they recognize as their rulers lord it over them, and their great ones are tyrants over them. But it is not so among you; but whoever wishes to become great among you must be your servant, and whoever wishes to be first among you must be slave of all. For the Son of man came not to be served but to serve, and to give his life a ransom for many (10:42-45).

No response of the disciples is narrated. The story moves on to Jericho, where Bartimaeus asks to see again, receives his sight, and follows Jesus "on the way"— to Jerusalem.

Although Bartimaeus was mentioned briefly above as a suppliant to whom the Markan Jesus responds, because his story is more elaborate than some and he becomes, at its end, one of the other followers of Jesus, his story deserves a more detailed look, especially in terms of deflected christology. Outside Jericho, blind Bartimaeus calls out to Jesus: "Son of David, Jesus [following the order of the appellations in Greek against the NRSV], have mercy on me!" (10:47); and, even though many try to silence him, he calls out again, "Son of David, have mercy on me!" (10:48). Neither the Markan Jesus nor the Markan narrator comments directly on the designation "Son of David."[25] Against Ferdinand Hahn and others, I have argued in the previous chapter that the Markan Jesus here ignores the phrase "Son of David." When Jesus stops and speaks to Bar-

---

25. Paul J. Achtemeier, "'And He Followed Him': Miracles and Discipleship in Mark 10:46-52," *Semeia* 11 (1978): 115–45, notes that "the negative trajectory of the Davidic ancestry of Jesus in Mark 11 and 12 . . . enables one to see more clearly the relative insignificance of the title ["Son of David"] within the story itself" (115; see also 118–19).

timaeus, the "Son of David" language drops out: Bartimaeus calls Jesus "My teacher" (Aramaic *Rabbouni*, 10:51); and, when Jesus restores his sight, Bartimaeus follows Jesus "on the way" (10:52). After his direct encounter with the Markan Jesus, Bartimaeus speaks and acts like a follower and no longer calls Jesus "Son of David."

The contrast between the Markan Jesus' response to the unclean spirits and demons and the crowds and his response to Bartimaeus is instructive. What the unclean spirits and demons, as transcendent characters, say—that Jesus is the Son or the Holy One of God—is also announced by the narrator (1:1[26]) and by God (1:11; 9:7), although the unclean spirits and demons are opposed to God and are thus in a struggle with God and Jesus. The Markan Jesus silences the unclean spirits and demons. What the crowds say, at least in the first half of the narrative, is that Jesus' teaching authority and healing power are amazing, on which the Markan narrator agrees. The Markan Jesus attempts to silence the crowds. This command becomes more understandable when applied also to the disciples when Peter confesses Jesus as the Christ but soon thereafter rejects Jesus' teaching about suffering persecution. What Bartimaeus says initially, calling out to Jesus as "Son of David," is not affirmed by the Markan narrator or the Markan Jesus. Jesus does not explicitly silence Bartimaeus, but Bartimaeus, after his direct and enlightening encounter with Jesus, drops the term and calls Jesus "*Rabbouni*," my rabbi or my teacher.[27] When the Markan narrative moves from the encounter of Jesus with Bartimaeus outside Jericho to the encounter with the crowds outside Jerusalem, the name David is invoked again (as will be discussed below) and again is not responded to by either the Markan Jesus or the Markan narrator.

It would appear that when the Markan Jesus commands silence it is to arrest half-knowledge, knowledge that focuses too much on the power of Jesus and not enough on the power of God. Centering on God is essential to deflected christology. The power of healing and authoritative teaching comes

26. The textual arguments about "Son of God" in Mark 1:1 were discussed earlier in chapter 2, on projected christology, in relation to what the narrator says about Jesus in Mark 1:1. See also Yarbro Collins, *Mark*, 130, who rejects the phrase as secondary.

27. Ian Henderson, "Reconstructing Mark's Double Audience," in Malbon, ed., *Between Author and Audience*, 6–28, observes that "BarTimaeus and those in Mark's audience like him can get away with addressing Jesus as 'Son of David' where Peter and those in Mark's audience like him must first learn servanthood" (24). I would also observe that Bartimaeus "gets away with" addressing Jesus as "Son of David" only in the sense that he is not directly reprimanded; he is healed by Jesus of Nazareth (not Bethlehem) because Jesus is a merciful healer and because the kingdom of God is breaking in. Henderson's larger point is well taken: not everyone in the Markan audience would be expected to understand the significance of "Son of David" when Bartimaeus uses it; but I would add that those who can follow that debate will need to listen carefully when Jesus does address the issue directly, not aimed negatively at Bartimaeus but at "the scribes" (see my comments below on 12:35-37).

from God. Suffering for the sake of service to those with the least power is not inconsistent with the will of God. Half-knowledge can be transformed into full understanding by those who attend to the entire Markan narrative, just as half-sight can become full sight under the Markan Jesus' care (8:22-26). False knowledge (e.g., Jesus as "Son of David") is silenced indirectly, by being ignored not only by the Markan Jesus but also by the Markan narrator and by (God), who are the three most valued authorities for the implied author and audience. Thus some of the commands to silence usually examined under the category "the messianic secret in Mark" might well be explored under the category deflected christology.

As we noted earlier in chapter 2, on projected christology, the Markan Jesus' response to "those who went ahead and those who followed"[28] as he entered into Jerusalem was profound silence when they shouted, "'Hosanna! Blessed is the one who comes in the name of the Lord! Blessed is the coming kingdom of our ancestor [Gk father] David! Hosanna in the highest heaven!'" (11:9-10). Perhaps the Markan Jesus' focus on the coming kingdom of *God* (the only one to whom the Markan Jesus refers as "father"; see 13:32 and 14:36) is de-centered by the crowd's acclamation of "the coming kingdom of our father [NRSV ancestor] David" (11:10). Thus Jesus' silence here, in concert with his continual emphasis on the kingdom of *God* up to this point, deflects attention away from "the one who comes in the name of the Lord" to the Lord, that is, God, directly.

At his entry into Jerusalem and once again as he prepares for the celebration of the Passover there, the Markan Jesus asks his disciples to make arrangements on his behalf, procuring a colt for the entry (11:2-3) and a room for the Passover (14:13-15). In their narrative contexts, these two "predictions" of the near future, immediately and exactly fulfilled, give credence to Jesus' larger predictions in the eschatological discourse that they frame (chapter 13). However, in the context of narrative christology, what is most intriguing about these two statements of the Markan Jesus is their use of a term or "title" used by other characters or the narrator to refer to Jesus. At 11:3, Jesus instructs two of his disciples what to do if anyone asks about their taking the colt: "[J]ust say this, 'The lord [the NRSV capitalization is an overtranslation] needs it and will send

28. In the previous chapter, on projected christology, the direct speech of these speakers was discussed along with that of anonymous characters in the broad category of the crowds/people/some. The anonymous terms "many" (Gk *polloi*) and "others" (Gk *alloi*) appear in 11:8, presumably describing the same characters as those who speak in 11:9-10. The term "crowd" (Gk *ochlos*) does not appear in this pericope. But here in the discussion of the Markan Jesus' response—or nonresponse—to these characters, they are grouped with "followers" because of the narrator's terminology in describing them as "those who followed" (11:9). It would appear this pericope is unique—and uniquely ambiguous—on several counts, including how to categorize the speakers (followers in what sense?) and how to evaluate their speech.

it back here immediately.'" At 14:14, Jesus instructs two of his disciples to say to the owner of the house into which the man carrying a jar of water enters, "'The teacher [again the NRSV capitalization is uncalled for] asks, Where is my guest room where I may eat the Passover with my disciples?'" The Markan Jesus is not explicitly calling himself "the lord" (and certainly not "the Lord," which he uses for God alone) or "the teacher" but giving the disciples exact words to use in making the necessary arrangements for their stay with him in Jerusalem. The Markan Jesus appears to recognize that his disciples and others would refer to him as "the master" (Gk *kyrios*) or "the teacher."

In Jerusalem, when Peter points out to Jesus that the fig tree he cursed ("May no one ever eat fruit from you again"; 11:14) has withered, the Markan Jesus deflects attention from himself to God: "Have faith in God. . . . [W]hatever you ask for in prayer [to God], believe that you have received it, and it will be yours" (11:22, 24).[29] If one asks God for forgiveness of one's trespasses, and also forgives others, one will receive forgiveness from God (11:25)[30] because to "repent, and believe in the gospel" are the appropriate responses to the "time [that] is fulfilled and the kingdom of God [that] has come near" (1:15). When he is departing the Jerusalem temple for the last time, the Markan Jesus points out to his disciples a poor widow who is putting two small copper coins into the treasury; Jesus is still trying to shift their attention to what it means to be last in order to be first, saying to them: "Truly I tell you, this poor widow has put in more than all those who are contributing to the treasury. For all of them have contributed out of their abundance; but she out of her poverty has put in everything she had, all she had to live on" (12:43-44).

Yet, when they are outside the temple, the disciples are still impressed by the grandeur of the temple complex itself (13:1), so the Markan Jesus again tries to deflect admiration, this time by referring to the future of this powerful institution and these grand buildings: "Do you see these great buildings? Not one stone will be left here upon another; all will be thrown down" (13:2). Undaunted, four of the disciples ask Jesus to tell them the "when" and "what" of "the sign" of "these things . . . to be accomplished" in the future (13:4). Equally undaunted, the Markan Jesus asserts his ignorance in contrast to God's

29. Cf. Michael L. Cook, S.J.: "The Temple and the power structure it represents are replaced with the exhortation: 'Have the faith of God!' Such faith empowers one with God's point of view" (*Christology as Narrative Quest* [Collegeville, Minn.: Liturgical Press, 1997], 89). Such empowerment with God's point of view is shared with the prophets. As Broadhead notes, "In his teaching activity [concerning the fig tree/temple/fig tree scene] Jesus employs citation of the prophets to interpret this prophetic drama. In this manner the condemnation of the temple originates not in the personality of Jesus, but in the prophetic tradition of the OT" (*Teaching with Authority*, 171).

30. On Mark 11:22-25 in context, see Sharyn Echols Dowd, *Prayer, Power, and the Problem of Suffering: Mark 11:22-25 in the Context of Markan Theology* (SBLDS 105; Atlanta: Scholars Press, 1988).

knowledge: "But about that day or hour no one knows, neither the angels in heaven, nor the Son, but only the Father" (13:32).[31] This statement is at the core of deflected christology. No matter who keeps pointing to Jesus, the Markan Jesus keeps pointing to God—and to the need for continual discipleship among those who would do the will of God: "Beware, keep alert; for you do not know when the time will come" (13:33).

The details of Jesus' eschatological discourse are beyond our present scope, although the "Son of Humanity" reference in 13:26 will be considered in the following chapter. However, one aspect of the discourse is of special relevance to narrative christology, the Markan Jesus' comment on "false Christs": "And if anyone says to you at that time, 'Look! Here is the Christ [NRSV Messiah]! or Look! There he is!'—do not believe it. False christs [NRSV messiahs] and false prophets will appear and produce signs and omens, to lead astray, if possible, the elect. But be alert; I have already told you everything" (13:21-23). Neither applying nor accepting the "title" Christ for himself, the Markan Jesus labels as "false" any who claim it by drawing attention to themselves by "signs and omens" to lead the elect astray, that is, away from God. Earlier, as part of the discipleship instruction in the second passion prediction unit, the Markan Jesus had said that those who "are of Christ" will graciously receive lowly service (a cup of water) from whoever offers it and those who give it "will by no means lose the reward" (9:41). Here he says that "false christs" will do just the opposite: produce powerful-looking signs and omens to lead others astray, away from God. These are the only two times the Markan Jesus speaks the term "Christ"; neither is applied directly to himself, but both are important to his presentation of deflected christology.

Once the passion narrative begins in chapter 14, the responses of the Markan Jesus to the disciples focus, not surprisingly, on his fast-approaching persecution and the implications of that persecution for them. Concerning the woman who anoints his head in the house of Simon the leper at Bethany, Jesus says to the disciples, "Let her alone; why do you trouble her. . . . She has done what she could; she has anointed my body beforehand for its burial. Truly I tell you wherever the good news is proclaimed in the whole world, what she has done will be told in remembrance of her" (14:6a, 8-9). At his final celebration of the Passover with his disciples, Jesus tells them, "[O]ne of you will betray me, one who is eating with me" (14:18). "It is one of the twelve, one who is dip-

---

31. On 13:32, see Donahue, "Neglected Factor," 590–92. "The ignorance of the day in 13:32 as well as the submission to the will of God in 14:36 are not ways of describing an ontological relationship but of portraying Jesus as a model of trusting fidelity. Even though Jesus will sit at the right hand of power (14:62) and share in the final judgment (13:26), and even though in his life he was the one who spoke uniquely for God, he still stands before the mystery and transcendence of God" (592). The deflected christology of the Markan Jesus is for the sake of God's transcendence.

ping bread into the bowl with me" (14:20). Also at the Passover table, Jesus says to the disciples, "Take; this is my body. . . . This is my blood of the covenant, which is poured out for many. Truly I tell you, I will never again drink of the fruit of the vine until that day when I drink it new in the kingdom of God" (14:22b, 24-25). All these stories will be told in remembrance.

A little later, at the Mount of Olives, Jesus warns his disciples, in the words of God's prophet Zechariah, "You will all become deserters; for it is written, 'I will strike the shepherd, and the sheep will be scattered'" (14:27; cf. Zech 13:7), but Jesus also comforts them: "But after I am raised up, I will go before you to Galilee" (14:28). Peter, not too surprisingly, seems to need a second warning (14:30), which he remembers too late (14:72). At Gethsemane, Jesus says to all his disciples, "Sit here while I pray [to God]" (14:32), and to Peter, James, and John, "I am deeply grieved, even to death; remain here, and keep awake" (14:34). At Jesus' next response, Peter, unable even to stay awake, loses his nickname (Peter, "rock"): "Simon, are you asleep? Could you not keep awake one hour? Keep awake and pray [to God] that you may not come into the time of trial; the spirit indeed is willing, but the flesh is weak" (14:37b-38). But the other disciples are included too in a final response: "Are you still sleeping and taking your rest? Enough! The hour has come . . ." (14:41a). What the Markan Jesus does as he faces his fast-approaching death is pray to God, and this is what he recommends to his disciples. Prayer does not make suffering easy, but prayer is a reaching out to God for whom "all things are possible" (10:27), although not all are willed (14:36). But the conversation between the Markan Jesus and the disciples that began on the shores of the Sea of Galilee with "Follow me" (1:17) ends at Gethsemane with Jesus' words: "Get up, let us be going. See, my betrayer is at hand" (14:42).

We have listened to the Markan Jesus' responses to his disciples, his unending attempts to help them understand the implications of the in-breaking rule of God—for joy and for suffering, for life and for death. Now we return to the beginning of Mark's Gospel to listen to the co-temporal conversation between the Markan Jesus and the Markan Jewish authorities, or rather, in considering deflected christology or what Jesus says in response, to the Markan Jesus' side of that conversation.

Jesus' Responses to the Jewish Authorities

Although the narrator sets the Markan Jesus' authority in contrast to that of the Markan scribes at Jesus' initial teaching and exorcizing in the Capernaum synagogue ("for he taught them as one having authority, and not as the scribes"; 1:22), his first reported verbal response to Jewish authorities is in the initial scene of his return "to Capernaum after some days" (2:1). There "some of the scribes" (2:6) respond to Jesus' statement to the paralytic, "Son, your sins are forgiven" (2:5) by (as the narrator explains in an inside view) "questioning in their hearts, 'Why does this fellow speak in this way? It is blasphemy! Who can forgive sins but God alone?'" (2:6-7). The Markan Jesus, however, also has this inside view of the scribes and thus can respond to them publicly:

> At once Jesus perceived in his spirit that they were discussing these questions among themselves; and he said to them, "Why do you raise such questions in your hearts? Which is easier, to say to the paralytic, 'Your sins are forgiven,' or to say, 'Stand up and take your mat and walk'? But so that you may know that the Son of Man has authority on earth to forgive sins"—he said to the paralytic—"I say to you, stand up, take your mat and go to your home" (2:8-11).

The Markan Jesus' announcement to the paralytic that "your sins are forgiven" uses the theological passive and probably should be read, "your sins are forgiven by God," in which case Jesus is not taking the initiative in forgiving the man's sins but proclaiming to the man the availability of forgiveness and healing, which are interconnected, as a consequence of the in-breaking rule *of God.* It is almost as if the implied audience is to assume that Jesus not only has an inside view of the scribes but of God; the Markan Jesus knows the forgiving and healing power of God and knows how to make it available to others. This is not the interpretation of the Markan scribes, however, and the Markan Jesus' response to them—"so that you may know that the Son of Man has authority on earth to forgive sins" (2:10)—is hardly designed to address their concerns. (The cryptic "Son of Humanity" statements of the Markan Jesus will be considered in the following chapter on refracted christology.) Although the Markan Jesus deflects attention to God by the theological passive, he also raises the question of how the authority of the Son of Humanity on earth is related to the authority of God. Yet the narrator confirms that the people witnessing the encounter understand the focus on God: "They were all amazed and glorified God" (2:12, one of the narrator's only two direct uses of "God"; cf. 1:14).

This scene of the healing of the paralytic and the controversy over forgiveness of sins is the first of five controversy stories involving the Markan Jesus and the Jewish authorities that are arranged chiastically, and also with linear progression, in 2:1–3:6.[32] In the second controversy story, "the scribes of the Pharisees" (a unique phrase) ask Jesus' disciples about him: "Why does he eat with tax-collectors and sinners?" (2:16). But Jesus hears of their question and responds to them directly: "Those who are well have no need of a physician, but those who are sick; I have come to call not the righteous but sinners" (2:17). As in his previous response, here again Jesus links the needs for health and forgiveness with God's concerns for people and thus with his own concerns as the proclaimer of the in-breaking rule *of God.*

---

32. For the classic study, see Joanna Dewey, *Markan Public Debate: Literary Technique, Concentric Structure, and Theology in Mark 2:1–3:6* (SBLDS 48; Chico, Calif.: Scholars Press for SBL, 1980).

Those who question Jesus in the third controversy story are only designated as "they" or "people" (reflecting the third-person plural ending of the Greek verb at 2:18a), but their question to Jesus clearly involves the Jewish authorities: "Why do John's disciples and the disciples of the Pharisees fast, but your disciples do not fast?" (2:18b). Jesus' response combines three metaphors: the bridegroom, new cloth, and new wine (2:19-22). Just as one cannot without loss sew a patch from new (unshrunk) cloth on an old cloak or put new wine into old (already stretched-out) wineskins, so, it would seem, one cannot without loss incorporate a new proclamation of the in-breaking rule of God into existing social structures. The image of the bridegroom with the wedding guests captures the joy of the new, but the statement that "[t]he days will come when the bridegroom is taken away from them" (2:20) foreshadows the loss that will also be entailed. The Markan Jesus deflects attention from the immediate activities of his disciples (not fasting) to a deeper issue: not only health, forgiveness, and joy but also loss and fasting result from the in-breaking of the rule of God.

In the second controversy story, "the scribes of the Pharisees" ask Jesus' disciples about his eating patterns (eating with sinners); in the fourth controversy story, the Pharisees ask Jesus about his disciples' eating patterns (plucking grain on the Sabbath): "Look, why are they doing what is not lawful on the sabbath?" (2:24). Although Gene Boring is correct to note that Mark, in contrast to Matthew 12:1, does not explicitly mention that the disciples were hungry or that they ate the grain heads they plucked,[33] it is not far-fetched to conclude that this is implied. The issue again is the Law—how to interpret the Law in one's daily practice of devotion to God. The Markan Jesus argues for a precedent for breaking the bounds of sacred and profane time (Sabbath rules) in David's breaking of the bounds of sacred and profane space (the temple showbread), suggesting from this use of God-given Scripture that the Jewish tradition has always had the flexibility to stretch its rules for the sake of human need because of God's care for people: "The sabbath was made for humankind, and not humankind for the sabbath" (2:27). Jesus' approach, however, is hardly accommodating of the Pharisees' concerns: "Have you never read . . ." (2:25) is clearly not a kindly overture to biblical interpreters! And, while citing Scripture for the first time, the Markan Jesus again raises the complex issue of how God's authority is related to the authority of the cryptic Son of Humanity: "so the Son of Man is lord even of the sabbath" (2:28).

The fifth and final story in this series raises again—and escalates—the controversy over Sabbath observance. Here "they" (presumably the Pharisees from the previous controversy story; see 3:6) are waiting in the synagogue (sacred space) on the Sabbath (sacred time) "to see whether he would cure him [the man with a withered hand] on the sabbath, so that they might accuse him"

33. M. Eugene Boring, *Mark: A Commentary* (The New Testament Library; Louisville: Westminster John Knox, 2006), 91.

(3:2). The Markan Jesus transforms the question that is implicitly theirs (Is it lawful to heal on the Sabbath?) in a way that builds on his consistent focus on God's care for persons and God's power for health and forgiveness as the rule of God breaks in—and also relies on storyteller's exaggeration: "Is it lawful to do good or to do harm on the sabbath, to save life or to kill?" (3:4). At this point the narrator takes over in order to bring the entire series of controversy stories to its culmination. The conversation with the Pharisees, the most active Jewish authorities in the first half of the narrative, comes to an end: "they were silent" (3:4). Jesus "looked around at them with anger; he was grieved at their hardness of heart," and he healed the man who had a withered hand with a word only ("Stretch out your hand") and no physical work (3:5). But this restoration of health as a mark of the in-breaking rule of God is not without loss: "The Pharisees went out and immediately conspired with the Herodians against him, how to destroy him" (3:6).

The next response of the Markan Jesus to the Jewish authorities comes in the complex passage concerned with the source of his healing power. We have already considered this intercalated pericope (3:19b-35) involving an array of human characters (Jesus, the crowd, his family [literally "those around him"], the scribes who came down from Jerusalem, his mother and brothers) and references to an array of transcendent characters (Beelzebul, demons, Satan, the Holy Spirit) from the point of view of enacted christology and projected christology. Here our focus is the Markan Jesus' response to the Markan "scribes who came down from Jerusalem [and] said, 'He has Beelzebul, and by the ruler of the demons he casts out demons'" (3:22).[34] Our focus is particularly on what Jesus' response manifests about deflected christology. Behind Jesus' metaphoric answer about "a kingdom . . . divided against itself" that "cannot stand" (3:24) is his proclamation about "the kingdom of God [that] has come near" (1:15). Satan's kingdom, surely under stress with Jesus' successful exorcisms as part of the in-breaking rule of God, is not in danger of an internal breakup but is being attacked from outside—by God. It is the radical confusion of these two strong kingdoms, these two opposed powers—God and Satan—that is the unforgivable sin in the Markan Jesus' response—blasphemy against the Holy Spirit (which came "into" Jesus at his baptism, 1:10), the Holy Spirit *of God*. To say of Jesus, as the Markan "scribes who came down from Jerusalem" do here, "He has an unclean spirit" (3:30), is to misunderstand completely the Markan implied author's view of this cosmic struggle and the role of the Markan Jesus in it. The response of the Markan Jesus is thus, and again, to deflect attention from himself, here as exorcist, to God, the source of such exorcisms. As we noted earlier concerning Jesus' response to the crowd around him in the following story (3:31-35), the story that closes this intercalation, the Markan Jesus also deflects

---

34. For a thorough literary analysis of 3:23-27 in context, see Shively, "The Story Matters," which is described in note 6.

attention from his own natural family to his new family as "[w]hoever does the will of God" (3:35). God is the measure of both cosmic and human relationships for the Markan Jesus.

In chapters 4, 5, and 6 the Markan Jesus is engaged with his disciples and various crowds and suppliants, one of whom, surprisingly, is a Jewish authority figure, "one of the leaders of the synagogue named Jairus" (5:22). After the consistent portrayal of Jesus in conflict with Jewish authorities from 1:22 to 3:30, this episode cracks open what might otherwise be a monolithic stereotype of Jewish authorities as only opponents of the Markan Jesus. Jesus' response to Jairus is, "Do not fear, only believe [have faith]" (5:36). Faith in what? Faith in the power of renewal in the in-breaking rule of God. Jairus' faith is exceptional for a Jewish authority figure, but it parallels the faith of the hemorrhaging woman with whom his story is intercalated. Because of her faith she is healed and welcomed back into the community of the people of God as "daughter" by the Markan Jesus (5:34), and because of Jairus' faith the life of his daughter is renewed. Health and renewed life are marks of the rule of God proclaimed by the Markan Jesus.

In chapter 7, the Markan Jesus and the Markan Pharisees encounter one another again. The last time they engaged in conversation—always one-sided because this is Jesus' story!—was in the fourth and fifth controversy stories of 2:1–3:6, involving Sabbath rules and the Markan Jesus' first bringing of Scripture to bear on his argument with the Jewish authorities (2:23–3:6). But in chapter 7 the Pharisees are with some of the scribes who had come down from Jerusalem (7:1), who last engaged the Markan Jesus in the dispute over whose power (God's or Satan's) is behind his exorcisms (3:22-30). This is an impressive coalition of Markan Jewish authorities. They put their question to Jesus in terms of his disciples' practices, but it is clear that they regard Jesus as responsible for such practices among his followers: "Why do your disciples not live according to the tradition of the elders, but eat with defiled hands?" (7:5). By again bringing Scripture to bear on the argument, the Markan Jesus is deflecting the challenge from the hand-washing habits of his disciples to a deeper issue concerning "the commandment of God":

> Isaiah prophesied rightly about you hypocrites, as it is written,
> "This people honors me with their lips,
> but their hearts are far from me;
> in vain do they worship me,
> teaching human precepts as doctrines."
> You abandon the commandment of God and hold to human tradition.
>
> 7:6-8

This way of arguing is at the core of the deflective christology manifested by the Markan Jesus. Attention is deflected from "human tradition" that some follow and others do not to "the commandment of God," which is regarded as foundational for everyone. After thus defending his disciples, the Markan Jesus goes on the offensive with a second example of the same principle, interpreting "Corban" as human tradition over against the scriptural commandment of God to "Honor your father and your mother" (7:10).

In their next appearance the Pharisees are alone, and they do not even receive from the implied author the opportunity for direct speech; the narrator simply reports: "The Pharisees came and began to argue with him, asking him for a sign from heaven, to test him" (8:11). The narrator prepares for Jesus' response by noting that "he sighed deeply in his spirit": "Why does this generation ask for a sign? Truly I tell you, no sign will be given to this generation" (8:12). In Mark's Gospel, "signs" are not positive, and those who seek them are misdirected (cf. 13:4, 22[35]). Here the Markan Jesus offers the Pharisees no redirection; perhaps the implied audience is to recall that God's presence is being made known in the powerful healing and teaching available through the Markan Jesus as the proclaimer of the in-breaking rule of God.

At 10:2-9 the Pharisees make their next appearance. Again they are alone; again the narrator comments that their motive was "to test him" (10:2; cf. 8:11); and again the Markan Jesus engages them in biblical interpretation. The Markan Pharisees raise the point of Law and practice: "Is it lawful for a man to divorce his wife?" (10:2). The Markan Jesus forces them to claim their scriptural basis and set forth their interpretation first: "What did Moses command you?" (10:3). This time the Pharisees have Scripture, not just "human tradition," to cite: "Moses allowed a man to write a certificate of dismissal and to divorce her" (10:4; from Deut 24:1). But Jesus asserts that this "commandment" was written only because of their "hardness of heart" (10:5) and that an earlier scriptural text gives God's intent: "from the beginning of creation, 'God made them male and female.' 'For this reason a man shall leave his father and mother and be joined to his wife, and the two shall become one flesh'" (10:6-8; from Gen 1:27; 2:24). When the Pharisees cite tradition, Jesus cites the commandment of God; when the Pharisees cite the commandment of God, Jesus cites an earlier commandment of God as primary!

The Markan Jesus quotes Scripture again, not so much in response to the Jewish authorities but in their seat of authority, the temple, and in the hearing of the chief priests and scribes (11:15-18): "Is it not written, 'My house shall be called a house of prayer for all the nations'? [Isa 56:7] But you have made it a den of robbers [Jer 7:11]" (11:17). This comment follows Jesus' action in the temple—more a clearing of the temple than a cleansing of it—and the scholarly literature on this episode is far-reaching. But in terms of the present focus on deflected christology, what is important to note is that the Markan Jesus quotes a text from Isaiah, with God as the speaker, that centers on prayer for all the

---

35. The word "sign" (Gk *sēmeion*) does appear with a positive valence in the longer ending of Mark (16:17, 20), another of many differences that characterize this text as a later addition.

nations (or Gentiles; Gk *ethnoi*) as the function of God's "house." The Markan Jesus' deflection of attention *from* the buying and selling that were essential to the role of the temple as a center of sacrifice *to* its role as a center of prayer for all nations would likely have had a profound effect on Mark's first-century audience if, as many scholars argue, this audience had recently experienced the destruction of the temple and the loss of a sacrificial center.

A second series of stories involving controversy between the Markan Jesus and the Markan Jewish authorities, recalling the series of controversy stories set in Galilee at 2:1–3:6, is presented at 11:27–12:34 with Jesus "walking in the temple" (11:27). Although there are five stories involving Jewish authorities as characters, only the first four result in controversy. In the first story "the chief priests, the scribes, and the elders" ask Jesus "[b]y what authority" he is doing "these things" (11:28). "These things" is a bit open-ended, and so is Jesus' response. Because they will not answer his question about whether the authority of John the baptizer was "from heaven," that is, of God, or "of human origin," Jesus refuses to answer their question about his authority. However, the choice is obvious: from God or not. God, and the authority of God, are the central focus. The second story is Jesus' parable of the wicked tenants told to "them," presumably the chief priests, scribes, and elders, who, according to the narrator, "realized that he had told this parable against them" (12:12). With his now usual rhetorical technique, Jesus adds a quotation from Scripture to the end of the parable, introduced by his repeated and unfriendly "Have you not read this scripture: 'The stone that the builders rejected has become the cornerstone; this was the Lord's doing, and it is amazing in our eyes'?" (12:10; from Ps 118:22-23). When the Markan Jesus quotes Scripture, the Markan implied audience is to recognize that he is citing the authority of God.

In the third story the Markan Pharisees and some Herodians heap up flattery of Jesus in an effort to trap him in his reply: "Teacher, we know that you are sincere [true], and show deference to no one; for you do not regard people with partiality, but teach the way of God in accordance with truth" (12:14). But the Markan Jesus, "knowing their hypocrisy" (12:15), turns their trick question about paying taxes to the emperor back on them and deflects attention away from both himself and the emperor to God: "Give to the emperor the things that are the emperor's, and to God the things that are God's" (12:17).[36] The

---

36. On 12:13-17, see Donahue, "Neglected Factor," 572–75. Donahue's powerful conclusion warrants quoting fully: "Thus, these three elements of the pericope: (a) the description of Jesus by attributes normally evocative of divine impartiality, (b) the picture of the encounter as a testing of Jesus and (c) the reaction to his saying (12:17) in language usually characteristic of the manifestation of the power of God in miracle stories (cf. 2:12 and 5:20)—all suggest theological dimensions to the pericope more significant than a bit of church-state parenesis. The test to which Jesus will be put is how he will speak of God and in so speaking how he implicitly defines his own relationship to God. This relationship is dialectical. The attributes and the reaction of the crowd show clearly the presence of

narrator comments that "they were utterly amazed at him" (12:17b). Are the Pharisees and Herodians amazed? What kind of amazement is this? Will this amazement relieve the growing tension? The implied audience must wonder. In the fourth story, when the Sadducees cite Scripture (Deut 25:5-6; but see also Gen 38:8) to form a trick question for Jesus concerning the resurrection (in which they do not believe), Jesus retorts that they "know neither the scriptures not the power of God" (12:24) and cites earlier Scripture, God's words to Moses from the burning bush (Ex 3:6), to focus on God as "God . . . of the living" (12:27).[37]

In the fifth and final story in this series of encounters between the Markan Jesus and the Markan Jewish authorities, one of the scribes, having seen that Jesus answered the Sadducees well (12:28) by focusing on God as God of the living, concurs with Jesus' focus on God in reciting the *Shema* (12:29-33; from Deut 6:4-5),[38] a portion of Scripture central to daily Jewish practice. At this point the Markan Jesus, having found a Jewish authority figure with whom he shares scriptural interpretation, finds nothing to deflect but rather commends the scribe: "You are not far from the kingdom of God" (12:34a). Like the synagogue leader Jairus amid the controversy stories of Jesus and Jewish authorities in Galilee, so here in the Jerusalem temple this one scribe is marked as exceptional, and his response to Jesus and Jesus' response to him prevent the ossifica-

---

God in the teaching of Jesus. Yet this presence remains veiled. Jesus explicitly accepts none of these attributes and the reader must be engaged in learning how they are true of Jesus. In the miracle stories titles of dignity which are addressed to Jesus and then put under the messianic secret are paradoxically true, that is, they are understood in a sense different from that intended by the speaker in the gospel. So here, the reader knows that Jesus has those attributes with which the scribes address him, but knows they are true in a sense different from that of the speaker. These attributes remain hidden under the veil of the human Jesus[,] and the nearness to God which Mark attributes to Jesus must be affirmed without compromising the sovereignty of God. Jesus himself is, then, the prime example of one who renders 'to God the things of God' (12:17)" (574). What Donahue describes here is close to what I am depicting as deflected christology.

37. Cf. Donahue: "The saying of Jesus in 12:26-27 also touches on the nature of God. God is the one who speaks through scripture and affirms his enduring power over death. At the center of his theological treatise on God [12:13-34], the Marcan Jesus reaffirms the core of Jewish monotheism, that God is a God of the living and a living God" ("Neglected Factor," 577).

38. As Donahue notes: "Most significantly the major thrust of this teaching is theistic rather than explicitly christological. Jesus in effect teaches that belief in the one God and service of him is the foundation of any further belief" ("Neglected Factor," 581). As Ferdinand Hahn observes, "For the primitive Jewish-Christian church, as for Jesus, the confession of the one God is a precondition which is taken for granted" ("The Confession of the One God in the New Testament," *HBT* 2 [1980]: 69–84, quotation from 73). What is distinctive is that the Markan Jesus makes the implicit confession of the one God explicit. After the *Shema*, the Markan Jesus also quotes Lev 19:18 in Mark 12:31.

tion of the portrayal of the Jewish authorities as *all* opponents of Jesus. "After that no one dared to ask him any question" (12:34b)—at least for a moment!

In fact, it is the Markan Jesus who asks the next question; however, both Jesus' question and its interpretation are so complex that we will examine that question under a separate subheading below. But first we may note briefly, in contrast to the specific encounter with the one exceptional scribe, the Markan Jesus' warning about the self-serving behaviors of scribes in general (12:38-40). This warning is followed by the last scene of Jesus in the temple: his pointing out to the disciples the self-sacrificing behavior of one poor widow (12:41-44), which was mentioned above in reference to Jesus' responses to the disciples and which will be commented on more fully in chapter 5, on reflected christology. In returning to the question Jesus asked when "no one dared to ask him any [other] question" (12:34), we note that the Markan Jesus moves, as it were, from a position of defense against various representatives of the Jewish authorities (11:27–12:27), to agreement with one scribe (12:28-34), to a position of offense against a view that is depicted by the Markan Jesus as typical of scribes (12:35-37).

JESUS' RESPONSE TO WHAT HE REPORTS THE SCRIBES SAY

The Markan Jesus seems to ask his question of the larger group of his followers, as the narrator's closing line indicates: "And the large crowd was listening to him with delight" (12:37b). But he asks it in the temple, the seat of authority of the Jewish authorities who have taken on the role of his opponents, and he asks it about an opinion he attributes to the scribes:

> While Jesus was teaching in the temple, he said, "How can the scribes say that the Christ [NRSV Messiah] is the son of David? David himself, by the Holy Spirit declared,
> 'The Lord said to my Lord,
> "Sit at my right hand,
> until I put your enemies under your feet."'
> David himself calls him Lord; so how can he be his son?"
> 12:35-37a

Rejection of the application of "Son of David" to the Christ is the obvious conclusion of the Markan Jesus' citation and interpretation of Psalm 110:1 in 12:35-37, despite its use elsewhere as a proof-text for Jesus' exaltation.[39] The logic of the argument of the Markan Jesus is as follows: If David, the inspired speaker of the psalm, reports that "the Lord," that is, the Lord God, said to David's Lord, that is, the Christ (made obvious by the content of God's address

---

39. Achtemeier's step-by-step description of how scholars resist this obvious conclusion is worth a trip to the library to read in full; see "'And He Followed Him,'" esp. 126–27 but also 127–30.

to him: "Sit at my right hand . . .")[40] then David is calling the Christ "my Lord," which David would not do if the Christ were his son and thus lower in status rather than higher in status, as "my Lord" indicates; thus the Christ cannot be the Son of David.[41]

Nevertheless, the pull of the use of Psalm 110:1 as a proof-text for Jesus' Davidic sonship elsewhere in and beyond the New Testament is strong on many Markan readers and interpreters. Clifton Black speaks for many when he observes of 12:37, "Mark's challenge to Jesus' Davidic lineage, given its assertion elsewhere (cf. 10.47-48; Mt 1.1-17; Lk 3.23-38; Rom 1.3; 2 Tim 2.8), is mystifying."[42] From the point of view of Matthew, Luke, Romans, and 2 Timothy, this aspect of the Markan narrative might be mystifying, but reading this text through those is not the best way to make sense of it. As we observed earlier in chapter 2 in relation to projected christology, Bartimaeus' use of the phrase "Son of David" (10:47-48) until the point when he encounters the Markan Jesus but not afterward does not on its own offer sure support for the idea of Jesus' "Davidic lineage." However, many readers and commentators resolve (or dissolve?) the mystery on which Black comments by reading Mark's Gospel against a strong background belief in Jesus as the Son of David that they bring with them to the narrative, a Christian belief that is simply assumed to be in all "Christian" materials.

Ferdinand Hahn is an example of a scholar who reads the straightforward textual meaning of 12:35-37, then rejects it for reasons beyond the text:

> Moreover, it would remain difficult to say how the concluding question ["David himself calls him Lord; so how can he be his son?"] about the relationship of the Son of David and [the Lord] is to be answered; there would only be the possibility of regarding it as improper [that is, as meaning the Christ is not the Son of David], but this again would not be compatible with the fact that precisely in the

---

40. Although the LXX uses the Greek word *kyrios* for both words (paralleled by "Lord" in the English translation), the Hebrew text uses Israel's proper name for God, *YHWH*, in the first instance, and the generic term for "lord" (including human lords), *adonai*, in the second. Also noted by Boring, *Mark*, 347.

41. Joel Marcus, *The Way of the Lord: Christological Exegesis of the Old Testament in the Gospel of Mark* (Louisville: Westminster John Knox, 1992), agrees that "[t]he implicit logic of our passage [12:35-37] is that no father refers to his own son as 'my lord'; therefore it is a misnomer to speak of Jesus as David's son" (139-40) and notes that "[t]his plain sense of the passage is recognized even by some who assert that it *cannot* mean that in its Markan context," citing Matera and Kingsbury as examples (140 n. 38). Marcus himself is in the same position, however, with his assertion that the Markan Jesus' "no" to the "Son of David" title (as linked with "the Christ") really means in Mark's Gospel "not only" (as linked with Jesus as the "Son of God").

42. C. Clifton Black, "Notes on the Gospel According to Mark," *The HarperCollins Study Bible: NRSV* (New York: HarperCollins, 1993), on 12:37.

Palestinian sphere Jesus' sonship of David was an argument brought forward and an attempt was made to prove it by genealogies.[43]

Here the incompatibility between what the Markan Jesus says and the history of the tradition of the "title" "Son of David" that Hahn has carefully researched is resolved in favor of the history of the tradition. In my view, the reconstructed background is permitted to overpower the foreground, the Markan narrative.

Hahn begins his history of the tradition of "Son of David" with the assumption that "[a]ssertions of the status of Jesus as Son of David go back to the early Palestinian church, where an important part must have been played by genealogical trees and the attempt to demonstrate the descent of Jesus from the house of David."[44] This "must have been" the case because "[i]t is indisputable that in the time of Jesus the question of family descent still played a part even among the people, and for the family of Jesus this is confirmed by the information of Hegesippus concerning the relations of Jesus who were introduced to the emperor Domitian," according to the retelling of Eusebius in the fourth century.[45] In support of this assumption, Hahn can cite no Markan texts, even though he considers Mark's Gospel the earliest, but must begin with the (rather late and conflicting) genealogies of Matthew and Luke, along with the earlier Romans 1:3 and the later Revelation 5:5. Hahn admits that "[i]t must not, of course, be forgotten that the description 'Son of David' is markedly infrequent and in a clearly pre-Christian context occurs only in *Psalms of Solomon* 17:21; only in post-Christian times does it become more frequent in Jewish traditions."[46] Yet he concludes that "it need not be assumed that 'Son of David' first struck root in the soil of earliest Christianity; it was certainly adopted but obviously goes back to a not very ancient linguistic use."[47] Hahn summarizes his argument in this way:

> but the descent of Jesus will have acquired quite simply the value of a legitimation, and not least will have contributed to the fact that the specifically this-worldly elements of the Davidic promise and the royal messianism in general were in spite of everything accepted and absorbed after some hesitation.[48]

It appears to me that Mark's Gospel gives witness to that hesitation.[49]

---

43. Ferdinand Hahn, *The Titles of Jesus in Christology: Their History in Early Christianity* (New York: World Publishing, 1969; first published in German in 1963), 105.

44. Hahn, *Titles of Jesus*, 240.

45. Hahn, *Titles of Jesus*, 241.

46. Hahn, *Titles of Jesus*, 242.

47. Hahn, *Titles of Jesus*, 242.

48. Hahn, *Titles of Jesus*, 245.

49. Hahn acknowledges Wrede's argument that in Mark 12:35-37 the title "Son of David" is "altogether rejected" and Wrede's invocation of "a series of later witnesses, the most important of which he regards as Barnabas 12:10f" (*Titles of Jesus*, 252), but Hahn

In Hahn's most direct commentary on Mark 12:35-37, his interpretation of Mark on the basis of material external to Mark is obvious:

> It is just this silence [that is, that no answer is given to the Markan Jesus' question in 12:37a] which gave rise to the supposition that the sonship of David was in general to be repudiated. But since elsewhere in the primitive Christian tradition there is no question of this and since we have Rom. 1:3f. as an outstanding parallel, we shall have to understand the answer implied in v. 37ab as something on the line of our two-stage Christology.[50]

This two-stage christology, based not on Mark but on other texts and what "must have been," is summarized by Hahn as follows:

> Messianic dignity and Lordship are assigned to the Risen and Exalted One; but this lofty dignity and function of rule over all mankind and the whole world does not exclude that Jesus in His lifetime was Son of David and that as such He occupied a quite special position of dignity. Consequently the sonship of David is a characteristic of the earthly reality of Jesus, and has the value of a prior stage of exaltation existing alongside the confession of the messianic power of the exalted One.[51]

Hahn also finds his two-stage christology a better solution than reading 12:35-37 paradoxically: "If we are not willing to accept a 'paradoxical unity' [Lohmeyer] between the Son of David and the transcendent Kyrios (which is an improbable hypothesis to postulate for the thinking of that time), then it must be considered whether the text cannot be explained in the sense of the two-stage Christology."[52]

As Hahn undercuts the Markan Jesus' rejection of the link between "Son of David" and "the Christ" by his creative reconstruction of the history of the tra-

---

is unconvinced. Hahn argues that "the point of view of the Letter of Barnabas is better explained against the background of the situation in the second century" and that "there is no plain indication that this kind of debate goes back to the earliest Christian times, for in the gospel of Mark and also in Matthew and Luke . . . affirmations of Jesus' being Son of David are calmly and unhesitatingly accepted" (252). I suspect such a reading of Mark is overly influenced by readings of Matthew and Luke; for my argumentation see the excursus to my article, "The Jesus of Mark and the 'Son of David,'" in Malbon, ed., *Between Author and Audience*, 181. The silence of the Markan Jesus (and the narrator) in relation to Bartimaeus' initial use of "Son of David" does not strike me as strong evidence for the "title" being "calmly and unhesitatingly accepted." For the text and translation of the relevant passage in *Barnabas*, see Yarbro Collins, *Mark*, 580; she regards *Barnabas* as "dependent on one or more of the Synoptic Gospels indirectly" (581). Dieter Zeller lists both Mark 12:35-37 and *Barn.* 12:10-11 as evidence that "some Jewish Christians already refused the title 'Son of David' for their transcendent *kyrios*" ("New Testament Christology in Its Hellenistic Reception," *NTS* 47 [2001]: 312–33, quotation from 315).

50. Hahn, *Titles of Jesus*, 253.
51. Hahn, *Titles of Jesus*, 253.
52. Hahn, *Titles of Jesus*, 252.

dition surrounding Mark's Gospel, so Joel Marcus makes a similar move based on his creative reconstruction of the theology of the redactor of Mark's Gospel. Marcus writes:

> In questioning the adequacy of the Davidic image of the Messiah, the Markan Jesus points to divine sonship and cosmic exaltation as the true horizons of the Messiah's identity. In Mark's eyes, Jesus is indeed the consummation of the centuries-old hope for a coming king from the line of David, a hope that [Jewish revolutionary] Simon [bar Giora] and all the other "messiahs" have falsely claimed to fulfill. But he is more than that because he has ascended not only the road to Jerusalem but also the way to the heavenly throne room, there to be enthroned at God's right hand and invited to wait until he has seen God put all his enemies under his feet.[53]

The creativity of Hahn's reconstruction of the history of the tradition and of Marcus' reconstruction of the theology of the redactor is obvious, but both overshadow the creativity of the Markan narrative itself. Neither Hahn nor Marcus recognizes a distinction between the Markan Jesus and the Markan narrator, a distinction I have found to be crucial to understanding Markan narrative christology. But, as I have argued earlier, I do not see even the Markan narrator arguing for Jesus as the "Son of David," a title against which the Markan Jesus clearly argues as linked to "the Christ."

---

53. Marcus, *Way of the Lord*, 151. Stephen P. Ahearne-Kroll, *The Psalms of Lament in Mark's Passion: Jesus' Davidic Suffering* (SNTSMS 142; Cambridge: Cambridge University Press, 2007), who focuses on the Markan narrative and not Markan redaction, also concludes that Jesus' saying does not really negate the "Son of David" connection but redefines it: "the earthly, militaristic images evoked by the 'Son of David' are downplayed and denied, but the royal imagery is still upheld by the quotation of Ps 110:1," and "Mark emphasizes the heavenly aspects in this messianic imagery" (164, 165). Despite significant differences, there seems to be a shared dichotomy between earthly and heavenly realms or aspects within the interpretations of "Son of David" by Hahn, Marcus, and Ahearne-Kroll; so also Yarbro Collins (*Mark*, 582: "He is son of David, but not in the way that many in this time would expect. His identity is best expressed in terms of the juxtaposition of and tension between the suffering Son of Man and the glorious Son of Man related to the vision of a heavenly one like a son of man in Dan 7:13") and Boring, *Mark* (see note 57). But I think Robin Griffith-Jones' caution is called for here: "Uncertain how to describe the understandings of, hopes for, and reliance on 'heaven' current in the first century CE, we readily draw distinctions between earth and heaven that leave earth as we now know and assess it; heaven can then be defined and described in some detail by its strangeness. . . . We need to recognize how dramatically strange the conceptual worlds of Jews and non-Jews in Jesus' time would be to us. . . . Mark was trying to disclose a *fullness* of divine and human together in Jesus that defied any then-current conceptual scale; the veil between heaven and earth that mattered was the veil over the eyes of the beholder who could not see in the life of Jesus what there was to be seen" ("Going Back to Galilee to See the Son of Man: Mark's Gospel as an Upside-Down Apocalypse," in Malbon, ed., *Between Author and Audience*, 82–102, quotation from 99).

The Markan narrative context of Jesus' question about what the scribes say about the "Son of David" both illustrates the creativity of the implied author and clarifies the point of view of the Markan Jesus. First, four episodes of confrontation with Jewish authorities in the temple are presented in Mark 11–12: (1) 11:27-33, with chief priests, scribes, and elders concerning authority; (2) 12:1-12, Jesus' parable of the wicked tenants; (3) 12:13-17, with Pharisees and Herodians concerning paying taxes; (4) 12:18-27, with Sadducees concerning the resurrection. Then, four linked sections of Jesus' teaching are presented: (1) 12:28-34, the mutual commendation between Jesus and the exceptional scribe discussing the "first" or greatest commandment; (2) 12:35-37, Jesus questioning how the scribes can say that the Christ/Messiah is the son of David; (3) 12:38-40, Jesus warning about the self-serving behaviors of scribes; (4) 12:41-44, Jesus pointing out the self-sacrificing behavior of the poor widow. The first three of these sections focus on scribes; the fourth, focused on the giving widow, is linked by the preceding reference to scribes who "devour widows' houses" (12:40).[54] A pattern emerges with the progression of the four passages: (1) a positive evaluation of what one scribe says and does, (2) a negative evaluation of what scribes generally say, (3) a negative evaluation of what scribes generally do, (4) a positive evaluation of what one poor widow, of the type victimized by scribes, does. The scribe in section 1, immediately preceding the Markan Jesus' argument in section 2, is clearly portrayed as exceptional. The scribes in section 2 and in the succeeding section 3 are portrayed as (stereo-)typical (they do not even appear directly as characters), and the view that the Christ is the Son of David is attributed to them (12:35) and thus rejected. Thus the Markan context of the Markan Jesus' questioning of what the scribes say about the Christ/Messiah as the Son of David reinforces its surface meaning, that is, the meaning most obviously understood from the logic of the Markan Jesus' words: The Christ cannot be the Son of David. The *ad hominem* argument (it cannot be true because the stereotypical scribes say it) is added to the exegetical argument (it cannot be true because David cannot call his son "my Lord").[55]

54. The Markan Jesus, however, unlike some Markan commentators, does not blame the victim; he calls attention to the widow not as another example of how scribes behave poorly, but as an example of how this poor woman gives richly. For the consideration of additional contexts of the poor widow passage, see Elizabeth Struthers Malbon, "The Poor Widow in Mark and her Poor Rich Readers," *CBQ* 53 (1991): 589–604, republished in Elizabeth Struthers Malbon, *In the Company of Jesus* (Louisville: Westminster John Knox, 2000), 166–88, and also in *The Feminist Companion to Mark* (ed. Amy-Jill Levine; Sheffield: Sheffield Academic, 2001), 111–27.

55. Ian Henderson, with his view of Mark's double audience, remarks, "The whole Markan audience would be able to recognize Jesus' textual reasoning as a parody of expert textual argumentation, whether within a Jewish cultural frame or within the frame of sophist Homeric questions. Yet only an audience with more expertise than Mark itself provides

When the Markan Jesus discredits what the scribes say about the Christ as the Son of David, is he deflecting attention away from himself and toward God as he frequently does? The case is not entirely clear. We noted earlier that the Markan Jesus seems to silence those proclaiming a half-truth (e.g., Peter's "You are the Christ") and ignore those proclaiming a false truth (Bartimaeus' "Son of David"). But here the Markan Jesus is hardly ignoring the scribes to whom he attributes the view that the Christ is the Son of David but arguing against them explicitly. When Peter confessed Jesus as "the Christ," the Markan Jesus did not reject the acclamation but silenced it. When Peter's response to Jesus' first passion prediction betrayed Peter's limited view of the Christ, the Markan Jesus rebuked Peter for setting his mind on human things and then deflected attention to "divine things" (8:33), including taking up one's cross and following Jesus (8:34). Could the Markan Jesus' rejection of the scribes' view that the Christ is to be the Son of David also represent a deflection of attention away from human things and more directly to divine things, away from a human, Davidic king to the kingdom of God? Not enough is indicated about the meaning of "Son of David" *internal to the Markan narrative* for the Markan implied audience (or, at least we latter-day interpreters of that implied audience) to be certain, but the Markan Jesus does raise the question just after the discussion of the first (greatest) commandment and the reciting of the *Shema* (12:29-30). Perhaps God is thought somehow to be decentered by an emphasis on the Christ as the "Son of David"[56] in a way not unlike the Markan Jesus' focus on the coming kingdom of God (the father) seems decentered by the crowd's acclamation of "the coming kingdom of our father David" (11:10). (I made this argument earlier in relation to the phrase "King of the Jews" in chapter 2, on projected christology.)

The commentary of Gene Boring moves in a similar direction in interpreting the Markan Jesus' rejection of the Christ as the Son of David:

---

would have recognized Psalm 110 as a central text for messianic speculation" ("Mark's Double Audience," 24–25).

56. Ian Henderson notes that "Jesus in Mark 12:35-37 is going out of his way to argue against the appropriateness of a scribal, royal Davidic Christology. Perhaps some of Mark's audience were expected to share the anti-hierarchical glee of Jesus' listeners (12:37). On the other hand, we ought also to imagine a category of . . . [elite readers for whom such a belief in Jesus' Davidic sonship] would pre-define 'anointedness' in positive terms of authority and power. For the latter readers—primary to Mark's overall argument—Mark is a lesson in relocating anointedness in harsh self-sacrifice and voluntary servitude as well as eschatological hope for the resolution of 14:62" ("Mark's Double Audience," 25). Richard A. Horsley argues that when Jesus "refutes the official scribes' view that 'the Messiah is the son of David,'" the "point is clearly to reject any notion of the messiah-king as an imperial ruler (just as Jesus had rejected James' and John's aspirations after imperial power and prestige in 10:35-45)" (*Hearing the Whole Story: The Politics of Plot in Mark's Gospel* [Louisville: Westminster John Knox, 2001], 251).

At the narrative level, the issue is not Jesus' own identity as the Christ, which has not yet been publicly disclosed. Nor does Jesus introduce the subject to respond to a challenge about his own Davidic descent, which is not an issue in Mark. There is no indication in Mark that the author or his community contends that Jesus is descended from David, and that this was disputed by Mark's opponents. The issue is the general image and mission associated with messianic faith: Son of David empowered by God to bring in the kingdom "from below," or suffering Son of Man who will return from heaven to establish God's kingdom "from above." . . .

. . . Biological descent is not at issue; the point is how the Christ is understood—as a David-like one who will fulfill Israel's national hopes, or as the transcendent Lord who will come again as Son of Man.[57]

The Markan Jesus refers to David one other time in the Markan narrative, when defending his disciples' plucking of grain on the Sabbath against the accusations of the Pharisees:

Have you never read what David did when he and his companions were hungry and in need of food? He entered the house of God, when Abiathar was high priest, and ate the bread of the Presence, which is not lawful for any but the priests to eat, and he gave some to his companions (2:25-26).

Like the Markan Jesus' exegesis of Psalm 110:1 at 12:35-37, here also the Markan Jesus interprets a passage from Scripture, 1 Samuel 21:1-6. (As we noted earlier in considering Jesus' responses to the Jewish authorities, this is the Markan Jesus' first instance of bringing Scripture to bear in a conflict with them.) Although the Markan Jesus makes an error in naming the high priest at the time of the story to which he refers (it should be Ahimelech, not his son Abiathar; see 1 Sam 22:20),[58] the name of the high priest is not essential to the Markan Jesus' analogy. The Markan Jesus is employing an ancient part of Jewish tradition, a David story, to confront a contemporary debate, the Pharisees' more stringent application of Sabbath regulations. As Boring notes, "[J]ust as the Scripture reports that David did 'what was not lawful' when he ate the sacred bread and shared it with those with him (1 Sam 21:1-9), so Jesus authorizes his disciples to transgress the biblical and traditional norms."[59] The David story serves the

57. Boring, *Mark*, 348–49; see note 53 for a critique of this earthly/heavenly dichotomy. Although there is a gap between, on the one hand, my interpretation and that of Boring concerning "Son of David" as rejected in Mark, and, on the other hand, the interpretation of "Son of David" as revised in Mark held by Marcus, Yarbro Collins, and Ahearne-Kroll—with other differences among all of us as well, it would appear we could all agree with this comment of Yarbro Collins: "The question about the messiah as son of David is thus part of a complex and nuanced narrative portrayal of Jesus as messiah" (*Mark*, 582).
58. Matthew (12:4) and Luke (6:4) leave out the name altogether, probably as a gentle correction of the Markan text.
59. Boring, *Mark*, 90–91. Achtemeier includes this passage (2:23-27), along with the discussion of Jesus' parentage in 6:1-3, as "other passages in Mark which point to his indifference,

Markan Jesus as a legitimization for questioning cultic regulations on the basis of God's care for hungry persons.[60] The saying of the Markan Jesus that follows his citation of the biblical story rests on this point: "The sabbath was made for humankind, and not humankind for the sabbath . . ." (2:27). The Markan Jesus' antagonism toward the Pharisees here, part of the pattern of controversy stories at 2:1–3:6 discussed earlier, is paralleled later by his argument against what he asserts the scribes say about the Christ as the son of David (12:35-37).

This long detour concerning "Son of David" is important to understanding the characterization of the Markan Jesus as narrative christology. Only at 12:35-37, concerning the scribal view of the Christ as the son of David (as reported by Jesus), does the Markan Jesus present a sustained argument about what might be considered a "christological title." Although two terms are at stake, "Christ" and "Son of David," it is the linking of the two that is argued against by the Markan Jesus at 12:35-37, and that subject will come up again as we complete our survey of the Markan Jesus' responses to the Jewish authorities. What I have argued here is that, in Mark's Gospel, the title "Son of David" is ignored by Jesus when offered by Bartimaeus (as is the "coming kingdom of our father David" when offered at his entrance into Jerusalem) and argued against by Jesus as linked to "the Christ," a view he attributes to the scribes. In addition, neither the Markan narrator nor the Markan voice (of God) has anything to say about "Son of David," positively or negatively. Because these three voices—the Markan voice of God, the Markan Jesus, and the Markan narrator—are the three most valued by the Markan implied author and implied audience, it seems inappropriate to go against them when interpreting Markan christology, especially Markan narrative christology.

Significant questions remain, including how these observations about the Jesus of Mark and the "Son of David" intersect with the observations of other Markan scholars.[61] For example, if the Markan narrative does not support

---

if not hostility, to Jesus' davidic background. In 2:23-27 . . . [t]he obvious statement, however, that a descendant of David should be permitted the same latitude as his forebear is not made. Had Mark, or the tradition, been intent on showing Jesus' davidic ancestry, this would have been an excellent place to make that point" ("'And He Followed Him,'" 127–28).

60. Although, as mentioned earlier, Boring is correct to note that Mark, in contrast to Matt 12:1, does not explicitly mention that the disciples were hungry or that they ate the grain heads they plucked, this is a reasonable implication, especially because in the analogous story the followers of David were hungry and did eat. Thus I would not exactly agree with Boring that "the Markan argument is not that 'human need is more important than Sabbath rules'" and that "[e]ven in this first saying, the focus is entirely on Jesus' authority" (91). The Markan argument seems twofold, like the two sayings juxtaposed at its conclusion (2:27)—based on human need *and* on Jesus' authority as Son of Humanity. Boring and I agree entirely on the larger issue: "Mark's Christology has no Davidic typology and is extremely cautious about interpreting Jesus in Davidic terms" (91).

61. I did not realize until my penultimate draft of the paper behind this chapter what an

interpreting Jesus as Son of David, how are we to interpret or reinterpret what many scholars have commented on as Mark's "royal messianism"?[62] This issue was raised in chapter 2 on projected christology in relation to interpretation of the term "King of the Jews." How does an interpreter tell the difference between the implied paradoxical presentation of an idea or image (Jesus as "Son of David" or Jesus as "king") and its implied critique and rejection? If, as I suggested earlier, "king" is not simply revised but in fact rejected as an appropriate way to understand the Markan Jesus, could it be that "Son of David" is also not simply revised but also rejected as an appropriate designation for the Markan Jesus? The Markan narrative evidence seems even stronger with regard to "Son of David."

---

important precursor I had in the 1978 *Semeia* article of Paul Achtemeier! Having rediscovered this critical essay, I am now wondering why it has not had more influence. Although Achtemeier asked redaction critical questions (it was 1978), and I am asking narrative critical questions, Achtemeier's priority in interpretation has been my own: "If we begin the investigation, however, not with the ambiguous statements about Jesus as son of David (in 10:46-52 the title is abandoned in v 51; in 11:1-10 it does not appear), but with the passage that most unambiguously speaks of Jesus as son of David, namely 12:35-37, and work from the clearer to the unclear passages, the results will be quite different" from the usual way of arguing against "the simplest interpretation" of 12:35-37 that "the Christ (for Mark clearly Jesus) is not the son of David the scribes await" ("'And He Followed Him,'" 126–27).

62. Donald Juel, *Messiah and Temple: The Trial of Jesus in the Gospel of Mark* (SBLDS, 31; Missoula, Mont.: Scholars Press, 1973); Frank J. Matera, *The Kingship of Jesus: Composition and Theology in Mark 15* (SBLDS, 66; Chico, Calif.: Scholars Press, 1982). The more recent work of Ahearne-Kroll (*Psalms of Lament*) reaffirms much of the previous discussion of Mark's "royal messianism," even extending it to the portrayal of the suffering of Jesus as Davidic suffering, based especially on the evocation of four Psalms of Lament (LXX 21, 40, 41–42, 68) in the Markan passion narrative. Like others, Ahearne-Kroll argues that Mark's Gospel revises this royal messianism, with his suggested revision being a rejection of a traditional militaristic image of "Son of David" for Jesus in favor of an image of a suffering, yet dissenting, Davidic messiah, concluding: "It seems to me that the suffering David who cries out to God for his saving action and challenges God to answer for his absence in the midst of suffering is the model that lends itself readily to Jesus' situation in Mark. The Davidic model carries the irony of royal depiction of Jesus throughout the trial, but it also accounts for how Jesus suffers in Mark. The Davidic model also adds the dimensions of faithful dissent and the search for an understanding of God's will for the one who suffers" (*Psalms of Lament*, 195–96). I find Ahearne-Kroll's argument about the "Son of David" image that Mark is revising, an argument that is rich in research about the cultural context as well as interested in the Markan narrative, quite intriguing; but, if my reading, which is focused more narrowly on the narrative christology of the Markan text, has merit, it may be that Mark's Gospel critiques the "Son of David" image more severely than Ahearne-Kroll imagines. Of course, knowledge of the cultural context is essential to any interpretation of any text, and the need for such knowledge about "Son of David" is especially clear in Mark's Gospel because so little of the background is inscribed in the text itself. But literary and historical investigations need to work not only in tandem but also as cross-checks, with critics from varying starting points on the literary-historical continuum challenging each other.

Another question raised by my understanding of "Son of David" in Mark's narrative involves the relationship between the Markan Jesus and the Markan narrator, who differ in their overall foci (God for the Markan Jesus, Jesus for the Markan narrator) but agree in ignoring "Son of David." We will return to this question at the conclusion of this chapter, and now—after this more detailed examination of Jesus' response to what he says the scribes (one group of Jewish authorities) say—we return to our overview of Jesus' responses to the Jewish authorities.

JESUS' RESPONSES TO THE JEWISH AUTHORITIES—CONTINUED

After the extensive collection of scenes in the Jerusalem temple from 11:27 through 12:44, with numerous responses to Jewish authorities, the Markan Jesus leaves the temple and interacts primarily with his disciples, or smaller groups of them, from 13:1 through 14:45. The narrator does note, at 14:1-2, the plotting of the chief priests and scribes against Jesus, but the Markan Jesus does not respond to the Jewish authorities again until 14:48-49, at the point of his arrest by "a crowd with swords and clubs, from the chief priests, the scribes, and the elders" (14:43). Is his response to the whole crowd? "Have you come out with swords and clubs to arrest me as though I were a bandit?" (14:48). Or is Jesus addressing the Jewish authorities specifically? "Day after day I was with you in the temple teaching, and you did not arrest me. But let the scriptures be fulfilled" (14:49). These phrases, "in the temple teaching" and "let the scriptures be fulfilled," remind the implied audience of the encounters with and discussions about the Jewish authorities in 11:27–12:44. Again and again in the temple teaching, the Markan Jesus had deflected attention from human authority to God, from the interpretations of Jewish authorities to his own scriptural interpretations, from contemporary challenges with the Romans to giving "to God the things that are God's" (12:17). Or is Jesus speaking to his followers? "All of them deserted him and fled" (14:50).

As the Markan Jesus moves toward his lowest point, he confronts the highest Jewish authority, the high priest. Jesus maintains silence (14:61) long enough to frustrate the high priest, ignoring his first question, "Have you no answer? What is it that they [those giving testimony the narrator twice identifies as "false"] testify against you?" (14:60). Finally Jesus does accede, although somewhat elliptically, to the high priest's second, and directly christological, question in a setting that will lead to his death, when to respond otherwise might well "save" his life (see 8:35). The high priest asks, "Are you the Christ [NRSV Messiah], the Son of the Blessed One?" (14:61), being too observant of Jewish tradition to pronounce the name of God. Jesus answers, "I am" (Gk *Egō eimi*, 14:62). Against Kingsbury,[63] it seems to me unlikely that this *Egō eimi* can be free of the connotations of the divine recognition formula (Exod 3:14, LXX; see also Isa 43:10-13) so clearly called upon in its one other Markan usage,

---

63. Kingsbury, *Christology*, 119 n. 202.

when Jesus, walking on the sea, tells the disciples *Egō eimi* (6:50; NRSV "It is I").[64] On the one hand, the Markan Jesus is consistently reticent to speak of himself or defend himself; but, on the other, when he does speak he echoes the words of God—which could also be considered observant of Jewish tradition, perhaps deflecting attention and honor to God.

Here an intriguing and relevant observation has been made by Elizabeth Shively:

> Though the Holy Spirit is not explicitly named when Jesus stands trial before the Council, these connections in the narrative [between Jesus and his followers, with reference to 13:11] imply that what Jesus says as a witness before the high priest is given to him in that hour. When the high priest asks him, "Are you the Christ, the Son of the Blessed One?" (14:61), the reader imagines that it is not Jesus who speaks but the Holy Spirit when he breaks his silence and answers, "I am, and you will see the Son of Man, seated at the right hand of Power, and coming with the clouds of heaven" (v. 62; cf. 13:11).[65]

In fact, I could add, the words "seated at the right hand" (14:62) are a second evocation of Psalm 110:1, which the Markan Jesus earlier quoted as the words of David "by the Holy Spirit" (12:35-36). If the Holy Spirit is understood by the implied audience to be speaking through the Markan Jesus, the deflection of attention from Jesus to God is even clearer.

Still, just what is the implied audience to understand the Markan Jesus is affirming about himself in his "I am" reply to the high priest's question, "Are you the Christ, the Son of the Blessed One?" Perhaps the two parts of the high priest's question will help the implied audience recall the two parts of the narrator's identification of Jesus in the opening line of the Gospel: "Jesus Christ, Son of God." Concerning "Son of God": Early on in the narrative, as the Markan Jesus manifests the power for health and forgiveness of the in-breaking rule of God, transcendent characters—unclean spirits and the voice (of God)—recognize the Markan Jesus as the "Son (or the Holy One) of (the Most High) God." Toward the end of the narrative, the Markan Jesus does respond affirmatively to the penultimate appearance in the Gospel of a term equivalent to "Son of God" ("Son of the Blessed One"), in the high priest's

---

64. Broadhead notes of the "I am" at 6:50, "the saying points directly to the unique identity and mission of Jesus in relationship to Yahweh" (*Teaching with Authority*, 125). However, the significance of the Markan Jesus' "I am" statement on the sea passes the disciples by, as Broadhead notes: "Ironically, Mk 6.47-53 employs a miracle story to narrate the failure of miracles to lead the followers of Jesus to faith and understanding" (*Teaching with Authority*, 127). The Markan Jesus' second "I am" statement, in the context of his persecution and imminent death, gives the implied audience what is needed to understand the statement more fully.

65. Shively, "The Story Matters," 138.

question—but not without immediately deflecting the focus elsewhere and refracting the high priest's terms with an allusive "Son of Humanity" statement (which will be discussed in the following chapter). At Jesus' death, the Roman centurion says, "Truly this man was Son of God [NRSV God's Son]!" (15:39). Concerning "Christ": At midpoint in the narrative, the Markan Jesus silences Peter's confession, "You are the Christ" (8:29), which likely represents as much misunderstanding as understanding on Peter's part, confusion as much as confession. Not long after that, in instructing his disciples about the way of discipleship, the Markan Jesus links lowly service and acceptance of others who offer such service with being "of Christ" (9:41). Later, Jesus labels those who say "the Christ" is here or there and "produce signs and omens" as "false Christs" (13:21-22). Toward the end of the narrative, the Markan Jesus does respond affirmatively to the penultimate appearance in the Gospel of the term Christ,[66] in the high priest's question—but not without immediately deflecting the focus elsewhere and refracting the high priest's terms with an allusive "Son of Humanity" statement. Just as the silencing of Peter's application of "Christ" does not invalidate the term entirely for the Markan Jesus, neither does his acceptance of it, or acquiescence to it, in the setting of his "trial" or administrative hearing make its meaning for the Markan Jesus entirely clear. It is the Markan narrative as a whole that must provide whatever clarity there is.

Is the context of persecution and suffering sufficient to make sense of the Markan Jesus' willingness to accept the term "Christ" when it is presented by the high priest at 14:60-61?[67] Or does Jesus' immediate juxtaposition of the term "Son of Humanity" refract what is meant by "Christ" in such a way that the Markan Jesus can accept the designation? Or does the separation of "Christ" and "Son of David" by the Markan Jesus at 12:35-37 have something to do with his final, if brief, acceptance of the term "Christ" in the presence of the high priest? Or is there a relation between the Markan Jesus' rejection of the "Christ"/"Son of David" connection and his opposition by the priestly establishment represented by the high priest's question? Responses to these questions may not be so much alternatives as layers of meaning.

---

66. The final use of "Christ" is in the mocking of the crucified Jesus by "the chief priests, along with the scribes" at 15:31-32, to which Jesus makes no response.

67. Observing the close association of Peter's denial and Jesus' confession, James R. Edwards comments, "The disciples have misunderstood Jesus (8:14-21), Judas has *secretly* betrayed him (14:10-11), but Peter's repudiation is the first open denial of Jesus. By contrast, Jesus' confession before the chief priest, 'I am [the Christ, the Son of the Most Blessed]' (v 62), is the first time in Mark that Jesus drops the veil of silence and openly confesses his identity. Jesus' identity is thus revealed at the moment of his deepest humiliation and weakness" ("Markan Sandwiches: The Significance of Interpolations in Markan Narratives," *NovT* 31 [1989]: 193–216, quotation from 212). Contra Scott, who provides an anachronistically Trinitarian reading of 14:62 ("Chiastic Structure," 23).

Jesus' Response to Pilate

Pilate is the sole Roman authority to whom the Markan Jesus responds.[68] Pilate, of course, asks Jesus a Gentile question: "Are you the King of the Jews?" (15:2). The Markan Jesus responds rather begrudgingly, "You say so" (15:2), a response positive enough to seal his death but noncommittal enough to disvalue the discourse. Whereas others speak sarcastically of Jesus as "*King* of the Jews"—Pilate (15:2, 9, 12; cf. 15:26), the soldiers (15:18), and even the chief priests and scribes (15:32, "the Christ [NRSV Messiah], the King of Israel")—Jesus speaks seriously of the *king*dom of God. The Markan Jesus consistently deflects honor away from himself and toward God.

Throughout the narrative the Markan Jesus tries to avoid acclamation and deflect honor to God; yet in the passion narrative Jesus accedes to those acclamations—or accusations—that lead to his death, accepted as the will of God (see 14:36; cf. 10:45). Thus even in his death the Markan Jesus deflects attention to God. As Donahue notes,

> Jesus is not simply a model to be followed on the way of suffering, but a model of one who in the midst of suffering can address God as *abba*, and who can see in suffering the will of God, even with the awareness that this will could be otherwise (14:34-36). The conjunction of suffering and discipleship leads one to the mystery of God and not simply to a contemplation of the cross of Jesus.[69]

"Therefore the problem of suffering for Mark is one of *theodicy*; the cross becomes the stumbling block because it cannot be reconciled with the way one thinks of God."[70]

---

68. Although Herod is "Jewish" in some sense, he is also the official representative ("king" in Mark's Gospel) appointed by the Roman Empire to oversee Galilee, and his words about Jesus were discussed along with those of Pilate as "the Roman authorities" in the previous chapter on projected christology. However, the Markan Jesus makes no response to Herod.

69. Donahue, "Neglected Factor," 587. Or, in the words of Eduard Schweizer, the conjunction of suffering and discipleship leads one to the hiddenness of God: "Here is the hiddenness of God at its most radical: 'My God, my God, why hast thou forsaken me?' . . . This fundamental hiddenness of God, which is disclosed only to the follower, is intended by Mark's messianic secret which he introduces four times with his characteristic word *diastellesthai* ('to charge'). But that the miracle of discipleship has really happened and that God's revelation will reach its goal, a Gentile, a few women, and a half-believing on-looker who buries Jesus are the sign" ("Mark's Theological Achievement" [trans. R. Morgan], in *The Interpretation of Mark* [2nd ed.; ed. William A. Telford; Edinburgh: T&T Clark, 1995], 63–87, quotation from 80; first published in *EvT* [1964]: 337–55).

70. Donahue, "Neglected Factor," 587, just prior to the previous quotation; italics original.

The Markan Jesus and God

The response of the Markan Jesus to what other Markan characters say to and about him illustrates deflected christology: the Markan Jesus attempts to deflect attention and honor from himself to God.[71] The Markan Jesus insists that it is God's power that heals and exorcises demons. The Markan Jesus also teaches about God with the authority of God and accepts persecution at the hands of the powerful on behalf of the powerless as the will of God. Although the Markan narrator opens with a bold statement about Jesus—"The beginning of the good news of Jesus Christ, the Son of God" (1:1)—only twice does the narrator speak about God, and then only in reference to Jesus ("Jesus came to Galilee, proclaiming the good news of God . . . ," 1:14; "they were all amazed [at Jesus' healing of the paralytic] and glorified God," 2:12). In the two would-be appearances of God in the Markan narrative, God does not actually appear; a voice from heaven or from a cloud, implicitly the voice of God, is heard by some of the characters. But for the Markan Jesus, God is as central as Jesus is for the Markan narrator. Here we will explore this centrality of God to the Markan Jesus by investigating what he says to and about God. Some overlaps with material previously discussed are inevitable. We considered what (God) says to and about Jesus in the previous chapter on projected christology, and now we will discuss what Jesus says in response. In the following chapter (refracted christology), we will examine what the Markan Jesus says instead of what is said to him, and this too is about God—concerning the Son of Humanity and the kingdom *of God*. In addition, what the Markan Jesus says *about* God, he says to various human audiences, and we have considered that aspect of his speech already in this chapter on deflected christology. So here we will explore how the relationship between the Markan Jesus and God is portrayed by Jesus' response to the voice (of God) at the baptism and transfiguration, his use of the expression *dei* (must), his reference to God as father, his use of "as it is written" in evoking Scripture, his use of theological passives, and his cry to God from the cross. We will conclude this chapter with reflection on the creative tension between the Markan Jesus and the Markan narrator concerning narrative christology.

---

71. For an intriguing exploration of "God's role as the Gospel's main actor and the way God's divergent modes of action come to bear upon the actions of Jesus and his disciples," see Ira Brent Driggers, *Following God through Mark: Theological Tension in the Second Gospel* (Louisville: Westminster John Knox, 2007), quotation from 99. Driggers illustrates the tension between God's invasive activity through Jesus—and the disciples—and God's transcendent activity over against Jesus—and the disciples. Both Jesus' passion and the disciples' failures are doubly explained in Mark—by divine and human causes, with these various tensions ultimately leading the quite human audience to a discipleship of responsibility and impossibility and an experience of the divine mystery.

Jesus' Response to the Voice (of God)
at the Baptism and Transfiguration

God is the one the Markan Jesus wishes to speak about, but twice God enters the Markan narrative as a character—or, rather as a voice[72]—and speaks to and/or about Jesus: at the baptism and at the transfiguration. The scenes are clearly and strongly interrelated. At the baptism scene, the heavens split, the Spirit descends, and a voice comes from heaven saying, "You are my Son, the Beloved; with you I am well pleased" (1:10-11). Jesus says nothing. "And the Spirit immediately drove him out into the wilderness" (1:12). The Markan Jesus makes no attempt to deflect what God says to him directly, perhaps because the words cannot be misunderstood by any of the other characters, who do not even hear them. Then, so it would seem, any possible misunderstanding by the implied audience to the effect that Jesus has been selected for an easy task or a glorious honor is dispelled directly by God's spirit, which throws (Gk *exballei*) Jesus out into the wilderness. At the transfiguration scene on "a high mountain" (9:2), a cloud overshadows Jesus (whose clothes are dazzling white) and Peter, James, and John; then a voice comes from the cloud saying, "This is my Son, the Beloved; listen to him!" (9:7). Jesus says nothing. But "[a]s they were coming down the mountain, he ordered them to tell no one about what they had seen, until after the Son of Man had risen from the dead" (9:9). Here, when other characters also hear the divine voice, the Markan Jesus does directly deflect the statement by insisting on present secrecy and bringing in the term "Son of Humanity" (to be discussed in the following chapter on refracted christology). In neither case (baptism or transfiguration) does the Markan Jesus ever proclaim what the voice says, as other characters and the narrator do. The two scenes are impressively high in drama, but amazingly low in content concerning what it *means* for Jesus to be called God's son.

The actions of Jesus (enacted christology) and the words of Jesus about God (deflected christology) confirm that the Jewish understanding of one obedient to God as a "son of God" is shared by the Markan Jesus.[73] The Markan Jesus, of course, never says, "I am the Son of God." Kingsbury makes much of Jesus' use

---

72. As Kingsbury observes, "One thing Mark does not do: he does not deal with God in the same manner in which he deals with the other characters of his story. With respect to the latter, Mark assumes the posture of the 'omniscient narrator.' . . . With respect to God, however, Mark does not permit the reader to imagine that he has 'unmediated access' either to heaven—God's abode (11:25)—or to his 'mind'" (*Christology*, 48). I might add that the Markan narrator parallels the Markan Jesus on this point; not even Jesus claims to know what God knows (13:32; cf. 10:40).

73. Black, "Mark," *HCSB*, on 1:1; Reginald H. Fuller, "son of God," in *HarperCollins Bible Dictionary* (ed. Paul J. Achtemeier; San Francisco: HarperSanFrancisco for the SBL, 1996), 1051. See also the earlier discussion of "Son of God" in chapter 2, on projected christology.

of the term "son" in the parable of the wicked tenants (12:1-11),[74] but it is good to remember that this is a parable. The Markan Jesus speaks of "the Son" in the third person in the eschatological discourse—precisely in order to deflect honor from "the Son" to "the Father": "But about that day or hour no one knows, neither the angels in heaven, nor the Son, but only the Father" (13:32).[75] And Jesus calls God "Abba, Father" in his prayer in Gethsemane (14:36), seeking release but accepting persecution and death in deference to God's will.[76] Whoever responds similarly, that is, "[w]hoever does the will of God" (3:35), is family to Jesus. Not "I am God's Son" but "Here are" (3:34) "my brother and sister and mother" (3:35) is the heart of the deflected christology of the Markan Jesus.[77]

The baptism and the transfiguration scenes are especially important in the Markan interpretation of Kingsbury. In *The Christology of Mark's Gospel*, he refers frequently to what God "thinks" about Jesus, but these two scenes offer the only two sentences that (God) says to or about Jesus in Mark (1:11; 9:7).

74. Kingsbury, *Christology*, 114–18. Even less convincing is Stephen H. Smith's assertion about the immediately preceding pericope, the question of authority (11:27-33): "For Jesus to act as judge of his people would be to claim the divine prerogative more openly and more bold[l]y than ever before, and, of course, this is precisely what Mark intends to assert: for him Jesus is God, no less" ("The Literary Structure of Mark 11:1–12:40," *NovT* 31 [1989]: 104–24, quotation from 122).

75. Donahue points out that this "disclaimer of Jesus about a role attributed to him equal to God at the end time" parallels Jesus' statement at 10:40, which is one of three occurrences of "a significant statement about God and Jesus' relation to him" that follows each passion prediction. "Peter does not think the things of God (8:33); the one who receives Jesus receives the one who sent him (9:37); and Jesus is not the one who assigns the places of honor in the new age (10:40). . . . Mark constantly relates proper instruction on discipleship not only to a proper understanding of the necessity of suffering but to a proper understanding of the relation of Jesus to God" ("Neglected Factor," 590). Christology deflected is theology proclaimed. Furthermore, as Dahl notes, "The concepts of Christ as the Son and Image of God, the mediator of creation, and the Word Incarnate represent not only developments of Christology but also affirmations of the oneness of God" ("The Neglected Factor," 7).

76. Fuller insists that "[t]he use of 'Son of God' as a Christological title should be clearly distinguished from the Father/Son language" ("son of God," *HCBD*, 1052).

77. Donahue also recognizes that 3:35 is the "key saying and one which provides a hermeneutical key" for the "number of sayings on the lips of Jesus which indicate that Mark roots this wider view of discipleship on the voice of Jesus addressing his church" ("Neglected Factor," 584, 583). Donahue's analysis of some of these sayings illustrates the Markan Gospel's "theistic grounding for discipleship which is a response to the gospel of God and fulfilling God's will" (585). Donahue concludes: "Mark's view of what it means to respond to the gospel is, therefore, wider than either an *imitatio Christi* or even an *imitatio discipulorum*. The essence of responding to the gospel is doing the will of God and the Marcan Jesus is one who summons people to such obedience rather than to literal imitation of his own life. Mark's understanding of God thus provides the way for a more comprehensive theology of discipleship" ("Neglected Factor," 586).

Kingsbury says very little about what Jesus says about God, about which Mark narrates considerably more. When the Markan Jesus deflects attention away from himself and to God, just what view of God does he present? John R. Donahue, S.J., in a critically important article on "God" as "A Neglected Factor in Markan Theology," draws this conclusion from an initial survey of God language in Mark—and a brief comparison with Matthew, Luke, and Paul:

> As one would expect, most references to God [in Mark] are on the lips of Jesus. Jesus speaks of God as the creator of the world and the human family (13:19; 10:6), who will bring human history to a close (13:20) and who prepares a place for the elect (13:20, 27; cf. 10:40). God has power to do what is beyond human conception (10:27); is alone good (10:18); issues commands and has a will which is to be followed (3:35; 7:8); is to be addressed as father in prayer (11:25; 14:36); and is the living God of Abraham, Issac [Isaac] and Jacob (12:27). The observation that there is nothing distinctively new or Christian in this picture of God in respect to the OT or Jewish thought of the time may be true. What is significant, however, is that in Mark, Jesus speaks of God without attributes or ascriptions. . . .
>
> Such reserved speech about God is strong especially in contrast to the anthropomorphism of Matthew and the interventionist or salvation history perspective of Luke. . . .
>
> The comparison of Mark, the other synoptics and Paul underscores the singularity of language about God in Mark. While Mark is closest to Paul in affirming the transcendence and mystery of God, his language is not as rich and nuanced as that of Paul. . . .
>
> . . . In surveying the way Jesus spoke of God, we saw that he speaks with reserve of a transcendent God with virtually no anthropomorphisms.[78]

The Markan Gospel shows reserve in reporting the action of God—the voice (of God) is heard directly only at Jesus' baptism and transfiguration. The Markan Jesus shows reserve not only in deflecting attention from himself to God but even in his speaking of God.[79]

---

78. Donahue, "Neglected Factor," 566, 567, 569, 592–93. This survey represents the first part of Donahue's article; in the other two parts he provides a detailed study of Mark 12:13-34, "Jesus' Jerusalem *didachē* . . . a virtual little treatise *De Deo Uno*" (570), and suggests some implications of the understanding of Mark's *theo*logy for christology and discipleship.

79. The Markan Jesus' reserve in speaking of God should be seen in relation to his tendency to speak in parables, and it is worth noting that Donahue, who has written most clearly about Jesus and God in Mark's Gospel, has also written persuasively on Jesus and the parables (see "Jesus as the Parable of God in the Gospel of Mark," in *Interpreting the Gospels* [ed. James Luther Mays; Philadelphia: Fortress, 1981], 148–67, first published in *Int* 32 [1978]: 369–86; and *The Gospel in Parable* [Philadelphia: Fortress, 1988]). What I am observing of the Markan Jesus' way of speaking of God has been claimed by other scholars for "the historical Jesus," e.g., Hahn, quoting H. E. Tödt's *Menschensohn:* "what is observable elsewhere in the teaching of Jesus, namely, a 'radical reduction of the tendency to picturesque

JESUS' USE OF *DEI* (MUST)

Perhaps another way to illustrate the Markan Jesus' reserve in speaking about God but especially his reserve in speaking about himself in relation to God is to consider how he employs the Greek term *dei* (must), generally assumed to signal "the divine will" or "the divine imperative."[80] When employed by the Markan Jesus, *dei* is a way of deflecting attention from himself to God, a way of interpreting events not in terms of human choices and consequences but in terms of God's ongoing activity in the world as God makes it known. There are six uses of *dei* in Mark, four of which are attributed to Jesus by indirect or direct speech. The first of these six (and these four) is found in the first passion and resurrection prediction, reported by the narrator as the indirect speech of Jesus: "Then he began to teach them that the Son of Man must (*dei*) undergo great suffering, and be rejected by the elders, the chief priests, and the scribes, and be killed, and after three days rise again" (8:31). About this teaching the Markan narrator notes—and this uniquely so: "Openly he was speaking the word" (8:32a, my translation; contrast "openly," *parrēsia*, at 8:32, with "in parables," *en parabolais*, at 4:2; see also 4:33). But Peter reacts strongly, rebuking Jesus and eliciting a rebuke in return and another strong teaching from Jesus: "you are setting your mind not on divine things [that *must* happen] but on human things [that you might like to happen]" (8:33).

The other three uses of *dei* attributed to the Markan Jesus occur in his direct speech within the eschatological discourse: "When you hear of wars and rumors of wars, do not be alarmed; this must (*dei*) take place, but the end is still to come" (13:7). "And the gospel [NRSV good news] must (*dei*) first be proclaimed to all nations" (13:10). "But when you see the desolating sacrilege set up where it ought not to be (let the reader understand), then those in Judea must (*dei*) flee to the mountains" (13:14). The events of the turn of the ages must happen as part of the in-breaking of God's rule (kingdom) on earth. This transitional time *must* include not only "wars and rumors of wars" (13:7) and various social and political crises from which followers *must* flee (13:14) but also—and first—proclaiming the gospel to all nations, a process in which those who do the will of God (3:35) *must* become involved. Thus *dei* connects both parts of the double ending of Mark's Gospel: the eschatological discourse (chapter 13—the passion of the community) and the passion of Jesus (chapters

---

description which is characteristic of all apocalyptic literature'" (Hahn, *Titles of Jesus*, 31). On the problems of assuming historicity for literary strands, see my concluding chapter.

80. Norman Perrin considers that *dei* makes "reference to divine necessity" and "certainly implies the fulfillment of scripture" ("Towards an Interpretation of the Gospel of Mark," in *Christology and a Modern Pilgrimage: A Discussion with Norman Perrin* [ed. Hans Dieter Betz; rev. ed.; Missoula, Mont.: SBL and Scholars Press, 1974; first published in 1971], 1–52, quotations from 19).

14–16).[81] As the divine imperative is behind the fulfillment of the end of the present age and the beginning of the new age, so the divine will is behind the end of Jesus' ministry and life and the new beginning represented by his empty tomb and resurrection.

The two Markan occurrences of *dei* not attributed to Jesus also connect to his passion. Coming down the mount of transfiguration, Peter, James, and John ask Jesus, "Why do the scribes say that Elijah must (*dei*) come first?" (9:11). Thus the scribes are asserted to share the general view of the divine imperative of coming events. But the Markan Jesus' interpretation of the Elijah image (with implicit reference to John the baptizer) is self-interrupted with a statement about the coming suffering of the Son of Humanity (9:11/12/13), fore-shadowing the passion predictions.[82] With heavy irony, Peter takes up the term *dei* for its final Markan usage, proclaiming—not only in spite of but as a result of Jesus' prediction of Peter's denial: "'Even though I must (*dei*) die with you, I will not deny you.' And all of them said the same" (14:31). Peter can perhaps imagine the things of God that *must* be, but he cannot affirm them in the face of personal danger—at least not the first time around.

Yet both parts of the Gospel's double ending indicate a second chance for Peter and other followers: "But go, tell his disciples and Peter that he [Jesus] is going ahead of you to Galilee; there you will see him; just as he told you" (16:7). "As for yourselves, beware; for they will hand you over to councils; and you will be beaten in synagogues; and you will stand before governors and kings because of me, as a testimony to them" (13:9). The divine imperative (*dei*) connects the transition of the present age/new age and the death/resurrection of Jesus—both of which implicate his followers. Both the passion and the eschaton are to be understood in relation to God's ruling activity. *Dei* puts the focus on God, not on Jesus. The Markan Jesus submits to the divine will (14:36) and proclaims that those who likewise do "the will of God" are his "brother and sister and mother" (3:35), and both actions deflect attention from Jesus to God.

JESUS' REFERENCES TO GOD AS FATHER

The Markan Jesus relates to "whoever does the will of God" as family and to God as father; the two are connected, and both deflect attention and honor from himself to God. In Mark's Gospel, Jesus refers to God as father only four

---

81. On the "double ending" of Mark, see Malbon, *Narrative Space*, 151–52 and 199–200 n. 6 and the literature cited there (Perrin, Trocmé, Pesch, Kermode). See also chapter 1, on enacted christology.

82. As Broadhead notes, "In view of this central focus ["the destiny of the Son of Man to suffer much and be despised (9.12)"], the issue of Elijah becomes intelligible: Elijah returned in the form of the Baptist, and they killed him. Thus, even the Elijah question points to the identity of Jesus and, beyond that, to the destiny of all who follow Jesus" (*Teaching with Authority*, 152).

times, fewer than in the other Gospels, but perhaps not so surprising given the Gospel of Mark's avoidance of anthropomorphism in relation to God.[83] The first reference concludes the Markan Jesus' discipleship instruction as part of the first passion prediction unit (8:31, passion prediction; 8:32-33, misunderstanding; 8:34–9:1, discipleship instruction): "Those who are ashamed of me and of my words in this adulterous and sinful generation, of them the Son of Man will also be ashamed when he comes in the glory of his Father with the holy angels" (8:38). Only through association with "his Father" in the age to come is the persecuted Son of Humanity of the passion prediction (8:31) to become the agent of future judgment. According to the Markan Jesus, persecution is the Son of Humanity's distinctive destiny; only in relation to God is the Son of Humanity associated with "glory." The second reference concludes the Markan Jesus' teaching in the intercalated fig tree/temple/fig tree scene and refers to another form of judgment, the forgiving—or not—of sins: "Whenever you stand praying, forgive, if you have anything against anyone; so that your Father in heaven may also forgive you your trespasses" (11:25). Again, attention is deflected to God, the father; it is God who forgives sins. Even earlier in the narrative, the Markan Jesus had used the theological passive in speaking to the paralytic: "your sins are forgiven [i.e., by God]" (2:5), only adding later, when questioned, "that the Son of Man has authority on earth to forgive sins" (2:10), authority clearly derivative from God now that the rule of God is breaking in upon the earth. In the future, when the temple itself is withered, the Markan Jesus asserts that "your Father in heaven" will forgive the sins of those who forgive others their sins. Attention is to be directed not toward Jesus but to the source of all authority and all forgiveness, God, the father.

It is the last two of the Markan Jesus' references to God as father that show most clearly deflected christology, refocusing attention and honor away from Jesus to God. As the eschatological discourse comes to its conclusion, that is, after Jesus has indicated various events that will happen as preludes to the arrival of the new age, Jesus insists on an important caveat: "But about that day or hour no one knows, neither the angels in heaven, nor the Son, but only the Father" (13:32). (The third-person reference to "the Son" here parallels the Markan Jesus' consistent third-person reference to "the Son of Humanity.") The distinction is crucial: Jesus does not know, the Son does not know, God knows. As Jesus' time with his disciples draws to a close in Gethsemane, that is, as Jesus' very life draws to a close, the Markan Jesus again distinguishes himself from God and deflects attention to God: "Abba,[84] Father, for you all things are

---

83. As observed by Donahue, "Neglected Factor," 593.

84. For a definitive critique of the earlier argument, associated especially with Joachim Jeremias, that the Aramaic term *abba* was unique to the historical Jesus and represented his "intimacy" with God, see Mary Rose D'Angelo, "*Abba* and 'Father': Imperial Theology and the Traditions about Jesus," *JBL* 111 (1992): 611–30, and "Theology in Mark and Q: *Abba*

possible; remove this cup from me; yet, not what I want [will, Gk *thelō*], but what you want [will]" (14:36). For God all things are possible—not for Jesus. What is possible for the Markan Jesus is to submit his will to the will of God, the father. This is also the requirement of whoever would be family to Jesus, to do the will of God (3:35).[85]

Michael Cook stresses Jesus' trust in God in these final two references to God as father. He views 13:32 as "an affirmation of trust that God will finally reconcile the seemingly irreconcilable opposition of good and evil." Of 14:36 he comments, "In the midst of his agony, confronted with the massive and overwhelming evil of his opponents' desire for a victim, Jesus is presented as one who fears that God will abandon him but who unwaveringly places absolute and unconditional trust in God imaged as *Abba*."[86] The Markan Jesus' *trust* in God is certainly an important aspect of the narrative at these points; however,

---

and 'Father' in Context," *HTR* 85 (1992): 149–74. The arguments of her first article are succinctly summarized in her second article: "(a) *abba* cannot be attributed with certainty to Jesus; the New Testament evidence suggests that *abba* functioned in and may have originated in the spiritual charismatic experience of the early Christian communities; (b) 'father' and 'my father' functioned as addresses to God in early Judaism, particularly in contexts of gentile persecution; (c) if Jesus used 'father' as an address to God, he is most likely to have done so in the context of resistance to the imperial claims made by Roman use of the title *pater* for the emperor" ("Theology in Mark and Q," 150 n. 4). For a brief but accessible look at the argument of Jeremias, see Joachim Jeremias, *The Central Message of the New Testament* (New York: Charles Scribner's Sons, 1965), 9–30, chapter 1, "*Abba*," and Hahn, "Confession of the One God," 77. My narrative analysis makes no claims about "the historical Jesus." What is relevant here is that 14:36 is the only occurrence of *abba* in Mark's Gospel (or any of the gospels for that matter), and it highlights the distinction between God, for whom all things are possible, and the Markan Jesus, for whom they are not. It may also be the case that a contrast is implied between God, the true father to whom all things are possible, and Caesar, the *pater patriae* (on which see D'Angelo) and head of the Roman imperium represented here by Pilate, an imperium that only seems to have power over the Markan Jesus. In this case there are Markan reverberations between implications and assertions that Jesus is only the son because God is the father (and not Caesar) and Jesus is not "king" because God is (and not Caesar), as discussed earlier in chapter 2. D'Angelo also notes that the foreignness of the Aramaic *abba* in Mark's Greek text "is a sign of its spiritual power," to be compared with Gal 4:6 and Rom 8:15-16 ("Theology in Mark and Q," 159; see 159–62)—spiritual power received from God of course.

85. See Abraham Smith, "Tyranny Exposed: Mark's Typological Characterization of Herod Antipas (Mark 6:14-29)," *BibInt* 14 (2006): 282–85, for an insightful examination of how cognates of *thelō* (will) connect and contrast Herod, Pilate, Jesus, and the disciples in Mark.

86. Cook, *Christology as Narrative Quest*, 97. D'Angelo makes clear the traditional Jewish background of this prayer: close examination of the use of "father" as a divine title in early Judaism indicates that "prayer using 'father' seems to be particularly appropriate for the afflicted and persecuted, especially for the righteous Jew (or proselyte) who is threatened by the wicked and haughty oppressor, especially the gentile oppressor." "In all these contexts, the

I am stressing that it is trust *in God*, not trust in himself or other human beings or leaders or the powers that be.[87] The Markan Jesus' trust is deflected to the only one who is trustworthy: the one God.

JESUS' USE OF "AS IT IS WRITTEN" IN EVOKING SCRIPTURE

In addition to the Markan Jesus' reference to God as father and his use of *dei* (must) as a way to signal divine necessity, deflected christology is manifest in the Markan Jesus' evocation of Scripture as God's revelation and in his use of theological passives. Although we have had occasion to comment on Jesus' use of Scripture and the theological passive above in discussing his responses to both followers and Jewish authorities, the subjects bear looking at again explicitly from the point of view of what is implied about the Markan Jesus' relationship to God. Because both of these subjects (and their scholarly literature) are expansive,[88] we can but sample them here—first the scriptural evocations, then the theological passives. In his survey of God language in Mark's Gospel, Donahue lists six passages that manifest "the assumption that scripture is God's revelation, especially when introduced by *gegraptai* (1:2; 7:6; 9:12-13; 11:17; 14:21, 27; cf. 4:11-12)."[89] A look at these occurrences of *gegraptai* (it is written) as they introduce scriptural quotations in Mark is revealing in terms of deflected christology.

Five of the six *gegraptai* quotations are on the lips of the Markan Jesus; however, the first one is presented by the narrator, just after the title (1:1) of the work:

> As it is written in the prophet Isaiah, "See, I am sending my messenger ahead of you, who will prepare your way; the voice of one crying in the wilderness: 'Prepare the way of the Lord, make his paths straight,'" John the baptizer appeared in the wilderness, proclaiming a baptism of repentance for the forgiveness of sins (1:2-4).

Much commentary has been written on problematic aspects of this long and complicated sentence! The "Isaiah" "quotation" actually conflates material from

---

title 'father' evokes both divine power and authority and a kinship that gives the suppliant a claim upon God" ("Theology in Mark and Q," 152, 153).

87. The language of "trust" also seems somewhat related to the traditional (from Jeremias) focus on the unique "intimacy" of Jesus and God that has been so thoroughly critiqued by D'Angelo (see note 84). Cook does assert that the first two references of the Markan Jesus to God as father "appear to be traditional formulations, but the last two touch the very core of Jesus' [unique? intimate?] relationship to God" (*Christology as Narrative Quest*, 97).

88. An appropriate starting point for this scholarly literature would be Marcus, *Way of the Lord*. See also Howard Clark Kee, "The Function of Scriptural Quotations and Allusions in Mark 11–16," in *Jesus und Paulus: Festschrift für Werner Georg Kümmel zum 70. Geburtstag* (ed. E. Earle Ellis and Erich Grässer; Göttingen, Germany: Vandenhoeck & Ruprecht, 1975), 165–88.

89. Donahue, "Neglected Factor," 566.

Isaiah 40:3 with Exodus 23:20 and Malachi 3:1. In addition, in Isaiah 40:3 in the Septuagint, the Greek translation of the Hebrew Scriptures and Mark's presumed source, "in the wilderness" is part of the cry itself, not the location of the one crying, and the term "Lord" is paralleled by the term "God," not "his." The first of these differences makes the Markan quotation apply more directly to John the baptizer who "appeared in the wilderness," and the second difference makes the term "Lord" open-ended enough to be applied by the implied audience to Jesus. Some commentators have argued that the "it is written" clause should be connected with what precedes it, 1:1, a move that requires the addition of a verb: The beginning of the gospel of Jesus Christ, the Son of God, *is* as it is written. . . . Others of us argue that 1:1 should be allowed to stand as the only Markan sentence without a verb (and thus as a proclamation, a title) and that the "it is written" clause should be connected to what follows it, as in the NRSV quoted above.[90] Nevertheless, nearly all would agree that, by this opening scriptural evocation voiced by the narrator, the implied author is establishing the renewing activity of God with the people of God as the context for hearing this narrative about Jesus.[91] The activity of God in sending the messenger results in the messenger calling for repentance from the people. Certainly the Markan Jesus affirms the activity of God as the context of his own activity and proclamation: "The time is fulfilled, and the kingdom of God has come near; repent, and believe in the good news" (1:15). And by this inaugural proclamation, the Markan Jesus deflects attention to God, in tune, it would seem, with the force of the narrator's opening with "as it is written" that focuses on the continuing activity of God but not with the title (1:1) of the narrative that focuses on Jesus.

The other five passages in Donahue's list of *gegraptai* quotations are voiced by the Markan Jesus. Two portions of Scripture introduced by "it is written" are directed by the Markan Jesus to Jewish authorities: first the Pharisees and scribes in Galilee (7:6), although these scribes "had come from Jerusalem" (7:1), and then the Jewish authorities in the temple, especially the chief priests and scribes (11:17). In the first instance, Isaiah 29:13 is applied to the Pharisees and scribes, designated as hypocrites, in a way "common" to "prophetic condemnation of empty worship."[92] In the second instance, Isaiah 56:7 and Jeremiah 7:11 are applied to the leaders of the temple, still in usual prophetic style. The Markan

90. For a somewhat fuller discussion of these problematic aspects of 1:2-4, see chapter 2, on projected christology, in relation to what the narrator says about Jesus in Mark 1:1.

91. Cf. Schweizer, "Mark's Theological Achievement," 65: "Precisely because Mark elsewhere hardly ever makes use of so-called scriptural proofs, the superscription for the whole Gospel is all the more astonishing. It says that Mark wants to present not the words and deeds of Jesus but the gospel of Jesus Christ (the Son of God), and that in it God's history with Israel, as the prophets announced it, has come to fulfilment. Therein consists the properly theological achievement of Mark" (see also 68).

92. Black, "Mark," *HCSB*, on 7:6-7.

Jesus deflects attention to God, just as the Hebrew prophets do. The remaining three passages in Donahue's list are addressed by Jesus to his disciples; however, the first two are linked not to a specific quotation from Scripture but to the "Son of Humanity." When Peter, James, and John ask Jesus why the scribes say that Elijah must come first, Jesus responds,

> Elijah is indeed coming first to restore all things. How then is it written about the Son of Man, that he is to go through many sufferings and be treated with contempt? But I tell you that Elijah has come, and they did to him whatever they pleased, as it is written about him (9:12-13).

In the absence of any particular scriptural text that can be brought to bear on the situation, the suffering of Elijah/John the baptizer and the Son of Humanity/Jesus is embedded in God's activity as "it is written" generally in Scripture. So also at 14:21: "For the Son of Man goes as it is written of him, but woe to that one by whom the Son of Man is betrayed!" As a prophet, the Markan Jesus calls the leaders of Israel to return to God (7:6 and 11:17); as one who, like prophets and others before him, will have to endure persecution as part of his calling, the Markan Jesus tries to prepare his followers for that intense focus on the will of God (9:12-13 and 14:21).

The Markan Jesus' final use of *gegraptai*, also addressed to his disciples, does introduce a specific biblical quotation. After his final meal with his disciples, Jesus departs with them to the Mount of Olives, where he says: "You will all become deserters; for it is written, 'I will strike the shepherd, and the sheep will be scattered'" (14:27, quoting Zechariah 13:7). Quoting and applying Scripture is a way of directing attention to the activity of God in the world, and the Markan Jesus employs this strategy with his disciples as well as with the Jewish authorities. The quotation from Zechariah in Mark 14:27 is particularly telling because it incorporates a theological passive (the sheep will be scattered, that is, by God) in parallel with a statement that identifies the actor as God (I will strike the shepherd; God is the speaker in Zech. 13:7), thus confirming the theological nature of the passive construction. Another biblical quotation by Jesus, with an introductory *tēn graphēn tautēn* ("the things written," that is, Scripture) in place of the introductory *gegraptai*, shares this pattern: "Have you not read this scripture: 'The stone that the builders rejected has become the cornerstone; this was the Lord's doing, and it is amazing in our eyes'?" (12:10-11). The reality that the stone has been made the cornerstone by God is confirmed in the statement that "this was the Lord's doing." These are certainly not the only quotations of or allusions to Scripture by the Markan Jesus (Donahue calls attention to 4:12; many others have been mentioned previously), but they are sufficient to make the point that quoting Scripture, understood as the written revelation of God's activity in the world, is taken up by the Markan Jesus as another way of deflecting attention from his own activity to its deeper grounding in the activity of God.

Jesus' Uses of Theological Passives

As a penultimate illustration of deflected christology, we may look at the Markan Jesus' use of theological passives, several examples of which we have already observed. Again following Donahue's inventory, we note twenty-seven "examples" of "passive verbs [that] suggest divine agency either as the 'theological passive' or more generally, as in the effecting of a miracle."[93] Of these twenty-seven, seventeen are found in the direct speech of the Markan Jesus, six are voiced by the narrator, and four are attributed to other characters. Not surprisingly, all of the narrator's uses of the theological passive have reference to actions of Jesus that may be attributed to divine action through him; four relate to healings (1:42; 3:5; 5:29; 6:56), one refers to the disciples' misunderstanding of Jesus' actions (6:52, "their hearts were hardened"), and one reports that Jesus "was transfigured before them" (9:2). In these cases even the narrator, who likes to focus on Jesus, must defer attention to God. One theological passive occurs in a question raised by the people in Jesus' hometown synagogue: "What is this wisdom that has been given to him?" (6:2), a form that may invite the implied audience to deflect the honor from Jesus to God, although that appears not to happen with the internal audience. Three additional uses by characters other than Jesus all employ the same verb: to be raised (*egeirō*). An unidentified "some" were "saying, 'John the baptizer has been raised from the dead'" (6:14) and appeared as Jesus, which is also the stated opinion of Herod (6:16). Both of these, of course, prove untrue in Mark's narrative. But the final use of "to be raised" as a theological passive is presented as the truly spoken message of the young man at the empty tomb: "Jesus of Nazareth, who was crucified . . . has been raised" (16:6) by God. The implied author has arranged for God's activity—from the prophecy of Isaiah presented by the narrator to the resurrection of Jesus proclaimed by the young man—to frame the activity of Jesus.[94]

The frequent use of theological passives is one more way in which the Markan Jesus moves within that frame to deflect attention and honor from himself to God, to proclaim not himself but the in-breaking of the rule (kingdom) of God as the present age gives way to the new age. Jesus' first words are "The

---

93. Donahue, "Neglected Factor," 566 and note 15. Although I have begun with Donahue's list (correcting 6:53 as 6:52), the categorization and analysis of these theological passives is my own.

94. Cf. Cook, *Christology as Narrative Quest*, 74: Mark 1:2-13 and 15:42–16:8, "which function as prologue and epilogue respectively, show a concern to begin and end with God's voice proclaiming the good news through a messenger or herald (John the Baptist dressed in camel's hair as the voice in the desert and the young man dressed in a white robe as the voice in the tomb). In each case there is a 'going before' (1:2; 16:7) that echoes the importance of the 'way,' but whereas John's voice is superseded by God's voice (1:11) Jesus' 'going before' at 16:7 calls attention to all that has preceded in the story world and evokes the expectation of a response that now only the listener/reader can give."

time is fulfilled [by God]" (1:15). Jesus recognizes God as the one by whom sins are forgiven (2:5; 3:28), by whom the Sabbath was created for humankind (2:27), by whom the ears of the deaf are opened (7:34), by whom followers are given "the mystery [Gk *mystērion*; NRSV secret] of the kingdom of God" (4:11) and will be given "still more" (4:24). The Markan Jesus also images God as the one by whom "whoever blasphemes against the Holy Spirit can never have forgiveness" (3:29); by whom, "for those outside, everything comes in parables" (4:11); by whom "no sign will be given to this generation" (8:12); by whom those who cause "little ones who believe" to stumble will be "thrown into hell" (9:42, 46, 47). Yet God is, for the Markan Jesus, also the one by whom places of honor and authority in the new age will be given to those for whom they are prepared (10:40); by whom (through the Holy Spirit) followers will be given words to speak in time of trial (13:11); by whom those who endure to the end will be saved (13:13). The Markan Jesus also points to God as the one by whom "the bridegroom is taken away" (2:20); by whom the Son of Humanity is handed over (9:31; 10:33); by whom the shepherd is struck and the sheep scattered (14:27). And yet Jesus also envisions God as the one by whom the rejected stone becomes the cornerstone (12:10) and the one by whom he will be raised up (14:28). The Markan Jesus' use of theological passives, of "*Abba*/Father" in addressing God, and *dei* (must) as a signal of the divine will all manifest a deflected christology through a consistent pattern of attempts to deflect attention and honor away from himself to the truly deserving source, God.

The Markan narrator knows all this. The narrator is aware of Jesus' reticence to receive attention and his desire to deflect honor to God,[95] but the Markan narrator does not entirely share that reticence. We will return to a consideration of this tension between the Markan narrator and the Markan Jesus at the close of this chapter, after a final example of how the Markan Jesus relates to God—in his final scene in the Gospel, his death.

JESUS' CRY TO GOD FROM THE CROSS

Only twice, at the baptism and the transfiguration, does (God) speak to the Markan Jesus; and only twice, at Gethsemane and the cross, does the Markan Jesus speak to God. There are two other points at which the Markan Jesus is said to be praying, that is, implicitly speaking with God (1:35; 6:46), but words are only given at Gethsemane and the cross, both including (at least some) Aramaic.[96] "Abba, Father, for you all things are possible; remove this cup from

95. Although Donahue does not make a point to distinguish between the narrator and Jesus in his study of *theos* in Mark, he does note that "[a]s one would expect, most references to God are on the lips of Jesus" ("Neglected Factor," 566). Donahue's most general observation is of "the sober and reserved way Mark speaks of God" (569), avoiding anthropomorphism (567) and stressing transcendence.

96. Aramaic terms are sprinkled throughout Mark's Gospel, all attributed to the

me; yet, not what I want [will; Gk *thelō*], but what you want [will]" (14:36). "At three o'clock Jesus cried with a loud voice, 'Eloi, Eloi, lema sabachthani?' which means, 'My God, my God, why have you forsaken me?'" (15:34). Both cries to God are incorporated into the passion narrative. Jesus' cry from the cross seems to confirm that at least one aspect of his prayer at Gethsemane, his request to God ("remove this cup from me"), goes unanswered by God. However, the fact that the Markan Jesus neither struggles with his captors nor tries to escape them suggests that another aspect of his prayer at Gethsemane, his promise to God (literally, "but not what I will but what you [will]"), is in force. The Markan Jesus is able to keep his promise to God, but he is not able to change the will of God.[97] This is not a surprising conclusion because the Markan Jesus has consistently insisted that it is only for God that "all things are possible" (14:36), not for human beings (10:27), and only for God that all things are known (10:40), not for "the Son" (13:32). As most commentators note, "My God, my God, why have you forsaken me?" manifests both the complete humanity of the Markan Jesus and the stark reality of his death. What is not always agreed upon by commentators is the state of the relationship between God and the Markan Jesus that is portrayed in this cry. Clearly the Markan Jesus is still talking to God—and talking to God by quoting the Scripture of God—but his experience of estrangement from God is equally clear.

The fact that the Markan Jesus' cry from the cross is the first line of Psalm 22 (Ps 21:2 in the LXX, which was the source for the Markan Gospel) does not resolve this situation.[98] Because only the first line of the Psalm is quoted, is one to assume the implied audience takes "My God, my God, why have you forsaken me?" at face value as communicating only Jesus' total despair and feeling

---

Markan Jesus except the narrator's Golgotha at 15:22. The narrator also employs Hebrew proper names: Satan at 1:13, Gethsemane at 14:32, and Boanerges at 3:17, although Boanerges may be Aramaic in derivation (see Yarbro Collins, *Mark*, 219); it is translated by the narrator, as are the clearly Aramaic terms. The use of Aramaic terms perhaps imparts an "authentic" flavor to the story of Jesus (5:41, Talitha cum; 7:11, Corban; 7:34, Ephphatha; 14:36, Abba; 15:34, Eloi, Eloi, lema sabachthani?). However, the use of Aramaic in the cry from the cross serves another function as well: explaining the misconception of "the bystanders" who hear "Eloi" as "Elijah" (15:35).

97. The comments of Paul Danove on this point are arresting: "Through the apprehension of the remoteness of God, the narrative rhetoric 'performs' for the narrative audience the experience of God's remoteness attributed to the character Jesus." "Identification with Jesus in these events invites the narrative audience to recognize that positive alignment with God guarantees no clarity concerning the nature of God's agency but demands fidelity to God even in the apprehension of abandonment and the threat of imminent death. The narratively indicated response to Jesus' and the narrative audience's final question to God comes not from God but from Jesus and, on the pattern of Jesus, from the narrative audience and, ultimately, the real reader" (*Rhetoric of Characterization*, 54 nn. 39 and 55).

98. For a review of the scholarly debate on the Psalm as it is used in Mark, see Ahearne-Kroll, *Psalms of Lament*, 207–8.

of abandonment by God? Or, because two other evocations of Psalm 22 occur in the passion narrative (Ps 22:18, "they divide my clothes among themselves, and for my clothing they cast lots"; cf. Mark 15:24; Ps 22:7, "All who see me mock at me; they make mouths at me, they shake their heads"; cf. Mark 15:29), is one to assume the implied audience is familiar with the entire Psalm? In that case, is the first line of the Psalm to be taken as a signal to the implied audience to consider the Psalm in its entirety, either as something of which the Markan Jesus could have been thinking or as something that the implied audience should have in mind? An interpreter's decision here is crucial because Psalm 22, which begins in rage if not despair, moves to a confident vow to praise God before people present and future when—not really "if"—God heeds the psalmist's plea for rescue.[99] The final situation portrayed in the Psalm (although hinted at as early as vv. 3–5) is dramatically different from the initial situation:

> All the ends of the earth shall remember and turn to the Lord;
> and all the families of the nations shall worship before him.
> For dominion belongs to the Lord, and he rules over the nations.
>
> . . .
>
> Posterity will serve him; future generations will be told about the Lord,
> and proclaim his deliverance to a people yet unborn,
> saying that he has done it.
> Psalm 22:27-28, 30-31

The psalmist, however, expects to live: "before him shall bow all who go down to the dust, and I shall live for him" (Ps 22:29b). The Markan Jesus expects to die.

Stephen Ahearne-Kroll is among those who argue for bringing the entire Psalm to bear in interpreting the Markan Jesus' cry from the cross ("it is highly unlikely that a biblically literate member of Mark's community would not have thought of the whole psalm when hearing this verse"[100]), but he bases his interpretation on a detailed and rather different reading of the Psalm:

> [The Markan Jesus' cry from the cross] is the first verse of the body of the psalm, which encapsulates the mood of the entire psalm—not despair, but outrage, anger, accusation, questioning, and pain at the thought that God has abandoned him in his time of greatest need. As we have seen, the sense of incomprehension and outrage is developed throughout the lament section of the psalm as David reflects on his relationship with God and describes his suffering in increasingly graphic and

99. Whitney T. Shiner, "The Ambiguous Pronouncement of the Centurion and the Shrouding of Meaning in Mark," *JSNT* 78 (2000): 3–22, asserts, "There is no particular reason for seeing these interpretations as mutually exclusive. . . . Thus the cry [of the Markan Jesus, quoting Ps 22:1] is parabolic, having a literal meaning in the story and another, more profound meaning for those who have ears to hear" (16, 17).
100. Ahearne-Kroll, *Psalms of Lament*, 209.

troubling terms. The psalm ends with a ten-verse promise of praise that is David's
last attempt to elicit God's response.[101]

> In the story of Jesus' crucifixion, Jesus embodies the suffering David from Psalm
> 21 [LXX] not to foreshadow Jesus' vindication at the resurrection, but to express
> the outrage of Jesus' suffering and God's abandonment in the midst of it. David
> rages against his abandonment, but not in rebellion against God; rather, he does
> so in a way that tries both to understand how and why God would do such a
> thing and to get God's attention so that God will deliver him from the suffering.
> He gains neither understanding nor deliverance from suffering in the psalm, and
> when read with Jesus' crucifixion, the search for understanding and deliverance
> becomes Jesus' and the audience's.[102]

The fact that the Markan passion story does show additional knowledge of Psalm
22 (Ps 21 LXX) does open up the possibility that the implied audience is to consider the entire Psalm in interpreting Jesus' use of its first verse. Ahearne-Kroll's
interpretation is intriguing, and his interpretation of the mood of the Psalm and
of the Markan Jesus' cry from the cross as outrage and questioning is convincing.
However, it may be that Ahearne-Kroll over-reads the "Davidic" implications of
the Psalms of Lament in Mark's passion narrative or, from the other side, under-
reads the Markan narrative's own internal clues. For example, the Markan Jesus,
unlike David, predicts his passion three times; and in the same Gethsemane
prayer "to get God's attention so that God will deliver him from the suffering"
(to use Ahearne-Kroll's words about David), the Markan Jesus also prays "but not
what I will, but what you [will]." And, as I noted above, the psalmist, whether
conceived of as David or not, expects to live, while the Markan Jesus expects to
die. So the David/Jesus analogy breaks down at some point, as all analogies do.

More certain interpretive help is given by the immediate narrative context
of the Markan Jesus' cry from the cross. The narrator sets the scene quite specifically: "When it was noon, darkness came over the whole land until three in the
afternoon" (15:33). Darkness at noon is an image of *God's action* in apocalyptic
judgment, as is suggested by this Markan allusion to Amos 8:9:

> On that day, says the Lord GOD,
> I will make the sun go down at noon,
> and darken the earth in broad daylight.[103]

At three, the Markan Jesus cries out, "My God, my God, why have you forsaken me?" The Markan Jesus' experience of abandonment is not to be denied

---

101. Ahearne-Kroll, *Psalms of Lament*, 209; see 87–109 for his detailed interpretation
of Ps 21 (LXX).

102. Ahearne-Kroll, *Psalms of Lament*, 210.

103. See also Zeph 1:15 and Joel 2:2; 3:15. Shiner, "Ambiguous Pronouncement," 10,
points out similar portents in the Greco-Roman tradition, in the stories of great men: Romu-
lus, Julius Caesar, Carneades, and Pelopidas.

or lessened; yet the implied audience also knows that God is present and acting. Immediately the bystanders, hearing "Eloi" as "Elijah," offer Jesus sour wine, perhaps to sustain him a bit longer to see "whether Elijah will come to take him down" (15:36). But the implied audience knows that "Elijah has come, and they did to him whatever they pleased, as it is written about him" (9:13). Then the narrator briefly reports two events in rapid succession, Jesus' last act and, implicitly, an act of God: "Then Jesus gave a loud cry and breathed his last. And the curtain of the temple was torn in two, from top to bottom" (15:37-38). The implied audience likely knows that a group of strong men could perhaps tear the curtain of the temple from bottom to top, but only God could tear the curtain "from top to bottom" (note also the theological passive construction: "was torn [i.e., by God]"). As Edwin Broadhead notes, "the miracle elements around the cross [darkness at noon and the torn temple veil] are employed to demonstrate the power and presence of God in the death of Jesus."[104] Finally, another character speaks, after being introduced by the narrator: "Now when the centurion, who stood facing him, saw that in this way he breathed his last, he said, 'Truly this man was Son of God [NRSV God's Son]!'" (15:39). The Markan Jesus certainly feels abandoned, and he certainly dies. But the implied audience also knows that the words of the centurion at his end echo the words of the narrator at the beginning—"Jesus Christ, Son of God" (1:1). Even if the Markan Jesus does not sense the presence of God in his death, the Markan narrator does. Even if the Markan Jesus is crying out only the first verse of Psalm 22, the Markan narrator seems aware of the entire Psalm—and is making sure that "future generations will be told about the Lord."

Irony depends on contrast, and the ironic contrast of the Markan Jesus' cry from the cross seems to move in the opposite direction from the irony of the centurion's statement at the foot of the cross. The Markan Jesus cries out, God, you have forsaken me; the Markan narrator presents a contrasting view: God is present—in the daytime darkness, in the torn temple curtain, and in the centurion's words. The Markan narrator affirms that the presence of God does not depend on the knowledge or emotional experience of the Markan Jesus. (Interestingly enough, the Markan Jesus had always insisted that only God knows all things.) The centurion, as a Gentile and as a minor representative of the Roman authorities responsible for Jesus' death, is an odd character to proclaim that Jesus is "Son of God" (without the definite article, like 1:1), but, whether the centurion is understood to be "sincere" or "sarcastic," the narrator has already confirmed the truth of his statement in advance. Thus the narrator disconfirms what the Markan Jesus says (although perhaps Jesus meant more) and confirms what the centurion says (although perhaps he meant less)—an ironic situation indeed. Yet in both cases the Markan narrator affirms that the presence of God is not dependent on the perception or sincerity of human

104. Broadhead, *Teaching with Authority*, 181.

beings, even when one of those human beings is the obedient Son of God and another is one of his executioners.

By this brief but careful arrangement of narrative events, the Markan implied author is able to proclaim a stereophonic message about Jesus' death: (1) Jesus dies a real and horrible death, abandoned by his disciples and by his God; and (2) in Jesus' death, God is still present—through Jesus' death God still acts. The implied author has put the first message on the lips of the Markan Jesus and the second in the words of the narrator. Some interpreters hear one voice louder than the other. The voices are not blended or harmonized but presented in tension, a tension that can be dramatically experienced by the implied audience. It would be a disservice to the simple complexity of the Markan narrative to drown out one voice or the other, or to otherwise "resolve" this tension. This tension is the mystery that is given in the Markan narrative.

The Markan Jesus and the Markan Narrator: Creative Tension in Markan Narrative Christology

Our look at projected christology, what others say, and deflected christology, what Jesus says in response, has illustrated a certain tension between what the Markan Jesus says and what other characters and the narrator say about him. Varying presentations of and responses to two terms, "Christ" and "Son of God," provide an easy illustration of this observation. The narrator opens the narrative boldly: "The beginning of the gospel [NRSV good news] of Jesus Christ [NRSV Messiah], the Son of God" (1:1).[105] This opening verse serves as a title for the entire narrative. All that is told here—from baptism through resurrection—is but the *beginning* of the gospel; the good news continues beyond the narrative world into the world of the implied audience, which is also, of course, the world of the implied author, at whose direction the narrator speaks. The narrator asserts from the beginning that Jesus is the Christ. Peter comes to this affirmation at midpoint (8:29), prompted and then silenced by Jesus. Jesus connects the phrase "of Christ" with those who receive and give lowly service (9:41) and "false christs" with those who produce powerful-looking "signs and omens" that lead others astray (13:21-22). Jesus reticently accepts the assignation "Christ" from the high priest in order *not* to "save" his own life (14:61-62). The chief priests and scribes apply the term "Christ" sarcastically to the only Jesus it really fits: the crucified Jesus (15:32).

The narrator also asserts from the beginning that Jesus is the Son of God. (God), so it is narrated, confirms this point of view (1:11; 9:7), and the unclean

---

105. On evaluating the textual variants of 1:1, that is, the presence or absence of *huiou theou*, Son of God, and for my decision to include "Son of God" at 1:1 in my analysis, see chapter 2, on projected christology, in relation to what the narrator says about Jesus in Mark 1:1.

spirits share it (1:24, 34; 3:11; 5:7). Jesus deflects attention from "the Son" to "the Father" (13:32), whose will is accepted and for whom "all things are possible" (10:27; 14:36), but accepts his naming by the high priest as "the Son of the Blessed One" as he faces death (14:61-62). The centurion, continuing the linkage of "Son of God" with death, gives voice to this affirmation at the narrative's climax, at the only point from which it is really true: the crucifixion (15:39). The tension between the speech of the Markan Jesus and other characters and the narrator, rarely discussed, highlights the often-discussed transformation of the implied audience's movement in understanding from the narrator's initial "Christ, the Son of God" to the end of the Markan Gospel.[106]

I am not asserting that the narrator's point of view is dramatically at odds with the point of view of the Markan Jesus, but they are clearly distinguishable. The narrator boldly asserts that Jesus is the Christ, the Son of God. Jesus is reticent. Perhaps this is why it is so important that the voice (of God) confirm the narrator's point of view; the Markan Jesus hardly does so! The only two times the narrator mentions God directly are both to attribute to God the power of the Markan Jesus, his teaching and healing (1:14; 2:12). Yet the Markan Jesus boldly proclaims the rule (kingdom) of God, about which the narrator speaks directly just once, and that after Jesus' death (15:43), and makes assertions about the Son of Humanity, about which the narrator is silent. (These statements are examined in the following chapter on refracted christology.) There is thus a tension between the Markan narrator who wants to talk about Jesus and the Markan Jesus who wants to talk about God.[107]

This tension between a reticent Markan Jesus and a bold Markan narrator is related to the tension that led William Wrede to his "discovery" of the

106. That the interpretation of Scott ("Chiastic Structures") is opposed to the "tension" in Mark's portrait of Jesus is clear in the way Scott sets up two alternative interpretations: "In strict logic, however, it can be said that the text presents one with alternatives: on the one hand, Jesus is both God and Christ and, on the other, Jesus is Christ but he is not God, although he exercises an authority that was thought to be exclusively the property of the Deity. . . . In other words: either Mark presents Jesus as God or his gospel presents us with more puzzles than doctrine. It leaves us wondering with the disciples, 'Who is this that the winds and the sea obey him?' and with the scribes, 'By what authority does he do these things or who has given him this authority?'" (20). Scott argues, without apparent concern for the anachronism of reading Mark through the lens of later church doctrine, for the first alternative—Jesus is both God and Christ, but, in his terms, I take the "more puzzles than doctrine" alternative to Markan interpretation, arguing precisely that the implied audience is left "wondering with the disciples."

107. In commenting on "God" as "The Neglected Factor in New Testament Theology," Dahl notes: "Oscar Cullmann has stated that 'Early Christian theology is in reality almost exclusively Christology.' It is not clear whether or not it has ever occurred to him that this statement might also be turned the other way round" (5). Perhaps the narrative christology of Mark's Gospel, especially deflected christology as manifested by the Markan Jesus, represents this "other way round": the narrative christology of the Markan Jesus is almost exclusively theology.

"messianic secret"—a tension between two levels of messianic claims about Jesus not easily smoothed over in Mark's Gospel. Wrede thought of these levels in historical terms as representing the conflict of early Jesus traditions (or the historical Jesus) and the theological convictions of the evangelist (or redactor). But I perceive them as literary aspects of the narrative—the Markan narrator and the Markan Jesus, both under the control of the Markan implied author. Suzanne Watts Henderson notes that, "[w]hile both Wrede and his critics have attempted to reconcile Mark's post-resurrection, sharply Christological agenda with the narrative's rather muffled, pre-resurrection Christological claims, Jesus' efforts to prevent full disclosure of his identity cohere with his role as God's faithful servant whose identity becomes most transparent in his most self-emptying act (Mk. 15:39)."[108] Henderson considers the error of commentators pursuing the motif of the messianic secret to be their narrow focus on Jesus' identity rather than his mission: "Simply put, once we challenge the prevailing assumption that Mark's gospel functions primarily to disclose Jesus' messianic *identity* with the claim that it depicts Jesus' messianic *mission*, the gospel's 'secrecy motif' (detected by Wrede in myriad forms) may well suit Jesus' own agenda, which is to focus attention on God's apocalyptic rectification of the world."[109] However, Henderson does not clarify her use of "Jesus" (the Markan character? the historical person?) or "Mark" (the implied reader? the narrator? the historical redactor?), leading to shifting boundaries between historical and literary categories and to this appended footnote: "Thus the chasm between the historical and narrative worlds may not be so sprawling after all: ironically, Mark may preserve, even develop, authentic traditions of Jesus' reticence precisely in service of the evangelist's own Christological purpose."[110] Here Henderson, like Wrede and his critics, slides too easily from literary to historical categories, a problem to which I will return in my concluding chapter. Conceiving of the messianic secret in a historical sense motivates the interpreter to resolve the tension; perceiving the tension as a narrative strategy questions such resolution.

And yet, amid this narrative tension between the Markan Jesus and the Markan narrator, there are also some intriguing correspondences. Sometimes it appears that the Markan Jesus takes on an ideological point of view first expressed by the Markan narrator. The usually reticent Markan Jesus does finally accede at the end to the title "Christ, Son of the Blessed One" (14:61-62), which the Markan narrator asserted at the beginning ("Christ, the Son of God," 1:1). The Markan narrator seems to link Scripture ("as it is written"), Elijah, and John the baptizer at 1:2-8, and the Markan Jesus links Scripture ("as it is written"), Elijah, and John the baptizer at 9:11-13. The Markan Jesus comments on the disciples' "hardened" "hearts" (8:17) only after the Markan narrator has

---

108. Henderson, *Christology and Discipleship*, 255–56.
109. Henderson, *Christology and Discipleship*, 256.
110. Henderson, *Christology and Discipleship*, 256 n. 20.

done so (6:52).[111] Sometimes it appears that the Markan narrator takes on an ideological point of view first expressed by the Markan Jesus. After the Markan Jesus silences the unclean spirit in the synagogue in Capernaum (1:25), the Markan narrator reports similar episodes of silencing (1:34; 3:12; and the drowning of the herd of swine into which the legion of unclean spirits had been sent, 5:13); thus the narrator seems to repeat and reflect Jesus' reticence in being made known (at the very least by *these* characters and perhaps more broadly) as the Son or Holy One of God. After the Markan Jesus notes, at the point of being rejected in his hometown, that "[p]rophets are not without honor, except in their hometown" (6:4), the narrator reports the transfigured Jesus talking with "Elijah with Moses" (9:4), two key prophets of Israel.

Sometimes the narrator's silence is filled in by the speech of the Markan Jesus. The Markan narrator never mentions the "Son of David," but the Markan Jesus argues against insisting that the Christ is the Son of David as he reports "the scribes" do. Thus in arguing that the Christ is *not* the Son of David, the Markan Jesus is *not* in tension with the Markan narrator, who presents Jesus as the Christ but not as the Son of David.[112] But sometimes the tension is unrelieved as the narrator opens up a way of honoring Jesus against the Markan Jesus' expressed intention or suggests something about Jesus' relationship with God other than what the Markan Jesus expresses. Although reporting the Markan Jesus' attempts to direct attention to God ("the Lord") after healing the Gerasene demoniac, the narrator seems more aligned with the point of view of the healed man, who the narrator reports "went away and began to proclaim in the Decapolis how much Jesus [the Lord?] had done for him" (5:20; cf. 1:3, the change in the Septuagintal text that allows the implied audience to read the one for whom John prepares the way, Jesus, as "Lord"). Although the Markan Jesus' last words are "My God, my God, why have you forsaken me?" the Markan narrator gives signals of God's presence and action in and through Jesus' death.

The Markan narrator's first acclamation at 1:1, which focuses on Jesus, is only reticently picked up by the Markan Jesus toward the end of the narrative—and of his life. However, the narrator's second acclamation, the composite "Isaiah" quotation at 1:2-3, which places the entire story of the Markan Jesus under the rubric of the story of God with the people of God, "as it is written," is picked up by the Markan Jesus immediately, in his first words in the narrative: "The time is fulfilled, and the kingdom of God has come near; repent, and

111. So also Norman R. Petersen, "The Composition of Mark 4:1–8:26," *HTR* 73 (1980): 185–217, quotation from 209: "Thus the reader here learns from the narrator what the character Jesus only verbalizes six episodes later."

112. The tension in this case is with an earlier Pauline statement—"Jesus Christ, . . . who was descended from David according to the flesh" (Rom. 1:1, 3) and later versions of the gospel story—Matthew and Luke. The Gospel of John, more in line with Mark on this point, presupposes that whether or not the Christ is the Son of David is a divisive issue; see John 7:40-44.

believe in the good news" (1:15). The Markan narrator evokes Scripture, which reveals God, just this once (1:2-3), but the Markan Jesus evokes Scripture again and again (2:25; 4:12; 7:6-7, 10; 10:6, 19; 11:9-10, 17; 12:10-11, 26, 29-30, 36; 13:24-25, 26; 14:27, 62; cf. 9:12-13; 14:21, 49). The implied author literally has the Markan Jesus—not the narrator, not other characters—make God known. The Markan narrator presents Jesus as the one who presents God—and (God) as the one who confirms Jesus in this role. The Markan Jesus speaks insistently of God, and (God) insists that others "listen to" Jesus (9:7). The narrator makes no direct claims to know God, offering no inside views and only two external views, or auditions, of the voice (of God). What the narrator knows about God comes from Jesus; Jesus knows God more directly. The narrator thus seems to follow the directions he narrates from the voice (of God): "listen to him" (9:7). At 1:2-3 the narrator points to the prophets, who point to John (1:4), who points to Jesus (1:7-8), who points to God (1:14-15). What the narrator tells in 1:1, the narrative as a whole shows, beginning with 1:2-15: the Markan Jesus makes God known.

From the beginning and consistently the Markan Jesus deflects honor to God; he accepts "honor" reticently at the end only when it does not conflict with honoring God. From the beginning the Markan narrator seeks to proclaim both Jesus and God; yet at the end he is reticent in speaking of the presence of the resurrected Jesus, not only in bodily form at the empty tomb, but even the presence of Jesus with his followers in the community after his death. The much-commented-on open ending of Mark's Gospel, however reticent, is dynamic, not static; at its close, the Markan Jesus is in process, on the way to Galilee, going there before his disciples—and especially Peter—as he told them (16:7; cf. 14:28). The other part of Mark's double ending, the eschatological discourse, also suggests this dynamism: when followers are brought to trial on account of the gospel, they are not to worry about what they are to say, for the Holy Spirit will speak through them (13:11). Especially when compared with the endings of the Gospels of Matthew and Luke—or Mark's own longer ending (16:9-20), which seems to be inspired by them—the narrator's account of the empty tomb seems subdued. At the end, the reticence of the Markan Jesus to proclaim himself even seems echoed by the Markan narrator! But the Markan Jesus was never reticent to proclaim the in-breaking rule (kingdom) of God, and, at the end, the implied author, through the message of the young man at the tomb, returns the implied audience's attention to Galilee where that proclamation began. Thus the relations of the Markan Jesus and the Markan narrator, as part of the implied author's way of communicating with the implied audience, are complex indeed. Even the Markan narrator, so focused on Jesus, seems to show, in describing Jesus' actions, some signs of the deflection of honor to God that is so strongly expressed in the Markan Jesus' words.

CHAPTER 4

REFRACTED CHRISTOLOGY:
WHAT JESUS SAYS INSTEAD

Not only does the Markan Jesus attempt to deflect attention and honor away from himself and toward God (the focus of the previous chapter on deflected christology), but the Markan Jesus also refracts—or bends—the christologies of other characters and the narrator. The image comes from the way a prism refracts "white" light and thus shows its spectral colors. When a thing is bent and looked at from another angle, something different appears. The most obvious way in which the Markan Jesus bends the christologies of others is by his statements about the "Son of Man"—or, to translate the Greek (*ho huios tou anthrōpou*) more literally, "Son of Humanity," especially in juxtaposition with "christological titles" offered by other characters. No other character or the narrator speaks of the "Son of Humanity."[1] The Markan Jesus' statements about the "kingdom of God" may also be seen as refracting the christologies of other characters and the narrator. No other character speaks of the "kingdom of God," and the narrator does so but once, just after Jesus' death (15:43). "Son of Humanity" and "kingdom (rule) of God" depict the Markan Jesus' distinctive point of

1. In all the canonical gospels, "the Son of man sayings are formulated in the third person singular and placed in the mouth of Jesus Himself. 'Son of man' is never found as a mode of address or in any formula of confession" (Ferdinand Hahn, *The Titles of Jesus in Christology: Their History in Early Christianity* [New York: World Publishing, 1969; first published in German in 1963], 32). However, Acts 7:56 narrates this speech of Stephen, "Look, I see the heavens opened and the Son of Man standing at the right hand of God!" (noted by Hahn, 49 n. 108).

view.[2] This chapter explores Markan narrative christology by examining what the Markan Jesus says instead of what the narrator and other characters say—what Jesus says about the "Son of Humanity" (with a preliminary word on the work of Kingsbury and Naluparayil on this designation) and the "kingdom of God."

Kingsbury and Naluparayil on the Markan "Son of Man"

Jack Dean Kingsbury's way of dealing with the "Son of Man" statements in Mark deserves an initial comment. He recognizes, of course, their uniqueness to Jesus, which is a literary critical observation, but his analysis of them is tremendously influenced by his negative reaction to theories of Markan "corrective christology" in which "Son of Man" statements are evaluated positively over against "Son of God" statements considered as reflective of a rejected "divine man" or *theios anēr* christology.[3] "Son of God" is, of course, one of two favorite "christological titles" of the Markan narrator—and *the* favorite title of Kingsbury. I am very much in agreement with Kingsbury's critique of "corrective christology" as ignoring and distorting much of the evidence of the Markan narrative and importing quite problematic "evidence" about the divine man christology of Mark's presumed opponents. However, I find Kingsbury's way of interpreting the "Son of Man" statements of the Markan Jesus, given Kingsbury's prior commitment to the point of view of the Markan narrator, completely unsatisfying.

Kingsbury deals with all the "titles" other than "Son of Man" in an integrated, chronological way; he deals with "Son of Man" alone in a final chapter or in a trailing excursus.[4] This isolation is a first step toward minimizing the signifi-

---

2. John R. Donahue, S.J., briefly discusses "the picture of Jesus as proclaimer of the kingdom and as Son of Man" as "[t]wo of the major metaphors by which Jesus is presented in the Gospel of Mark" ("Jesus as the Parable of God in the Gospel of Mark," *Interpreting the Gospels* [ed. James Luther Mays; Philadelphia: Fortress, 1981], 148–67, quotation from 156; first published in *Int* 32 [1978]: 369–86).

3. On three phases of the "divine man" discussion, see M. Eugene Boring, "Markan Christology: God-Language for Jesus?" (unpublished paper distributed to members of the Mark Seminar of the SNTS, 1998, 7–8 n. 21; these comments are not included in the version published later under the same title: *NTS* 45 [1999]: 451–71). Over against the proponents of Markan "corrective christology" (e.g., Weeden, Perrin), Werner H. Kelber argues in *The Kingdom in Mark: A New Place and a New Time* (Philadelphia: Fortress, 1974) that it is not "Son of God" that is "corrected" in Mark's Gospel but a false, apocalyptic understanding of "Son of Man." For my comment on how Kelber, in other publications, sees other aspects of tradition (church politics, linguistic medium, genre) "corrected" by Mark's Gospel, see "Texts and Contexts: Interpreting the Disciples in Mark," *Semeia* 62 (1993): 81–102, esp. 87–88; republished in Elizabeth Struthers Malbon, *In the Company of Jesus: Characters in Mark's Gospel* (Louisville: Westminster John Knox, 2000), 100–130, esp. 110.

4. Jack Dean Kingsbury, *The Christology of Mark's Gospel* (Philadelphia: Fortress, 1983),

cance of the "title." Kingsbury asserts that "'the Son of Man' does not function 'confessionally' to specify 'who Jesus is.'"[5] As evidence for this view, Kingsbury argues that (1) "Son of Man" is never "conjoined" with the name "Jesus." "Thus, never does Mark write 'Jesus Son of Man,' and never does any character in his story call upon Jesus with the words, 'Jesus Son of Man.' . . ."[6] Kingsbury further argues that (2) "[t]he absence of 'the Son of Man' from the predication formulas of Mark's narrative is an exceedingly strong indication that, again, Mark does not use this term to specify 'who Jesus is.'"[7] (Kingsbury lists but does not define "[s]tatements or questions answered in the affirmative which function in Mark as predication formulas."[8]) Because christology for Kingsbury is a matter of "who Jesus is" and "the Son of Man" does not bear upon Jesus' "identity," how does it function? In *The Christology of Mark's Gospel*, Kingsbury concludes that "'the Son of Man' may be defined as the title of majesty by means of which Jesus refers to himself 'in public' or in view of the 'public' (or 'world') in order to point to himself as 'the man,' or 'the human being' (earthly, suffering, vindicated), and to assert his divine authority in the face of opposition."[9] I am not fond of Kingsbury's reified term "identity," but it is not clear to me how this description does not comment on Jesus' "identity."[10] In *Conflict in Mark*, Kingsbury takes the final step by concluding that

> "the Son of man" is best understood not as a christological title but as a technical term. The very purpose of a christological title is to set forth, wholly or partially, both the identity and the significance of Jesus. By contrast, a technical term is, less grandly, some word or expression bearing a precise meaning. Whereas "the Son of man" does bear a precise meaning ("the man," or "the human being") and also can be said to convey something of the significance of Jesus, it does not set forth his identity.
>
>   . . . In Mark's story, therefore, the designation "the Son of man" emphasizes the twin features of repudiation and vindication.[11]

chapter 4; Jack Dean Kingsbury, *Conflict in Mark: Jesus, Authorities, Disciples* (Minneapolis: Fortress, 1989), 58–61.

5. Kingsbury, *Christology*, 159.
6. Kingsbury, *Christology*, 160.
7. Kingsbury, *Christology*, 164.
8. Kingsbury, *Christology*, 163.
9. Kingsbury, *Christology*, 168.
10. With Kingsbury, contrast Edwin K. Broadhead: "Within the Gospel of Mark, the Son of Man title is never a confessional statement, either on the lips of Jesus or any other character. Further, the title is never used directly of Jesus in the Gospel of Mark. Nonetheless, the narrative identification of the Son of Man with Jesus is clear. Thus, the Gospel of Mark, confirms the Son of Man title as a mysterious but valid description which belongs appropriately to the mission and identity of Jesus" (*Naming Jesus: Titular Christology in the Gospel of Mark* [Sheffield: Sheffield Academic, 1999], 131).
11. Kingsbury, *Conflict*, 60–61.

In overreacting to the attempt of "corrective christology" to replace one set of "titles" with another, Kingsbury has failed to realize that all the "titles" (and "technical terms"!), or what *all* the characters and the narrator say, must be interrelated if it is the *whole* Gospel of Mark we wish to interpret. Kingsbury loses sight of his initial—and literary—observation of the uniqueness of "the Son of Man" statements to the character Jesus: "'the Son of Man' constitutes, literarily, the 'phraseological point of view' of exclusively Jesus, occurring in his mouth alone and referring solely to him."[12] Kingsbury's christology overwhelms Mark's narrative.[13]

In his understanding of Markan christology, Kingsbury privileges the titles of Jesus privileged by the narrator in 1:1—Christ and Son of God. In contrast, Jacob Chacko Naluparayil, in his book, *The Identity of Jesus in Mark*,[14] privileges the title or designation privileged by Jesus—Son of Man. However, as I mentioned in my brief discussion of Naluparayil's book in my introductory chapter, because Naluparayil interprets all other titles and designations as "qualifying" the "Son of Man," his resulting narrative christology is an amalgam that dissolves the Markan implied author's tension between what the narrator and various characters say and what Jesus says instead. Toward the close of his book, Naluparayil investigates the character Jesus directly by identifying separately the traits of Jesus identified from the views of other characters and the traits of Jesus identified from what he does and says. Then Naluparayil "brings together" these two lists of traits, along with "other evidences appearing in the narrative that would assist our comprehension of Jesus' character traits"[15] (a problematic methodological step), into a list of "prominent traits" and the "designation" that "answer[s] the question 'what Jesus is like'":[16] a human person; a superior dignitary in disguise; divine Sonship, Christhood, and the destiny of death

---

12. Kingsbury, *Christology*, 178.

13. Kingsbury comments that his critique of the "corrective christology" interpretation presents "a 'clash' between a tradition-critical approach to Mark [theirs] and a literary-critical approach [his]" (*Christology*, 41). Because their approach finds "the interpretive key to Mark's presentation of Jesus" (40) outside of Mark in the Hellenistic concept of the divine man it is "suspect from the outset" (41). Kingsbury's approach, however, suffers a similar problem; in the attempt to balance a literary-critical approach with attention to "titles of majesty," which are part of a christological/theological system outside of Mark, sometimes a "clash" occurs. Cf. Boring's comment that Kingsbury "overplays his opponents' purported domination by matters 'outside the text' while he bases his view on 'the Gospel of Mark itself'" ("Markan Christology," unpublished version, 3 n. 7; comment not included in the version published later).

14. Jacob Chacko Naluparayil, *The Identity of Jesus in Mark: An Essay on Narrative Christology* (Jerusalem: Franciscan Printing Press, 2000). For further comments, see my review of Naluparayil in *Biblica* 4 (2001): 569–73.

15. Naluparayil, *Identity*, 540.

16. Naluparayil, *Identity*, 540.

and resurrection; loyalty and obedience of the divine Son; teacher with *exousia* (authority) and *dynameis* (power), and the possessor of the Holy Spirit; divine wisdom (*sophia*); divine *exousia* and *sophia* operating as the liberating mercy; savior; establisher of the reign of God on earth. In his final paragraph before his triple conclusion (to chapter 6, to part 2, to the book), Naluparayil asks his final (and initial) question and gives his final (and initial) answer: Given "the insufficiency of the protagonist's name [Jesus of Nazareth] to carry the divine character traits," "does the narrator provide us with another narrative noun or designation which can function as the receptacle of all the supernatural traits of Jesus? Yes, 'the Son of Man' functions in the narrative as the designation, as the locus of all the above-said divine character traits of the protagonist, as the name of the divine person."[17]

Naluparayil's use of the term "divine person" seems more Chalcedonian than Markan. Jesus' identity seems abstracted from the telling of a story and reified as a collection of christological propositions. Thus Naluparayil's quest for Jesus' identity is quite abstract and theological. It also seems to me that his understanding of Jesus' identity is anachronistic and reified. I find the book's subtitle, *An Essay on Narrative Christology*, subordinate indeed. At 600-plus pages, it is hardly an essay, and narrative christology not only is not its sole content (considerable attention is given to source and redaction critical issues), but the christology (with "Son of Man" serving as "the name of the divine person") overwhelms the narrative. Naluparayil, like Kingsbury, is interested in the identity of Jesus—a rather abstract and theological quest.[18] I am interested in the narrative of Mark on a more concrete and literary level of how the story works.

A Narrative Critical Reading of the Markan Jesus' "Son of Humanity" Sayings

To return to the obvious fact of Mark's narrative: Jesus and only Jesus speaks of the "Son of Humanity," but Jesus never says, "I am the Son of Humanity"; rather, he speaks only and always in the third person of the "Son of Humanity."

---

17. Naluparayil, *Identity*, 547.

18. Comparable to Naluparayil is an article with an intriguing title and a disappointing argument, Harry L. Chronis, "To Reveal and to Conceal: A Literary-Critical Perspective on 'the Son of Man' in Mark," *NTS* 51 (2005): 459–81: "'[T]he Son of Man' serves essentially as a paradoxical incognito. It belongs to a whole pattern of speech that the Markan Jesus employs to resist disclosure of his identity as 'the Son of God'" (459). Like Naluparayil, Chronis functionally fuses the meaning and significance of "Son of Man" and "Son of God," ignoring any narrative distinctions between characters and narrator; for the so-called "narrative's logic" of this merger, see 463. In fact, Chronis appears to commit the intentional fallacy (reading in the intentions) not in reference to the author but in reference to Jesus (whether the character Jesus or the historical Jesus is not always clear), about whom he makes anachronistic conclusions about his "full divinity" (Son of God) and "full humanity" (Son of Man).

Self-reference is implicit, never explicit, needing completion by the implied audience.[19] Because the Markan Jesus has just said to the paralytic "your sins are forgiven" (2:5)[20] when he adds, to the questioning scribes, "But so that you may know that the Son of Man has authority on earth to forgive sins" (2:10), the implied audience concludes that, having such authority, Jesus must be "the Son of Man."[21] Similarly, in the narration of the controversy over the disciples'

---

19. Cf. M. Eugene Boring: Son of Man "occurs exclusively on the lips of Jesus himself, i.e., in the Markan narrative it represents Jesus' own christology which the author urges upon the reader" ("The Christology of Mark: Hermeneutical Issues for Systematic Theology," *Semeia* 30 [1984]: 125–53, quotation from 131). As I argued at the conclusion of the previous chapter and will argue again later, the implied author presents the implied audience with a creative tension between the view of the Markan Jesus and other Markan voices (the narrator and other characters).

20. With Broadhead (*Naming Jesus*, 131 n. 16) and others, I read *aphientai* ("forgiven") at 2:5 as a divine or theological passive referring to *God's* forgiveness, which Jesus announces. Such a reading is consistent with the deflected christology whereby the Markan Jesus attempts to deflect attention and honor away from himself and toward God, as discussed in the previous chapter.

21. Robert M. Fowler (*Let the Reader Understand: Reader Response Criticism and the Gospel of Mark* [Minneapolis: Fortress, 1991], 102–3) argues that the "Son of man" at 2:10 should be attributed not to the Markan Jesus but to the Markan narrator. (It should be noted that Fowler is especially interested in locating and commenting on "explicit commentary by the narrator" and is not utilizing the available distinction between the narrator and the implied author, concerning which see the conclusion of this chapter.) I do not find Fowler's argument convincing. As he himself must admit, the "second-person plural verb form ('you may know'; *eidēte*) is [no more than] ambiguous, possibly referring either to Jesus' intranarrative or to the narrator's extranarrative narratees." Fowler finds the "decisive evidence" in the last three words of verse 10: "he says to the paralytic." Of course, everyone recognizes those words as the narrator's because of the third-person form, "he says." (It seems to me—and this reasoning appears not to be considered by Fowler—that the narrator's "he says" intrudes at this point to make clear the change in the protagonist's reference for "you": from "you scribes" at "so that you may know" back to "you paralytic" at "I say to you.") But Fowler argues further that because the "Son of man" statement is also in the third person, it "makes excellent sense" as the narrator's comment as well. Yet all of the Markan Jesus' "Son of Man" statements are in the third person! Does that mean all of them should be attributed to the narrator? In fact, Fowler does suggest such a reading for 2:28 (see 103–4) and 14:62 (see 118–19; his point about Jesus' second-person *plural* comment to the high priest at 14:62 is interesting but not decisive for his case; note that the high priest employs the first-person *plural* in his response to Jesus). As Fowler himself notes (130), the three "Son of man" sayings he wishes to attribute to the Markan narrator are the first two and the last one, the framing uses. The broader issue for Fowler seems to be that all the "Son of man" sayings (like many other important aspects of Mark's Gospel) achieve no "uptake" at the story level and thus function at the discourse level, "taken up only by the reader." Granted, the entire narrative is for the implied audience, but attention is well paid to how the implied author develops differently the comments of the narrator and those of the protagonist—either of which may not

plucking grain on the Sabbath, Jesus, having just argued that David's setting aside of the sacred/profane distinction in response to human need serves him as a precedent with regard to his disciples' behavior, states that "[t]he sabbath was made for humankind, and not humankind for the sabbath; so the Son of Man is lord even of the sabbath" (2:27-28). The implied audience is invited to deduce that Jesus is "the Son of Man."[22]

The narrative effect of the narrator's failure to pick up the "Son of Humanity" designation directly is twofold: (1) Jesus is presented as having a unique phraseological point of view, and (2) the implied audience can be drawn into the story to take responsibility for applying "Son of Humanity" to Jesus. The present authority of the "Son of Humanity," which might well be translated the Human Being (literally, the son of the human being), includes pronouncing that sins are forgiven and abrogating sacred/profane distinctions in favor of meeting human needs. Later in the narrative, these topics recur in ways that again engage the implied audience. As they stand by the withered fig tree, Jesus says to his disciples: "So I tell you, whatever you ask for in prayer, believe that you have received it, and it will be yours. Whenever you stand praying, forgive, if you have anything against anyone; so that your Father in heaven may also forgive you your trespasses" (11:24-25).[23] In the midst of Jesus' explanation to his disciples of the parable of what defiles, the narrator interjects a parenthetical statement: "(Thus he declared all foods clean.)" (7:19). Not only is Jesus involved with forgiveness and with setting aside traditional distinctions, so is the implied audience, which recognizes in Jesus' authoritative actions the "Son of Humanity," the Human One.

If the corporate aspect of the phrase "Son of Humanity" or the Human One is stressed, the representative nature of Jesus' humanity is clear. Thus Mark's Gospel raises intriguing questions: Is it just Jesus who has authority over the Sabbath, or is it by implication human beings who have authority over the Sabbath? Is it just Jesus who can forgive sins in the name of God, or is it human beings who have authority on earth to forgive sins in the name of God?[24] Certainly it is not just Jesus who is called upon to risk persecution by the powerful

---

be taken up by the characters in the story—so that the implied audience must deal with the resulting tension. Fowler is not the first, of course, to argue that "Son of man" at Mark 2:10 is not on the lips of Jesus; for others, see the citations in William O. Walker, Jr., "The Son of Man: Some Recent Developments," *CBQ* 45 (1983): 584–607, esp. 589 n. 29.

22. Cf. the implied audience's deduction that John is the "voice" "in the wilderness" in Mark 1:2-4.

23. On the movement from the disciples to the implied audience, see Elizabeth Struthers Malbon, "Disciples/Crowds/Whoever: Markan Characters and Readers," *NovT* 28 (1986): 104–30; republished in *The Composition of Mark's Gospel: Selected Studies from Novum Testamentum* (ed. David E. Orton; Leiden, The Netherlands: Brill, 1999), 144–70; also republished in Malbon, *In the Company of Jesus*, 70–99.

24. David Rhoads has raised these interpretive questions in personal correspondence.

in service to the powerless. Such a reading of the corporate humanity aspect of the Markan Jesus' phrase "Son of Humanity" stands parallel to his consistent deflection of honor away from himself and to God. The Markan Jesus is a human being who is responsive to God, obedient to God, and empowered by God, but the Markan Jesus is not God.

Would that the "Son of Man" were simply a "technical term" "bearing a precise meaning," as Kingsbury suggests, rather than the ambiguous phrase with a range of potential meanings most New Testament scholars find it to be.[25] Some Markan commentators even argue that the author of Mark's Gospel chose the term because of its plasticity, and then proceeded to fill it with the desired content within the narrative itself.[26] Literally, the phrase *ho huios tou anthrōpou* means "the son of the human being."[27] *Literarily*, it can be an allusion to the "one like a human being" or "one like a son of man" of the eschatological vision of Daniel 7:

25. The scholarly literature on "Son of Man"—its background and its New Testament use—is vast. Two excellent overviews are Walker, "The Son of Man," and John R. Donahue, S.J., "Recent Studies on the Origin of 'Son of Man' in the Gospels," *CBQ* 48 (1986): 484–98. Donahue (494 n. 48) notes that studies of "Son of Man" have virtually ignored redaction critical work on the Synoptics. For a classic philological and history-of-traditions study of "Son of Man," see Hahn, *Titles of Jesus*, chapter 1, "Son of Man," 15–67. Hahn opens his study with this observation: "Of all Christological titles, that of the Son of man has been the most thoroughly investigated. The reason for this is that is has been hoped, by means of this predicate of dignity, to penetrate most deeply to the preaching of Jesus Himself" (15). Among older studies, the final chapter of Morna D. Hooker's *The Son of Man in Mark: A Study of the Background of the Term 'Son of Man' and Its Use in St Mark's Gospel* (Montreal: McGill University Press, 1967), 174–98, offers a condensed and interesting presentation of "The Marcan Pattern" of the Son of Man sayings and "Jesus' Own Use of the Term." On the problem of moving from literary patterns to historical layers, see my final chapter.

26. Boring, for example, notes that "[m]ost important of all, when others use christological titles of Jesus which he wishes to affirm but develop and elaborate, Jesus responds in terms of the Son of Man. . . . It is clear that the content of 'Christ' and 'Son of God' is to be determined by the meaning of 'Son of Man.' . . ." ("Christology of Mark," 132). Cf. Donahue: "It [Son of Man] serves to unite the three stages of Jesus' life—his coming in power and glory, the hiddenness of this power during his suffering and death, and the proleptic exercise of it during his ministry. Son of Man also gives the proper interpretation to Son of God and provides a structural unity to the Gospel" ("Parable of God," 158).

27. *The New Testament and Psalms: An Inclusive Version* (ed. Victor Roland Gold et al.; New York: Oxford University Press, 1995) translates *ho huios tou anthrōpou* as the "Human One," and *The Complete Gospels: Annotated Scholars Version* (ed. Robert J. Miller; Sonoma, Calif.: Polebridge, 1992) translates it as "son of Adam." For a discussion of Jewish ideas about Adam, the first and representative human one, as important background for *ho huios tou anthrōpou* in Mark, see Joel Marcus, "Mark and Paul: The Evidence of Markan Christology; A Response to Martin Werner," unpublished paper distributed to members of the Mark Seminar of the SNTS, 1998, 8–11; much of this paper was later published as "Mark—Interpreter of Paul," *NTS* 46 (2000): 473–87, but not the part cited here.

> As I watched in the night visions,
> I saw one like a human being
> coming with the clouds of heaven.
> And he came to the Ancient One
> and was presented before him.
> To him was given dominion
> and glory and kingship,
> that all peoples, nations, and languages
> should serve him.
> His dominion is an everlasting dominion
> that shall not pass away,
> and his kingship is one
> that shall never be destroyed.
>
> Daniel 7:13-14

Of the Markan Jesus' fourteen uses of "Son of Humanity,"[28] the first two, quoted earlier (2:10, 28), approach the literal pole of the term's range of meanings. Three uses, including the last one (8:38; 13:26; 14:62), present clear allusions to Daniel 7:13-14. The other nine uses refer to the "Son of Humanity" as one who will suffer at the hands of men, which seems fairly distinct from both meaning poles and equally typical of the central thrust of Mark's Gospel.[29] As John Donahue notes, "Son of Man" "brings from the tradition a connotation of one who is both an individual and a corporate figure who will be exalted after a period of struggle."[30]

The involvement of "Son of Humanity" statements in Markan refracted christology becomes clear when the context of each statement is observed and especially when the pattern of all the contexts is laid out. The Markan Jesus applies the first two "Son of Humanity" statements in contexts of controversy with Jewish authorities—scribes (2:6) and Pharisees (2:24). It is clear that Jesus' words exacerbate the controversy (see 3:6). More particularly, the first controversy concerns "blasphemy" (2:7), which is, later in the narrative, the judgment of the high priest (14:64) in response to Jesus' answer to the high priest's question and Jesus' final "Son of Humanity" statement (14:62). Thus controversies over blasphemy, over determining the boundaries of God's authority and Jesus' authority, frame the "Son of Humanity" statements in Mark's narrative.

---

28. Broadhead observes: "The Son of Man title is the most frequent of the christological images in the Gospel of Mark" (*Naming Jesus*, 129).

29. Hahn, *Titles of Jesus*, whose goal is to trace the tradition history of the "Son of Man" sayings, suggests a chronological development from "words concerning the future action of the Son of man," to "words concerning the earthly deeds of the Son of man," to "words concerning the passion and resurrection of the Son of man," with possible connections to "the historical Jesus" for the first group and only church formulations for the last.

30. Donahue, "Parable of God," 158.

Twelve of the "Son of Humanity" statements occur in the second half of the Gospel, with an especially critical one occurring at about the midpoint. In response to Jesus' query, Peter has spoken up for the disciples: "You are the Christ [NRSV Messiah]" (8:29). One might assume the narrator is pleased with this designation (cf. 1:1), but the Markan Jesus commands secrecy (8:30) and immediately refracts the meaning Peter (and anyone else who has been following the narrative thus far) presumably gives to the title "Christ": God's anointed one, a powerful teacher and healer. The title "Christ" is bent, approached from a different angle, by the juxtaposition of Jesus' statement that the "Son of Humanity" must (Gk *dei*) suffer at the hands of men—as well as rise again after three days (8:31). This statement Peter cannot affirm as he affirmed Jesus as the Christ. Within the span of five verses, Peter moves from answering a significant question with a confession the implied audience can only regard as correct ("You are the Christ," 8:29) to being rebuked like an unclean spirit and called "Satan" by Jesus (8:33). The bright light of "Christ" appears as a complex red/orange/yellow/green/blue/violet spectrum when refracted by Jesus' "Son of Humanity" statement, his first of three passion predictions. *The* christological surprise of Mark's Gospel is that the powerful healer and teacher accepts his own persecution, suffering, and death at the hands of men as the will of God. "Peter's fault," as John Donahue observes, "is not lack of courage nor any fascination with a *theologia gloriae*. It is rather that he does not see the passion as a thing of God. . . ."[31] After the fact, the centurion links Jesus' death with the phrase "Son of God" (15:39). Before the fact, predicting the fact, the Markan Jesus links what turns out to be his suffering and death with the phrase "Son of Humanity."

Three additional "Son of Humanity" statements are presented prior to the second passion prediction, and together they frame and refract the significant "christological title" "Son of God" in the form "This is my Son, the Beloved" spoken by the voice from the cloud at Jesus' transfiguration (9:7). Just prior to the narration of the transfiguration story, the Markan Jesus concludes his renewed teaching of the disciples (8:34–9:1), following their misunderstanding (8:32-33) of his first passion prediction (8:31), with a "Son of Humanity" statement linked with a "kingdom of God" statement:

> "Those who are ashamed of me and of my words in this adulterous and sinful generation, of them the Son of Man will also be ashamed when he comes in the glory of his Father with the holy angels." And he said to them, "Truly I tell you, there are some standing here who will not taste death until they see that the kingdom of God has come with power" (8:38–9:1).

The allusion to Daniel 7:13-14 at 8:38 ("come," "glory") is not as strong as at 13:26 and 14:62, but the powerful Danielic "Son of Man" does seem to set the

---

31. John R. Donahue, S.J., "A Neglected Factor in the Theology of Mark," *JBL* 101 (1982): 563–94, quotation from 586.

context for this statement, especially because it is joined to the only Markan reference to "the kingdom of God" coming "with power" (9:1).[32]

Just after the narration of the transfiguration story, the Markan Jesus orders Peter, James, and John "to tell no one about what they had seen, until after the Son of Man had risen from the dead" (9:9). As part of a follow-up conversation about Elijah, Jesus comments: "How then is it written about the Son of Man, that he is to go through many sufferings and be treated with contempt?" (9:12). As in the passion predictions, suffering and rising from the dead are linked to the "Son of Humanity." Jesus' injunction to silence about Peter's confession of Jesus as the Christ was made understandable by Peter's inability to accept Jesus' statement about the suffering of the "Son of Humanity."

At the transfiguration, God tells Peter, James, and John to "listen" to Jesus "my Son." What Jesus says next is not to tell about this manifestation of power until the suffering/rising "Son of Humanity" statements have been experienced fully: first challenging the authorities on behalf of the weak, then suffering and death, then rising from the dead, then telling, then coming with "glory" (8:38; 13:26) and "power" (13:26; cf. 9:1; 14:62). This is the context for understanding Jesus as God's "Son," the prism for refracting "Son of God": glory and power, yes; but first challenging the status quo and enduring suffering. Yet suffering is not the last word.

The next "Son of Humanity" statements are the second and third passion predictions. The three passion prediction units (passion prediction, misunderstanding by the disciples, instruction in discipleship) give structure to the "way" section of Mark's Gospel, 8:22–10:52, with its recurrent references to Jesus and his disciples being "on the way," literally "on the way" to Jerusalem, but metaphorically much more. As John Donahue points out,

> in each case where discipleship misunderstanding is being countered, there is not only a statement on the proper meaning of discipleship (bearing of cross, 8:34-36; receiving of little ones, 9:35-36; being willing to be baptized and drink the cup, 10:38-39), but there is also a significant statement about God and Jesus' relation to him. Peter does not think the things of God (8:33); the one who receives Jesus receives the one who sent him (9:37); and Jesus is not the one who assigns the places of honor in the new age (10:40).[33]

What Donahue calls "disclaimer[s] of Jesus," I am calling elements of deflected and refracted christology.

The second and third passion prediction/"Son of Humanity" statements introduce a term not included in the first: *paradidōmi*, translated as both will

---

32. Power is an issue here. As Michael L. Cook, S.J., observes, the Son of Man according to Daniel 7 "is vindicated by God against the four 'beasts' that represent the imperial powers" (*Christology as a Narrative Quest* [Collegeville, Minn.: Liturgical Press, 1997], 86).

33. Donahue, "Neglected Factor," 590.

be "betrayed" (9:31) and will be "handed over" (10:33). "Handed over" is the more literal rendering, but the reason for the translation "betrayed" comes into view with three additional "Son of Humanity" statements linked with two additional *paradidōmi* references. In his final table fellowship with all his disciples, the Markan Jesus announces that one of them, "one of the twelve" (14:20), will "betray [hand over]" him (14:18) and then comments: "For the Son of Man goes as it is written of him, but woe to that one by whom the Son of Man is betrayed! It would have been better for that one not to have been born" (14:21). At the close of his final moments at Gethsemane with Peter, James, and John (as they sleep and he prays), the Markan Jesus announces that "[t]he hour has come; the Son of Man is betrayed into the hands of sinners" (14:41). The sad irony is that the suffering of the "Son of Man" at the hands of men begins at the hands of one of his own men, "one of the twelve" (14:10, 20, 43), who hands him over. This turn of events is prepared for in the second and third passion predictions (each joining "Son of Humanity" and *paradidōmi*) and culminates in the two "Son of Humanity" statements in the Last Supper scene (one with *paradidōmi*) and one "Son of Humanity" statement in the Gethsemane scene (with *paradidōmi*). Here (9:31; 10:33; 14:21 *bis*, 41) the "Son of Humanity" statements do not refract a particular statement about Jesus made by a character or the narrator. Rather they refract their context of discipleship; the white light of following Jesus "on the way" is refracted to reveal a red to violet blur of betrayal—and later denial and abandonment. But the three passion predictions also assert that the "Son of Humanity" will rise up, and this reality is echoed by the Markan Jesus to the disciples about to abandon him at Gethsemane: "But after I am raised up, I will go before you to Galilee" (14:28).

In looking ahead from the second and third passion predictions to other pairings of "Son of Humanity" and *paradidōmi*, we skipped over what might in fact be the most important of all the Markan Jesus' "Son of Humanity" statements. It comes at the end of the "way" section, just before the story of the healing of the blind Bartimaeus closes the frame (8:22-26/8:27–10:45/10:46-52). It comes as the last word of Jesus' third and final discipleship instruction: "For the Son of Man came not to be served but to serve, and to give his life a ransom for many" (10:45).[34] The self-giving service of the "Son of Humanity" is the

---

34. Norman Perrin, in a postscript to his republished discussion of "The Use of (*Para*)*didonai* in Connection with the Passion of Jesus in the New Testament," in *A Modern Pilgrimage in New Testament Christology* (Philadelphia: Fortress, 1974), 94–103 (first published in *Der Ruf Jesu und die Antwort der Gemeinde: Festschrift für Joachim Jeremias* [ed. Edward Lohse, Christoph Burchard, and Berndt Schaller; Göttingen, Germany: Vandenhoeck & Ruprecht, 1970], 204–12), notes that one can "not distinguish between *paradidonai* as, for example, in the passion predictions, and *didonai*, as, for example, in Mark 10:45. The parallelism of meaning between Gal. 1:4, which uses *dontos*, and Gal. 2:20, using *paradontos*, shows that the two forms of the verb are synonymous, as indeed we would expect in *koine* Greek" (103; also mentioned in Perrin, "Towards an Interpretation of the Gospel of Mark,"

capstone of the teaching of the Markan Jesus in the three passion prediction units. The disciples are to serve others as does Jesus, who must be the "Son of Humanity."[35] Like the other "Son of Humanity" statements around it (9:31; 10:33; 14:21 *bis*, 41), this one refracts no specific "title" offered by a character or the narrator; it refracts the disciples' argument about who is the greatest (9:34); it refracts John's report to Jesus of turning away one who exorcised demons in Jesus' name but who was not following the disciples (9:38). It bends the image the disciples have of their leader in order to shine light on discipleship from a new angle.[36]

The last two "Son of Humanity" statements to be examined, including the last one to be uttered by the Markan Jesus, reflect the "Son of Humanity" imagery from Daniel 7:13-14. These statements (13:26 and 14:62), like earlier ones (8:31, 38; 9:9, 12), occur in close connection with another "christological title" and serve to refract it, to bend and reshape the christology it assumes or presents. As part of his eschatological discourse, addressed literally to Peter, James, John, and Andrew (13:3) but by extension to "all" (13:37), the Markan Jesus warns of the appearance of false "Christs" (NRSV messiahs; 13:22) and of anyone who might say "Look! Here is the Christ!" (NRSV Messiah; 13:21). Then he employs cosmic imagery and a Danielic "Son of Humanity" statement: "Then they will see 'the Son of Man coming in clouds' with great power and glory. Then he will send out the angels, and gather his elect from the four winds, from the ends of the earth to the ends of heaven" (13:26-27). Just as Peter's answer, "You are the Christ," elicits Jesus' refracting response about the suffering "Son of Humanity," so here Jesus' own warning against those who say, "Here is the Christ!" seems to elicit a "Son of Humanity" statement. But this time, with

---

in *Christology and a Modern Pilgrimage: A Discussion with Norman Perrin* [rev. ed.; ed. Hans Dieter Betz; Missoula, Mont.: SBL and Scholars Press, 1974], 49 n. 26). Like the second and third passion predictions then, Mark 10:45, the climax of the Markan Jesus' discipleship instruction in the "way" section, combines "Son of Humanity" and (*para*)*didonai*.

35. The verb "serve" (*diakoneō*), as Edwin K. Broadhead notes, "is commonly used to speak of table service, but it takes on extraordinary meaning in Mark. The destiny of the Son of Man is to serve (10.45), and followers of Jesus can accomplish greatness only through service (10.43-44). Thus, service becomes the most crucial character trait of the narrative. Only three characters are called servants in the Gospel of Mark: the Son of Man (10.45), angels (1.13) and women (1.31; 15.40-41)" (*Teaching with Authority: Miracles and Christology in the Gospel of Mark* [JSNTSup 74; Sheffield: Sheffield Academic, 1992], 63 n. 1).

36. Cf. Donahue: "The story of Jesus is also to be the story of his followers. Mark uses the title [Son of Man] to give a particular theological understanding to Jesus as Son of God too. . . . Mark, by showing in what sense Jesus is to be Son, shows in what sense also his followers are to be 'son.' Ultimately then the christological titles in Mark are not simply descriptions of Jesus but are metaphors of what God has done in Jesus. Mark's Jesus points to the mystery of the divine-human encounter; he is a paradigm of that encounter" ("Parable of God," 158–59).

the three passion predictions behind him and his death inexorably before him, the Markan Jesus speaks of the renewed power of the "Son of Humanity"—a power, however, still used for others.[37] The "Son of Man" will come "with great power and glory" in order (through the agency of angels) to "gather his elect" from wherever they are scattered. Beware of false Christs who may scatter. The true anointed one of God, like the Danielic "Son of Humanity," will *gather* those who are scattered—perhaps even those scattered by betrayal, denial, and abandonment of the one they knew to be the Christ.

The final "Son of Humanity" statement, 14:62, is the fourth one to be juxtaposed with a form of "Son of God" (8:38; 9:9, 12—surrounding "my Son" at 9:7; 14:62—responding to "Son of the Blessed One" at 14:61) and the second one to be linked with an accusation of blasphemy (2:10; 14:62). No "Son of Humanity" statement illustrates more clearly the refracted christology of Mark's Gospel.[38] The high priest has been asking questions; Jesus has been keeping silent (14:60-61). Perhaps Jesus will "save" his life! Then the high priest asks the final question, "Are you the Christ [NRSV Messiah], the Son of the Blessed One?" (14:61), echoing in his high priestly way the narrator's first assertion (1:1, "Jesus Christ, the Son of God"). To his almost cryptic reply, "I am," the Markan Jesus immediately adds a Danielic "Son of Humanity" statement, as if to refract both "Christ" and "Son of God [the Blessed One]," to bend the traditional "titles" to which he gives reticent assent only in order to lose his life in order to save it (cf. 8:35). When Peter applied the term "Christ" to the Jesus he knew as powerful teacher and healer, Jesus responded with a suffering "Son of Humanity" statement. But here, as in the eschatological discourse, when the way of Jesus as the way of service—even if it leads to persecution and suffering—has been clearly revealed (most clearly to the implied audience), Jesus responds with a powerful "Son of Humanity" statement.[39] Suffering is a word that must be heard, but it is

37. Broadhead notes that "the contrasting images of lowliness and power which circulate around the Son of Man title are merged within the narrative itself"; "the narrative links the contrasting sides of the Son of Man precisely in the condemnation and death of Jesus" (*Naming Jesus*, 133).

38. Perrin notes: "In the trial before the Sanhedrin, the messianic secret is finally and formally abandoned as Jesus accepts and publicly acknowledges the designation Son of God. Then that designation is reinterpreted by the last and hence climactic use of Son of Man in the gospel" ("Towards an Interpretation," 32). The Markan Jesus is depicted as "refusing to allow Son of God to be applied to him until the conditions are such that is can be used properly" (34), an observation related to my discussion of deflected christology in the previous chapter. "When the narrative has reached the point where these conditions are fulfilled, Jesus accepts the designation and gives it its final reinterpretation [14:62]" (34). I understand this "reinterpretation" as "refracted christology," a literary critical category, not, as Perrin did, as "corrective christology," a redaction-critical category with emphasis on the historical context of the evangelist (see 15, 38).

39. Cf. Eduard Schweizer, "Mark's Theological Achievement" (trans. R. Morgan), in

not the last word. The last word is given by "the Power" at whose "right hand" the "Son of Humanity" is to come (14:62).[40]

As Edwin Broadhead perceptively concludes in his short but rich chapter on "Son of Man" as part of Markan "Titular Christology": "The mystery of the Son of Man as it is embedded in the story of Jesus explores the depth of the sovereignty of God and exposes the narrative to the claim of the future. This move exceeds the plot line, and the story is opened to a new dimension of power and to a new era of hope."[41] A narrative critic (Broadhead describes his analysis as "formalist") would add—a new era of hope for the implied audience. The projection of the story of the "Son of Humanity" beyond the end of Mark's Gospel is one of many ways the implied author involves the implied audience in the narrative. Broadhead continues:

> While the other Gospels narrate the victory of Jesus over death (Mt. 28.16-20; Lk. 24.13[-53]; Jn 20.11–21.25), the Gospel of Mark transcends the death of Jesus through its Son of Man imagery. . . . The death of Jesus, as his whole story, is taken up into the sovereign power of God and into the unfinished narrative of the future. Operating within the realm of the narrative, the Son of Man title also becomes the vehicle through which the narrative moves beyond itself and its own limitations.[42]

Thus Broadhead observes of the function of the "Son of Man" in Mark's Gospel what I and others have noted about its parables and its overall thrust: It is "as much a christological question and challenge as it is an answer or a description."[43]

In summary: The narrator proclaims "Jesus Christ, the Son of God" (1:1). Peter confesses to Jesus, "You are the Christ" (8:29), and the unclean spirits have known all along that Jesus is the "Son of God" (1:24; 3:11; 5:7). The high priest asks, "Are you the Christ [NRSV Messiah], the Son of the Blessed One?" (14:61). The centurion admits, "Truly this man was God's Son!" (15:39). The Markan Jesus is not in a position to respond to the first (the narrator's opening line) or the last (because he has just died). But in between, he silences the unclean spirits and Peter and breaks his own silence with the high priest—and all for the same reason: to turn answers into questions, to refract the sometimes

---

The Interpretation of Mark (2nd ed.; ed. William A. Telford; Edinburgh: T&T Clark, 1995), 63–87, quotation from 77: "Since now the suffering of the Son of Man is already under way, only his exaltation and parousia are proclaimed here [at 14:62], as at 8:38."

40. As Broadhead notes, in particular reference to 14:62, the Gospel of Mark connects the mystery of the "Son of Man" to the working of God; thus, "the Son of Man title . . . holds a theological point of reference in priority over its christological imagery" (*Naming Jesus*, 132). Or, in my terms, Markan narrative christology—especially as it is deflected and refracted by the Markan Jesus—is theology.

41. Broadhead, *Naming Jesus*, 134.

42. Broadhead, *Naming Jesus*, 134.

43. Broadhead, *Naming Jesus*, 134.

blinding light of the traditional "titles" into the colorful story of one who comes not to be served but to serve.

Thus the Markan Jesus and the Markan narrator (both creations of the implied author) present quite different "christological titles" in quite different ways. The Markan narrator (among other things) proclaims Jesus as "Son of God." The Markan Jesus (among other things) proclaims the in-breaking of the kingdom of God and the coming of the powerful yet suffering "Son of Humanity." The Markan implied author presents the implied audience with this creative tension. To resolve the tension in favor of the Markan narrator (as does Kingsbury by subordinating "Son of Man" to "Son of God") or in favor of the Markan Jesus (as does Naluparayil by amalgamating all traits to the "Son of Man") would be to flatten the multidimensional narrative and its multilayered christology. The implied author of Mark sets up this tension to draw in the implied audience—not to resolve the tension but to see the story of Jesus in its full spectral colors of commitment to God and God's rule, to hear of the story of Jesus in its full complexity and mystery.[44]

A Narrative Critical Reading of the Markan Jesus' "Kingdom of God" Sayings

In terms of systematic theology, one would distinguish, perhaps dramatically, between theology and christology. Such abstract distinctions seem less relevant when the task is to understand the narrative christology of the Markan Gospel.[45] My investigation of deflected and refracted christology in Mark shows that the Markan Jesus is more eager to speak of God (theology) than of himself (christology). This narrative fact tells us as much (or more!) about Jesus

---

44. Donahue, in his conclusion to his review of recent studies on the origin of "Son of Man," notes a christological "tension" in the gospels generally (without narrative critical reference to implied author, narrator, and characters): "The Gospels in varying degrees reflect concern over a Christology where Jesus as a figure of power is misappropriated by different groups. A Christology where Jesus constantly describes himself as 'the Son of man' with its overtones of solidarity with the human condition underscores the true humanity of the one who was proclaimed as risen Lord. It holds in creative tension the dual stages of the career of Jesus, a tension which was to unfold dramatically in the next four centuries of church history—a tension which, like the Son of man problem itself, resists resolution, yet remains a summons to continued engagement" ("Recent Studies," 498).

45. Cf. Boring: "For Mark, to tell the story of *Jesus* is to talk about *God*, the *one* God. Thus to dispute whether the Markan narrative is theocentric or christocentric is a misplaced question" ("Markan Christology," *NTS* version, 471). Suzanne Watts Henderson develops this observation in relation to the discipleship passages in Mark 1–6, concluding that "Mark predicates true discipleship not on full knowledge of Jesus' precise identity but rather on his followers' full participation in his kingdom-of-God agenda" (*Christology and Discipleship in the Gospel of Mark* [SNTSMS 135; Cambridge: Cambridge University Press, 2006], 245.

(christology) as it does about God (theology). What the character Jesus says about the "kingdom of God" is thus an important element of Markan narrative christology.[46]

There are fourteen Markan references to "kingdom of God,"[47] the same number as "Son of Man" references. I do not mention this to suggest some fantastical numerical symbolism—although that would be easy enough to do: fourteen is twice seven; seven is the number of completeness; fourteen represents double completeness; etc.—let the reader smile! But I mention the numbers to note that, at least by frequency, "Son of Humanity" and "kingdom of God" have a similar weight in the Markan narrative. All fourteen "Son of Humanity" statements are on the lips of Jesus; all but one (15:43) of the fourteen "kingdom of God" statements are his as well. As "Son of Humanity" is the Markan Jesus' unique perspective, so "kingdom of God" is his unique proclamation.[48]

The term "kingdom" comes from the secular world—where David (11:10) and Herod (6:23) can have kingdoms, along with other nations (13:8). Herod offers to give Herodias' dancing daughter up to half of his kingdom (6:23). The crowd welcoming Jesus into Jerusalem anticipates "the coming kingdom of our ancestor David!" (11:10). Jesus warns four of his disciples (13:3; but see 13:37) in his eschatological discourse that "nation will rise against nation, and kingdom against kingdom" (13:8a). "Kingdom" can also be applied metaphorically[49] to the reign of Satan. The Markan Jesus argues with the scribes who come down from Jerusalem, who accuse him of casting out demons "by the ruler of

46. In offering "Some Proposals" as an antidote to the neglect of "God" in New Testament theology, Nils A. Dahl includes this statement that combines God (theology), Christ (christology), and Jesus' kingdom sayings: "The Easter faith did not render Jesus' preaching about God and His kingdom obsolete but rather caused the sayings of Jesus to be remembered and reshaped as words of the Lord (Paul) or of 'the living Jesus' (Gospel of Thomas, Introduction). The evangelists integrated parts of the sayings-tradition into the story of the crucified and risen Christ, each in his own way" ("The Neglected Factor in New Testament Theology," *Reflection* [Yale Divinity School] 73 [1975]: 5–8, quotation from 7).

47. Donahue presents the following data on the Markan use of *theos* (God): "The text of Mark contains the term *theos* forty-eight times. There are fourteen kingdom of God sayings[,] of which thirteen are on the lips of Jesus, and five appellations of the phrase Son of God, of which three are on the lips of demons, one is the superscription and one is the final reference by the centurion. Apart from the kingdom sayings Jesus speaks of God directly seventeen times and *theos* is explicitly used in seven OT citations on the lips of Jesus while in two citations God is the presumed speaker without being explicitly mentioned (7:6 = Isa 29:13; 11:17 = Isa 56:7). There are five other usages of *theos*, two by the narrator (1:14, 2:12) and three by others in the gospel" ("Neglected Factor," 565).

48. Donahue asserts that "[i]n taking over the proclamation of the kingdom of God, Mark is doubtless close to the historical Jesus. However, he does not simply record this tradition but makes kingdom into a major theological motif which spans the whole Gospel" ("Parable of God," 156).

49. Obviously there is a metaphorical dimension to the Markan reference to "the

demons" (3:22), that "[i]f a kingdom is divided against itself, that kingdom cannot stand. . . . And if Satan has risen up against himself and is divided, he cannot stand, but his end has come" (3:24, 26). This is a profound image for Mark's Gospel, for, as we noted in relation to enacted christology, the actions of the Markan Jesus as powerful exorcist of demons and healer, and as authoritative preacher and teacher as well, serve as evidence that the kingdom of Satan *is beginning to* come to an end because the kingdom of God has begun.[50]

In Mark's Gospel, *basileia*, kingdom, is predominantly used to refer to the *basileia tou theou*, the "kingdom (or rule, or reign) of God." Jesus is often said to preach or to teach, and he is often called "teacher" in Mark. These narrative facts have clear significance for the enacted christology of Mark's Gospel whereby Jesus' deeds reveal more than others' words. The dominant theme of Jesus' preaching and teaching is the in-breaking of the "kingdom of God."[51] The Gospel's first "kingdom" reference, the first narrated activity of Jesus' ministry after his baptism and testing have established his commission from God, presents the archetype of Jesus' preaching: ". . . Jesus came to Galilee, proclaiming the good news of God, and saying, 'The time [*kairos*] is fulfilled, and the kingdom of God has come near; repent, and believe in the good news" (1:14-15). This proclamation, of course, raises more questions than it answers: What is the significance of *kairos?* How is it fulfilled? If the kingdom of God has come near, is it already here, or not yet here? How is Jesus' demand for repentance related to John's (cf. 1:4-5)? What does it mean to *believe* in the good news? Yet, as Robert Tannehill notes, "This scene relates the whole mission of Jesus to the coming of God's kingdom."[52]

The second "kingdom of God" reference is equally significant—and equally cryptic. Whereas the first reference establishes Jesus as the kingdom's proclaimer, the second establishes his followers as its participants. The Markan Jesus, "[w]hen he was alone," said to "those who were around him along with the twelve" (4:10): "To you has been given the mystery [Gk *mystērion*; NRSV secret] of the kingdom of God, but for those outside, everything comes in par-

coming kingdom of our ancestor David" (11:10) as well, because David is long dead, but his "kingdom" is still "coming."

50. For a careful literary analysis of Mark 3:23-27, see Elizabeth Shively, "The Story Matters: Solving the Problem of the Parables in Mark 3:23-27," in *Between Author and Audience in Mark: Narration, Characterization, Interpretation* (ed. Elizabeth Struthers Malbon; New Testament Monographs 23; Sheffield: Sheffield Phoenix, 2009), 122–44.

51. According to Donahue, "By making the kingdom proclamation and sayings such a dominant motif and integrative factor in the Gospel, Mark gives a radically new referent to kingdom" ("Parable of God," 157).

52. Robert C. Tannehill, "The Gospel of Mark as Narrative Christology," *Semeia* 16 (1979): 57–95, quotation from 64. The essay has been republished in Robert C. Tannehill, *The Shape of the Gospel: New Testament Essays* (Eugene, Ore.: Cascade Books, 2007), 161–87.

ables . . ." (4:11). As it turns out, being given the *mystērion* is not unlike being given a parable; it is more like being enabled to experience the right questions than knowing the right answer. In fact, receiving the *mystērion* of the "kingdom of God" makes life no easier for Jesus' followers than being the proclaimer of its arrival does for Jesus himself. Although the news of God's nearness is good, it is also shocking and demanding. It is for this reason that parables are especially appropriate for communicating news of the "kingdom of God."

"The kingdom of God is as if . . ." (4:26) and "With what can we compare the kingdom of God . . . ?" (4:30) serve as introductory formulae for the Markan Jesus' parabolic speaking in chapter 4. Much has been written about the parables of Jesus, the parables in Mark, and even Jesus as the parable of God in Mark.[53] The present work is not the place to review or attempt to extend those discussions, although I acknowledge my dependence on what I have learned from them. My question is, rather, how does what the Markan Jesus says about the "kingdom of God" influence the narrative christology of Mark's Gospel? Do Jesus' images of the "kingdom of God" refract any other conceptions of it? Certainly anyone expecting "kingdom" images of power and glory (conquering armies of celestial beings and cosmic battles) will have been disappointed with the Markan Jesus' talk of planting seeds. Adding to the surprise are the observations that not all the seeds flourish, that we do "not know how" (4:27) those that manage to grow do so, and that a tiny seed grows not into the mighty tree one might expect of a storyteller but into a common shrub, or even a good-sized weed! The images of Jesus' parables in chapter 4 grow out of his proclamation that "the kingdom of God has come near" (1:15). God is a real presence in the world, but God's rule is not (or not yet) overwhelming the world. In terms of narrative christology, Jesus is one who experiences God's nearness in this surprising way and tries to enable others to experience it as well. One has to have ears to hear, says the parabolic speaker of chapter 4.[54]

In chapter 10, Jesus' metaphoric speaking (and acting) also relies on "kingdom of God" language. The Markan Jesus blesses the little children whom the disciples had apparently tried to turn away (10:13-16) and affirms that "the kingdom of God belongs" "to such as these" (10:14)—powerless children, expected to do as others require—and that "whoever does not receive the kingdom of God as a little child will never enter it" (10:15). Children, low in social status, are the models for those who would enter the kingdom of God. Similarly, and equally surprisingly, the rich, high in social status, present an image

---

53. For bibliography see John R. Donahue, S.J., *The Gospel in Parable* (Philadelphia: Fortress, 1988).

54. As Donahue puts it: "The kingdom of God is not simply as Perrin notes a 'tensive symbol' for God's sovereignty, but is now a metaphor of that power manifest in the life and teaching of Jesus. Jesus is the proclaimer of the kingdom, but in Mark's presentation the kingdom also proclaims Jesus" ("Parable of God," 157).

of those for whom such entry is somewhere between difficult and impossible. "How hard it will be for those who have wealth to enter the kingdom of God!" (10:23), Jesus tells his disciples after the man who "had many possessions" "was shocked and went away grieving" (10:22) at Jesus' request to give his possessions away to the poor and come follow him (10:21). The disciples too are perplexed at such words (10:24a). But Jesus refracts their status quo thinking with a colorful image: "It is easier for a camel to go through the eye of a needle than for someone who is rich to enter the kingdom of God" (10:25). If the "kingdom of God" challenges the status quo to this extent, it is no wonder that the established authorities challenge its proclaimer.

It may not be just the rich who have difficulty entering the "kingdom of God." Sandwiched between Jesus' two sayings about this difficulty of the rich is a saying that could have more general import: "Children, how hard it is to enter the kingdom of God!" (10:24b). Although there are textual variants that blunt the general impact by adding "for those who trust in riches," the dialogue of Jesus and his disciples in the following verses (10:26-27) suggests the broader application. Disciples: "Then who can be saved?" (10:26). Jesus: "For mortals it is impossible, but not for God; for God all things are possible" (10:27). But however difficult the entry, sacrificing one's power, one's wealth, even—with the Jewish storyteller's usual hyperbole—one's eye is worthwhile, for "it is better for you to enter the kingdom of God with one eye than to have two eyes and to be thrown into hell . . ." (9:47). If the "kingdom of God" is this demanding, it is no wonder that its proclaimer infuriates his foes and challenges his followers.

Because the kingdom of Satan is being overthrown (see 3:23-27), choices must be made. Those who hear Jesus' proclamation, like the Jesus who proclaims it, live at a decisive moment in time—a *kairos*. Just after the baptism and testing scenes in the wilderness, the Markan Jesus announces that the *kairos* is fulfilled (1:15). Just before the transfiguration scene on the high mountain, Jesus announces that "there are some standing here who will not taste death until they see that the kingdom of God has come with power" (9:1). At the close of the Last Supper scene, Jesus announces that "I will never again drink of the fruit of the vine until that day when I drink it new in the kingdom of God" (14:25). The kingdom of God has come, and yet the kingdom of God is still to come. It is not a mere matter of chronology, in which already and not yet are mutually exclusive, but a *kairos*.[55]

---

55. Cf. Boring on the tensive nature of history and eschatology in Mark: "The eschatological battle with Satan has already been won and demons flee before the triumphant Christ, for the eschaton has arrived and the world is different. But also the world still goes on as before. To speak of this situation as 'zwischen den Zeiten' [between the times] is to make it more chronological than Mark in fact wants to make it. . . . [D]iachronic language cannot do justice to the synchronic reality which struggles to be expressed . . ." ("Christology of Mark," 140).

The kingdom of God has come near, but one must be given its *mystērion*; one must have eyes to see and ears to hear. Some do. The Markan Jesus says to a scribe (surprisingly enough) with whom he has been discussing the greatest commandment, "You are not far from the kingdom of God" (12:34). Not only has the kingdom of God come near you, but you have come near the kingdom of God! One must receive the *mystērion* that one is given. And after Jesus can say no more about the kingdom, having "breathed his last" (15:39), the *narrator* picks up the phrase for the first—and only—time, in describing Joseph of Arimathea, "a respected member of the council" (presumably the council who condemned Jesus to death[56]), as one "who was also himself waiting expectantly [or looking; Gk *prosdechomenos*] for the kingdom of God" (15:43). The kingdom has come and is coming. The narrator, picking up Jesus' "kingdom" language, invites the implied audience to share the position of Joseph of Arimathea.

The kingdom has come (1:15); the kingdom is coming (9:1; 12:34; 14:25; cf. 15:43)—that is what the Markan Jesus says. And what the Markan Jesus says is a significant clue to the Markan Gospel's christology. Although the Markan narrator proclaims Jesus as the "Christ, the Son of God," the Markan Jesus proclaims the in-breaking of the "kingdom of God." The enacted, deflected, and refracted christology of the Markan Jesus is theology.[57] The one anointed by God (messiah, Christ), chosen by God (Son of God; see Psalm 2), and obedient to God (a son of God in Jewish usage) is the one who senses that God is near, even if others do not, and faithfully proclaims God's presence as good news.

Refracted Christology and Parable

As proclaimer of the surprising "kingdom (or rule) of God" and speaker of the puzzling "Son of Humanity" statements, the Markan Jesus is, as John Donahue has artfully shown, presented as the parable of God in the Gospel of Mark.[58] Following C. H. Dodd's influential definition of a parable, Donahue illustrates how each element applies to an aspect of Mark's portrayal of Jesus. I could also suggest that Dodd's definition of a parable correlates with the aspects of Markan

56. Contra Kingsbury, *Conflict*, 123–24 n. 46; 125 n. 87.

57. In the sense of *narrative* theology, not systematic theology. Cf. Cook: "In an ultimate sense the most important character in Mark's story world is God. . . . Jesus' view of God, inseparable from God's view of Jesus, is expressed throughout the gospel" (*Christology as a Narrative Quest*, 96). Cf. also Boring: "In the Markan narrative, to encounter Jesus is to deal with God . . ." ("Christology of Mark," 139).

58. "Since parable has now become not simply a description of a select group of sayings of Jesus, but an independent hermeneutical and theological category," Donahue argues, "we will propose that Mark's Gospel can be presented as a narrative parable of the meaning of the life and death of Jesus." "Such a [parabolic] reading means that the Gospel's presentation of Jesus is always 'open-ended' and always calls for revisioning and restatement" ("Parable of God," 149, 155).

narrative christology I have labeled deflected and refracted christology. Dodd wrote, in *The Parables of the Kingdom:* "At its simplest the parable is a metaphor or simile drawn from nature or common life, arresting the hearer by its vividness or strangeness, and leaving the mind in sufficient doubt about its precise application to tease it into active thought."[59] The story of Jesus of Nazareth has metaphoric significance but is "drawn from . . . common life."[60] Enacted christology stresses how much is revealed about Jesus in his actions within the common life of Galilee and Jerusalem. Reflected christology (to be discussed in the following chapter) illustrates within the narrative the metaphoric power of Jesus' life that extends beyond the narrative. But the Markan Jesus' actions and words—especially his words about the "Son of Humanity" and the "kingdom of God," explored here in relation to refracted christology—are so vivid and strange, even in relation to the Markan narrator, that they arrest the audience, leave doubt, and tease the audience into active thought.

In the terms of Tannehill, who initiated the discussion of Markan narrative christology:

> To a surprising degree Jesus' action, rather than replacing the action of others, calls forth the action of others. Jesus becomes the ameliorator of others in that he incites them to become ameliorators for themselves and others. In other words, Jesus functions frequently as an influencer, one who moves others to action.[61]

The key issue involving Jesus is not "identity" but influence. Markan narrative christology focuses not on essence (What is Jesus' nature?) but on process (What are the dynamics of the relationships Jesus establishes and encourages?). In Markan terms, the central issues are authority (*exousia*) in relation to the inbreaking rule of God and following (*akolouthein*), following Jesus in the proclamation of and participation in the gifts and risks of that kingdom. The parables of the kingdom of God demand response, and so does their Markan parabler. Although the Markan narrator does show interest in the christological question "Who is Jesus?" the Markan Jesus focuses on other questions: "What is God doing?" and "What will the hearers of this good news do?" Markan narrative christology raises all these questions, resolves none, and thus teases the implied audience into active thought and thoughtful action.

In the terms I have applied to Markan narrative christology here, the deflected and refracted christology of the Markan narrative challenges the implied audience to deal with the tension between an assertive narrator who proclaims

---

59. C. H. Dodd, *The Parables of the Kingdom* (Glasgow: Collins, 1961), 16.

60. Cf. Donahue: "In Mark, Jesus is truly the parable of God, but the way to God is not through any docetic circumvention of the human Jesus. In the case of Jesus himself, no less than in the parables he utters, the scandal of the human is the starting point for the unfolding of the mystery of God" ("Parable of God," 160).

61. Tannehill, "Narrative Christology," 63.

"Jesus Christ, the Son of God" and focuses on his actions and a reticent Jesus who deflects attention and honor, challenges traditional views, and insistently proclaims not himself but God. By creating this tension between narrator and protagonist, the Markan implied author is able to present Jesus the parabler as a parable, as one who teases others into active thought. The implied author of Mark sets up this tension to draw in the implied audience—not to resolve the tension but to receive it as the *mystērion* that is given, to receive it, in Tannehill's words, "with full appreciation of its power to challenge."[62]

62. Tannehill, "Narrative Christology," 60.

CHAPTER 5

REFLECTED CHRISTOLOGY:
WHAT OTHERS DO

The final aspect of the Markan narrative christology presented here is reflected christology, that is, christology reflected in what some characters other than Jesus in the Markan narrative do that reflects what the Markan Jesus says and does. We began the exploration of Markan narrative christology with a consideration of what Jesus does, enacted christology (chapter 1). However, I made no attempt in that chapter to discuss individually and specifically every action of the Markan Jesus. Such a task would have made this book considerably longer than it already is, as well as redundant with work already presented elsewhere. This chapter is even more constrained in what it attempts—but for the same reasons: scale and redundancy. Not only do I not seek to provide an analysis of all that every other character does in relation to Jesus (in parallel with the limits of chapter 1), but I do not even seek to provide an overview or outline of the generalized actions of all the characters in relation to Jesus (as I attempted to do in chapter 1 concerning Jesus' actions). First, such work would involve some redundancy with the analysis and commentary provided in chapter 2 (projected christology) on what other characters and the narrator say to, about, or in relation to Jesus. Speaking too is a form of doing. Second, a discussion of actions of all the characters and character groups would prove redundant with work I have presented elsewhere on the characters around Jesus.[1] In addition, other Markan

---

1. See the essays collected in *In the Company of Jesus: Characters in Mark's Gospel* (Louisville: Westminster John Knox, 2000).

scholars have reflected and commented on the actions of the Markan characters in helpful articles, monographs, and commentaries too numerous to name, a third source of potential redundancy.[2]

Yet the most obvious constraint here is not redundancy but scale: the sheer number of actions that would need to be considered. Certainly, all the actions of all the characters in relation to Jesus influence the characterization of the Markan Jesus in a number of ways, but I will focus here on only one aspect of that complex whole, an aspect based on the foregoing discussions of the deflected and refracted christology of the Markan Jesus as it is enacted in the Markan narrative in tension with the christology projected by other characters and the narrator. This aspect of Markan narrative christology based on what some characters do in relation to Jesus I call reflected christology. And, although I will discuss specific characters and their actions at the level of Mark's story, I will be especially attentive to the discourse level of the narrative. It is at the discourse level that the implied author communicates with the implied audience by means of the overall arrangement of episodes and the overarching ("hypertactic") presentation of themes in the plot. This focus also parallels my treatment of Jesus' actions, in chapter 1.

In the discussion of enacted christology in chapter 1, I sketched out a general schema of the Markan cast of characters, highlighting who is in conflict with whom and who interacts positively with whom. The human characters range from opponents to disciples to suppliants to exemplars, with the final three groups being included in the more plastic category of fallible followers. The relation of the fallible followers to the Markan Jesus forms the background for reflected christology, but in the foreground of reflected christology are those minor characters who are exemplary. After an overview of the category and functioning of exemplary characters, I will focus here on three pairs of minor characters who serve as exemplars of Jesus' words and deeds for the rest of his followers. Deflected and refracted christology (discussed in chapters 3

2. But here are some starting points. For a useful overview of the characters around Jesus, see David Rhoads, Joanna Dewey, and Donald Michie, *Mark as Story: An Introduction to the Narrative of a Gospel* (2nd ed.; Minneapolis: Fortress, 1999), 116–36. For a commentary sensitive to issues of the characters in the narrative, see M. Eugene Boring, *Mark: A Commentary* (The New Testament Library; Louisville: Westminster John Knox, 2006). On the disciples, see Suzanne Watts Henderson, *Christology and Discipleship in the Gospel of Mark* (SNTSMS 135; Cambridge: Cambridge University Press, 2006), and Ira Brent Driggers, *Following God through Mark: Theological Tension in the Second Gospel* (Louisville: Westminster John Knox, 2007). On the women characters, see Hisako Kinukawa, *Women and Jesus in Mark: A Japanese Feminist Perspective* (Maryknoll, N.Y.: Orbis, 1994), and David Rhoads, "Jesus and the Syrophoenician Woman in Mark: A Narrative Critical Study," *JAAR* 62 (1994): 343–75, republished in *Reading Mark: Engaging the Gospel* (Minneapolis: Fortress, 2004), 63–94. On the minor characters, see Joel F. Williams, *Other Followers of Jesus: Minor Characters as Major Figures in Mark's Gospel* (JSNTSup 102; Sheffield: Sheffield Academic, 1994).

and 4) have to do primarily with the Markan Jesus' focus on God, particularly as distinct from the focus of everyone else (characters and narrator) on Jesus (projected christology, discussed in chapter 2). Reflected christology suggests that how other characters relate to Jesus may in fact mirror how Jesus relates to God. The mirror the opponents of Jesus hold up is distorted; sensing that Jesus is involved in a conflict of cosmic proportions involving God, they link Jesus with the wrong pole (3:22-30). The mirror the disciples hold up is dim, but good enough to see Jesus—and themselves!; in shock, they drop the mirror. The mirror the exemplars hold up is small, but polished; in their brief and specific actions, they mirror how Jesus relates to God and thus to others—or perhaps how Jesus relates to others and thus to God.

Exemplary Characters

In Mark's Gospel, the exemplary characters are minor characters, which does not at all mean that they are unimportant.[3] For my purposes, a "minor" character is one who lacks a continuing or recurrent presence in the story as narrated. Minor characters, alongside the major characters, extend the continuum of potential responses to Jesus in an open-ended way, providing implicit narrative comparisons and contrasts with the responses of the continuing or recurrent characters and providing a bridge from the (internal) characters to the (borderline) implied audience. As the Jewish authorities are *generally* depicted as opponents of Jesus in Mark, and the disciples are *generally* portrayed as fallible followers, so the minor characters are *most often* presented as exemplars. In their brief moments of narrative time, they serve as models for attitudes and behaviors appropriate also for the major characters of the narrative and especially for the implied audience.

The minor characters around Jesus, generally presented as exemplars, occur in three sequential sets in the Markan narrative. From 1:1 through 8:21 the minor characters are generally suppliants who exemplify faith in Jesus' healing power and authority as proclaimer of the kingdom (rule) of God. In 8:22 through 10:52, the middle section of Mark, three suppliants appear—all with rich connotative and symbolic significance for understanding the nature of followership, especially fallible followership—as well as the rich man who is a negative exemplar of followership. From 11:1 through 16:8, the passion

---

3. I have discussed the minor characters in "The Major Importance of the Minor Characters in Mark," in *The New Literary Criticism and the New Testament* (ed. Elizabeth Struthers Malbon and Edgar V. McKnight; Sheffield: Sheffield Academic and Valley Forge: Trinity, 1994), 58–86, republished in Malbon, *In the Company of Jesus*, 189–225. The following brief synopsis of exemplary characters is drawn from that article, which may be consulted for reference to the secondary literature, but see esp. Rhoads, Dewey, and Michie, *Mark as Story*, 129–35, and Williams, *Other Followers*.

narrative, the minor characters are generally exemplars of suffering and service as paradoxical aspects of the messiahship of Jesus and the rule of God, although Pilate and the soldiers, of course, act as opponents.

Like the disciples as fallible followers and the Jewish authorities as opponents, the minor characters as exemplars manifest a certain rhythm in their appearance, but the rhythm of each group is distinctive. If the disciples may be said, schematically, to move from their best to worse to their worst, and the Jewish authorities from bad to worse to the worst, the minor characters as exemplars might be said to move from good to mixed to best. The implied author is concerned to illustrate who Jesus is as the Christ and who can be his followers and how. The unfolding of the plot demands and depends on changes in the characters and groups of characters. The opponents must become increasingly aggressive in order for the plot to be carried out. As the disciples increasingly manifest the difficulty of followership by their fallibility, the minor characters are increasingly called on to manifest the possibility of even difficult followership.

The disciples of the Markan Jesus reflect his dynamic relationship with God. The suppliants mirror his trust in God's healing power and confidence that God's kingdom has come near. The exemplars reflect the Markan Jesus' self-giving service and his openness to the kingdom of God as having come near and yet still coming. Disciples, suppliants, and exemplars all fall into the broader category of fallible followers, as distinguished from opponents. The category of fallible followers itself is more a continuum than a series of cubbyholes. A suppliant, like Bartimaeus, for example, might also be an exemplar; exemplary women characters, like those at the cross, might also be acting as disciples. Here we will look briefly at one pair of suppliants/exemplars and two pairs of exemplars in Mark's Gospel with the goal of seeing how their relationships to the deeds and words of the Markan Jesus contribute to the reflected christology of Mark's Gospel.

TWO MEN HEALED OF BLINDNESS

Although many interpreters have noted that the only two stories of the healing of blindness in Mark's Gospel (8:22-26 and 10:46-52) form a frame for the "way" section, many commentators still suggest a break at 8:27, Peter's "confession," when making a Markan outline. In fact, the pericope just prior to 8:27, the healing of the blind man of Bethsaida (8:22-26), has strong connections to both what precedes it and what follows it. Because Bethsaida was mentioned as the goal of the disciples' would-be journey across the Sea of Galilee at 6:45, a journey detoured first by the disciples' difficulty in rowing in "an adverse wind" (6:48) and later by Jesus' journeys with them into Gentile territory, their narrated arrival at Bethsaida at 8:22 gives closure to the preceding events. Because the narrative impact of the preceding events serves to illustrate Jesus' outreach—in teaching, healing, and feeding—to Gentiles as well as Jews, the two-stage healing might well be interpreted by the implied audience to refer symbolically to understanding (insight) of these two stages of Jesus' ministry.

However, after the dialogue between Jesus and the disciples about who Jesus is said to be (8:27-30), followed immediately by the first passion prediction (8:31) and the disciples' misunderstanding (8:32-33), it is clear that the two-stage healing of blindness may also be interpreted by the implied audience to refer symbolically to the two stages of insight needed to understand Jesus not only as powerful healer and teacher (Peter's "Christ") but also as one who serves, even when persecuted (Jesus' "Son of Humanity").

As I argued in chapter 1, I see no reason to suggest that the implied audience would be asked to choose one interpretation over the other. In a chronological (1:1–16:8) reading or hearing, the connection of 8:22-26 to the preceding material would occur first; the connection to succeeding material would come as an afterthought, but with the persuasive force of 20/20 hindsight. Naturally, the blind man of Bethsaida is a suppliant, but because of the strong symbolic meanings of his two-stage healing, he serves also as an exemplar of one who sees not only the obvious and the obviously good (Jesus is a powerful healer and teacher among the Jews, that is, the "Christ") but also, after a second healing touch and a deeper look, the not-so-obvious and the not-so-obviously good (Jesus is also a powerful healer and teacher among Gentiles, and Jesus is the "Son of Humanity," who as such must suffer persecution and die). One might also see two stages in Bartimaeus' terms of address for Jesus: "Son of David," used initially but ignored by the Markan Jesus, and "*Rabbouni*" (my rabbi), employed after his direct encounter with Jesus.[4] If the writers of the Gospels of Matthew and Luke knew and used Mark's Gospel, it does not surprise me that they did not use the story of the two-stage healing.[5] Perhaps they realized just how intertwined in the Markan narrative it was, not at all like a pearl on a string, but more like a thread in a tapestry.[6]

---

4. As discussed earlier in chapter 2 on projected christology and chapter 3 on deflected christology.

5. Joanna Dewey, "Mark as Interwoven Tapestry: Forecasts and Echoes for a Listening Audience," *CBQ* 53 (1991): 221–36, see 230, treats Mark 9:14-27, the healing of the boy with a spirit, as a two-stage healing as well as 8:22-26; I have not run into this terminology elsewhere. Presumably she considers the first stage to be indicated at 9:26 and the second stage at 9:27. Although resurrection language is present ("like a corpse," "He is dead," "lifted up"), the story is not a resuscitation (contrast 5:35-43, where Jairus' daughter is dead before Jesus' arrival) but an exorcism, which is complete at 7:26. It is the crowd that assumes, wrongly, that the boy is dead. It is not irrelevant that this final exorcism in Mark's Gospel points symbolically forward to the resurrection. Both Matthew (17:14-21) and Luke (9:37-43a) include shorter versions on the exorcism; neither has the level of Mark's detail, including the reference to the crowd mistaking the boy for a corpse.

6. It is possible that Matthew, who does seem to worry about every little thing that *might* suggest Jesus' weakness, also rejected the two-stage healing because it made Jesus' healing power seem deficient. But clearly, Matthew and Luke do not follow Mark's way of suggesting the extension of Jesus' ministry from Jews to Gentiles because each has his own way:

The importance of the two-stage healing of blindness to Markan narrative christology, especially reflected christology, becomes even more plain when it is viewed from a second perspective, that of its connection with the healing of Bartimaeus to form a frame around the "way" section. From 8:27 through 10:45, Jesus and his disciples (and, of course, the implied audience) are "on the way"—geographically, to Jerusalem, christologically and theologically, to an understanding that the one who would be greatest must be the least. The pericope of the closing frame opens with an exact parallel to the pericope of the opening frame:

> [And] they came to Bethsaida (8:22).
> [And] they came to Jericho (10:46).[7]

The parallel seems intentional because a second reference to Jericho, in fact "leaving Jericho," occurs in the following sentence. In discussing both projected and deflected christology earlier (chapters 2 and 3), I have commented on how Bartimaeus' twofold cry to Jesus as "Son of David" is to be interpreted. Here I want to focus on Bartimaeus' action after he arrests Jesus' attention.

The Markan Jesus recognizes Bartimaeus as a suppliant, asking, "What do you want me to do for you?" (10:51a). But Bartimaeus now recognizes Jesus with the words of a disciple or follower: "My teacher [Aramaic *Rabbouni*], let me see again" (10:51b). Bartimaeus was not born blind; he once had sight, but blindness overwhelmed him; now he wants to see anew. Given the blindness of the disciples in the entire preceding section, the possible symbolic meaning of renewed sight is not hard for the implied audience to see. Jesus observes to the man, "your faith has made you well"—would-be followers, take note—and "immediately he regained his sight" (10:52). Jesus had said to Bartimaeus, "Go," but Bartimaeus, with new sight, "followed him on the way" (10:52). "On the way" (*en tē hodō*) are the very last words of this well-defined section of the Markan narrative, during which "on the way" has been repeatedly articulated (8:27; 9:33, 34; 10:17, 32; cf. 10:46) as the setting for Jesus' discipleship teaching about the call to service and risk of suffering and the disciples' struggles to see that clearly and anew. I am simply unable to imagine, as Kingsbury and others are, how the implied audience could be expected *not* to take "on the way" metaphorically or symbolically as indicating the proper discipleship response to Jesus.[8]

Matthew, the Great Commission (Matt 28:18-20), and Luke, the sending out of the seventy (Luke 10:1-16) and the book of Acts.

7. Here, as elsewhere, the NRSV unfortunately eliminates the typical Markan *kai parataxis*, beginning sentences with *kai*, "and."

8. Jack Dean Kingsbury, *The Christology of Mark's Gospel* (Philadelphia: Fortress, 1983), 104 n. 159. In contrast, see Edwin K. Broadhead, *Teaching with Authority: Miracles and Christology in the Gospel of Mark* (JSNTSS 74; Sheffield: Sheffield Academic, 1992), 166, on the connection between miracle and discipleship with reference to the Bartimaeus story.

Thus Bartimaeus, like the man from Bethsaida, is presented as a suppliant turned exemplar. What they ask for at the story level is sight; what their actions suggest at the discourse level is insight. The Bethsaida man looks at things again; Bartimaeus follows "on the way." The framing position of their stories cues the implied audience to look again at these two characters and see not suppliants walking but exemplars following on the way.

Two Giving Women

The characters of the second pair, in my list of exemplars reflecting the christology of the Markan Jesus, ask for nothing but give all. For this reason they are obviously not suppliants, and for this very reason they are exemplars of Jesus' self-giving service. The two characters are, interestingly enough, unnamed women: the poor widow (12:41-44) and the anointing woman (14:3-9).[9] Their gender implies their low status; their lack of names confirms it. But, as the Markan Jesus notes, "many who are first will be last, and the last will be first" (10:31). Like the two stories of the healed blind men, the two stories of the giving women form a frame, here around Jesus' eschatological discourse in chapter 13. It is actually the two stories of giving women in contrast to two stories of selfish men that form the frame.

At the close of Jesus' teaching in the temple (11:27–12:44), he warns his listeners about the selfish behavior of scribes "who like to walk around in long robes, and to be greeted with respect in the marketplaces, and to have the best seats in the synagogues and places of honor at banquets! . . . [and to] devour widows' houses"! (12:38-40). In the very next scene, Jesus sits down opposite the treasury in the temple and calls to his disciples' attention the poor widow's gift of two small coins, adding his own interpretation: ". . . she has put in all she had, her whole life (my translation; Gk *panta hosa eichen ebalen, holon ton bion autēs*; 12:44). Norman Perrin refers to this verse as "the climactic allusion to the cross in the woman's sacrifice."[10] The contrast between these scribes, opponents of the Markan Jesus, and this woman, an exemplar of what the Markan Jesus offers and demands, could hardly be more dramatic.

---

9. In addition to their inclusion in my article on minor characters, referenced in note 3, I have discussed the poor widow and the anointing woman in these two articles: "Fallible Followers: Women and Men in the Gospel of Mark," *Semeia* 28 (1983): 23–49, republished in Malbon, *In the Company of Jesus*, 41–69; "The Poor Widow in Mark and Her Poor Rich Readers," *CBQ* 53 (1991): 589–604, republished in Malbon, *In the Company of Jesus*, 166–88, and also in *The Feminist Companion to Mark* (ed. Amy-Jill Levine; Sheffield: Sheffield Academic, 2001), 111–27.

10. Norman Perrin, "Towards an Interpretation of the Gospel of Mark," in *Christology and a Modern Pilgrimage: A Discussion with Norman Perrin* (rev. ed.; ed. Hans Dieter Betz; Missoula, Mont.: SBL and Scholars Press, 1974), 1–52, quotation from 22.

After the close of Jesus' eschatological discourse (13:3-37), during which time he had been "sitting on the Mount of Olives opposite the temple" (13:3), the narrator relates briefly the activities and discussions of the chief priests and scribes as they search for a way to arrest Jesus (14:1-2). In the very next scene, Jesus sits at table in the house of Simon the leper and calls his disciples' attention to the anointing woman's gift of ointment worth more than three hundred denarii, adding his own interpretation: "She has performed a good service for me. . . . She has done what she could; she has anointed my body beforehand for its burial. Truly I tell you, wherever the good news is proclaimed in the whole world, what she has done will be told in remembrance of her" (14:6b, 8-9). The parallels between the opening frame (scribes/poor widow) and the closing frame (chief priests and scribes/anointing woman) are obvious, but the symmetry is broken for an additional contrast to the anointing woman. The narrator reports that "Judas Iscariot, who was one of the twelve" (14:10), hands over Jesus for money, in contrast to the unnamed woman who hands over money for Jesus. Thus the story of the anointing woman, which, with the story of the poor widow, frames Jesus' eschatological discourse, is itself framed by two stories of selfish men, an elaborate but not inappropriate setting for a story that is to be told "wherever the good news is proclaimed in the whole world" (14:9).[11]

Both the women give money, although the amounts differ greatly: two lepta (about a penny) and more than three hundred denarii (about a year's wages for a laborer). Money (or money spent for an act of hospitality) is the literal gift of the characters at the level of the story, who speak no words in explanation of their actions. Their symbolic gifts are made manifest at the level of the Markan Jesus' commentary and/or the Markan implied author's arrangement of episodes. The Markan Jesus seems to accept the gesture of the anointing woman as acknowledgment of his approaching death—that is, the gift of his life. For the implied audience, the poor widow gives the gift of "her whole life" as exemplary of Jesus. The two healed blind men are suppliants/exemplars. The Bethsaida man and Bartimaeus request literal sight (at the story level) and seem to receive metaphorical insight (at the discourse level). The two giving women are simply exemplars, asking for nothing. The poor widow and the anointing woman give literally their money (at the story level) and metaphorically (at the discourse level) the one gives acknowledgment of Jesus' approaching gift of his life, while the other gives her own "life"—both as proleptic reflections for the implied audience of Jesus' imminent action in giving his life.[12]

11. Tom Shepherd observes this additional contrast between the anointing woman and Judas: "The woman makes a gift of her valuable asset (*didōmi*) while the disciple Judas receives a promise of money for his betrayal of Jesus (*paradidōmi*)" ("The Narrative Function of Markan Intercalation," *NTS* 41 [1995]: 522–40, quotation from 537).

12. One pair of characters that also "frames" an event presents an interesting contrast to these two pairs. Although the actions of Simon of Cyrene (15:21) and the centurion at the foot of the cross (15:39) "frame" the crucifixion narrative, and Simon's action of carry-

Two Exceptional Jewish Authorities

The third and final pair of characters by whom I will illustrate the reflective christology of Mark's Gospel are, like the pair of giving women, exemplars. But, unlike both the pair of giving woman and the pair of healed blind men, this third pair does not form an obvious frame around a narrative unit. The two characters are paired in their reflection of an aspect of Jesus' teaching about the kingdom of God, which is an important element of the refracted christology of the Gospel of Mark, based on what Jesus says instead. This third pair consists of the exceptional scribe and Joseph of Arimathea, who is an exceptional "member of the council."[13]

Thus both the scribe and Joseph of Arimathea are leaders in the Jewish establishment. The scribe's place in the narrative is at the end of the lineup of leaders who try to entrap Jesus as he teaches in the temple: chief priests, scribes, and elders (11:27–12:12), Pharisees and Herodians (12:13-17), Sadducees (12:18-27), and "[o]ne of the scribes" (12:28-34). At this point, the scribe's favorable attitude toward Jesus and Jesus' favorable response to him are clearly marked as exceptional. Joseph of Arimathea's place in the narrative is at the end of the crucifixion, after the Jewish and Roman leaders have managed to entrap, arrest, condemn, and crucify Jesus. At this point, the implied audience is likely surprised to learn that Joseph of Arimathea who "went boldly to Pilate and asked for the body of Jesus" was, in fact, "a respected member of the council" (15:43). Although the noun used here for "council member," *bouleutēs*, is not the same as the noun used at 15:1 for "council," *sunedrion*, it is from the same root as the verb used at 15:1, *sumboulion*, "held a consultation." It is exceptional that a member of the council that turned Jesus over to death by the Roman authorities would soon thereafter ask *the* Roman authority, Pilate, for the body of Jesus in order to bury it—an act frequently not permitted by the Romans for those crucified.[14] But it is also exceptional that a Roman centurion, having just

---

ing Jesus' cross echoes to some extent the Markan Jesus' words (8:34), the centurion's words echo the words not of the Markan Jesus but of the Markan narrator (1:1) and/or the voice (of God) (1:11; 9:7).

13. For my more detailed analysis and reference to the secondary literature, see "The Jewish Leaders in the Gospel of Mark: A Literary Study of Marcan Characterization," *JBL* 108 (1989): 259–81, republished in Malbon, *In the Company of Jesus*, 131–65.

14. I am not convinced that Raymond E. Brown's argument that Joseph of Arimathea's concern was not for Jesus but for the requirements of the Jewish law, makes sense as a reading of Mark's narrative (see "The Burial of Jesus [Mark 15:42-47]," *CBQ* 50 [1988]: 233–45), contra Sharyn Dowd, *Reading Mark: A Literary and Theological Commentary on the Second Gospel* (Macon, Ga.: Smyth & Helwys, 2000), 164–65. Brown's careful discussion is of great interest in tracing the larger historical and literary development of the tradition of Jesus' burial; however, Brown's category of "disciples" seems to me less plastic than Mark's category of "followers," all of whom are fallible. In addition, I think Brown's linking of "waiting

put Jesus to death, would refer to him as "God's Son." This is the point exactly: this is an exceptional story.

Both the exceptional scribe and Joseph present ironic contrasts to the suppliants of the Markan Jesus. The scribe asks not for healing but for teaching, in the form of interpretation of the Law: "Which commandment is the first of all?" (12:28). Joseph can ask nothing of Jesus, but he asks Pilate for all that would appear to be left of Jesus, his body. Both the exceptional scribe and Joseph take up roles appropriate to disciples. The scribe debates the Law with Jesus, whom he calls "Teacher" (12:32); as a disciple, he commends his teacher (12:32), and his teacher commends and encourages him as a disciple (12:34). Joseph, very much like the disciples of the beheaded John the baptizer, who "came and took his body, and laid it in a tomb" (6:29), came to Pilate to ask for Jesus' body, then took the body and wrapped it in a linen cloth and laid it in a tomb, and rolled a stone against the door of the tomb (15:42-46). Before being tempted to chastise Jesus' twelve chosen disciples for their poor showing in comparison with the exceptional scribe and Joseph of Arimathea, one must remember that the implied author has made the disciples "round" in their journey of faith and failure and the exceptional scribe and Joseph "flat" for their one exemplary scene. The implied author is more interested in discipleship than in the disciples, more concerned to produce new disciples than to portray the twelve disciples as heroes.

The most striking similarity between the exceptional scribe and Joseph of Arimathea is that both are described in relation to "the kingdom of God." Once the scribe recognizes that Jesus has spoken rightly and "truly" (12:32), and Jesus sees that the scribe has answered "wisely" (12:34a), Jesus says to the scribe, "'You are not far from the kingdom of God.' After that no one dared to ask him any question" (12:34b). Jesus and this one scribe have silenced all the Jewish authorities who questioned the Markan Jesus in the temple. Jesus' teaching has come back to its beginning. It is clear that "the kingdom of God has come near" (1:15) because this scribe is "not far from the kingdom of God." The challenge to the kingdom of Satan manifest in Jesus' powerful exorcising of demons is one piece of evidence that the kingdom of God has come near. Another is Jesus' powerful teaching "as one having authority, and not as the scribes" (1:22)— except for the present scribe, who teaches in harmony with Jesus that God "'is one, and besides him there is no other'; and 'to love him with all the heart, and with all the understanding, and with all the strength,' and 'to love one's neigh-

---

expectantly for the kingdom of God" (15:43) with "the category of being a pious observer of the law" ignores the Markan context of the "kingdom of God" sayings, all of which except 15:43 are spoken by the Markan Jesus and none of which assumes pious observance of the law. Certainly the changes made in the description of Joseph of Arimathea in Matthew and Luke suggest discomfort with the tension of the Markan account of an exceptional Jewish leader, a discomfort often shared by other Markan readers.

bor as oneself,'—this is much more important than all whole burnt offerings and sacrifices" (12:32-33). This scribe reflects the deflected and refracted christology enacted by the Markan Jesus. Like Jesus, the exceptional scribe wishes to give honor to God and to challenge traditional views.

Joseph of Arimathea is also described in relation to "the kingdom of God," not by the Markan Jesus as was the exceptional scribe, but by the Markan narrator, who, at Jesus' death, picks up the phrase that had been Jesus' unique proclamation. The narrator presents three descriptive phrases after Joseph's name. The first is simple: "of [or from] Arimathea." The second and third are in paradoxical tension: "a respected member of the council" and "who was also himself waiting expectantly for the kingdom of God" (15:43). The tension is like that of the centurion who recognized Jesus as God's Son, narrated just two pericopai back. And it is also like the tension implicit between Peter's denial and the reminder at the tomb that Jesus is going before Peter to Galilee (16:7; cf. 14:28), narrated just two pericopai ahead. It is a tension resolved in repentance and forgiveness. The "kingdom of God has come near; repent, and believe in the good news" (1:15). Believing in such good news, Joseph "was also himself waiting expectantly for the kingdom of God."

Some interpreters have judged "waiting expectantly for the kingdom" or being "not far from the kingdom" to be negative portrayals, as if Joseph should already be *in* the kingdom or at least *see* the kingdom, and as if the exceptional scribe should also be *in* the kingdom or at least *very close* to the kingdom.[15] These interpretations, however, seem to ignore the contexts the Markan narrative provides for understanding "kingdom of God" statements. In relation to refracted christology (chapter 4) we noted that, according to the Markan Jesus, who is the only one to speak of "the kingdom of God" until 15:43, the kingdom has already come and is still coming. At his final Passover meal with his disciples, Jesus both acknowledges the finality of the present celebration and looks forward to a new celebration: "Truly I tell you, I will never again drink of the fruit of the vine until that day when I drink it new in the kingdom of God" (14:25). In being "not far from the kingdom" and in "waiting expectantly for the kingdom," the exceptional scribe and Joseph of Arimathea are in good company, and they reflect the company they keep—the Markan Jesus.

Exemplary Characters and the Implied Audience

The Markan implied author sets up different relationships between the implied audience and the various characters in the narrative. The Markan Jesus, of

---

15. David Rhoads has noticed from years of experience performing the Gospel of Mark that the scribe, when he repeats what Jesus says, omits "loving God with one's whole life" (Gk *psychē*), and Rhoads interprets this to mean that the scribe is thus distanced from Jesus and from the kingdom of God (e-mail correspondence, 2009).

course, takes center stage, and the implied audience is encouraged to focus on him, admire him, identify with his side in the cosmic and human struggle, and follow him. Likewise, the implied audience is expected to distance itself from those who struggle against Jesus in the transcendent realm (Satan, demons, unclean spirits) and those who come to oppose him in the human realm (the Roman leaders and, for the most part, the Jewish leaders). The implied audience is enticed to identify with the disciples, and other fallible followers, not only in the earnest desire to follow Jesus but also in the surprising difficulty of the task of following—and thus reflecting—one who chooses to serve rather than be served, even in the face of persecution and death. At the point in the narrative when the disciples manifest their greatest struggle, in response to Jesus' most paradoxical demands, the exemplars supply the implied audience with positive images of what following entails. The clear reflection of what it means for Jesus to be the Christ shines through in the exemplary actions of the healed blind man from Bethsaida and Bartimaeus, the poor widow and the anointing woman, and the exceptional scribe and Joseph of Arimathea. Through reflected christology, these exemplary characters mirror how Jesus relates to God and thus to others—or perhaps how Jesus relates to others and thus to God.

The Markan Jesus, Mark's Jesus, and the Historical Jesus

> . . . *Mark is a strong witness to the enigmatic*
> *and exclusive character of narrative,*
> *to its property of banishing interpreters*
> *from its secret places.*
>
> *Frank Kermode*[1]

As a narrative critic, my goal in this book has been to understand how Jesus is characterized in the Gospel of Mark. At the beginning was a simple observation: characters are known by what they say, by what they do, and by what others (the narrator and other characters) say and do to, about, or in relation to them. The result is a *multilayered* Markan narrative christology, focusing not only on what the narrator and other characters say about Jesus (projected christology), but also on what Jesus says in response to what these others say to and about him (deflected christology), what Jesus says instead about himself and God (refracted christology), what Jesus does (enacted christology), and *how* what other characters do is related to what Jesus says and does (reflected christology). By "the Markan Jesus" I refer to the character who speaks and acts in the Gospel of Mark, but by "Mark's Jesus" I refer to that more complicated presentation by the implied author that encompasses what the Markan Jesus says and does

---

1. Frank Kermode, *The Genesis of Secrecy: On the Interpretation of Narrative* (Cambridge, Mass.: Harvard University Press, 1979), 33–34.

and what all the other characters and the Markan narrator say and do in relation to the Markan Jesus. Two implications of this resulting portrait of "Mark's Jesus"—and a portrait is all any of us can offer—concern the layering process, both the process by which we literary critics label various "narrative" layers or strands within the text and the process by which other scholars label various "historical" layers within the same text. On the one hand, my observations call into question two frequent assumptions of narrative critics: (1) that the point of view of the Markan Jesus is aligned with the point of view of the Markan narrator and (2) that there is no distinction between the Markan narrator and the Markan implied author. Such assumptions now seem to me to collapse "layers" or aspects of the Markan narrative that fruitfully bear distinction. On the other hand, I can but raise a question about whether New Testament scholars who paint portraits of the "historical Jesus" make a category mistake in reading strands that are identified by literary means as "historical layers." At this point the hazards of our metaphors are obvious: literary *strands* are conceived as interwoven and hard to take apart without destroying the fabric of the narrative, but historical *layers* are imaged on the analogy of archaeological excavation and may lull us into thinking we can separate layers with dedicated work.

The Markan Jesus, Narrator, and Implied Author

Some years ago, in introducing Markan narrative criticism in the book *Mark and Method* (1992), I wrote:

> The distinctions between the implied author and the narrator and between the narratee and the implied reader were developed in secular literary criticism for the close analysis of nineteenth- and twentieth-century novels. Ishmael is the narrator of *Moby Dick*, but he is the creation of the implied author. Most narrative critics of the first-century Gospels have not found these distinctions as useful. Most narrative critics have observed little or no difference between the implied author and narrator or between the narratee and implied reader of Matthew, Mark, Luke, and John. The implied author of *Moby Dick* knows more than Ishmael, but a similar separation is not obvious in Mark.[2]

The powerful and influential introduction to narrative criticism, *Mark as Story*, in both its first (1982) and second (1999) editions, gives evidence of this view by not even employing the term "implied author," only "narrator."[3] Some-

2. Elizabeth Struthers Malbon, "Narrative Criticism: How Does the Story Mean?" in *Mark and Method: New Approaches in Biblical Studies* (ed. Janice Capel Anderson and Stephen D. Moore; Minneapolis: Fortress, 1992), 23–49, quotation from 28, republished in Malbon, *In the Company of Jesus*, 1–40.

3. David Rhoads and Donald Michie, *Mark as Story: An Introduction to the Narrative of a Gospel* (Philadelphia: Fortress, 1982), where the narrator is the first topic in the second chapter, "Rhetoric." David Rhoads, Joanna Dewey, and Donald Michie, *Mark as Story: An*

what later I had occasion to add to my statement that a separation between the implied author and the narrator is "not obvious" in Mark: "'Not obvious' indeed—but subtle and important!"[4] And later still I was able to revise the latter part of that paragraph, for a new edition of *Mark and Method* (2008), to read:

> Initially, many narrative critics of the first-century Gospels did not find these distinctions as useful. Many narrative critics observed little or no difference between the implied author and narrator or between the narratee and implied reader of Matthew, Mark, Luke, and John. Thus some narrative critics used the terms *narrator* and *narratee*, while others employed *implied author* and *implied reader.* However, it is important to note, with Mark Allan Powell, that "The narrator and the narratee are not identical with the implied author and the implied reader. They are rhetorical devices, created by the implied author. They are part of the narrative itself, part of the discourse through which the story is told."[5]

As should be clear at the close of this book, I regard the distinction between the narrator and the implied author as essential to perceiving and expressing Markan narrative christology.

The practical need for this theoretical distinction between implied author and narrator became obvious as I realized that the Markan Jesus and the Markan

---

Introduction to the Narrative of a Gospel (2nd ed.; Minneapolis: Fortress, 1999), where "The Narrator" has become the title of the second chapter instead of "Rhetoric," and a new chapter on "The Reader" has been added; in that chapter the authors discuss the "ideal reader" (137–43), which is used synonymously with the "implied reader" in two footnotes (n. 2 and n. 4, 173). The fact that the category "narrator" has been joined with the category "implied author" is clear in this statement: "The ideal reader is the mirror image of the narrator" (138) instead of the implied reader/audience being the mirror image of the implied author, and the narratee being the mirror image of the narrator. Intriguingly, Stephen H. Smith states: (1) "As it so happens, however, there is essentially no difference between implied author and narrator in the Gospel of Mark, and there is thus no problem in treating them as one" (*A Lion with Wings: A Narrative-Critical Approach to Mark's Gospel* [Sheffield: Sheffield Academic, 1996], 23 n. 28); (2) "In speaking of the narrator, it is important not to confuse him or her with the implied author" (27–28); and (3) "In Mark's Gospel narrator and narratee are, for all practical purposes, identical with the implied author and implied reader respectively, and need not be considered separately from them" (39)! Apparently Smith's view, not untypical, is to recognize the theoretical distinction between implied author and narrator given in Chatman's model but to disavow its usefulness to Markan interpretation.

4. Elizabeth Struthers Malbon, "The Christology of Mark's Gospel: Narrative Christology and the Markan Jesus," in *Who Do You Say That I Am? Essays on Christology* (in honor of Jack Dean Kingsbury; ed. Mark Allan Powell and David R. Bauer; Louisville: Westminster John Knox, 1999), 33–48, quotation from 48 n. 26.

5. Elizabeth Struthers Malbon, "Narrative Criticism: How Does the Story Mean?" in *Mark and Method: New Approaches in Biblical Studies* (2nd ed.; ed. Janice Capel Anderson and Stephen D. Moore; Minneapolis: Fortress, 2008), 33, quoting Mark Allan Powell, *What Is Narrative Criticism?* (GBS; Minneapolis: Fortress, 1990), 27.

narrator do not speak with the same voice. Presumably one could say that the
narrator has created a character with a different voice from himself, but it seems
more helpful to understand both the Markan Jesus and the Markan narrator
as creations of the Markan implied author, following the use of these terms by
literary critic Seymour Chatman.[6] Both the distinction between the implied
author and the narrator and the nonalignment of the Markan Jesus and the
Markan narrator are important to my understanding of how Jesus is characterized in Mark, and both challenge a frequently assumed or stated narrative
critical view of Mark's Gospel. For the root of these assumptions, we may look
back to the now-classic essay on "'Point of View' in Mark's Narrative" by Norman Petersen, in which Petersen asserts that the Markan narrator's "ideological
standpoint is identical with that of his central character, Jesus, with whom he
shares the power of knowing what is in the minds of others."[7] In fact, Petersen
argues that "[t]hrough this commonality of psychologically internal points of
view, and with the support of the plotting of the story by which one actor is
rendered central, the narrator is aligned—if not identified—with the central
actor."[8]

There are at least three significant differences between Petersen's assumptions and mine that lead him to this conclusion. First, the central argument of
Petersen's 1978 essay is that the "intrusive omniscience of the narrator in Mark's
Gospel [and his unified point of view] is the principal guarantee that it is a literary narrative, and that its author is a bona fide narrator."[9] It no longer seems
necessary, thanks, of course, in part to the work of Petersen, to argue with most

6. Seymour Chatman, *Story and Discourse: Narrative Structure in Fiction and Film* (Ithaca: Cornell University Press, 1978). In seeking to understand differences in the ways critics
use Chatman's diagram, Harry E. Shaw, "Why Won't Our Terms Stay Put? The Narrative
Communication Diagram Scrutinized and Historicized," in *A Companion to Narrative Theory*
(ed. James Phelan and Peter J. Rabinowitz; London: Blackwell, 2005), 299–311, points out
that they bring to it "two different implicit models of the communication situation" (299):
an emphasis on the modality of information or an emphasis on the modality of rhetoric.
Shaw argues that "[t]he implied author [as distinct from the narrator] fits only the rhetoric
view." "We never, the information argument would go, read the implied author's words, or
hear his or her voice telling the story"; the implied author is a "mere redundancy" with the
narrator from the point of view of the modality of information (301). To ask, as I have been
here, *how* the narrative characterizes Jesus is indeed to ask a question about the rhetoric of the
narrative rather than an information question about *what* christology is presented.

7. Norman R. Petersen, "'Point of View' in Mark's Narrative," *Semeia* 12 (1978): 97–
121, quotation from 107.

8. Petersen, "'Point of View,'" 102.

9. Petersen, "'Point of View,'" 97. For a recent look at the issue of the narrator's "omniscience" from the point of view of orality studies, see Philip Ruge-Jones, "Omnipresent, not
Omniscient: How Literary Interpretation Confuses the Storyteller's Narrating," in *Between
Author and Audience in Mark: Narration, Characterization, Interpretation* (ed. Elizabeth Struthers Malbon; New Testament Monographs 23; Sheffield: Sheffield Phoenix, 2009), 29–43.

audiences that Mark's Gospel is a narrative. And I would argue that expressing more than one point of view would seem to add to a narrative's complexity, rather than challenging its narrativity. Second, Petersen assumes that "Mark [as narrator] never explicitly claims any title [for Jesus] as his own, except for the name 'Jesus' ('son of God' in 1:1 is textually suspect)."[10] Although there is textual variation with regard to the presence of *huiou theou* (Son of God) in 1:1, the phrase is included in brackets in the current United Bible Societies text.[11] And what of "Christ" in 1:1? That is not "textually suspect." Third, and more problematically, Petersen asserts that the Markan narrator's "ideological, temporal and spatial, and psychological identification of his point of view with Jesus's, aligns him [on the phraseological plane] with the one appellation used only by Jesus, 'son of Man.'"[12] I find just the opposite. It is the narrator's failure to pick up this significant term (as well as "kingdom of God," except for 15:43) that draws attention to the distinction between the Markan narrator and the Markan Jesus, a distinction also noted in the reticence of the Markan Jesus to pick up the narrator's terms, "Christ, the Son of God."

The main point of Petersen's article is to argue that the Gospel of Mark is, in fact, a narrative and not just a pearls-on-a-string redactional collection of traditional stories. His method of argumentation is to show that the Gospel manifests a unified "point of view," which can be attributed to the narrator, meaning that the text is a narrative, with the narrator understood as the author. As Petersen explains, "What is at stake in this distinction is the larger question of whether Mark is the author of a *narrative* text, and therefore its *narrator*. . . . If Mark's text is a narrative told by a single voice, Mark's use of sources is irrelevant for understanding his text as a narrative."[13] In 1978 Petersen was one of the biblical scholars involved in the paradigm shift from form- and redaction-critical approaches to literary critical approaches to the Gospels, and in that major reconceptualizing of what we would now call the "real author," clear distinctions between the real author, the implied author, and the narrator were not in focus.

The title of Petersen's article, "'Point of View' in Mark's Narrative," not only manifests his conclusion (Mark *is* a narrative) but also pays tribute to the work

10. Petersen, "'Point of View,'" 111.

11. On this textual variation, see chapter 2, on projected christology, in relation to what the narrator says about Jesus in Mark 1:1.

12. Petersen, "'Point of View,'" 111. I note that the narrator and Jesus are aligned on the spatial plane except for the two brief (but important) episodes centered on John the baptizer (1:2-8; 6:14-29). On the temporal plane, only the Markan Jesus (and the young man at the tomb, 16:7, who recalls his words, 14:28) speaks of the future beyond the close of the narrative in 16:8. On the psychological plane, the narrator and Jesus share the capacity to have inside views. On the ideological plane, it is primarily Jesus who speaks of and to God, not the narrator. It is on the phraseological plane that the distinction between the narrator and Jesus is most obvious.

13. Petersen, "'Point of View,'" 103.

of Boris Uspensky on "point of view."[14] Because Uspensky's theory of "point of view" is focused on the narrator and I am interested in characterization in a broader sense, I have not relied on his work in my own; however, a somewhat closer look at two of Uspensky's categories will help me explain where I agree and where I disagree with Petersen's application of Uspensky's theory to Mark's Gospel and his assertions about Jesus and the narrator in Mark. As Petersen points out, Uspensky understands "point of view" to function on five planes: ideological, phraseological, spatial, temporal, and psychological. I will comment on Petersen's observations of the ideological and the phraseological planes in Mark.

Petersen concludes that "Mark's ideological [or evaluative] standpoint is identical with that of his central character, Jesus" and is best expressed in Jesus' accusation of Peter (Mark 8:33) as "thinking in terms of the things of men rather than of the things of God."[15] This conclusion has frequently been echoed in narrative critical studies of the Gospels, not just Mark.[16] Gary Yamasaki, who has written an extensive book on "point of view" in biblical exegesis, comments

14. Boris Uspensky, *A Poetics of Composition: The Structure of the Artistic Text and Typology of a Compositional Form* (trans. Valentina Zavarin and Susan Wittig; Berkeley: University of California Press, 1973).

15. Petersen, "'Point of View,'" 107–8.

16. On Mark, see Rhoads, Dewey, and Michie, *Mark as Story*, 44–45; Smith, *A Lion with Wings*, 56; Jack Dean Kingsbury, *Conflict in Mark: Jesus, Authorities, Disciples* (Minneapolis: Fortress, 1989), 2, 14, 26. Jack Dean Kingsbury, *The Christology of Mark's Gospel* (Philadelphia: Fortress, 1983), even says that Petersen does not go far enough in linking the point of view of Jesus and the narrator: "This description of 'evaluative point of view' in Mark is, as far as it goes, sound. The problem, however, is that it basically leaves out of account the factor that is most crucial. It is not solely with the evaluative point of view of Jesus that Mark identifies his own evaluative point of view. He goes further and makes certain that both his evaluative point of view and that of Jesus are in accord with the evaluative point of view of God" (47–48). On Matthew, see Jack Dean Kingsbury, *Matthew as Story* (2nd ed.; Philadelphia: Fortress, 1988), 34. For a careful argument that the Matthean Jesus is aligned with the Matthean narrator along some of Uspensky's planes, see Janice Capel Anderson, *Matthew's Narrative Web: Over, and Over, and Over Again* (JSNTSup 91; Sheffield: Sheffield Academic, 1994), 53–74; she concludes: "The points of view of the narrator and the character Jesus are aligned on the ideological plane. They are partially aligned on the phraseological, temporal, spatial, and psychological planes. These partial alignments support the ideological alignment. The choice of the term 'alignment' is deliberate. The narrator never simply assumes the point of view of Jesus or vice versa" (56). On John, see R. Alan Culpepper, *Anatomy of the Fourth Gospel: A Study in Literary Design* (Philadelphia: Fortress, 1983), 33. For a detailed and creative exploration of the *distinction* between the voice of Jesus and the voice of the narrator in Luke, see James M. Dawsey, *The Lukan Voice: Confusion and Irony in the Gospel of Luke* (Macon, Ga.: Mercer University Press, 1986). Although Dawsey does not employ the term "the implied author," he does use the term "author" in this sense: "Obviously the author was an accomplished artist who could control the language of his characters. It is also a credit to his ability as a storyteller that the author allowed his narrator and Jesus to hold different views concerning some elements of the story" (75).

that "[t]his is an astute observation of the workings of ideological point of view in Mark, and constitutes the most valuable contribution of Petersen's article."[17] Although of course I agree that the Markan narrator and the Markan Jesus are aligned in valuing thinking in the way of God over against human thinking, I would submit that there is more to the ideological plane in Mark's Gospel than this broad value statement. The Markan narrator and the Markan Jesus are not aligned on the key issue of the value and importance of the Markan Jesus: while the narrator boldly announces the main character as "Jesus Christ, the Son of God" and insistently reports his amazing actions and words, Jesus, just as insistently, resists attention and deflects honor to God. Thus I see ideological overlap but not ideological "identity" between the Markan narrator and the Markan Jesus. Ideological overlap rather than ideological identity gives room for creative tension—without the loss of "reliability" for either the Markan narrator or the Markan Jesus, except that neither occupies the place of God! John Donahue perceptively notes that "the nearness to God which Mark attributes to Jesus must be affirmed without compromising the sovereignty of God."[18] But how can this be accomplished? One way is for the implied author to have the narrator focus on Jesus as near to God and to have Jesus focus on God as sovereign. Both are asserted on the ideological plane of Mark's Gospel, but the former is manifest in the Markan narrator, the latter in the Markan Jesus.

As I mentioned earlier, Petersen's comment on the phraseological plane is more problematic: concerning "point of view" on the phraseological plane, the Markan narrator's "ideological, temporal and spatial, and psychological identification of his point of view with Jesus's, aligns him with the one appellation used only by Jesus, 'son of Man.'"[19] Although Uspensky's own comments on the phraseological plane are not easy to understand (Yamasaki finds this plane the most misunderstood by biblical exegetes), observation of "point of view"

17. Gary Yamasaki, *Watching a Biblical Narrative: Point of View in Biblical Exegesis* (New York and London: T&T Clark, 2007), 69. For Yamasaki's extremely clear and helpful explanation of Uspensky's five planes, see 30–34. Yamasaki's book also systematically reviews other literary and linguistic theories of point of view and articles, books, and dissertations by biblical scholars (both "New Testament" and "Old Testament") who address point of view, before presenting his own detailed "methodology for analyzing point of view in biblical narratives" and an application of that methodology to Luke 19:1-10. Petersen's article is the first item by a biblical scholar reviewed by Yamasaki (68–74), and it reveals the pattern: every comment is measured against the standard of Uspensky (or another theorist referenced by the author), and every "misunderstanding" is laid bare; less attention is paid to whether or not the author is trying to say something different from Uspensky and whether that might be interesting. Yamasaki (95–99, 107) awards his highest praise for the explication of "point of view" in New Testament exegesis to Anderson for her discussion of "point of view" in Matthew referenced in the preceding note.

18. John R. Donahue, S.J., "A Neglected Factor in the Theology of Mark," *JBL* 101 (1982): 563–94, quotation from 574.

19. Petersen, "'Point of View,'" 111.

functioning on the phraseological plane does involve noting, first, the differing speech characteristics or stylistic features of the narrator and the various
characters and, then, noting if the narrator picks up a speech characteristic of a
character and includes it in the narrator's own speech. If so, a shift toward the
"point of view" of that character is indicated at that point in the narrative.[20]
But the Markan narrator never picks up "Son of Humanity" from the Markan
Jesus.[21] (And the Markan Jesus only reticently accedes to the initial proclamation of the narrator, "Christ, the Son of God," when transformed into the final
accusation of the high priest, "Are you the Christ, the Son of the Blessed?" as he
faces death.[22]) However, the Markan narrator does pick up "kingdom of God"
from the Markan Jesus once, just after Jesus' death, noting that Joseph of Arimathea "was also himself waiting expectantly for the kingdom of God" (15:43).
At this point in the story the Markan Jesus can no longer speak for himself,
but, according to Uspensky's theory of "point of view," the narrator, in using
Jesus' characteristic phrase, now shifts the narrative to Jesus' "point of view."[23]
Thus when Jesus faces death, he accedes to a phrase nearly like the narrator's,
and after Jesus dies, the narrator applies a phrase that had been uniquely his.

20. For Uspensky's comments concerning the phraseological plane, see *Poetics of
Composition*, 17–56, esp. 32; for Yamasaki's explanation of Uspensky's comments on the
phraseological plane, see *Watching a Biblical Narrative*, 31–32; for Yamasaki's critique of
Petersen's application of the phraseological plane to Mark, see 70–72. Yamasaki comments
that Petersen shows a basic misunderstanding of Uspensky's concept of "point of view" on the
phraseological plane (which he later [80, 107] notes is common among biblical exegetes) and
also the tendency to gravitate toward discussion of "point of view" on the ideological plane
(another tendency among biblical exegetes [80, 107], because, Yamasaki speculates, ideology
is closer to something familiar—theology [107]). Yamasaki does not critique Petersen at the
points I do because I am critiquing Petersen's reading of Mark over against my own whereas
Yamasaki is critiquing Petersen's reading of Uspensky over against his own.
21. So also Kingsbury, *Christology*, 178: "'the Son of Man' constitutes, literarily, the
'phraseological point of view' of exclusively Jesus, occurring in his mouth alone and referring
solely to him." After the transfiguration, the narrator comes close to using the Markan Jesus'
unique term, "Son of Man" (9:9); however, it remains clear that the narrator intends these
words as an indirect report of Jesus' speech.
22. There are other distinctive speech characteristics of the narrator and Jesus as well;
for example, the Markan Jesus talks about God a great deal; the narrator only twice, both
connected to the mission and ministry of Jesus (1:14; 2:12). For other examples, including
some "shifts" between their uses of phrases, see the comments on creative tension between
the narrator and Jesus in the conclusion to chapter 3, on deflected christology.
23. Uspensky, *Poetics of Composition*, 32. Although the fourteen uses of "kingdom of
God" by the Markan Jesus are surely enough to establish it as a speech characteristic for him,
Yamasaki might be nervous about making too much of this single occurrence of the narrator's use of the phrase (see *Watching a Biblical Narrative*, 97, for a somewhat parallel case).
However, if so, that may be a weakness in Yamasaki's interpretation (or Uspensky's theory);
frequently a single exception to what is usual is of critical importance in Mark's Gospel.

Apparently, even Uspensky's theory of "point of view" recognizes Jesus' death as the turning point.

Uspensky's theory of "point of view" was developed to discuss how the narrator leads or directs the reader through the narrative. It was not developed as a theory of characterization.[24] Uspensky does not make a distinction between the implied author and the narrator, and he speaks of the power of the narrator in ways that include the overall control of the narrative that would be assigned to the implied author in a theory making use of that term. It is little wonder that Petersen does not introduce the implied author/narrator distinction into his comments based on Uspensky, especially given his concern in that article simply to justify calling Mark's author a narrator and his work a narrative. My work in Markan narrative criticism certainly confirms the crucial area of agreement pointed out by Petersen thirty years ago between the Markan Jesus and the Markan narrator over against many of the other characters: valuing thinking in the way of God over the human way of thinking. But my work on the characterization of Jesus has uncovered some relevant distinctions between the Markan Jesus and the Markan narrator, especially concerning how to value Jesus in relation to God and God in relation to Jesus. To clarify these observations, I have found it necessary to avoid equating the points of view of Jesus and the narrator and to avoid collapsing the distinction between the narrator and the implied author. Thus I employ a distinction we narrative critics have had all along but have not generally found helpful or necessary—the implied author

24. I have considered whether what Uspensky has to say in his fifth chapter, "The Interrelations of Points of View on Different Levels in the Work," might shed light on the tension between the narrator and Jesus I see in the Markan characterization of Jesus. The first of two categories of interrelations, "the nonconcurrence of points of view articulated in the work on different levels of analysis" (*Poetics of Composition*, 102–8), seems not to apply to the Markan situation. The explanation of the second category, "the combination of points of view on the same level" (108–19), offers a promising metaphor: "the narration is produced directly from two or more different positions on the same plane [in Mark, the positions of the Markan Jesus and the Markan narrator on both the ideological plane and the phraseological plane]; this phenomenon may be compared to the use of two sources of light—double-lighting—in painting" (108). However, I am less clear about the implications of Uspensky's use of the term "combination" and the language used to explain it: "We are talking now . . . about the combination of points of view—that is, about the simultaneous use of several different positions. This instance occurs when there are several superimposed discrete compositional structures [such as the Markan narrator's proclamation of Jesus and the Markan Jesus' deflection of honor to God?], articulated on the same level of analysis [the ideological plane of Mark's Gospel?]" (108–9). Again, Uspensky's explication is as spare as his illustrations from Dostoevsky are rich. In his final chapter, however, Uspensky does note: "In respect to literature, and contrary to some widely-held opinions (that trace the description constructed from a plurality of viewpoints to the beginnings of the realistic social and psychological novel), the use of several different points of view in narration may be noted even in relatively ancient texts" (171).

and the narrator—to make sense of this new distinction in Markan narrative christology. This distinction is perhaps best expressed as the implied author's creative tension between the Markan Jesus and the Markan narrator, as summarized at the conclusion to chapter 3, on deflected christology.[25]

Although it is beyond the scope of my present study to explore them fully, I wish to suggest briefly two possibilities that might be investigated for describing theoretically this creative tension between the Markan narrator and the Markan Jesus. The first possibility is Menakhem Perry's theory of literary dynamics.[26] Could the Markan narrator's point of view and the Markan Jesus' point of view be understood as two "frames" in the sense conveyed in the reader-oriented theory of Perry? The theory of "frames" and "repatterning" of frames does seem to be applicable to a more frequent observation of Mark's Gospel: the image of Jesus as a powerful Christ and Son of God, initially supported by his powerful words and deeds, is challenged by the image of Jesus as one who serves the powerless and thus suffers at the hands of the powerful; here the order of the text clearly contributes to its meaning, which is the focus of Perry's article. However, it is not so clear that this theory of "frames" works as well with the two points of view, that of the narrator and the main character, where both are revealed to the implied audience throughout most of the narrative. In addition, although the image of Jesus as one who serves does transform but not replace the image of Jesus as powerful healer, through what Perry labels "retrospective additional patterning,"[27] resolution of the tension between the narrator's focus on Jesus and Jesus' focus on God, or creating a new "frame" that incorporates them both, seems not to be the point of Mark's Gospel. Perhaps the best way to understand this ongoing tension in terms of Perry's theory is simply to appreciate Mark's Gospel as a narrative with "[r]hetorical or reader-oriented motivations: the structure of the text-continuum here is not motivated in terms of a model which the text imitates and the reader must identify or in terms of a frame which the reader has to construct. Here the text is grasped as a message which is supposed to be experienced."[28] Perry illustrates his theory with a detailed analysis of Faulkner's "A Rose for Emily," which he concludes with this comment about Faulkner's narratives in general: "Sometimes there is no deciding which angle of vision is true and which is false, but most often the reader experiences

---

25. I have been concerned to clarify the distinction between the narrator and the implied author; for an equally concerned plea for distinguishing the implied author and the (real) author, see Wayne C. Booth, "Resurrection of the Implied Author: Why Bother?" in *A Companion to Narrative Theory* (ed. James Phelan and Peter J. Rabinowitz; Oxford: Blackwell, 2005), 75–88.

26. Menakhem Perry, "Literary Dynamics: How the Order of a Text Creates Its Meanings (with an Analysis of Faulkner's 'A Rose for Emily')," *Poetics* 1 (1979): 35–64 and 311–61.

27. Perry, "Literary Dynamics," 59.

28. Perry, "Literary Dynamics," 40.

the tension between the 'appropriate' angle of vision and the other one from which he cannot escape."[29] In the case of the Gospel of Mark, neither angle of vision is false, but their truths must be experienced in creative tension.

A second possibility for describing theoretically this creative tension between the Markan narrator and the Markan Jesus is the rather complicated "typological circle" presented by F. K. Stanzel in *A Theory of Narrative*,[30] which focuses on the role of the narrator and thus has more links with the work of Petersen and Uspensky. To present Stanzel's intriguing but complex model briefly, I will rely on the carefully condensed explication of it by Yamasaki,[31] even simplifying my explanation beyond his. At the beginning of Stanzel's theory is the concept of "mediacy," that everything that is communicated is done so by a mediator. The culmination of Stanzel's theory is the description of three actualized narrative situations depicting three different ways narratives are mediated. The first narrative situation is not relevant to Mark's Gospel: "the *first-person* narrative situation, in which the narrator speaks in the first person . . . as a character in the story world . . . in a way that makes the reader aware of the fact that he or she is being told a story. . . ."[32] The second is "the *authorial* narrative situation, in which the narrator tells the story from a position outside the story world . . . in the third person . . . in a way that makes the reader aware of the fact that he or she is being told a story. . . ."[33] This is the category in which narrative critics place Mark's Gospel; however, it might be more appropriately applied to the situation of the Markan narrator—rather than the Markan implied author or the narrative as a whole. The third is "the *figural* narrative situation, in which the reader loses the sense of being told the story as the events are filtered through the consciousness of a character ('reflector') who exists in the story world . . . though the narration is given in the third person. . . ."[34] This figural narrative situation might be applied to the situation of the Markan Jesus; Stanzel's description of it is inviting for that purpose: In the figural narrative situation

> the mediating narrator is replaced by a reflector: a character in the novel who thinks, feels and perceives, but does not speak to the reader like a narrator. The reader looks at the other characters of the narrative through the eyes of this reflector-character. . . . Thus the distinguishing characteristic of the figural narrative situation is that the illusion of immediacy is superimposed over mediacy.[35]

29. Perry, "Literary Dynamics," 354.

30. F. K. Stanzel, *A Theory of Narrative* (trans. Charlotte Goedsche; Cambridge: Cambridge University Press, 1984).

31. Yamasaki, *Watching a Biblical Narrative*, 38–40, 101, 211 (Yamasaki's adaptation of Stanzel's diagram of the "typological circle").

32. Yamasaki, *Watching a Biblical Narrative*, 101.

33. Yamasaki, *Watching a Biblical Narrative*, 101.

34. Yamasaki, *Watching a Biblical Narrative*, 101.

35. Stanzel, *Theory of Literature*, 5.

Stanzel's typology is intended to describe three different types of actual narratives, not two or three aspects of one narrative, so I am pushing Stanzel's model in a new direction here. The Markan narrator is not "replaced by" the Markan Jesus, but perhaps Mark's Gospel could be thought of as involving certain aspects of both the authorial narrative situation (the Markan narrator's situation) and the figural narrative situation (the Markan Jesus' situation); not as merging them, but as presenting them both to the implied audience; not as harmony, with each voice lined up with the other, but as polyphony, with each voice singing its own melody.[36] As Robert Tannehill noted in introducing the concept

36. The metaphor of polyphony might suggest also the model of what Uspensky, following Mikhail Bakhtin (English translation: *Problems of Dostoevsky's Poetics* [ed. and trans. Caryl Emerson; Minneapolis: University of Minnesota Press, 1984]), calls "polyphonic narration," that is, narration in which "the various viewpoints [in the present example, just two, those of the Markan Jesus and the Markan narrator, the viewpoints of other characters being subordinated] are not subordinated, but are presented as essentially equal ideological voices" (*Poetics of Composition*, 10). Uspensky's comments on this subject are extremely brief, and it may be that his theory would not accommodate the narrator as one of the "essentially equal ideological voices"; he writes, "The points of view in a polyphonic work must belong directly to characters who participate in the narrated events (in the action). In other words, there must be no abstract ideological position outside of the personalities of the characters" (10). Investigating Bakhtin's theory properly would take us too far afield at this point. I note that the doctoral dissertation of Geoff Robert Webb, "Reading Mark with a Vulgar Mind: Applying Bakhtinian Categories to Markan Characterisation" (Melbourne College of Divinity, 2003) asserts (incidental to its chief argument that Mark's Gospel "can be considered 'dialogic' at both first *and* second levels") that "the Markan narratorial/authorial stance would therefore normally demand that much of the discourse within the Gospel is, by nature, authoritative, and therefore excluded by definition from being polyphonic" (30–31). Webb certainly knows more about Bakhtin's theory than I do; however, what I am questioning is the presumed "narratorial/authorial stance" of Mark's Gospel, so I do not necessarily agree with his judgment about the nonapplicability of Bahktin's concept of "polyphonic narration" to Mark's Gospel. Cf. Petri Merenlahti, *Poetics for the Gospels? Rethinking Narrative Criticism* (London: T&T Clark, 2002), 33: "At first sight, as ideological literature whose omniscient narrators constantly seek to control their characters and readers, the gospels may not seem likely to qualify as dialogic narratives in the full Bakhtinian sense of the word. Rather, they present a paradigm case of what Bakhtin called *monologic*, or *authoritative* discourse. On the other hand, however, it is exactly the multivoicedness of the biblical text that decades of historical biblical criticism have brought to daylight. . . . It is not difficult to see that, in contemporary literary avant-garde culture with its resistance to stability, closure and dominance, this dissonant, unsettled appearance of the gospels might find a perfect match." And also: "Even when playing with mystery, secrecy and indirection, the narrator [of Mark] displays ideological interests that give the narrative a serious monologic tone. . . . Paradoxical as it is, while fiercely calling for an entirely monologic narrative, ideology points out the many voices present in the text. This peculiar dualism is, I think, the very essence of all gospel narratives" (Merenlahti, *Poetics*, 75–76).

of Markan narrative christology years ago, "The study of Mark as a narrative reveals more unity and art in this Gospel than is commonly recognized."[37]

A narrative christology of Mark's Gospel should reflect not just the point of view of the narrator but the creative tension between the point of view of the narrator (and the characters as well) and that of the Markan Jesus. In Kingsbury's *Christology of Mark's Gospel*, concern for the "titles of majesty" applied to Jesus by the other characters, and especially by the narrator, dominates. Kingsbury takes "the narrator's point of view" to be the only "correct" point of view on "christology" in the Gospel of Mark; all differing points of view expressed by characters (Jesus is not considered in the same way) are wrong; all similar points of view, including God's, are congruent and thus "correct." Although Kingsbury purports to describe the Christology of Mark's Gospel, his focus is actually the Christology of the Markan *narrator*. Taking my lead from Tannehill's call for a "narrative christology" of Mark and focusing on the characterization of Jesus, I have come to appreciate a more complicated narrative arrangement whereby the protagonist Jesus presents a unique point of view about himself in relation to God. It is a point of view *enacted* in his words and deeds, more than *projected* in what others say about him (e.g., "titles"). It is a point of view from which honor and attention are *deflected* from himself to God and from which traditional understandings (and "titles") attributed to him are *refracted* or bent into new meanings. And it is a point of view that can be *reflected* in the actions of other characters who share, even if in one exemplary moment, the deflected and refracted christology enacted by the Markan Jesus.

In addition, and contrary to what has generally been observed about Mark's Gospel, the narrator is not identical with the implied author. The implied author controls the narrator and all the characters. It is the implied author who juxtaposes the christology of the Markan Jesus and the christology of the Markan narrator and other characters, and it is the Markan implied audience who has to hold the two together. The tension is essential to the narrative christology of Mark's Gospel. Projected christology cannot stand alone as Markan narrative christology; what others say about Jesus is not more important than what Jesus says in response (deflected christology) or instead (refracted christology). What Jesus does (enacted christology) and what others do in relation to him (reflected christology) also play important roles. The implied author is the one who allows a character, even the main character, to have a point of view distinct from the narrator—and vice versa: A Jesus who talks like the narrator could hardly be a Jesus who "came not to be served but to serve" (10:45), but a Jesus who affirms

37. Robert C. Tannehill, "The Gospel of Mark as Narrative Christology," *Semeia* 16 (1979) 57–95, quotation from 88. The essay has been republished in Robert C. Tannehill, *The Shape of the Gospel: New Testament Essays* (Eugene, Ore.: Cascade Books, 2007), 161–87.

only what the Markan Jesus says could hardly bear the full weight of "the gospel of Jesus Christ, the Son of God."

"Mark's Jesus" and the "Historical Jesus"[38]

This study of "Mark's Jesus" is a venture in narrative criticism, which, at least in the United States, has been an important scholarly development of the past thirty years. Because the "renewed" or "third" quest for the historical Jesus has also been an important development during the same period, one might expect that narrative critical approaches would have been utilized as one among other helpful tools in the quest for the historical Jesus, at least in the United States. This expectation would be further suggested by the early appreciation of the "poetic" nature of Jesus' sayings by scholars who have become key figures in the renewed quest for the historical Jesus, for example, Robert Funk[39] and John Dominic Crossan.[40] However, this concern for the poetic language of the Jesus sayings has been largely taken up after the manner of form criticism, with its interest in the smallest units of tradition, and not in the manner of redaction criticism, with its interest in the Gospels as edited wholes.[41] In addition, both form criticism and redaction criticism, while manifesting aspects of literary interest (at different levels of the Gospel texts: pericope/larger units or an entire Gospel), are at heart historical critical approaches, interested in the history of the tradition (at different periods of the Gospels' histories: pre-Gospel traditions/redacted Gospels).[42] Whereas Jesus researchers approach the Gospels

38. This section is adapted (rather freely) from portions of Elizabeth Struthers Malbon, "New Literary Criticism and Jesus Research," in *The Handbook of the Study of the Historical Jesus, Vol. 1: How to Study the Historical Jesus* (ed. Tom Holmén and Stanley E. Porter; Leiden, The Netherlands: Brill, forthcoming).

39. Robert W. Funk, *Language, Hermeneutic, and the Word of God: The Problem of Language in the New Testament and Contemporary Theology* (New York: Harper & Row, 1966).

40. John Dominic Crossan, *In Parables: The Challenge of the Historical Jesus* (New York: Harper & Row, 1973); Crossan, *The Dark Interval: Towards a Theology of Story* (Niles, Ill.: Argus Communications, 1975; Sonoma, Calif.: Polebridge, 1988).

41. David S. du Toit concludes his survey of current trends in Jesus research with a brief remark on the methodological crisis caused by the severe erosion of "confidence in form criticism as a tool for historical analysis" ("Redefining Jesus: Current Trends in Jesus Research," in *Jesus, Mark and Q: The Teaching of Jesus and Its Earliest Records* [ed. Michael Labahn and Andreas Schmidt; JSNTSup 214; Sheffield: Sheffield Academic, 2001], 82–124, quotation from 122).

42. Edwin K. Broadhead points out this irony: Form criticism and redaction criticism, "which snatched the Gospels from the quest for the historical Jesus attempted to re-historicize the Gospels. Moving quickly through the process of literary analysis, form and redaction criticism employed the Gospel material in a second type of historical quest" (*Teach-*

as source materials to be excavated and sifted for valuable evidence, narrative critics approach the Gospels as creations in themselves to be explored and appreciated holistically, including their gaps and tensions. Thus one finds in key English-language scholars of the quest for the historical Jesus little interest in or use of the results of narrative criticism. Narrative criticism and historical Jesus research, at least in the United States and England, seem to have begun and remained as parallel tracks rather than as intersecting approaches.[43]

As evidence and qualification of this generalization, I present here brief comments on the stated methodological approaches of perhaps the two most well-known current Jesus researchers: John Dominic Crossan and N. Thomas Wright, who might be seen as representing opposite ends of a spectrum.[44] Obviously I am not presuming here to do justice to the complexity of the extensive research and publications of Crossan and Wright but rather, by reference to their influential work, to raise a question about the relation of the broader quest for the historical Jesus to literary analysis of the Gospel narratives.

John Dominic Crossan has found it crucial to work out an explicit and systematic methodology for Jesus research, which, as he carefully outlines in the prologue to *The Historical Jesus: The Life of a Mediterranean Jewish Peasant*, involves examining three levels of material: (1) the macrocosmic level of cross-cultural and cross-temporal social anthropology, (2) the mesocosmic level of Greco-Roman and especially Jewish history of the first part of the first century, and (3) the microcosmic level of literary or textual study of the specific traditions about Jesus, both within and beyond the canon.[45] The third level receives the greatest methodological elaboration, beginning with the affirmations that "[t]he Gospels are neither histories nor biographies, even within the ancient tolerances for those genres"[46] and that both canonical and extracanonical gospels

---

ing with Authority: Miracles and Christology in the Gospel of Mark [JSNTSup 74; Sheffield: Sheffield Academic, 1992], 23).

43. Likewise, historical Jesus research has not intersected with feminist biblical criticism—because, so Elisabeth Schüssler Fiorenza forcefully argues, feminist scholarship rejects both the positivist, empiricist foundation of historical Jesus research and its privileged stake in preserving the sociopolitical status quo. For her overview, see "The Rhetorics and Politics of Jesus Research: A Critical Feminist Perspective," in Labahn and Schmidt, eds., *Jesus, Mark and Q*, 259–82; for her fuller discussion, see *Jesus and the Politics of Interpretation* (New York: Continuum, 2001).

44. Both Crossan and Wright differ significantly in their methodology from a more "classical" approach, e.g., that of John P. Meier.

45. John Dominic Crossan, *The Historical Jesus: The Life of a Mediterranean Jewish Peasant* (San Francisco: HarperSanFrancisco, 1991). The prologue of Crossan's popular book, *Jesus: A Revolutionary Biography* (San Francisco: HarperSanFrancisco, 1994), presents a shortened version of this methodological outline; as a whole, the popular book represents a distillation of Part III of the scholarly book.

46. Crossan, *Historical Jesus*, xxx.

are made up of "original, developmental, and compositional layers" or "reten-
tion, development, and creation."[47] In addition, Crossan "reject[s] absolutely
any pejorative language for those latter processes. Jesus left behind him thinkers
not memorizers, disciples not reciters, people not parrots."[48] These statements,
not surprisingly, given Crossan's earlier work on Jesus' parables under the influence of the New Criticism, suggest an openness to literary criticism (which
deals with "development" and "composition" or "creation") as a tool in Jesus
research. However, the language of layers is more in tune with the trajectory
from source to form to redaction criticism than with more recent literary criticism, including narrative and reader-response criticism, of the New Testament.

Crossan's methodology specifies in detail how one examines this literary or
textual level, both strategically and tactically. The complexity of the Jesus tradition itself calls for a strategy of (1) inventory, listing all the sources to be used,
(2) stratification, positioning each source or text in a chronological sequence
with a date range,[49] and (3) attestation, presenting the now-stratified data base
in terms of multiplicity of independent attestation. Crossan does not claim that
placing texts "in their historical situation and literary relationship" (notice the
redaction-critical ring) will eliminate controversy, only that it must be done by
the Jesus researcher "so that a reader knows where one stands on every issue."[50]
Although Crossan admits that, "in abstract theory there could be just as much
development and creation in that first stratum as in any of the other three," his
"method postulates that, at least for the first stratum, everything is original until
it is argued otherwise."[51]

Why has Crossan felt it necessary to develop and explicate such an elaborate
methodology (barely sketched here) as a Jesus researcher? Because "[h]istorical
Jesus research is becoming something of a scholarly bad joke,"[52] "an academic
embarrassment. It is impossible to avoid the suspicion that historical Jesus research is a very safe place to do theology and call it history, to do autobiography
and call it biography."[53] Thus, because Crossan is suspicious of what theology
can do and has done to history in the quest for the historical Jesus, he strives to
separate history and theology, using literary criticism as a tool. However, from

---

47. Crossan, *Historical Jesus*, xxxi.

48. Crossan, *Historical Jesus*, xxxi.

49. Crossan admits that "[c]hronologically most close does not, of course, mean historically most accurate" (*Historical Jesus*, xxxii), but he argues that study must begin with the
chronologically first stratum.

50. Crossan, *Historical Jesus*, xxxi.

51. Crossan, *Historical Jesus*, xxxii. Because Crossan shifts the burden of proof between
the first stratum and the later ones, a great deal depends on how complexes (content-related
clusters of sayings or deeds rather than single sayings) are assigned to strata.

52. Crossan, *Historical Jesus*, xxvii.

53. Crossan, *Historical Jesus*, xxviii.

a narrative critical point of view, although Crossan's literary critical sensibility is refreshing and challenging, his presumed literary critical tools are largely source-, form-, and redaction-critical approaches employed to establish historical layers or strata in the Jesus tradition, and Crossan trusts these presumed literary tools in the work of suggesting historical layers far beyond what a literary or narrative critic would. Although many literary critics might share Crossan's suspicion of theology, few share his level of trust of literary criticism as a tool for reconstructing history because, more basically, literary criticism begins with a healthy suspicion of history, that is, history as it has been reconstructed by scholars from the literature of the New Testament.

At the other end of the spectrum of current Jesus research is N. Thomas Wright, now Bishop of Durham, Church of England. Because Wright is suspicious of what history can do and has done to theology in the quest for the historical Jesus, he strives to integrate theology and history, rejecting literary or narrative criticism as a tool at the level of the Gospels as wholes and using it selectively at the level of Jesus' parables. Wright does not trust even the earlier literary tools of form and redaction criticism, which place limits on the history that can be reconstructed.[54] He does find some parables research, influenced by the New Criticism (and perhaps mediated through the work of Crossan), useful in his theological/historical reconstruction. Although literary criticism begins with a suspicion of history, that is, history as it has been reconstructed by scholars from the literature of the New Testament, it is not, like Wright's, a suspicion based on valuing theology, which has also seemed suspicious to literary critics in its dominating influence in New Testament interpretation (especially in redaction criticism). For Wright, redaction criticism is too literary in its scope; for narrative critics, redaction criticism is too theological and too historical in its interests. The spectrum of Jesus research is indeed broad.

For Wright there are two major ways of knowing about Jesus: history and faith.[55] Furthermore, these two ways are not to be understood as in conflict, or even as separate. As Wright affirms early on in *Jesus and the Victory of God,*

---

54. In regard to Wright's work, the warning of Norman Perrin is still appropriate: "The questions, answers, and teaching [of Mark 8:27-33] are on the lips of Jesus and Peter, but the titles involved are from the christological vocabulary of the early church. . . . So we come to the all-important point so far as a redaction-critical view of the narrative is concerned: it has the form of a story about the historical Jesus and his disciples but a purpose in terms of the risen Lord and his church" (*What Is Redaction Criticism?* [GBS; Philadelphia: Fortress, 1969], 42).

55. For a succinct presentation of history and faith as ways of knowing Jesus, see N. T. Wright, "Knowing Jesus: Faith and History," in Marcus J. Borg and N. T. Wright, *The Meaning of Jesus: Two Visions* (San Francisco: HarperSanFrancisco, 1999), 15–27. In *Jesus and the Victory of God*, Vol. 2 of *Christian Origins and the Question of God* (Minneapolis: Fortress, 1996), Wright employs the terms "history" and "theology" as the two modes of

> The underlying argument of this book is that the split [between history and theology, elsewhere between history and faith] is not warranted: that rigorous history (i.e. open-ended investigation of actual events in first-century Palestine) and rigorous theology (i.e. open-ended investigation of what the word 'god,' and hence the adjective 'divine,' might actually refer to) belong together, and never more so than in discussion of Jesus.[56]

Even putting aside the question of whether this is too much togetherness of the categories history and theology/faith, one may note that literature (or narrative or story), an obvious, although complex, category of the Gospels, our best sources for both history and theology about Jesus, is not mentioned here. There is a promising mention of the mediating role of language:

> One important feature of bringing together the worlds of history and faith, and recognizing that other people (notably first-century Jews) did so, too, is that we should make ourselves conscious of the way in which we, and they, use language to do both at the same time.[57]

However, this promise seems to apply only to recognizing the importance of language in the stories Jesus is reported to have told, not in relation to the stories told about him.[58] A brief discussion of the parable of the Prodigal Son in Wright's popular book *The Original Jesus* exclaims that "[s]tories create worlds"

---

knowing about Jesus, and even works out an interpretation (allegory?) of the parable of the Prodigal Son relevant to historical Jesus research in which the younger son/brother is history (124), "Enlightenment historiography" (117), or "the historical task itself" (137), and the older son/brother is theology (137). Wright sees his historical method as "a penitent history" that "offers itself as the long and dusty road back to reality, to confrontation, and perhaps to reconciliation" (144).

56. Wright, *Jesus and the Victory of God*, 8. Any boundary between history and theology seems totally dissolved in Wright's popular book (based on a British television special), *The Original Jesus* (Oxford: Lion/Grand Rapids: Eerdmans, 1996), where the subcategories do not appear specifically and the sermon-like essay flows in a presumed historical mode from the Lukan Jesus' parable of the Prodigal Son to Ezekiel's vision of the valley of the dry bones, and from the Matthean Jesus' Sermon on the Mount to the Lukan Mary's Magnificat. Another popular book by Wright, *Who Was Jesus?* (London: SPCK, 1992; Grand Rapids: Eerdmans, 1993), is not a presentation of his own research but a review and critique of the books of three "maverick popularizers" (viii) that appeared in 1992: Barbara Thiering, A. N. Wilson, and John Spong.

57. Wright, "Knowing Jesus," 18–19.

58. A connection between parable and gospel, although recognized by some Markan literary critics, is denied explicitly by Wright: "My point remains that the genre of the gospels, and that of the individual stories in which Jesus figures, lies along the continuum of history and biography, not of parable" ("The Truth of the Gospel and Christian Living," in *The Meaning of Jesus*, 216).

(sounding very like an echo of Crossan's *The Dark Interval*),[59] and a chapter that employs the parable of the Prodigal Son as a paradigm in *Jesus and the Victory of God* opens, "History proceeds by telling stories."[60] But no mention is made in either place of the world created by the author of Luke 15 by presenting together three parables of the lost and found, nor of how that might complicate our understanding of "the original Jesus."[61]

In Wright's survey of the quest for the historical Jesus in the opening chapters of *Jesus and the Victory of God*, he divides questers into two (largely heuristic) categories: followers of Wrede, manifesting a thoroughgoing skepticism, and followers of Schweizer, manifesting a thoroughgoing eschatology. It is telling for me to realize that Wright, as a Jesus researcher following Schweizer, links the work of Wrede with thoroughgoing skepticism, that is, skepticism of Mark's Gospel as a source for the historical Jesus, and employs negatively in relation to Wrede's heritage the phrase "Mark as pure fiction."[62] I, on the other hand, as a Markan narrative critic, link the work of Wrede positively with the beginning of an appreciation of literary characteristics of Mark's Gospel.[63] Although Wright critiques form criticism and those Jesus researchers who apply criteria to one saying or story at a time (preferring instead a "method of hypothesis and verification"[64]), it is still the smaller units of the gospel tradition that form criticism isolates that he focuses on as well. Wright is also suspicious of redaction criticism as it is generally practiced, which, he complains, "has sometimes misled

59. Wright, *Original Jesus*, 36.

60. Wright, *Jesus and the Victory of God*, 125. In this final chapter of the introductory part of *Jesus and the Victory of God*, the parable of the Prodigal Son serves as a paradigm (allegory?) of both the history of Jesus research (see my note 55) and of the historical Jesus that Wright constructs: "Thus, in a nutshell, the parable of the prodigal father points to the hypothesis of the prophetic son: the son, Israel-in-person, who will himself go into the far country, who will take upon himself the shame of Israel's exile, so that the kingdom may come, the covenant be renewed, and the prodigal welcome of Israel's god, the creator, be extended to the ends of the earth" (132). In volume 1 of *Christian Origins and the Question of God*, entitled *The New Testament and the People of God* (London: SPCK/Minneapolis: Fortress, 1992), Wright performs a Greimasian (French structuralist) analysis of the Markan parable of the Wicked Tenants (69–77).

61. However, in that chapter in *Jesus and the Victory of God*, Wright does comment: "Luke, to be sure, has used the story within his own larger story. There is an interesting parallel, again not always observed, between Luke 15 and Acts 15. In both, people are being welcomed in from beyond the boundaries of normal acceptability" (128).

62. Wright, *Jesus and the Victory of God*, 81.

63. Cf. Petersen, "'Point of View,'" 104: "Paradoxically, the illusion demolished by Wrede can be transformed into a literary entity, namely the narrative 'world' created by Mark. In other words, although Mark's text does not accurately depict *history*, it may coherently depict *his story*."

64. Wright, *Jesus and the Victory of God*, 87.

scholars into supposing that they [the Gospels] are therefore of less historical value."[65] New Testament narrative criticism, redaction criticism's latter-day
stepchild, Wright seems to reject in theory and ignore in practice.[66]

Obviously, such a cursory look at two scholars engaged in painting portraits of the "historical Jesus" is extremely limited. However, this brief glimpse
of the work of two of the foremost practitioners of historical Jesus research,
who are in many ways poles apart, may suggest the current gap between Jesus
research and narrative criticism. To recapitulate, because Crossan is suspicious
of what theology can do and has done to history in the quest for the historical
Jesus, he strives to separate history and theology, using literary criticism as a
tool—perhaps trusting too much how well those presumed literary tools work
in delineating historical sources and layers. On the other hand, because Wright
is suspicious of what history can do and has done to theology in the quest for
the historical Jesus, he strives to integrate theology and history, rejecting literary
criticism as a tool at the level of the Gospels as wholes and using it selectively
at the level of Jesus' parables—perhaps trusting too little what literary criticism in general or narrative criticism in particular might add to both history
and theology. Narrative criticism, for its part, is suspicious of what history and
theology can do and have done to literary critical appreciation of the Gospels as
stories—perhaps trusting too little in both.

Biblical literary criticism has roots in source, form, and redaction criticism
on the biblical studies side as well as roots in the New Criticism and structural-
ism on the side of literary criticism more generally. However, New Testament

---

65. Wright, *Jesus and the Victory of God*, 89.

66. I find myself somewhat mystified by Wright's rich chapter on "Literature, Story
and the Articulation of Worldviews" (chapter 3 in *The New Testament and the People of God*,
volume 1 of *Christian Origins and the Question of God*), especially in light of his claim in the
preceding chapter that "the study of the New Testament involves three disciplines in particular: literature, history and theology" (31) and his insistence elsewhere that the *two* sources of
knowledge of the historical Jesus are theology and history (with no reference to literature). In
this third chapter, Wright ranges over a wide variety of modern and postmodern literary theories, but, somewhere between the incredibly long sentences and the sustained sarcastic tone
in describing other literary theories or strategies of reading, I realize I do not know what to
believe about what he believes about the inherent importance of literature and the power of
story as story. In Wright's usage, "story" is connected with worldviews—and with knowledge
and verification (see vol. 1, 31–46, esp. 45), but not especially connected with literature or
with the Gospels as narratives. I wonder: Is Wright's proposed theory of reading, "critical
realism," a cipher for rescuing authorial intent and historical reference from the onslaughts of
modern and postmodern literary critical theory? Is he using "story" as a temporary stand-in
for history (which is, in his view, quite connected to theology)? Is "literature" subsumed by
theology? These are my questions of Wright. The questions Wright raises about literary theories of reading are pertinent, but the proposals he offers seem equally problematic, especially
in light of his integration of history and theology without sustained reference to literature or
literary criticism in volume 2, *Jesus and the Victory of God.*

literary criticism, including two of its strongest branches—narrative criticism and reader-response criticism—has grown up in reaction against certain excesses of historical criticism. It is no wonder that suspicion remains between those questing for the *historical* Jesus and those questioning the *literary*-ness of the Gospels.[67] Perhaps we all need to recognize the necessity and positive value of a hermeneutic of suspicion not only of our ancient texts but of our contemporary texts as well! Jesus researchers have been most interested, of course, in isolating the earliest layer of tradition, while narrative critical scholars have been especially interested in the rhetorical moves of the implied author throughout the narrative as it has come down to us in its so-called "final form." However, narrative criticism raises the question of whether the historical categorization of tradition and redaction is the only or the best way to understand the layers or strands within Gospel texts.[68] All strands or layers in a text need not be evidence of *historical* differences (as literary critics of the Hebrew Bible have pointed out with reference to JEDP[69]), but all such layers or strands clearly have *literary* effects.[70]

One wonders, for example, if the historical Jesus that some scholars have reconstructed might be more fairly described as the Markan Jesus.[71] Because

67. David M. Gunn, "Narrative Criticism," in *To Each Its Own Meaning: An Introduction to Biblical Criticisms and Their Application* (revised and expanded ed.; ed. Stephen R. Haynes and Steven L. McKenzie; Louisville: Westminster John Knox, 1999), 201–29, comments: "Nevertheless, an acute problem remains in biblical studies, namely, that much of the data for any kind of historical discourse (including reconstruction of ancient social locations) must come from texts whose provenance is, despite nearly two centuries of historical investigation, a matter of mere speculation. In short, the question of literary criticism's relation to historical criticism is an important one, but it requires a more sophisticated discussion than it has generally been afforded so far" (228). John R. Donahue, S.J., "The Literary Turn and New Testament Theology: Detour or New Direction?" *JR* 76 (1996): 250–75, proposes "that within biblical studies the developments within rhetorical criticism and the new historicism [see 262–72] offer the best combination of historical research, literary sophistication, and concern for religious experience. . . . Concretely, the new historicism, which views texts at the intersection of historical and social forces, recommends dialogue between biblical 'literary critics' and those engaged in the application of social scientific methods to biblical texts" (273).

68. C. Clifton Black, *The Disciples According to Mark: Markan Redaction in Current Debate* (JSNTSup 27; Sheffield: Sheffield Academic, 1989), does an excellent job of demonstrating the amazing lack of consensus among redaction critics themselves in distinguishing tradition and redaction.

69. See, for example, the comparative source-critical and literary critical analyses of Gen 37:18-30 by Adele Berlin, *Poetics and Interpretation of Biblical Narrative* (Sheffield: Almond, 1983), 113–21.

70. For an impassioned argument against attributing tensions within a text too easily to separate sources, see chapter 5 of Berlin's book mentioned in the preceding note: "Poetic Interpretation and Historical-Critical Method," 111–39.

71. See, e.g., Richard A. Horsley, *Hearing the Whole Story: The Politics of Plot in Mark's Gospel* (Louisville: Westminster John Knox, 2001), who understands the author of Mark to be

Markan priority is affirmed by most New Testament scholars—both Jesus researchers and narrative critics, both those who assume the two-source hypothesis (Mark + Q) and those who find the Farrer-Goulder hypothesis (Mark without Q) more convincing—Mark's Gospel has remained a key source for historical Jesus scholars. As I pointed out earlier, narrative critics have frequently claimed that the Markan narrator and the Markan Jesus share the same point of view, but my own work on the characterization of Jesus in the Gospel of Mark finds a distinction between the Markan narrator and the character Jesus. This literary distinction parallels one that Jesus researchers often take as a distinction between the evangelist and the historical Jesus. For example, even though narrative critics of Mark do not always take note of the uniqueness of "Son of Humanity" and "kingdom of God" to the Markan Jesus, Jesus researchers usually do isolate these phrases in the "earliest layer" of the Markan Gospel, the layer closest to, if not identical with, the "historical Jesus."[72] However, simply to convert this literary tension to a historical distinction would be to make a category mistake.

---

writing in Palestine within the generation of the historical Jesus and thus operating from the same social location and context; thus Horsley sees barely any distance between the "'author' of the story," the narrator, Jesus, and "the trusting and well-informed audience" (17). Marcus Borg's portrait of Jesus may manifest a partiality toward the Lukan Jesus; see Marcus J. Borg, *Jesus: A New Vision: Spirit, Culture, and the Life of Discipleship* (San Francisco: Harper & Row, 1987), and *Meeting Jesus Again for the First Time: The Historical Jesus and the Heart of Contemporary Faith* (San Francisco: HarperSanFrancisco, 1994).

72. Although it is Crossan, not Wright, who speaks of "layers," Wright assumes that "son of man" and "kingdom of God" reflect the usage of the historical Jesus; on "Son of Man," see Wright, *Jesus and the Victory of God*, 360–65 and 512–19; on "kingdom of God," see Wright, *Jesus and the Victory of God*, chapter 10, "The Questions of the Kingdom," 443–74. Even Edwin K. Broadhead, a formalist (literary) critic and not a historical Jesus scholar, comments: "Historical hypothesis and literary technique cohere in the Son of Man title. This title, which is judged by many as the term most likely to have been used by Jesus, is Jesus' most frequent self-designation in the Gospel of Mark. It is found within the story exclusively on the lips of Jesus, and this term did not prove popular in Church confessions" (*Naming Jesus: Titular Christology in the Gospel of Mark* [JSNTSup 175; Sheffield: Sheffield Academic, 1999], 170). However, Crossan concludes that "Jesus' own use of the generic 'son(s) of man' greatly facilitated the transition to the titular Son of Man as almost a favorite self-designation in both the *Sayings Gospel Q* and Mark" (*Historical Jesus*, 258) but that "[i]t was Mark, therefore, and Mark alone, who created the suffering and rising Son of Man and placed all those [passion prediction] units . . . on the lips of Jesus, whence they were accepted and expanded by both Matthew and Luke" (*Historical Jesus*, 259; see also 454–56, "Appendix 4: Inventory for Son of Man Sayings"). A sense of the importance of "kingdom of God" in Crossan's reconstruction of the historical Jesus can be seen in the high frequency of "kingdom of God" sayings in the "overture" presented at the beginning of *The Historical Jesus* (xiii–xxvi; see also 457–60, "Appendix 5: Inventory for Kingdom Sayings").

Thus a brief look at the categories is in order. Historical Jesus research and narrative criticism note different distinctions for their respective tasks. To oversimplify for heuristic purposes, for redaction criticism the great divide is between the evangelist or redactor and tradition; for historical Jesus research, following a form-critical model, tradition is further subdivided into early church tradition and the historical Jesus. But narrative criticism theorizes distinctions that are blurred within the category of evangelist/redactor: real author, implied author, narrator. Unfortunately, when narrative critics blur our own theoretical categories (noting no distinction between implied author and narrator), we make it that much easier for some interpreters to imagine an analogy between historical and literary categories: the Markan evangelist/redactor is to the historical Jesus as the implied author/narrator is to the character Jesus.

History	*Narrative*
evangelist/redactor	implied author/narrator
- - - - - - - - - - - -	- - - - - - - - - - - - - - -
historical Jesus	character Jesus

Such an alignment makes it appear that the distance between the narrator and the redactor and between the character Jesus and the historical Jesus is not great.[73]

However, by refusing to blur the theoretical distinction between narrator and implied author, narrative critics could help clarify the situation, making it obvious that both the narrator and the characters are under the direction of the implied author, who, along with the real author, is analogous to the evangelist/redactor.

History	*Narrative*
	real author
evangelist/redactor	
	implied author:
	narrator
	characters, including Jesus
- -	
tradition	
- -	
historical Jesus	

73. I raised this issue in relation to the "messianic secret" in the final section of chapter 3, where I argued that the creative tension of Markan narrative christology (e.g., its bold Markan narrator and reticent Markan Jesus), a literary observation, cannot on its own serve as evidence for the hypothesis of the "messianic secret" as an awkward historical resolution of messianic and non-messianic claims about Jesus.

Thus the presumed analogous position of the character Jesus and the historical Jesus is a category mistake, an illusion. Narrative criticism recognizes the
character Jesus as just as much a creation of the implied author as the narrator
is. Narrative critical theory elaborates analysis at the level of the author of the
narrative as the author (real author) is manifest in the literary text (implied
author, narrator, characters)—and, although not shown in the above diagram,
their counterparts (real audience, implied audience, narratee). Historical Jesus
research elaborates analysis at the level of tradition, as even the above thumbnail
sketch of the detailed work of Crossan illustrates. Narrative analysis does not
provide ready-made "data" for historical conclusions about redaction or tradition or the historical Jesus. This does not mean, of course, that narrative criticism denies the reality or importance of tradition or the historical Jesus. It does
illustrate, however, the concern of narrative criticism that narrative or literary
distinctions not be automatically labeled as historical layers.

Literary critic Frank Kermode notes that "there are some fairly simple ideas
that we find it difficult to keep hold of; they require (from me at any rate) a
special effort I am unwilling to make. One such is the proposition that no narrative can be transparent on historical fact."[74] One reason we find it so hard to
keep hold of this proposition is that narrative itself makes it so easy to ignore or
even forget! With Mark's Gospel specifically in mind, Kermode continues: "The
advantage of third-person narration is that it is the mode which best produces
the illusion of pure reference. But it *is* an illusion, the effect of a rhetorical de-
vice."[75] Indeed, "[w]e are so habituated to the myth of transparency [narrative's
transparency to history] that we continue, as Jean Starobinski neatly puts it, to
ignore *what is written* in favor of *what it is written about*. One purpose of this
book is to reverse that priority. . . ."[76] Kermode is speaking, of course, of his
book, *The Genesis of Secrecy: On the Interpretation of Narrative*. But I too have
been trying to pay attention to what is written—the *how* of Markan narrative christology, *how* Jesus is characterized—rather than to what it is written
about—Markan Christology in the theological sense or the development of
Christology in the historical sense.

From this focus on narrative christology, I argue that it is not epistemo-
logically appropriate simply to assign the point of view of the Markan Jesus to
"the historical Jesus" and the point of view of the narrator to the Markan evangelist, as if the first-century author valued our twenty-first-century historical
consciousness over immediate rhetorical strategies and kerygmatic goals.[77] Both

74. Kermode, *Genesis of Secrecy*, 116. Kermode's fifth and penultimate chapter is entitled "What Precisely Are the Facts?"

75. Kermode, *Genesis of Secrecy*, 117, italics original.

76. Kermode, *Genesis of Secrecy*, 118–19, italics original.

77. By minimizing both the difference between ancient and contemporary "historians"
and the distance between history and theology, C. Clifton Black appears to me to do just that
in his recent essay, "Mark as Historian of God's Kingdom," *CBQ* 71 (2009): 64–83.

the point of view of the Markan Jesus and that of the Markan narrator are under the jurisdiction of the Markan implied author; that is, they are manifestations of the literary text whose historical reference could be queried and hypothesized but must not be assumed at face value.[78] To move from the literary observation of a distinctive term associated with the character Jesus (Son of Humanity) to a conclusion about a historical person named Jesus a generation earlier seems to be as foolhardy as the movement from the hypothesis of Markan priority to the judgment of Markan historicity turned out to be. Admittedly, it is safer to suggest, based on literary observations of Mark's Gospel, that even the implied narrative christology of the Markan Jesus derives from "the early church" in general rather than from "the historical Jesus."[79] Yet even that historical deduction from literary clues runs the risk of ending the search for an appropriate literary interpretation. The historical quest must be carried out in ways that do not short-circuit the hermeneutical one.[80]

Surely the "literary turn" in biblical studies has warned us against resolving literary tensions by historicizing them. In fact, tensions in a narrative need not be "resolved" at all. By means of the tension between the Markan narrator, who proclaims Jesus the "Christ, the Son of God" but mostly talks about Jesus, and the Markan Jesus, who proclaims the coming of the kingdom of God and the "Son of Humanity" and mostly talks about God, the Markan implied author offers the implied audience a powerful portrayal of one truly and obediently focused not on himself but on God.

Realistically, of course, in this age of specialization it has become impossible for researchers to keep up with the scholarly literature of both the quest for the historical Jesus, which has increased exponentially in the past thirty years,

---

78. At the conclusion of his book on the rhetoric of characterization, Paul L. Danove makes this point about the difficulty of moving from the implied author to the real author: "Although the previous studies [in his book] of the beliefs cultivated for the narrative audience would seem to provide direct access to the beliefs that may be attributed to the real author, the limitations on applicability still apply. There is no way to guarantee that these cultivated beliefs actually characterized the real author and every reason to assume that this narrative communication [Mark's Gospel], like all communication, projects an idealized portrait of the author (the implied author) and that the communication itself is directed as much to its real author as to its original real audience" (*The Rhetoric of the Characterization of God, Jesus, and Jesus' Disciples in the Gospel of Mark* [JSNTSup 290; New York: T&T Clark, 2005], 161).

79. So Broadhead (*Naming Jesus*, 170–71): "In the Gospel of Mark most titles are not statements *from* Jesus, but statements *about* him. . . . The central focus of his message and his activity is not himself, but the kingdom of God. . . . A clear narrative pattern emerges: concern for christological clarity belongs more to those who surround him than to Jesus himself. This literary canon most likely presents an accurate reflection of the historical situation: the creeds, confessions and titles which highlight christological values belong more to the faith statements of the early Church about Jesus than to the message of Jesus himself."

80. See Elizabeth Struthers Malbon, "Texts and Contexts: Interpreting the Disciples in Mark," *Semeia* 62 (1993): 81–102; republished in *In the Company of Jesus*, 100–130.

and narrative criticism of the Gospels, enjoying its initial growth in these years. Yet the relative isolation of literary criticism and Jesus research is not accidental or based solely on the demands of specialization.[81] Narrative criticism and Jesus research differ in their basic approaches to the Gospels. For Jesus researchers, the challenge is to analyze the Gospels for traces of something else of great interest to them—the historical Jesus. For narrative critics, the Gospels themselves are of great interest, and the challenge is to appreciate them in relation to their multiple audiences. For the former, the Gospels are means, for the latter, ends.[82] Thus the tension between those who search for "Mark's Jesus" and those who search for the "historical Jesus" may be as strong as the tension between the Markan Jesus and the Markan narrator. It remains to be seen whether this tension will be as creative.

Mark's Jesus: Characterization as Narrative Christology

My introductory chapter opened with an epigraph from literary critic and intriguing Markan interpreter, Frank Kermode: "To be blessedly fallible, to have the capacity to subvert manifest senses, is the mark of good enough readers and good enough texts."[83] Any reader who is still with me at this point is aware of my fallibility, which I hope is in some sense "blessed." But my stronger hope is that my readers share with me a sense of Mark's Gospel as not only "blessedly fallible" but as having "the capacity to subvert manifest senses." Mark's Gospel subverts its own narrator's manifest sense of what it means for Jesus to be the Christ, the Son of God, by its protagonist's manifest sense of what it means for God to be God.

This concluding chapter also opens with an epigraph from Frank Kermode: ". . . Mark is a strong witness to the enigmatic and exclusive character of narrative, to its property of banishing interpreters from its secret places."[84] This statement also reminds us, as members of the incredibly diverse audience of Mark's Gospel, that we are never finished, can never finish, interpreting this good enough text, even if we are good enough readers. Mark's Gospel maintains

---

81. Compare Mark Alan Powell's description of the situation in which "literary criticism and Jesus scholarship . . . often placed scholars committed to either enterprise at a distance from those dedicated to the other, with an unfortunate lapse in opportunities to learn from each other" ("Authorial Intent and Historical Reporting: Putting Spong's Literalization Thesis to the Test," *Journal for the Study of the Historical Jesus* 1 [2003]: 225–49, quotation from 225). Although I do not find Powell's argument about authorial intent entirely convincing, I do find his attempt to engage both literary critics and Jesus researchers in the conversation admirable and encouraging.

82. As Broadhead, *Teaching with Authority*, 33, notes, "The end of literary analysis is literature—what it presents and how it presents it."

83. Kermode, *Genesis of Secrecy*, 14.

84. Kermode, *Genesis of Secrecy*, 33–34.

its secret places from which we are banished, and yet we are brought back again and again by its enigmatic character. My study of the characterization of Jesus as Markan narrative christology draws attention to the enigmatic nature of a story told in such a way that the narrator's commendation of the central character is tempered by that character's commitment to a character who, even though minimally present in the action, is more central to it—God. Despite the tension between the Markan Jesus and the narrator, (God) confirms the narrator's application of "Son of God" to the Markan Jesus and also confirms that what the Markan Jesus does and says is pleasing to (God), serving almost as a mediating character between them, confirming them both in different ways. Thus it is the implied author's point of view, not that of either the Markan Jesus or the Markan narrator alone, that is closest to the point of view of (God). The implied author, like (God), can handle the diversity and tension of multiple points of view.[85] And both the implied author's creation and (God) seem to share the "enigmatic and exclusive character" of which Kermode speaks.

In the Gospel of Mark the tension between the narrator's point of view and Jesus' point of view enables the implied author to present a Jesus whose focus

---

85. It might seem that Michael L. Cook, S.J., is in agreement when he asserts, "The point of view of the narrative is the point of view of God . . ." (*Christology as Narrative Quest* [Collegeville, Minn.: Liturgical Press, 1997], 70). However, my words are carefully chosen: Thus it is the implied author's point of view, not that of either the Markan Jesus or the Markan narrator alone, that is closest to the point of view of (God). In respecting the Markan narrative, it seems I must also respect and follow the hesitancy of both the Markan Jesus and the Markan narrator when speaking of God, who never appears except as a voice and to whom Jesus always defers. Thus I would not say, as Cook does, "Mark's primary concern is to communicate the significance of Jesus as *God* sees him. . . . For Mark, God is indeed the one who tells this tale" (70). Rather, it is the implied author who tells the tale, and the implied author's primary concern is to communicate the significance of Jesus to the implied audience by means of the tension of what the Markan Jesus says and does *and* what the Markan narrator (and all the other characters) say and do in relation to him. In presenting that creative tension, the implied author is most like (God), who confirms both the Markan narrator and the Markan Jesus—and then lets the audience listen. Thus it is clear that I also do not agree with Cook when he agrees with Kingsbury's assertion that Mark (the real author? the implied author? the narrator?) "aligns both his own evaluative point of view and that of Jesus with the evaluative point of view of God" (Kingsbury, *Christology*, 49, as quoted in Cook, 80); I have already argued that the Markan Jesus and the Markan narrator are not completely aligned on the ideological or phraseological plane. Neither Kingsbury nor Cook is making use of the distinction of the implied author and the narrator, which I have found essential to describing the Markan narrative. However, I see Cook's Christological focus on the "beloved Son," using the words of the voice (of God) as his central image, as somewhat different from Kingsbury's Christological focus on the "Christ, the Son of God," using the narrator's proclamation as his central assertion. I would agree with Cook on the larger issue of the Markan narrative: "For those who have eyes to see, ears to hear, and feet to walk, this is a story about the faithfulness of God embodied in Jesus and available to all who listen and obey" (70).

is always on God, even though the narrator keeps focusing on Jesus. One could hardly present the story of Jesus without focusing on Jesus; the narrator is thus not to be blamed. But neither is the implied author to be ignored in creating the gap, the tension, between the narrator's point of view and that of the main character, Jesus. It is not the Markan Jesus' point of view or the Markan narrator's point of view that is the point of view of Mark's Gospel. It is the implied author's point of view as this is received by the implied audience. Thus the tension between the narrator and Jesus is not a problem to be resolved, not a gap to be filled in, but a narrative christological confession offered by the implied author to the implied audience as a challenge and a mystery.

BIBLIOGRAPHY

Achtemeier, Paul J. "'And He Followed Him': Miracles and Discipleship in Mark 10:46-52." *Semeia* 11 (1978): 115–45.

Achtemeier, Paul J. *Jesus and the Miracle Tradition.* Eugene, Ore.: Cascade Books, 2008.

Achtemeier, Paul J., gen. ed. *The HarperCollins Bible Dictionary.* San Francisco: HarperSanFrancisco for the SBL, 1996.

Ahearne-Kroll, Stephen P. *The Psalms of Lament in Mark's Passion: Jesus' Davidic Suffering.* SNTSMS 142. Cambridge: Cambridge University Press, 2007.

Aland, Kurt, et al., ed. *The Greek New Testament.* 3rd ed. New York: United Bible Societies, 1975.

Anderson, Janice Capel. *Matthew's Narrative Web: Over, and Over, and Over Again.* JSNTSup 91. Sheffield: Sheffield Academic, 1994.

Anderson, Janice Capel, and Stephen D. Moore, eds. *Mark and Method: New Approaches in Biblical Studies.* 2nd ed. Minneapolis: Fortress, 2008.

Arndt, William F., and F. Wilbur Gingrich. *A Greek-English Lexicon of the New Testament and Other Early Christian Literature.* 2nd ed. Chicago: University of Chicago Press, 1979.

Austin, J. L. *How to Do Things with Words.* Cambridge, Mass.: Harvard University Press, 1975.

Bakhtin, Mikhail. *Problems of Dostoevsky's Poetics.* Edited and translated by Caryl Emerson. Minneapolis: University of Minnesota Press, 1984.

Berlin, Adele. *Poetics and Interpretation of Biblical Narrative.* Sheffield: Almond, 1983.

Best, Ernest. *The Temptation and the Passion: The Markan Soteriology.* SNTSMS 2. Cambridge: Cambridge University Press, 1965.

Betz, Hans Dieter. "The Early Christian Miracle Story: Some Observations on the Form Critical Problem." *Semeia* 11 (1978): 69–81.

Black, C. Clifton. *The Disciples According to Mark: Markan Redaction in Current Debate.* JSNTSup 27. Sheffield: Sheffield Academic, 1989.

Black, C. Clifton. "Mark as Historian of God's Kingdom." *CBQ* 71 (2009): 64–83.

Black, C. Clifton. "Notes on the Gospel According to Mark." *The HarperCollins Study Bible: NRSV.* New York: HarperCollins, 1993.

Boomershine, Thomas E. "Mark, the Storyteller: A Rhetorical-Critical Investigation of Mark's Passion and Resurrection Narrative." Ph.D. diss., Union Theological Seminary, New York, 1974.

Booth, Wayne C. "Resurrection of the Implied Author: Why Bother?" Pp. 75–88 in *A Companion to Narrative Theory.* Edited by James Phelan and Peter J. Rabinowitz. Oxford: Blackwell, 2005.

Borg, Marcus J. *Jesus: A New Vision: Spirit, Culture, and the Life of Discipleship.* San Francisco: Harper & Row, 1987.

Borg, Marcus J. *Meeting Jesus Again for the First Time: The Historical Jesus and the Heart of Contemporary Faith.* San Francisco: HarperSanFrancisco, 1994.

Borg, Marcus J., and N. T. Wright. *The Meaning of Jesus: Two Visions.* San Francisco: HarperSanFrancisco, 1999.

Boring, M. Eugene. "The Christology of Mark: Hermeneutical Issues for Systematic Theology." *Semeia* 30 (1984): 125–53.

Boring, M. Eugene. "Mark 1:1-15 and the Beginning of the Gospel." *Semeia* 52 (1990): 43–81.

Boring, M. Eugene. *Mark: A Commentary.* The New Testament Library. Louisville: Westminster John Knox, 2006.

Boring, M. Eugene. "Markan Christology: God-Language for Jesus?" *NTS* 45 (1999): 451–71.

Broadhead, Edwin K. *Naming Jesus: Titular Christology in the Gospel of Mark.* JSNTSup 175. Sheffield: Sheffield Academic, 1999.

Broadhead, Edwin K. *Prophet, Son, Messiah: Narrative Form and Function in Mark 14–16.* JSNTSup 97. Sheffield: Sheffield Academic, 1994.

Broadhead, Edwin K. *Teaching with Authority: Miracles and Christology in the Gospel of Mark.* JSNTSup 74. Sheffield: Sheffield Academic, 1992.

Brown, Raymond E. "The Burial of Jesus (Mark 15:42-47)." *CBQ* 50 (1988): 233–45.

Burnett, Fred W. "Characterization and Reader Construction of Characters in the Gospels." *Semeia* 63 (1993): 1–28.

Camery-Hoggatt, Jerry. *Irony in Mark's Gospel: Text and Subtext.* SNTSMS 72. Cambridge: Cambridge University Press, 1992.

Chantraine, Pierre. *Dictionnaire étymologique de la langue grecque: Histoire des mots.* Supplement under the direction of A. Blanc, C. de Lamberterie, J.-L. Perpillou. Paris: Klincksieck, 1999.

Chatman, Seymour. *Story and Discourse: Narrative Structure in Fiction and Film.* Ithaca: Cornell University Press, 1978.

Chronis, Harry L. "To Reveal and to Conceal: A Literary-Critical Perspective on 'the Son of Man' in Mark." *NTS* 51 (2005): 459–81.

Cook, Michael L., S.J. *Christology as Narrative Quest.* Collegeville, Minn.: Liturgical Press, 1997.

Crossan, John Dominic. *The Dark Interval: Towards a Theology of Story.* Niles, Ill.: Argus Communications, 1975; Sonoma, Calif.: Polebridge, 1988.

Crossan, John Dominic. *The Historical Jesus: The Life of a Mediterranean Jewish Peasant.* San Francisco: HarperSanFrancisco, 1991.

Crossan, John Dominic. *In Parables: The Challenge of the Historical Jesus.* New York: Harper & Row, 1973.

Crossan, John Dominic. *Jesus: A Revolutionary Biography.* San Francisco: HarperSanFrancisco, 1994.

Culpepper, R. Alan. *Anatomy of the Fourth Gospel: A Study in Literary Design.* Philadelphia: Fortress, 1983.

Culpepper, R. Alan. "Mark 10:50: Why Mention the Garment?" *JBL* 101 (1982): 131–32.

Dahl, Nils A. "The Neglected Factor in New Testament Theology." *Reflection* (Yale Divinity School) 73 (1975): 5–8.

D'Angelo, Mary Rose. "*Abba* and 'Father': Imperial Theology and the Traditions about Jesus." *JBL* 111 (1992): 611–30.

D'Angelo, Mary Rose. "Theology in Mark and Q: *Abba* and 'Father' in Context." *HTR* 85 (1992): 149–74.

Danove, Paul L. "The Characterization and Narrative Function of the Women at the Tomb (Mark 15,40-41, 47; 16,1-8)." *Biblica* 77 (1996): 375–97.

Danove, Paul L. *Linguistics and Exegesis in the Gospel of Mark: Applications of a Case Frame Analysis and Lexicon.* JSNTSup 218. SNTG 10. Sheffield: Sheffield Academic, 2001.

Danove, Paul L. "The Narrative Function of Mark's Characterization of God." *NovT* 43 (2001): 12–30.

Danove, Paul L. "The Narrative Rhetoric of Mark's Ambiguous Characterization of the Disciples." *JSNT* 70 (1998): 21–38.

Danove, Paul L. *The Rhetoric of the Characterization of God, Jesus, and Jesus' Disciples in the Gospel of Mark.* JSNTSup 290. New York: T&T Clark, 2005.

Danove, Paul L. "The Rhetoric of the Characterization of Jesus as the Son of Man and Christ in Mark." *Biblica* 84 (2003): 16–34.

Danove, Paul L. "A Rhetorical Analysis of Mark's Construction of Discipleship." Pp. 280–96 in *Rhetorical Criticism and the Bible: Essays from the 1998 Florence Conference.* Edited by Stanley D. Porter and Dennis L. Stamps. JSNTSup 195. Sheffield: Sheffield Academic, 2002.

Darr, John A. "Narrator as Character: Mapping a Reader-Oriented Approach to Narration in Luke-Acts." *Semeia* 63 (1993): 43–60.

Darr, John A. *On Character Building: The Reader and the Rhetoric of Characterization in Luke-Acts.* Louisville: Westminster John Knox, 1992.

Davidsen, Ole. *The Narrative Jesus: A Semiotic Reading of Mark's Gospel.* Aarhus, Denmark: Aarhus University Press, 1993.

Dawsey, James M. *The Lukan Voice: Confusion and Irony in the Gospel of Luke.* Macon, Ga.: Mercer University Press, 1986.

Dewey, Joanna. "The Gospel of Mark as an Oral-Aural Event: Implications for Interpretation." Pp. 145–63 in *The New Literary Criticism and the New Testament.* Edited by Elizabeth Struthers Malbon and Edgar V. McKnight. JSNTSup 109. Sheffield: Sheffield Academic, 1994; Valley Forge, Pa.: Trinity, 1994.

Dewey, Joanna. "Mark as Aural Narrative: Structures as Clues to Understanding." *STRev* 36 (1992): 45–56.

Dewey, Joanna. "Mark as Interwoven Tapestry: Forecasts and Echoes for a Listening Audience." *CBQ* 53 (1991): 221–36.

Dewey, Joanna. *Markan Public Debate: Literary Technique, Concentric Structure, and Theology in Mark 2:1–3:6.* SBLDS 48. Chico, Calif.: Scholars Press, 1980.

Dewey, Joanna. "Oral Methods of Structuring Narrative in Mark." *Int* 53 (1989): 32–44.

Dewey, Joanna. "The Survival of Mark's Gospel: A Good Story?" *JBL* 123 (2004): 495–507.

Dewey, Joanna, and Elizabeth Struthers Malbon. "Mark." Pp. 311–24 in *Theological Bible Commentary.* Edited by Gail R. O'Day and David L. Petersen. Louisville: Westminster John Knox, 2009.

Dodd, C. H. *The Parables of the Kingdom*. Glasgow: Collins, 1961.

Donahue, John R., S.J. *Are You the Christ? The Trial Narrative in the Gospel of Mark*. SBLDS 10. Missoula, Mont.: SBL, 1973.

Donahue, John R., S.J. *The Gospel in Parable*. Philadelphia: Fortress, 1988.

Donahue, John R., S.J. "Jesus as the Parable of God in the Gospel of Mark." Pp. 148–67 in *Interpreting the Gospels*. Edited by James Luther Mays. Philadelphia: Fortress, 1981. First published in *Int* 32 (1978): 369–86.

Donahue, John R., S.J. "The Literary Turn and New Testament Theology: Detour or New Direction?" *JR* 76 (1996): 250–75.

Donahue, John R., S.J. "A Neglected Factor in the Theology of Mark." *JBL* 101 (1982): 563–94.

Donahue, John R., S.J. "Recent Studies on the Origin of 'Son of Man' in the Gospels." *CBQ* 48 (1986): 484–98.

Donahue, John R., S.J. "Temple, Trial, and Royal Christology (Mark 14:53-65)." Pp. 61–79 in *The Passion in Mark: Studies on Mark 14–16*. Edited by Werner H. Kelber. Philadelphia: Fortress, 1976.

Dowd, Sharyn. *Prayer, Power, and the Problem of Suffering: Mark 11:22-25 in the Context of Markan Theology*. SBLDS 105. Atlanta: Scholars Press, 1988.

Dowd, Sharyn. *Reading Mark: A Literary and Theological Commentary on the Second Gospel*. Macon, Ga.: Smyth & Helwys, 2000.

Dowd, Sharyn, and Elizabeth Struthers Malbon. "The Significance of Jesus' Death in Mark: Narrative Context and Authorial Audience." *JBL* 125 (2006): 271–97. Republished as pp. 1–31 in *The Trial and Death of Jesus: Essays on the Passion Narrative in Mark*. Edited by Geert Van Oyen and Tom Shepherd. Leuven, Belgium: Peeters, 2006.

Driggers, Ira Brent. *Following God through Mark: Theological Tension in the Second Gospel*. Louisville: Westminster John Knox, 2007.

Edwards, James R. "Markan Sandwiches: The Significance of Interpolations in Markan Narratives." *NovT* 31 (1989): 193–216.

Fowler, Robert M. *Let the Reader Understand: Reader-Response Criticism and the Gospel of Mark*. Minneapolis: Fortress, 1991.

Fuller, Reginald H., and Pheme Perkins. *Who Is This Christ? Gospel Christology and Contemporary Faith*. Philadelphia: Fortress, 1983.

Funk, Robert W. *Language, Hermeneutic, and the Word of God: The Problem of Language in the New Testament and Contemporary Theology*. New York: Harper & Row, 1966.

Gold, Victor Roland, et al., eds. *The New Testament and Psalms: An Inclusive Version*. New York: Oxford University Press, 1995.

Gooder, Paula. *Searching for Meaning: A Practical Guide to New Testament Interpretation*. London: SPCK, 2008; Louisville: Westminster John Knox, 2009.

Graham, Helen R. "A Passion Prediction for Mark's Community: Mark 13:9-13." *BTB* 16 (1986): 18–22.

Griffith-Jones, Robin. "Going Back to Galilee to See the Son of Man: Mark's Gospel as an Upside-Down Apocalypse." Pp. 82–102 in Malbon, ed., *Between Author and Audience in Mark*.

Guida, Annalisa. "From *Parabolē* to *Sēmeion*: The Nuptial Imagery in Mark and John." Pp. 103–20 in Malbon, ed., *Between Author and Audience in Mark*.

Gunn, David M. "Narrative Criticism." Pp. 201–29 in *To Each Its Own Meaning: An Introduction to Biblical Criticisms and Their Application*. Rev. and expand. ed. Edited by Steven L. McKenzie and Stephen R. Haynes. Louisville: Westminster John Knox, 1999.

Hahn, Ferdinand. "The Confession of the One God in the New Testament." *HBT* 2 (1980): 69–84.

Hahn, Ferdinand. *The Titles of Jesus in Christology: Their History in Early Christianity.* New York: World Publishing, 1969.

Harrington, Daniel J., S.J. *What Are They Saying about Mark?* 2nd ed. Mahwah, N.J.: Paulist, 2004.

Havelock, Eric. "Oral Composition in the *Oedipus Tyrannus* of Sophocles." *New Literary History* 16 (1984): 175–97.

Henderson, Ian. "Reconstructing Mark's Double Audience." Pp. 6–28 in Malbon, ed., *Between Author and Audience in Mark.*

Henderson, Suzanne Watts. *Christology and Discipleship in the Gospel of Mark.* SNTSMS 135. Cambridge: Cambridge University Press, 2006.

Hooker, Morna D. *The Gospel According to Saint Mark.* BNTC. Peabody, Mass.: Hendrickson, 1991.

Hooker, Morna D. *The Son of Man in Mark: A Study of the Background of the Term 'Son of Man' and Its Use in St Mark's Gospel.* Montreal: McGill University Press, 1967.

Horsley, Richard A. *Hearing the Whole Story: The Politics of Plot in Mark's Gospel.* Louisville: Westminster John Knox, 2001.

Iersel, Bas M. F. van. "Concentric Structures in Mark 1:14–3:35 (4:1) with Some Observations on Method." Translated by W. H. Bisscheroux. *BibInt* 3 (1995): 75–97.

Iersel, Bas M. F. van. "De betekenis van Marcus vanuit zijn topografische structuur." *Tidschrift voor Theologie* 22 (1982): 117–38.

Iersel, Bas M. F. van. *Mark: A Reader-Response Commentary.* Translated by W. H. Bisscheroux. Sheffield: Sheffield Academic, 1998.

Iersel, Bas M. F. van. *Reading Mark.* Translated by W. H. Bisscheroux. Collegeville, Minn.: Liturgical Press, 1988.

Jeremias, Joachim. *The Central Message of the New Testament.* New York: Charles Scribner's Sons, 1965.

Johnson, Sherman E. *A Commentary on the Gospel According to St. Mark.* London: Adam & Charles Black, 1960.

Juel, Donald. *Messiah and Temple: The Trial of Jesus in the Gospel of Mark.* SBLDS 31. Missoula, Mont.: Scholars Press for the SBL, 1977.

Keck, Leander. "Christology and History: A Review Essay." *Theology Today* 57 (2000): 232–38.

Keck, Leander. "The Task of New Testament Christology." *Princeton Seminary Bulletin* 26 NS (2005): 266–76.

Keck, Leander. "Toward the Renewal of New Testament Christology." *NTS* 32 (1986): 362–77.

Kee, Howard Clark. *Community of the New Age: Studies in Mark's Gospel.* Philadelphia: Westminster, 1977.

Kee, Howard Clark. "The Function of Scriptural Quotations and Allusions in Mark 11–16." Pp. 165–88 in *Jesus und Paulus: Festschrift für Werner Georg Kümmel zum 70. Geburtstag.* Edited by E. Earle Ellis and Erich Grässer. Göttingen, Germany: Vandenhoeck & Ruprecht, 1975.

Kelber, Werner H. "Jesus and Tradition: Words in Time, Words in Space." *Semeia* 65 (1994): 139–67.

Kelber, Werner H. *The Kingdom in Mark: A New Place and a New Time.* Philadelphia: Fortress, 1974.

Kelber, Werner H. *The Oral and the Written Gospel: The Hermeneutics of Speaking and Writing in the Synoptic Tradition, Mark, Paul, and Q.* Philadelphia: Fortress, 1983.

Kermode, Frank. *The Genesis of Secrecy: On the Interpretation of Narrative.* Cambridge, Mass.: Harvard University Press, 1979.

Kingsbury, Jack Dean. *The Christology of Mark's Gospel.* Philadelphia: Fortress, 1983.

Kingsbury, Jack Dean. *Conflict in Mark: Jesus, Authorities, Disciples.* Minneapolis: Fortress, 1989.

Kingsbury, Jack Dean. *Matthew as Story.* 2nd ed. Philadelphia: Fortress, 1988.

Kinukawa, Hisako. *Women and Jesus in Mark: A Japanese Feminist Perspective.* Maryknoll, N.Y.: Orbis, 1994.

Malbon, Elizabeth Struthers. "The Christology of Mark's Gospel: Narrative Christology and the Markan Jesus." Pp. 33–48 in *Who Do You Say That I Am? Essays on Christology.* In honor of Jack Dean Kingsbury. Edited by Mark Allan Powell and David R. Bauer. Louisville: Westminster John Knox, 1999.

Malbon, Elizabeth Struthers. "Disciples/Crowds/Whoever: Markan Characters and Readers." *NovT* 28 (1986): 104–30. Republished as pp. 144–70 in *The Composition of Mark's Gospel: Selected Studies from Novum Testamentum.* Edited by David E. Orton. Leiden, The Netherlands: Brill, 1999. Also republished as pp. 70–99 in *In the Company of Jesus.*

Malbon, Elizabeth Struthers. "Echoes and Foreshadowings in Mark 4–8: Reading and Re-reading." *JBL* 112 (1993): 213–32.

Malbon, Elizabeth Struthers. "Fallible Followers: Women and Men in the Gospel of Mark." *Semeia* 28 (1983): 29–48. Republished as pp. 41–69 in *In the Company of Jesus.*

Malbon, Elizabeth Struthers. *Hearing Mark: A Listener's Guide.* Harrisburg, Pa.: Trinity, 2002.

Malbon, Elizabeth Struthers. *In the Company of Jesus: Characters in Mark's Gospel.* Louisville: Westminster John Knox, 2000.

Malbon, Elizabeth Struthers. "The Jesus of Mark and the Sea of Galilee." *JBL* 103 (1984): 363–77.

Malbon, Elizabeth Struthers. "The Jesus of Mark and the 'Son of David.'" Pp. 162–85 in Malbon, ed., *Between Author and Audience in Mark.*

Malbon, Elizabeth Struthers. "The Jewish Leaders in the Gospel of Mark: A Literary Study of Markan Characterization." *JBL* 108 (1989): 259–81. Republished as pp. 131–65 in *In the Company of Jesus.*

Malbon, Elizabeth Struthers. "The Major Importance of the Minor Characters in Mark." Pp. 58–86 in *The New Literary Criticism and the New Testament.* Edited by Elizabeth Struthers Malbon and Edgar V. McKnight. JSNTSup 109. Sheffield: Sheffield Academic; Valley Forge, Pa.: Trinity, 1994. Republished as pp. 189–225 in *In the Company of Jesus.*

Malbon, Elizabeth Struthers. "Markan Narrative Christology and the Kingdom of God." Pp. 177–93 in *Literary Encounters with the Reign of God* (in honor of Robert C. Tannehill). Edited by Sharon H. Ringe and H. C. Paul Kim. New York/London: T&T Clark International, 2004.

Malbon, Elizabeth Struthers. "Narrative Christology and the Son of Man: What the Markan Jesus Says Instead." *Biblnt* 11 (2003): 373–85.

Malbon, Elizabeth Struthers. "Narrative Criticism: How Did the Theory Develop and What Are Its Main Features?" Pp. 80–82 in *Searching for Meaning: A Practical Guide to New Testament Interpretation.* By Paula Gooder. London: SPCK, 2008; Louisville: Westminster John Knox, 2009.

Malbon, Elizabeth Struthers. "Narrative Criticism: How Does the Story Mean?" Pp. 29–57 in *Mark and Method: New Approaches in Biblical Studies*. 2nd ed. Edited by Janice Capel Anderson and Stephen D. Moore. Minneapolis: Fortress, 2008. First edition (1992) republished as pp. 1–40 in *In the Company of Jesus*.

Malbon, Elizabeth Struthers. *Narrative Space and Mythic Meaning in Mark*. San Francisco: Harper & Row, 1986; volume 13 of The Biblical Seminar; Sheffield: Sheffield Academic, 1991.

Malbon, Elizabeth Struthers. "New Literary Criticism and Jesus Research." In *The Handbook of the Study of the Historical Jesus, Vol. 1: How to Study the Historical Jesus*. Edited by Tom Holmén and Stanley E. Porter. Leiden, The Netherlands: Brill, forthcoming.

Malbon, Elizabeth Struthers. "The Poor Widow in Mark and Her Poor Rich Readers." *CBQ* 53 (1991), 589–604. Republished as pp. 166–88 in *In the Company of Jesus*. Also republished as pp. 111–27 in *The Feminist Companion to Mark*. Edited by Amy-Jill Levine. Sheffield: Sheffield Academic, 2001.

Malbon, Elizabeth Struthers. "'Reflected Christology': An Aspect of Narrative 'Christology' in the Gospel of Mark." *Perspectives in Religious Studies* 26, in honor of Edgar V. McKnight (1999): 127–45.

Malbon, Elizabeth Struthers. Review of Naluparayil, *The Identity of Jesus in Mark. Biblica* 4 (2001): 569–73.

Malbon, Elizabeth Struthers. "Texts and Contexts: Interpreting the Disciples in Mark." *Semeia* 62 (1993): 81–102. Republished as pp. 100–130 in *In the Company of Jesus*.

Malbon, Elizabeth Struthers, ed. *Between Author and Audience in Mark: Narration, Characterization, Interpretation*. New Testament Monographs 23. Sheffield: Sheffield Phoenix, 2009.

Malbon, Elizabeth Struthers, and Adele Berlin, eds. *Characterization in Biblical Literature. Semeia* 63 (1993).

Marcus, Joel. "Mark—Interpreter of Paul." *NTS* 46 (2000): 473–87.

Marcus, Joel. *The Mystery of the Kingdom of God*. SBLDS 90. Atlanta: Scholars Press, 1986.

Marcus, Joel. *The Way of the Lord: Christological Exegesis of the Old Testament in the Gospel of Mark*. Louisville: Westminster John Knox, 1992.

Marguerat, Daniel, and Yvan Bourquin. *How to Read Bible Stories: An Introduction to Narrative Criticism*. With the collaboration of Marcel Durrer. Illustrated by Florence Clerc. Translated by John Bowden. London: SCM, 1999.

Matera, Frank J. *The Kingship of Jesus: Composition and Theology in Mark 15*. SBLDS 66. Chico, Calif.: Scholars Press, 1982.

Merenlahti, Petri. *Poetics for the Gospels? Rethinking Narrative Criticism*. Edinburgh: T&T Clark, 2002.

Metzger, Bruce M. *A Textual Commentary on the Greek New Testament*. N.p.: United Bible Societies, 1971.

Miller, Robert J., ed. *The Complete Gospels: Annotated Scholars Version*. Sonoma, Calif.: Polebridge, 1992.

Moore, Stephen D. *Literary Criticism and the Gospels: The Theoretical Challenge*. New Haven: Yale University Press, 1989.

Moore, Stephen D. "The SS Officer at the Foot of the Cross: A Tragedy in Three Acts." Pp. 44–61 in Malbon, ed., *Between Author and Audience in Mark*.

Muecke, D. C. *The Compass of Irony*. London: Methuen, 1969.

Muller, P. *"Wer ist dieser?" Jesus in Markusevangelium*. BThSt 27. Neukirchen-Vluyn, Germany: Neukirchner Verlag, 1995.

Myers, Ched. *Binding the Strong Man: A Political Reading of Mark's Story of Jesus.* Maryknoll, N.Y.: Orbis, 1988.

Naluparayil, Jacob Chacko. *The Identity of Jesus in Mark: An Essay on Narrative Christology.* Studium Biblicum Franciscanum Analecta 49. Jerusalem: Franciscan Printing Press, 2000.

Naluparayil, Jacob Chacko. "Jesus of the Gospel of Mark: Present State of Research." *Currents in Research: Biblical Studies* 8 (2000): 191–226.

Neirynck, Frans. *Duality in Mark: Contributions to the Study of the Markan Redaction.* BETL 31. Leuven, Belgium: Leuven University Press, 1972.

Ong, Walter J. *Orality and Literacy: The Technologizing of the Word.* London and New York: Methuen, 1982.

Oyen, Geert Van. "Intercalation and Irony in the Gospel of Mark." Vol. 2, pp. 949–74 in *The Four Gospels 1992: Festschrift Frans Neirynck.* 4 volumes. Edited by F. Van Segbroeck et al. Leuven, Belgium: Leuven University Press, 1992.

Perrin, Norman. "Towards an Interpretation of the Gospel of Mark." Pp. 1–52 in *Christology and a Modern Pilgrimage: A Discussion with Norman Perrin.* Edited by Hans Dieter Betz. Rev. ed. Missoula, Mont.: SBL and Scholars Press, 1974.

Perrin, Norman. "The Use of (*Para*)*didonai* in Connection with the Passion of Jesus in the New Testament." Pp. 94–103 in *A Modern Pilgrimage in New Testament Christology.* Philadelphia: Fortress, 1974. First published in pp. 204–12 in *Der Ruf Jesu und die Antwort der Gemeinde: Festschrift für Joachim Jeremias.* Edited by Edward Lohse, Christoph Burchard, and Berndt Schaller. Göttingen, Germany: Vandenhoeck & Ruprecht, 1970.

Perrin, Norman. *What Is Redaction Criticism?* Philadelphia: Fortress, 1969.

Perry, Menakhem. "Literary Dynamics: How the Order of a Text Creates Its Meanings (with an Analysis of Faulkner's 'A Rose for Emily')." *Poetics* 1 (1979): 35–64 and 311–61.

Petersen, Norman R. "The Composition of Mark 4:1–8:26." *HTR* 73 (1980): 185–217.

Petersen, Norman R. "'Point of View' in Mark's Narrative." *Semeia* 12 (1978): 97–121.

Pokorny, Petr. "Markan Christology." Unpublished paper distributed to members of the Mark Seminar of the SNTS, 1998.

Powell, Mark Allen. "Authorial Intent and Historical Reporting: Putting Spong's Literalization Thesis to the Test." *Journal for the Study of the Historical Jesus* 1 (2003): 225–49.

Powell, Mark Allen. *What Is Narrative Criticism?* GBS. Minneapolis: Fortress, 1990.

Rabinowitz, Peter J. "Truth in Fiction: A Reexamination of Audiences. "*Critical Inquiry* 4 (1974): 121–41.

Resseguie, James L. *Narrative Criticism of the New Testament: An Introduction.* Grand Rapids: Baker Academic, 2005.

Rhoads, David. "Jesus and the Syrophoenician Woman in Mark: A Narrative Critical Study." *JAAR* 62 (1994): 343–75. Republished as pp. 63–94 in Rhoads, *Reading Mark: Engaging the Gospel.* Minneapolis: Fortress, 2004.

Rhoads, David, and Donald Michie. *Mark as Story: An Introduction to the Narrative of a Gospel.* Philadelphia: Fortress, 1982.

Rhoads, David, Joanna Dewey, and Donald Michie. *Mark as Story: An Introduction to the Narrative of a Gospel.* 2nd ed. Minneapolis: Fortress, 1999.

Rhoads, David, and Kari Syreeni, eds. *Characterization in the Gospels: Reconceiving Narrative Criticism.* JSNTSup 184. Sheffield: Sheffield Academic, 1999.

Robbins, Vernon K. "The Healing of Blind Bartimaeus (10:46-52) in the Marcan Theology." *JBL* 92 (1973): 224–43.

Robbins, Vernon K. *Jesus the Teacher: A Socio-Rhetorical Interpretation of Mark.* Philadelphia: Fortress, 1984.

Robinson, James M. *The Problem of History in Mark.* SBT 21. London: SCM, 1957. Repr., Philadelphia: Fortress, 1982.

Ruge-Jones, Philip. "Omnipresent, not Omniscient: How Literary Interpretation Confuses the Storyteller's Narrating." Pp. 29–43 in Malbon, ed., *Between Author and Audience in Mark.*

Schneidau, Herbert N. "Biblical Narrative and Modern Consciousness." Pp. 132–50 in *The Bible and the Narrative Tradition.* Edited by Frank McConnell. Oxford: Oxford University Press, 1986.

Schüssler Fiorenza, Elisabeth. *Jesus and the Politics of Interpretation.* New York: Continuum, 2001.

Schüssler Fiorenza, Elisabeth. "The Rhetorics and Politics of Jesus Research: A Critical Feminist Perspective." Pp. 259–82 in *Jesus, Mark and Q: The Teaching of Jesus and Its Earliest Records.* Edited by Michael Labahn and Andreas Schmidt. JSNTSup 214. Sheffield: Sheffield Academic, 2001.

Schweizer, Eduard. "Mark's Theological Achievement." Translated by R. Morgan. Pp. 63–87 in *The Interpretation of Mark.* 2nd ed. Edited by William A. Telford. Edinburgh: T&T Clark, 1995. First published in *EvT* (1964): 337–55.

Schweizer, Eduard. "The Portrayal of the Life of Faith in the Gospel of Mark." Pp. 168–82 in *Interpreting the Gospels.* Edited by James Luther Mays. Philadelphia: Fortress, 1981. First published in *Int* 32 (1978): 387–99.

Scott, M. Philip, O.C.S.O. "Chiastic Structure: A Key to the Interpretation of Mark's Gospel." *BTB* 15 (1985): 17–26.

Shaw, Harry E. "Why Won't Our Terms Stay Put? The Narrative Communication Diagram Scrutinized and Historicized." Pp. 299–311 in *A Companion to Narrative Theory.* Edited by James Phelan and Peter J. Rabinowitz. London: Blackwell, 2005.

Shepherd, Tom. "The Narrative Function of Markan Intercalation." *NTS* 41 (1995): 522–40.

Shiner, Whitney T. "The Ambiguous Pronouncement of the Centurion and the Shrouding of Meaning in Mark." *JSNT* 78 (2000): 3–22.

Shiner, Whitney Taylor. *Follow Me! Disciples in Markan Rhetoric.* SBLDS 145. Atlanta: Scholars Press, 1995.

Shiner, Whitney Taylor. *Proclaiming the Gospel: First-Century Performance of Mark.* Harrisburg, Pa.: Trinity, 2003.

Shively, Elizabeth. "The Story Matters: Solving the Problem of the Parables in Mark 3:23-27." Pp. 122–44 in Malbon, ed., *Between Author and Audience in Mark.*

Smith, Abraham. "Tyranny Exposed: Mark's Typological Characterization of Herod Antipas (Mark 6:14-29)." *BibInt* 14 (2006): 259–93.

Smith, Stephen H. *A Lion with Wings: A Narrative-Critical Approach to Mark's Gospel.* Sheffield: Sheffield Academic, 1996.

Smith, Stephen H. "The Literary Structure of Mk 11:1–12:40." *NovT* 31 (1989): 104–24.

Stanzel, F. K. *A Theory of Narrative.* Translated by Charlotte Goedsche. Cambridge: Cambridge University Press, 1984.

Stock, Augustine, O.S.B. "Hinge Transitions in Mark's Gospel." *BTB* 15 (1985): 27–31.

Swete, Henry Barclay. *The Gospel According to Mark.* London: Macmillan, 1913. Repr., *Commentary on Mark.* Grand Rapids: Kregel Publications, 1977.

Tannehill, Robert C. "The Disciples in Mark: The Function of a Narrative Role." *JR* 57 (1977): 386–405. Republished as pp. 135–59 in *The Shape of the Gospel: New Testament Essays*. Eugene, Ore.: Cascade Books, 2007.

Tannehill, Robert C. "The Gospel of Mark as Narrative Christology." *Semeia* 16 (1979): 57–95. Republished as pp. 161–87 in *The Shape of the Gospel*.

Taylor, Vincent. *The Gospel According to St. Mark*. 2nd ed. New York: St. Martins, 1966. Repr., Grand Rapids: Baker Book House, 1981.

Telford, W. R. *The Theology of the Gospel of Mark*. New Testament Theology. Cambridge: Cambridge University Press, 1999.

Toit, David S. du. "Redefining Jesus: Current Trends in Jesus Research." Pp. 82–124 in *Jesus, Mark and Q: The Teaching of Jesus and Its Earliest Records*. Edited by Michael Labahn and Andreas Schmidt. JSNTSup 214. Sheffield: Sheffield Academic, 2001.

Tuckett, Christopher, ed. *The Messianic Secret*. Philadelphia: Fortress and London: SPCK, 1983.

Uspensky, Boris. *A Poetics of Composition: The Structure of the Artistic Text and Typology of a Compositional Form*. Translated by Valentina Zavarin and Susan Wittig. Berkeley: University of California Press, 1973.

Walker, William O., Jr. "The Son of Man: Some Recent Developments." *CBQ* 45 (1983): 584–607.

Webb, Geoff Robert. "Reading Mark with a Vulgar Mind: Applying Bakhtinian Categories to Markan Characterisation." Th.D. diss., Melbourne College of Divinity, 2003.

Weeden, Theodore J., Sr. *Mark—Traditions in Conflict*. Philadelphia: Fortress, 1971.

Williams, Joel F. "Does Mark's Gospel Have an Outline?" *JETS* 49 (2006): 505–25.

Williams, Joel F. "Jesus' Love for the Rich Man (Mark 10:21): A Disputed Response toward a Disputed Character." Pp. 145–61 in Malbon, ed., *Between Author and Audience in Mark*.

Williams, Joel F. *Other Followers of Jesus: Minor Characters as Major Figures in Mark's Gospel*. JSNTSup 102. Sheffield: Sheffield Academic, 1994.

Wrede, William. *The Messianic Secret*. Translated by J. C. C. Grieg. Cambridge and London: James Clarke, 1971.

Wright, N. T. *Jesus and the Victory of God*, Vol. 2 of *Christian Origins and the Question of God*. Minneapolis: Fortress, 1996.

Wright, N. T. *The New Testament and the People of God*, Vol. 1 of *Christian Origins and the Question of God*. London: SPCK/Minneapolis: Fortress, 1992.

Wright, N. T. *The Original Jesus*. Oxford: Lion/Grand Rapids: Eerdmans, 1996.

Wright, N. T. *Who Was Jesus?* London: SPCK, 1992; Grand Rapids: Eerdmans, 1993.

Yamasaki, Gary. *Watching a Biblical Narrative: Point of View in Biblical Exegesis*. New York and London: T&T Clark, 2007.

Yarbro Collins, Adela. "Establishing the Text: Mark 1:1." Pp. 111–27 in *Texts and Contexts: Biblical Texts in Their Textual and Situational Contexts: Essays in Honor of Lars Hartman*. Edited by Tord Fomberg and David Hellholm. Oslo: Scandinavian University Press, 1995.

Yarbro Collins, Adela. *Mark: A Commentary*. Hermeneia. Minneapolis: Fortress, 2007.

Zeller, Dieter. "New Testament Christology in Its Hellenistic Reception." *NTS* 47 (2001): 312–33.

INDEX OF BIBLICAL CITATIONS

INDEX OF AUTHORS

202, 210, 215n56, 224, 224n8, 236n16, 238n21, 243, 257n85
Kinukawa, Hisako, 220n2

Malbon, Elizabeth Struthers, ix–x, 4n9, 6n15, 7nn17–18, 8nn20–21, 9nn22–27, 10n33, 21n1, 27n20, 33n36, 35n40, 37n44, 39n47, 40nn48–51, 42nn52&54, 43n58, 46–47n64, 48n68, 49n70, 51nn74–75, 61n9, 63n16, 72n48, 74n51, 77n59, 84n72, 89n83, 91n92, 92n94, 98n107, 110n121, 116n127, 121n137, 122n141, 135n10, 140n21, 162n49, 164n54, 178n81, 196n3, 201n23, 219n1, 221n3, 225n9, 227n13, 232n2, 233nn4–5, 244n38, 255n80
Marcus, Joel, 70n42, 120n136, 140n18, 160n41, 163, 163n53, 166n57, 181n88, 202n27
Marguerat, Daniel, 8n20, 10n33
Matera, Frank J., 119, 119n131, 160n41, 168n62
Merenlahti, Petri, 8n20, 242n36
Metzger, Bruce M., 58, 58n2, 118n130
Michie, Donald, 5, 5n11, 8n20, 10n33, 43, 43n55, 57n1, 60n6, 78n61, 220n2, 221n3, 232n3, 236n16
Miller, Robert J., 202n27
Moore, Stephen D., 3nn5–6, 8n20, 123n144
Muecke, D. C., 28n21, 116n126, 121, 121n138, 123, 123n143
Muller, P., 9n29
Myers, Ched, 31n29, 43, 43n57

Naluparayil, Jacob Chacko, 5, 6n14, 9, 9nn29&31, 11, 11nn38–41, 12, 13, 14, 196, 198, 198nn14–16, 199, 199nn17–18, 210
Neirynck, Frans, 39, 42, 42n53

Ong, Walter J., 23n4
Oyen, Geert Van, 28n21, 122–23n141

Perkins, Pheme, 17, 17n60
Perrin, Norman, 24n7, 32–33n34, 35n40, 37, 37n43, 177n80, 178n81, 196n3,

206n34, 208n38, 213n54, 225, 225n10, 247n54
Perry, Menakhem, 12n42, 240, 240nn26–28, 241n29
Petersen, Norman R., 11, 11n38, 15, 15n54, 30n28, 45n61, 69n41, 72n47, 193n111, 234, 234nn7–9, 235, 235nn10&12–13, 236, 236nn15–16, 237, 237nn17&19, 238n20, 239, 241, 249n63
Pokorny, Petr, 53n78
Powell, Mark Allen, 8n20, 10n33, 233, 233n5, 256n81

Rabinowitz, Peter J., 13, 13n48
Resseguie, James L., 8n20, 10n33
Rhoads, David, x, 5, 5n11, 8n20, 10n33, 43, 43n55, 57n1, 60, 60n6, 78n61, 88n82, 90n86, 138n15, 201n24, 220n2, 221n3, 229n15, 232n3, 236n16
Robbins, Vernon K., 13n49, 89n83, 99n109
Robinson, James M., 44n60
Ruge-Jones, Philip, 60, 61n8, 83n69, 234n9

Saldarini, Anthony J., 91n90
Schneidau, Herbert N., 4n7
Schüssler Fiorenza, Elisabeth, 245n43
Schweizer, Eduard, 32–33n34, 76n57, 172n69, 182n91, 208n39
Scott, M. Philip, O.C.S.O., 52n76, 134–35n9, 171n67, 191n106
Shaw, Harry E., 234n6
Shepherd, Tom, 28n21, 226n11
Shiner, Whitney Taylor, 13n49, 60n7, 93n95, 121, 121–22n139, 122, 122nn140–41, 123, 187n99, 188n103
Shively, Elizabeth, 44n60, 131n6, 138n16, 154n34, 170, 170n65, 212n50
Smith, Abraham, 51n75, 74n52, 120, 120nn133–135, 180n85
Smith, Stephen H., 7n19, 8n20, 10n33, 29n26, 32n31, 35n39, 175n74, 233n3, 236n16
Stanzel, F. K., 241, 241nn30-31&35, 242
Stock, Augustine, O.S.B., 34n37